Corporate Governance and Accountability

Corporate Governance and Accountability

Jill Solomon and Aris Solomon

John Wiley & Sons, Ltd

Other Wiley Editorial Offices

John Wiley & Sons Inc., 111 River Street, Hoboken, NJ 07030, USA

Jossey-Bass, 989 Market Street, San Francisco, CA 94103-1741, USA

Wiley-VCH Verlag GmbH, Boschstr. 12, D-69469 Weinheim, Germany

John Wiley & Sons Australia Ltd, 33 Park Road, Milton, Queensland 4064, Australia

John Wiley & Sons (Asia) Pte Ltd, 2 Clementi Loop #02-01, Jin Xing Distripark, Singapore 129809

John Wiley & Sons Canada Ltd, 22 Worcester Road, Etobicoke, Ontario, Canada M9W 1L1

Wiley also publishes its books in a variety of electronic formats. Some content that appears in print may
not be available in electronic books.

British Library Cataloguing in Publication Data

A catalogue record for this book is available from the British Library

ISBN 0-470-84365-9

Project management by Originator, Gt Yarmouth, Norfolk (typeset in 10/13pt Times)
Printed and bound in Great Britain by Cromwell Press, Trowbridge, Wiltshire
This book is printed on acid-free paper responsibly manufactured from sustainable forestry in which at
least two trees are planted for each one used for paper production

We dedicate this book to our parents and our daughter

Contents

Preface

Interest in corporate governance is growing at an exponential rate. Improvements in corporate governance practice are being orchestrated at a global level. International bodies such as the Organization for Economic Development (OECD) are developing internationally acceptable standards of corporate governance. In the UK, companies are continuing to strengthen their generally sound corporate governance systems, focusing on shareholder and stakeholder relations and accountability, improvements in the performance of boards of directors, auditors and the accounting function, and paying attention to the ways in which their companies are controlled and run. Similarly, institutional investors, accountants, auditors and the general public are increasingly aware of a continuing need to promote corporate governance reform. Recent scandals such as Enron have driven home this need for constant reform.

As a result of increasing interest in corporate governance matters within the practitioner community, academic research has burgeoned in the area. At universities across the UK, new modules are springing up on corporate governance-related issues, with corporate governance as a subject in its own right becoming central to many business-related degree courses. We therefore felt that a general text on corporate governance and accountability was overdue and that students needed an up-to-date reference book covering theory and practice in the area. In this text we aim to provide an overview of corporate governance as a growing academic discipline. We attempt to give a flavour of the academic research in the field, with reference to theoretical frameworks. We also aim to demonstrate the close relationship between academic research and professional practice in the area. The text includes a number of contemporary illustrations and case studies, and provides students with questions for reflection and discussion at the end of each chapter.

The text is designed specifically to accompany a one-semester module in corporate governance and is oriented toward undergraduates studying accounting and finance, business and management, as well as toward MBA (Master of Business Administration) and other postgraduate students taking modules with a corporate governance component. However, given the growing interest in corporate governance issues, we hope that a wide range of other readers may find the book useful. For example, given the growing emphasis on corporate governance training for pension fund trustees, following the Myners Review (2001) we hope that this book will be a useful guide for trustees on the many training courses that are being developed for them around the country, as well as for other professionals in the institutional investment community who require a reference text on corporate governance issues. Further, as can be seen from the international orientation of the text, we do not intend the book to be limited to UK students but hope that students of corporate governance in other countries may find it useful. We focus throughout the book on the relevance of corporate governance reform to countries all over the globe. There is an emphasis on corporate governance reform in East Asian economies, reflecting the specific research interests of the authors. We have set aims and learning outcomes at the beginning of each chapter so that students have a clear picture of what they are expected to assimilate and how their learning should progress at each stage of the book. There is also a summary at the end of each chapter bringing together the main concepts learned and providing continuity throughout the text.

This book represents the culmination of a decade of research into corporate governance and corporate accountability to stakeholders by the authors. Throughout the book we have referred to the results of our own research activities, including numerous postal questionnaires and a long-term series of in-depth research interviews, principally with members of the institutional investment community. We are extremely grateful for the financial support we have received for our research, from a number of institutions including the ESRC-funded centre for Business Relationships, Accountability, Sustainability and Society (BRASS) at Cardiff University, the Nuffield Foundation and the ESRC.

Acknowledgements

We are grateful to the many people who have helped us throughout the development of this text. We are especially grateful to a number of people for their input and guidance on the writing of this book. First and foremost, we are grateful to Brenda Thompson for her regular reading of drafts and for her careful editing. We also thank her for her moral support, without which the book would never have been published. We are also extremely grateful to several close friends and colleagues at Cardiff Business School who have devoted time and energy to helping us write this text. Special thanks to Mark Clatworthy for his careful comments on the final draft, especially on style. Thanks to Howard Mellett for comments on structure and academic content, as well as some careful editing. We also thank Simon Norton for his careful reading of the final draft, his insightful comments and suggestions, and his continuing friendship and support.

We are also grateful to Nathan Joseph from Aston Business School for his comments and advice—as always, he has provided constant moral and academic support. We thank Linda Lewis (Sheffield University Management School) for her guidance in our work, and friendship, over the years. Thanks are extended to David Owen (Nottingham Business School), Nikolaos Milonas (University of Athens and Cardiff Business School) and Nickolaos Travlos (ALBA, Greece and Cardiff Business School) for their comments on the book's structure and orientation. We are also grateful to a number of people who have acted (some anonymously) as reviewers on this book, especially to Michael Mumford (University of Lancaster) for his suggestions and for the extra literature he provided, especially his course notes on corporate governance, used at Lancaster University.

We also thank the many people from the UK institutional investment community who have contributed to this book through their participation in our research projects, especially our questionnaire surveys and research interviews. This has provided us with the rich, in-depth knowledge of corporate governance developments and issues that are essential for any text on such a wide and far-reaching subject as corporate governance and accountability. We thank our students, who attended the module 'Corporate Governance and Accountability' at Cardiff University in 2001–2002 and 2002–2003, for their feedback and suggestions on early drafts of the text. We are also grateful to our PhD student, Shih Wei Lin, for his comments on drafts of the book, and thank our MBA students who have commented on sections of the text. Special thanks to Monalisa Vora, who commented on Part II of the text. We thank Gil Powell for transcribing the interview data on which our empirical data are based. We also thank Lauren Darby for research assistance in our projects and in helping us gather references and data. Thanks also to Derek Thompson for his insightful comments on the historical sections of this text. We are also extremely grateful to the people at John Wiley & Sons who have worked hard to publish the final product, especially Steve Hardman, who have provided support and guidance at every stage of the writing. Thanks also to our copy-editor, Bruce Shuttlewood of Originator, for his help and hard work in the final stages of the book's production.

The *Combined Code on Corporate Governance* (2003) has been reproduced in full as an appendix to this book with the kind permission of the Financial Reporting Council. For further information regarding *The Combined Code* please contact the Financial Reporting Council on 020 7611 9700. To order a copy of *The Combined Code* please call 0870 777 2906.

Introduction

Corporate governance is a central and dynamic aspect of business. The term 'govern-ance' derives from the Latin *gubernare*, meaning 'to steer', usually applying to the steering of a ship, which implies that corporate governance involves the function of direction rather than control. There are many ways of defining corporate govern-ance, ranging from narrow definitions that focus on companies and their share-holders, to broader definitions that incorporate the accountability of companies to many other groups of people, or 'stakeholders'. In Chapter 1, we discuss a large array of definitions, but for the purposes of this introduction we use a general definition that corporate governance concerns *the way in which companies are directed and controlled.*[1]

The importance of corporate governance for corporate success as well as for social welfare cannot be overstated. Recent examples of massive corporate collapses resulting from weak systems of corporate governance have highlighted the need to improve and reform corporate governance at an international level. In the wake of Enron and other similar cases, countries around the world have reacted quickly by pre-empting similar events domestically. As a speedy response to these corporate failures, the USA issued the Sarbanes–Oxley Act in July 2002, whereas in January 2003 the Higgs Report and the Smith Report were published in the UK, again in response to recent corporate governance failures. The impact of their recommenda-tions are discussed throughout this book. We also spend time discussing the differ-ence between the rules-based approach to corporate governance adopted by the USA and the comply or explain approach chosen by the UK. Our main aim is to consider why such initiatives are being pursued and why continuing reform of the corporate governance system in the UK and elsewhere is necessary. In this introduction, we set the scene by placing the evolution of corporate governance in its historical and theoretical context, focusing mainly on the UK case. We now outline the contents of the chapters in more detail.

---

[1] This definition is taken from the Cadbury Report (1992).

Part I   Corporate governance: frameworks and mechanisms

Defining corporate governance

Part I of this book examines the frameworks and mechanisms of corporate govern-ance, mainly from a UK perspective. In *Chapter 1* we consider a range of definitions of corporate governance and provide our own definition of what corporate govern-ance entails. We also introduce a number of theoretical frameworks that have been used in the literature to analyse corporate governance issues. The study of corporate governance is principally the study of the mechanics of capitalist systems. As will become clear throughout this text, however, the US and UK forms of capitalism represent only one type of framework among many. There are as many variations of capitalism and corporate governance as there are countries in the world. However, corporate governance research has tended to focus predominantly on the Anglo-American (often termed the Anglo-Saxon) system of corporate governance, where companies are listed on stock exchanges and shareholders can trade freely in the shares. Traditionally, in this system, share ownership has been widely dispersed and management of companies has been distinctly separate from ownership. We now discuss the development of the Anglo-American system of corporate governance from a historical perspective.

A historical perspective

Corporate ownership structure has been considered as having the strongest influence on systems of corporate governance, although many other factors affect corporate governance, including legal systems, cultural and religious traditions, political en-vironments and economic events. All business enterprises need funding in order to grow, and it is the ways in which companies are financed which determines their ownership structure. It became clear centuries ago that individual entrepreneurs and their families could not provide the finance necessary to undertake developments required to fuel economic and industrial growth. The sale of company shares in order to raise the necessary capital was an innovation that has proved a cornerstone in the development of economies worldwide. However, the road toward the type of stock market seen in the UK and the US today has been long and complicated. Listed companies in their present form originate from the earliest form of corporate entity, namely the sole trader. From the Middle Ages, such traders were regulated by merchant guilds, which oversaw a diversity of trades.[2] The internationalization of trade, with traders venturing overseas, led gradually to regulated companies arising from the mediaeval guild system. Members of these early companies could trade

---

[2]   See Farrar and Hannigan (1998) for a detailed history of the development of companies in the UK from a legal perspective.

their own shares in the company, which led ultimately to the formation of joint stock companies.[3]

The first company to combine incorporation, overseas trade and joint stock was the East India Company, which was granted a Royal Charter in 1600, for Merchants of London trading into the East Indies. The early governance structures of this company were reminiscent of corporate governance structures and mechanisms in today's companies (see Farrar and Hannigan, 1998; Cadbury, 2002). International trade and interest in investment overseas led to the infamous South Sea Bubble of 1720, where the general public in Britain, who had invested in 'shares' in the Company of Merchants of Great Britain Trading to the South Seas, realized they had lost their hard-earned money in the first stock market overvaluation and subsequent collapse. At one point during the Bubble's growth the amount invested in companies involved in the South Seas reached £500 million, double the value of all the land in England at the time. Investors did not realize the lack of solid foundation underlying their investment. The bubble in UK information technology stocks in the late 1990s was another example of investor irrationality and the ways in which the markets could be fooled. The Bubble Act, which followed the bursting of the South Sea Bubble, prevented companies from acting as a body corporate and from raising money by selling shares, without the legal authority of an Act of Parliament or Royal Charter. Inevitably, this halted the development of joint stock companies. It was the development of the railway network in Britain in the 1800s that again instigated the development of companies as we know them today, as they needed to attract funds to feed their growth.

A total of 910 companies were registered from the introduction of the first modern Joint Stock Companies Act in 1844 (Farrar and Hannigan, 1998). However, these companies were 'unlimited'. This implied that their shareholders bore unlimited liability for their investee company's debts, and this was not an effective means of encouraging people to place their monies into the hands of company management. Greater enticement was required. This came with the Limited Liability Act of 1855. Limited liability implied that shareholders could only lose the amount they had invested in the company, rather than be liable for their entire wealth, as had been the case with unlimited companies. These events represented a major breakthrough for the growth of capitalism. This was introduced as a progressive reform measure aimed at revitalizing British business, as at that time companies were seeking incorporation in the USA and France in preference to the UK, in order to obtain limited liability for their shareholders. The number of incorporations rose dramatically following these changes.

---

[3] Joint stock companies have been defined as companies consisting of individuals organized to conduct a business for gain and having a joint stock of capital represented by shares owned individually by the members and transferable without the consent of the group (Longman, 1984).

In the USA the managerially controlled corporation evolved at a similar time, following the Civil War in the second half of the 19th century. It was from this time that the notorious 'divorce' of ownership and control began to emerge. This corporate malaise was first outlined in Berle and Means' (1932) seminal work, *The Modern Corporation and Private Property*, which showed that the separation of ownership from control had engendered a situation where the true owners of companies, the shareholders, had little influence over company management and were rendered impotent by the wide dispersion of ownership and by a general apathy among shareholders toward the activities of investee company management. It was the dispersion of ownership that created the root of the problem rather than the separation *per se*. The influence of companies was growing at the time of Berle and Means' work and many feared the potential impact of their influence on society, unless their power was checked by their owners, the shareholders. They considered that companies were growing to such an extent that they were almost becoming 'social institutions'. Yet, there was little incentive for shareholders to involve themselves in their investee companies. They held relatively small shares in a broad portfolio of companies. If they were dissatisfied with the companies' behaviour they could sell their shares. This approach to share ownership has been termed 'exit' as opposed to a more proactive approach of using their 'voice'. The 'problem' revealed in Berle and Means formed the basis of the 'agency problem', where shareholders (the principals) struggle to control and monitor the activities of managers (the agents) in order to align managerial interests and objectives with their own. An important implication of these observations was to focus increasing attention on the role of companies' boards of directors, as a mechanism for ensuring effective corporate governance.

Although the ownership structure underlying the traditional agency problem was prevalent in the USA, the situation was extremely similar in the UK, where share ownership flourished following the introduction of the Joint Stock Companies Act of 1844 and the Limited Liability Act of 1855. Problems arising from separation of ownership and control were recognized in Adam Smith's *The Wealth of Nations* (Smith, 1838). In his discussion of joint stock companies, he explained that company directors were the managers of their shareholders' money, and not their own. He considered it likely that these directors would be less concerned about someone else's investment than they would be about their own and that this situation could easily result in 'negligence and profusion' in the management of company affairs. Further, in his personal exposition of corporate governance, Sir Adrian Cadbury (Cadbury, 2002) pointed out that there were allusions to the 'agency problem' in the UK that predated Berle and Means' writing. Indeed, Cadbury explained that in the Liberal Industrial Inquiry of 1926–1928 in the UK, a significant problem was detected because management and responsibility were in different hands from the provision of funds, the risk taking and the financial rewards. A study by Florence (1961) also suggested similarity between the UK system of corporate governance and that of the USA, as he showed that two-thirds of large companies were not controlled by their owners.

When companies within the capitalist system of the UK and the USA demonstrate effective systems of corporate governance, they can be productive and efficient, and can have a positive impact on society as a whole. Efficiently functioning capital markets can, theoretically at least, lead to efficient allocation of resources and a situation of optimal social welfare. However, ineffective, weak corporate governance can have the opposite result. The 'yin and yang' of the capitalist system are widely known. On the positive side, capitalism is associated with wealth production, economic prosperity and corporate success. On the negative side, capitalism is associated with greed, despotism, abuse of power, opaqueness, social inequality and unfair distribution of wealth. Some of the negative aspects of global capitalism and its impact on society have been explored at some length in the literature (Hutton, 1995; Hutton and Giddens, 2001). It is the functioning of internal and external corporate governance that determines whether a company, or even a country, displays more of the negative or the positive aspects of the capitalist system. The level of inherent trust within the business sector and within society as a whole has been questioned in recent times, with a general acknowledgement by sociologists of a decline in social cohesion[4] and community. Specifically, there has been a decline in society's confidence in institutions, such as corporations and institutional investment organizations.[5] This decline in trust, so prevalent in UK society, and its implications for financial institutions are alluded to throughout this text, as they represent one major driving force behind corporate governance reform.

The traditional Anglo-American system of corporate governance described above has not remained stable and has undergone dramatic changes in recent years. The main aspect of change has involved transformation of ownership structure in the UK and the USA. The rise of the global institutional investor as a powerful and dominant force in corporate governance has transformed the relationship between companies and their shareholders and has created a completely different system of corporate governance from that described above. Ownership structure is no longer widely dispersed, as in the model presented by Berle and Means, but is now concentrated in the hands of a few major institutional investors.

---

[4] McCann et al. (2003) defined social cohesion as the degree of integration and bondedness of a society at large. They considered that social cohesion involves face-to-face interactive connections and the integration of shared values. To measure social cohesion is to measure the degree to which members of a society feel connected and integrated into communities and to general norms and values of the social world. Social cohesion is the opposite state to Durkheim's *anomie*, see Durkheim (1952).

[5] Giddens (1991) and Fukuyama (1995) discussed the decline in social cohesion and trust in society.

The Enron debacle

In *Chapter 2* we provide a case study focusing on the fall of Enron. This was a salient case of corporate governance failure, which led to the collapse of one of the most successful companies in the world. In the case study, we show that corporate governance mechanisms such as the function of non-executive directors, auditors, the internal audit committee and the board of directors all failed in certain respects. We also highlight the importance of ethical behaviour in business, explaining that corporate governance checks and balances serve only to detect, not cure, unethical activity. Most importantly, we show that the fall of Enron accelerated the worldwide agenda for corporate governance reform.

Corporate governance reform: a UK perspective

In *Chapter 3* we outline the principal codes of practice and policy documents that have been developed within the UK agenda for corporate governance reform, considering their motivation and main objectives. In *Chapter 4* we examine the role of boards of directors in corporate governance. Within the context of our preceding historical discussion, the need for a well-functioning board at the head of companies became evident as companies grew in size and their owners became more dispersed and less involved in companies' operations. We look specifically at initiatives that have been implemented to maximize board effectiveness, such as splitting the role of chairman and chief executive, as well as the extent to which they have been successful in improving corporate governance in the UK and elsewhere. *Chapter 5* investigates the role of institutional investors in UK corporate governance, focusing on the instruments of shareholder activism, especially voting and engagement. In *Chapter 6* we consider the role of transparency in corporate governance, examining the importance of corporate disclosure, internal control and auditing to effective corporate governance. Having analysed corporate governance reform within a UK context, we move on to discuss approaches to corporate governance reform in different countries around the world.

Part II Global corporate governance

The Anglo-American model of corporate governance is by no means the only model, despite suggestions and indeed concerns that it is becoming dominant internationally. In the second part of this book we consider the various categorizations used to describe and analyse different systems of corporate governance around the world. There are many more forms of corporate governance, based on different structures of ownership and influenced by vast variations on cultural and religious background, legal framework and political climate. For example, some systems of corporate governance are characterized traditionally by state ownership influence. These are typical of countries such as Russia and China, which have experienced hefty state control due to their political climates. Further, corporate governance in many East Asian countries has been influenced heavily by cultural and legal factors. Confucian ethics has had a significant and lasting impact on the development of business in South Korea, for example. Corporate governance in the other countries in the European Union also represents a patchwork of different systems, with many countries characterized by founding family ownership structures, and extremely different legal structures from that in the UK. Other corporate governance systems have been characterized traditionally by bank relationships, such as Japan and Germany, as well as by 'pyramidal' ownership structures, where companies are ultimately owned, through complicated chains, by other companies. Specifically, in *Chapter 7* we discuss the 'insider–outsider' categorization of corporate governance, examining the characteristics of the most extreme forms of these systems. *Chapter 8* provides a 'Reference Dictionary' of a selection of corporate governance systems around the world. Given the number of countries in existence, we cannot hope to provide exhaustive coverage of global corporate governance, as that would represent a book *per se*. However, we summarize the main characteristics of corporate governance in a number of countries in order to illustrate the diversity of corporate governance systems around the world.

Part III   Broadening the corporate governance agenda

Part III examines ways in which the concept of corporate governance has broadened to incorporate stakeholder concerns as well as shareholder accountability. In *Chapter 9* we consider the development of corporate social responsibility and the ways in which companies are discharging a broader accountability. Corporate failures such as Enron have rocked global confidence in business activities and have only served to fan the flames of distrust in corporate integrity. Corporate governance weaknesses, which perhaps passed unnoticed in earlier times, have led to massive corporate collapses, affecting countries around the world. How many Enrons would it take to destroy global capitalism by leading shareholders to withdraw their financial support for the corporate community? Clearly, corporate governance systems require urgent attention and companies need to smarten up their act. Investor confidence must be regained if society in its current form is to endure.

We are in a climate of change with corporate governance at the centre of this transformation. Not only is there a worldwide effort to improve corporate governance, but even countries that have been long-term communist states, such as China and Russia, are embracing a market-oriented system with shareholder accountability and greater corporate transparency, as can be seen from the discussion in *Chapter 8*. Capitalism has survived into the 21st century and seems to be becoming the dominant system in corporate governance. This is a difficult political issue, as it implies dominance of one political and economic system over another. This is not necessarily the most appropriate route for many countries in the world, as they need to retain their own character and culture in the face of change. However, this is not the only trend. The whole corporate discourse is metamorphosing. Whereas the shareholder-based model of corporate governance has dominated the 20th century, with attention being focused principally on making companies more accountable to their shareholders, there is now an increasing emphasis on satisfying the needs of a broad range of stakeholders.

Stakeholder concerns are gradually taking on a central position in corporate governance across the globe. Even countries with developing stock markets are concentrating not only on improving shareholder accountability but also on embracing stakeholder concerns. A new reality is dawning in the corporate world. The directors' discourse for the 21st century is very different from that of 20th century directors. Directors are being forced to be concerned with far more than simply running their business and increasing shareholder value. Directors now have far-reaching responsibilities to wide stakeholder groups. Directors worry about pollution, social issues, stakeholder engagement and the impact of their company's operations in countries at the other side of the world. Companies that do not take account of social and environmental issues are faced with direct shareholder and stakeholder action. Corporate social responsibility is becoming a primary concern of business, whether through a desire to be ethical or through a belief that being ethical actually improves profitability. Social and environmental issues have become significant risks requiring careful management. There is a growing body of empirical evidence that suggests that companies which are more socially responsible are also more profitable, as we see from empirical evidence presented throughout this text. In *Chapter 9* we explore ways in which businesses are becoming more socially responsible and we examine the metamorphosis of the directors' discourse in the UK and elsewhere. We consider the increasing importance of accountability, not only to shareholders but to a wide range of stakeholders.

Chapter 10 is concerned with the rise of socially responsible investment, whereby institutional investors are realizing the impact of social, ethical and environmental issues on their investment return and are therefore encouraging companies to treat these issues with more gravity. We consider the dawning of a new corporate reality in the 21st century, involving a complete paradigm shift away from individual introvert corporate groups toward a global corporate community that is outward-looking and all-encompassing. Companies are assuming a role in society, by embracing corporate social responsibility and actively pursuing improvements in social welfare, by discharging greater accountability to a broad range of stakeholders. Furthermore, they are pursuing this inclusive approach with the full endorsement of their primary shareholders, the institutional investors.

In *Chapter 11* we conclude the text with a discussion of the possible future route that corporate governance and accountability may take in the UK and elsewhere. We make a number of suggestions for policy makers.

Part I

Corporate governance: frameworks and mechanisms

Chapter 1

Defining corporate governance

Aims and objectives

This chapter provides an introduction to the corporate governance discipline, pre-dominantly from a UK perspective. The specific objectives of this chapter are to:

- discuss a range of definitions of corporate governance in order to arrive at a definition that is appropriate for this text;

- appreciate the development of corporate governance from a historical perspective;

- compare and contrast several theoretical frameworks that are applied to the corporate governance discipline.

Introduction

'Corporate governance' has become one of the most commonly used phrases in the current global business vocabulary. This raises the question, 'is corporate governance a vital component of successful business or is it simply another fad that will fade away over time?' The notorious collapse of Enron in 2001, one of America's largest companies, has focused international attention on company failures and the role that strong corporate governance needs to play to prevent them. The UK has responded by producing the Higgs Report (2003) and the Smith Report (2003), whereas the US produced the Sarbanes–Oxley Act (2002). Nations around the world are instigating far-reaching programmes for corporate governance reform, as evidenced by the proliferation of corporate governance codes and policy documents, voluntary or mandatory, both at the national and supra-national level. We believe that the present focus on corporate governance will be maintained into the future and that, over time, corporate governance issues will grow in importance, rather than fade into insignificance. The phenomenal growth of interest in corporate governance has been accompanied by a growing body of academic research. As the discipline matures, far greater definition and clarity are being achieved concerning the nature of corporate governance. In this chapter we consider the broad-ranging nature of corporate governance and the many ways of defining the subject. We discuss corporate governance from a theoretical perspective, setting the scene for the following chapters.

What is corporate governance?

There is no single, accepted definition of corporate governance. There are substantial differences in definition according to which country we are considering. The main focus of this chapter and the following five is the agenda for corporate governance reform, mainly from a UK perspective. However, we use the US case of Enron in Chapter 2 to demonstrate the need to improve corporate governance mechanisms. However, even within the confines of one country's system, such as the UK, arriving at 'a' definition of corporate governance is no easy task. Corporate governance as a discipline in its own right is relatively new. We consider that the subject may be treated in a narrow or a broad manner, depending on the viewpoint of the policy maker, practitioner, researcher or theorist. It seems that existing definitions of corporate governance fall on to a spectrum, with 'narrow' views at one end and more inclusive, 'broad' views placed at the other. One approach toward corporate governance adopts a narrow view, where corporate governance is restricted to the relationship between a company and its shareholders. This is the traditional finance paradigm, expressed in 'agency theory'. At the other end of the spectrum, corporate governance may be seen as a web of relationships, not only between a company and its owners (shareholders) but also between a company and a broad range of other 'stakeholders': employees, customers, suppliers, bondholders, to name but a few. Such a view tends to be expressed in 'stakeholder theory'. This is a more inclusive and broad way of treating the subject of corporate governance and one which is gradually attracting greater attention, as issues of accountability and corporate social responsibility are brought to the forefront of policy and practice in the UK and elsewhere.

In Table 1.1 we consider some published definitions of corporate governance, each of which adopt a different view of the subject and provide a consensus on the relative importance of these definitions. The consensus derives from a questionnaire survey that sampled a large number of UK institutional investors (Solomon et al., 2000b). In the questionnaire survey we evaluated institutional investors' views of corporate governance. We presented them with a number of established definitions of corporate governance. These definitions were not intended to discriminate completely between different views, but rather each was chosen to emphasize slightly different interpretations of the corporate governance function. The selection represents a range of definitions, starting from the narrowest which described the basic role of corporate governance (The Cadbury Report, 1992; see also, Cadbury, 2002), to a solely financial perspective involving only shareholders and company management (Parkinson, 1994) and extending to a broader definition that encompassed

Table [1.1]   Definitions of corporate governance: institutional investors' views

Rank	Corporate governance is . . .	Average response
1	. . . the process of supervision and control intended to ensure that the company's management acts in accordance with the interests of shareholders (Parkinson, 1994).	Strongly agree
2	. . . the governance role is not concerned with the running of the business of the company *per se*, but with giving overall direction to the enterprise, with overseeing and controlling the executive actions of management and with satisfying legitimate expectations of accountability and regulation by interests beyond the corporate boundaries (Tricker, 1984).	Agree
3	. . . the governance of an enterprise is the sum of those activities that make up the internal regulation of the business in compliance with the obligations placed on the firm by legislation, ownership and control. It incorporates the trusteeship of assets, their management and their deployment (Cannon, 1994).	Agree
4	. . . the relationship between shareholders and their companies and the way in which shareholders act to encourage best practice (e.g., by voting at AGMs and by regular meetings with companies' senior management). Increasingly, this includes shareholder 'activism' which involves a campaign by a shareholder or a group of shareholders to achieve change in companies (The Corporate Governance Handbook, 1996).	Some agreement
5	. . . the structures, process, cultures and systems that engender the successful operation of the organization (Keasey and Wright, 1993).	Some agreement
6	. . . the system by which companies are directed and controlled (The Cadbury Report, 1992)	Slight agreement

Reproduced by permission of Academic Press

corporate accountability to a wide range of stakeholders and society at large (Tricker, 1984). We also included a definition that emphasized the importance of shareholder activism, as this allowed us to gauge institutional investors' views on their own role in corporate governance (The Corporate Governance Handbook, 1996). The selection also included definitions that were regulation-centred (Cannon, 1994) or focused on corporate success (Keasey and Wright, 1993). The definitions in Table 1.1 are ranked according to the institutional investors' views of their relative importance.[1] The table illustrates that the finance paradigm is probably the most easily acceptable to UK institutional investors, as Parkinson's (1994)

---

[1] Specifically, the ranking was achieved by calculating the mean average response to a question in the questionnaire asking institutional investors the extent to which they agreed or disagreed with each definition. Institutional investors were asked to select a score from 1 (strongly disagree) to 7 (strongly agree).

shareholder-oriented definition received strongest support. This is not surprising as they are major shareholders and are likely to give themselves priority in terms of corporate governance relationships.

In general the definitions of corporate governance found in the literature tend to share certain characteristics, one of which is the notion of accountability. Narrow definitions are oriented around corporate accountability to shareholders. Some narrower, shareholder-oriented definitions of corporate governance focus specifically on the ability of a country's legal system to protect minority shareholder rights (e.g., La Porta et al., 1998). However, such definitions are mainly applicable to cross-country comparisons of corporate governance, and at present we are focusing on corporate governance within the UK. We return to the legal influence on different systems of corporate governance around the world in Chapters 7 and 8.

Broader definitions of corporate governance stress a broader level of accountability to shareholders and other stakeholders. We can see that Tricker's (1984) definition, encompassing accountability to a broader group of people than just the shareholders, was also supported strongly by institutional investors from the results in Table 1.1. This demonstrates an interest within the financial community in a broader, stakeholder-oriented approach to corporate governance. The broadest definitions consider that companies are accountable to the whole of society, future generations and the natural world. We have agreed on our own, relatively broad, definition of corporate governance for the purposes of this book, based on our research and our views concerning corporate governance issues. We suggest that *corporate governance is the system of checks and balances, both internal and external to companies, which ensures that companies discharge their accountability to all their stakeholders and act in a socially responsible way in all areas of their business activity.*

Throughout this book we attempt to show that theoretical frameworks that suggest companies should be accountable only to their shareholders are not necessarily inconsistent with theoretical frameworks that champion stakeholder accountability. The reason underlying this argument is that shareholders' interests can only be satisfied by taking account of stakeholder interests, as companies that are accountable to all of their stakeholders are over the long term more successful and more prosperous. Our definition of corporate governance therefore rests on the perception that companies can maximize value creation over the long term, by discharging their accountability to all of their stakeholders and by optimizing their system of corporate governance. This view is supported by the emerging literature. We discuss some of this literature in Chapters 9 and 10, specifically. Indeed, our own empirical research has provided substantial support for the view that corporate financial performance is positively related to corporate governance. We have found substantial evidence to suggest a growing perception among institutional investors in the City of London that there is a corporate governance dividend as well as a dividend attached to stakeholder accountability. Indeed, we have found from our research that one reason 'good' corporate governance, as well as corporate social responsibility, are linked significantly to good corporate financial performance is its link with management quality. Better managers instigate better corporate governance and pay attention to their stakeholders. Better managers also manage companies more effectively and produce higher financial returns. This view was expressed by an investment analyst in a large UK investment institution, in response to a questionnaire, who commented that:

> I feel that organisations that demonstrate a commitment to a broad range of stakeholders are likely to show better management skills than those that do not . . .[2]

The Higgs Report (1993) reflected a similar sentiment, emphasizing a strong link between good corporate governance, accountability and value creation, in the following:

> . . . the UK framework of corporate governance . . . can clearly be improved . . . progressive strengthening of the existing architecture is strongly desirable, both to increase corporate accountability and to maximise sustainable wealth creation.
>
> (Higgs Report, p. 12, para. 1.13)

Overall, this perception is growing among the professional community and academic research is beginning to provide empirical evidence in support of this view of corporate governance, accountability and corporate profitability. However, this is the 'business case' for corporate governance and, more generally, for corporate social responsibility. Should companies improve corporate governance and discharge accountability to all of their stakeholders purely because it is ethical? We discuss these ethical issues in the subsection on stakeholder theory on p. 23. In the real world, it is unlikely that businessmen and investors will be interested in acting ethically unless there are positive financial returns to be made from so doing. As there appears to be a strong business case underlying corporate governance reform and stakeholder accountability, then the corporate and financial communities are more likely to embrace these approaches. Having provided an introduction to corporate governance and a sample of the many approaches to defining the subject, we now move on to discussing a number of theoretical frameworks that are used to analyse corporate governance issues.

---

[2] This view was expressed in a questionnaire we received. The questionnaire survey was conducted in January 2003 and was distributed to all of the members of the Society of Investment Professionals, who amount to over 4,000 investment analysts, fund managers, trustees, *inter alia*. The survey focused specifically on social, ethical and environmental disclosure and socially responsible investment, as an important aspect of corporate governance.

Theoretical frameworks

A number of different theoretical frameworks have evolved to explain and analyse corporate governance. Each of these frameworks approaches corporate governance in a slightly different way, using different terminology, and views corporate governance from a different perspective, arising from a different discipline (e.g., the agency theory paradigm arises from the fields of finance and economics, whereas transaction cost theory arises from economics and organizational theory). Other frameworks, such as stakeholder theory, arise from a more social-orientated perspective on corporate governance. Although there are marked differences between the various theoretical frameworks, as they each attempt to analyse the same problems but from different perspectives, they do share significant commonalities. Further, the frameworks overlap theoretically. In this section we intend to outline some of the most commonly used theoretical frameworks in accounting and finance-related disciplines and to specify some of the commonalities and differences between these competing paradigms. We examine agency theory, transaction cost theory and stakeholder theory. Other approaches include organization theory and stewardship theory (see Tricker, 1998). It is also important to recognize that there are cultural and legal influences on corporate governance, which we consider in Part II, where relevant.

To appreciate fully the various theories of corporate governance, it is useful to review briefly the development of stock markets, as their structure and operations have led to the development of agency theory. In the introductory chapter, we summarized the historical development of corporate governance in the UK. For the purposes of this chapter, we revisit the development of limited liability with the aim of laying the foundations of agency theory.[3] Before stock markets developed, companies relied on finance from wealthy individuals, usually relatives of the entrepreneur. Companies were owned and run by the same people. For economies to grow, it was necessary to find a large number of different investors to provide money for companies, so that they could expand. The principal element of today's stock markets, which has encouraged investors to buy shares, thereby ensuring a steady flow of external finance for companies, is known as limited liability. This was developed in 1855 and means that *shareholders are not responsible for the debts* of the companies in which they invest. The development of limited liability meant that investors were more prepared to buy shares, as all they would risk was their investment—not their entire wealth. A stock market is a means by which a company can raise capital by selling shares to investors, who become shareholders. Not only can investors buy shares but also these financial securities may be traded on the stock market. It is important to remember that the only time the company receives any funds is when the shares are sold for the first time. The important

---

[3] Arnold (1998) provided a detailed history of the development of stock markets as a way for companies to obtain finance and is a useful text for students to read in order to appreciate the links between the development of UK capitalism and corporate finance.

issue from a theoretical viewpoint is that in buying a share, even though an investor does not jeopardize his entire wealth, he is becoming an 'owner' of the company. However, although the majority of shareholders own, in part, the investee company, they have little to do with running the company, as this is the job of the company directors, to whom they entrust their funds.

Agency theory

The introduction of limited liability and the opening up of corporate ownership to the general public through share ownership had a dramatic impact on the way in which companies were controlled. The market system in the UK and the USA, *inter alia*, is organized in such a way that the owners, who are principally the shareholders of listed companies, delegate the running of the company to the company management. There is a 'divorce' of ownership and control that has led to the notorious 'agency problem'. Berle and Means (1932) discussed the extent to which there was a dispersion of shareholding, which consequently led to a separation of ownership and control in the USA. Prais (1976) showed that a similar structure of ownership and control operated in the UK. The agency problem was first explored in Ross (1973), with the first detailed theoretical exposition of agency theory presented in Jensen and Meckling (1976). They defined the managers of the company as the 'agents' and the shareholder as the 'principal' (in their analysis there is one shareholder versus the 'managers'). In other words, the shareholder, who is the owner or 'principal' of the company, delegates day-to-day decision making in the company to the directors, who are the shareholder's 'agents'. The problem that arises as a result of this system of corporate ownership is that the agents do not necessarily make decisions in the best interests of the principal. One of the principal assumptions of agency theory is that the goals of the principal and agent conflict. In finance theory, a basic assumption is that the primary objective for companies is shareholder wealth maximization. In practice this is not necessarily the case. It is likely that company managers prefer to pursue their own personal objectives, such as aiming to gain the highest bonuses possible. Managers are likely to display a tendency towards 'egoism' (i.e., behaviour that leads them to maximize their own perceived self-interest: Boatright, 1999). This can result in a tendency to focus on project and company investments that provide high short-run profits (where managers' pay is related to this variable), rather than the maximization of long-term shareholder wealth through investment, in projects that are long term in nature. Hence British industry has been notorious for 'short-termism'.

Short-termism has been defined as a tendency to foreshorten the time horizon applied to investment decisions, or raise the discount rate above that appropriate to the firm's opportunity cost of capital (Demirag and Tylecote, 1992). It is considered to characterize countries that are classified generally as 'outsider-dominated' (see Franks and Mayer, 1994; Short et al., 1998) where this means that the economy is not only dominated by large firms controlled directly by their managers but also indirectly through the actions of outsiders, such as institutional investors. We discuss this categorization of corporate governance systems in more detail in Chapter 7. Further, short-term pressure on companies has arisen from the institutional investment community, who have been more interested in gaining quick profits from portfolio investment than in the long-term survival and growth of their investee companies. They have been accused of 'churning' shares in order to make high returns on investment, regardless of the effects of their actions on managers, who as a consequence have been under pressure to focus on short-term performance (Sykes, 1994). This aspect of institutional investment is covered in more depth in Chapter 5.

In this corporate governance environment, managers are tempted to supplement their salaries with as many perquisites (such as holidays through the company, office equipment and the like) as possible—again leading to a reduction in shareholder value. The reduction in the shareholder's welfare is known as the 'residual loss' in agency theory terminology. Overall, we can see that the ownership structure in the UK (and in other countries with similar market systems) leads to a significant problem of divergent objectives. This 'agency problem' presents shareholders with a need to control company management.

An important question is therefore, 'how can shareholders exercise control over company management?' Another important and basic assumption of agency theory is that it is expensive and difficult for the principal to verify what the agent is doing (see Eisenhardt, 1989). There are a number of ways in which shareholders' and managers' interests may be aligned, but these are costly. Agency costs arise from attempts by the shareholder to 'monitor' company management. Monitoring by the shareholder is expensive, as it involves initiating activities such as shareholder engagement (expensive on resources and time-consuming). Incentive schemes and contracts are examples of monitoring techniques. The literature shows that solutions to agency problems involve establishing a 'nexus' of optimal contracts (both explicit and implicit) between management and the company's shareholders. These include remuneration contracts for management and debt contracts. These contracts seek to align the interests of the management with those of the shareholder. Although agency costs arise from establishing these contracts, costs are also incurred from the agents' side. Managers are keen to demonstrate to the shareholder that they are accountable and that they are following the shareholder wealth maximization objective. They may provide extra information about risk management in their annual reports, for example, which will add costs to the accounting process. They may expend additional resources in arranging meetings with primary shareholders. The costs associated with such initiatives are referred to as *ex-ante* bonding costs. The total agency cost arising from the agency problem has been summarized as comprising of: the sum of the principal's monitoring expenditures; the agent's bonding expenditures; and any remaining residual loss (see Hill and Jones, 1992). One of the main reasons that the desired actions of principal and agent diverge is their different attitude toward risk. This is referred to as the problem of 'risk sharing', as managers and shareholders prefer different courses of action because of their different attitudes toward risk (see Shankman, 1999).

We now introduce briefly the direct ways in which shareholders can 'monitor' company management and help to resolve agency conflicts. These methods of share-holder activism and their impact are discussed in more detail in Chapter 5. First, as owners of the company, shareholders have a right to influence the way in which the company is run, through voting at AGMs. The shareholder's voting right is an important part of his or her financial asset. An area of the finance literature is devoted to investigating the use of voting rights by shareholders, particularly institutional investors, and we discuss some of this literature in Chapter 5. Shareholders can influence the composition of the board of directors in their investee companies (the companies in which they invest) through voting at AGMs. There is also a range of other issues on which shareholders may vote. Voting by shareholders constitutes 'shareholder activism'. Although the voting right is seen to constitute part of a shareholder's financial asset, institutional investors do not necessarily consider it to be a benefit, but rather an albatross around their necks. One pension fund director we interviewed commented that:

> There is a weakness in the present system of corporate governance in that responsibility for ownership rests with people who don't want it and are not seeking it. We are investing in shares because they give us a good return and it is coincidental really that they bring with them this responsibility. I am not saying we don't want this responsibility. I am just saying it is difficult to handle that sort of thing.

However, the same interviewee also suggested that one important result from the most recent code of corporate governance practice in the UK (the Combined Code, 1998) was that fund managers are taking more interest in corporate governance and in particular are voting at AGMs. Connected to shareholder voting rights is the takeover mechanism, which represents another means of controlling company management. Jensen and Ruback (1983) emphasize the importance of the stock market as a means of disciplining company management through the takeover mechanism. If shareholders are dissatisfied with a company's management structure they can vote in favour of a takeover. Clearly, the threat of takeover is *per se* a disciplining force on managers, as they are unlikely to want to lose their jobs. Directors' contracts represent one means by which they can gain some security, although lengthy contracts are becoming less popular as corporate governance reform continues.

Another way in which shareholders may attempt to align managers' interests with their own is through the passing of shareholder resolutions, where a group of shareholders collectively lobby the company on issues with which they are dissatisfied. This is an extreme form of shareholder activism which has been employed infrequently in the UK. An illustration of shareholder activism can be seen in the BP-Amoco case in Chapter 10 (see Illustration 10.2). Of course, shareholders also have the option of divesting (selling their shares). This is the ultimate action and represents a failure on the part of the company to retain investors, where the divestment is due to dissatisfaction with management activities. An example of this was the case of Huntingdon Life Sciences, a company that conducts scientific research through animal experimentation. Not only did this company lose its principal UK institutional investors, as they were forced to divest following lobbying by animal rights groups, but it also lost investment from institutions in the USA. We discuss this case in more detail in Chapter 10 in the context of socially responsible investment (see Illustration 10.1). Clearly, if companies lose major shareholders, the market loses confidence in the company, more shareholders sell their shares and the share price plummets. Without financial support the company will fail. It is in the interests of listed companies not only to attract potential investors but also to retain them. Divestment is the ultimate threat.

Another way in which core institutional investors can influence investee company management is through one-to-one meetings between a representative from the investment institution and a manager from the company. Such meetings are taking place more and more frequently and seem to be influencing corporate behaviour in a significant way. Holland (1998) considered the function of such meetings from an accounting perspective, showing that private disclosure through engagement and dialogue was developing to supplement public corporate disclosure. There is a distinct link between these one-to-one meetings and managerial decision making, although the Hampel Report (1998)[4] suggested that institutional investors do not want to be involved in companies' business decisions. However, there are important legal issues involved in the content and results of these meetings. If any price-sensitive information is revealed by company management (i.e., information which, if traded on, could affect share prices) to the institutional investors, then it is against the law for the investor to trade on this information until it becomes publicly available. This has led to many controversies in the past and occasionally results in 'insider dealing', where an investor (or a member of the family of an investment manager, for example) sells or buys shares in a company on receipt of private information, in order to make personal profit. Such events are high profile and result in court cases, if information becomes public. We discuss the legal framework relating to insider dealing in more detail in Chapter 5.

If the market mechanism and shareholders' ability to express themselves are not enough to monitor and control managerial behaviour, some sort of regulation or formal guidance is needed. Indeed, if markets were perfectly efficient and companies could compete in an efficient market for funds, artificial initiatives aimed at reforming corporate governance would be redundant, as:

> ... we should not worry about governance reform, since, in the long run, product market competition would force firms to minimize costs, and as part of this cost minimization to

---

[4] This Report is the third significant report on corporate governance in the UK. We discuss the report in detail in Chapter 3.

adopt rules, including corporate governance mechanisms, enabling them to raise external capital at the lowest cost ... competition would take care of corporate governance.

(Shleifer and Vishny, 1997, p. 738)

However, markets are not perfectly competitive and therefore intervention is necessary in order to improve corporate governance, help companies to raise finance and make companies more accountable to their shareholders and other stakeholders. Agency problems do exist between companies and their shareholders throughout the world, and governments are intervening by producing policy documents and codes of corporate governance best practice at an amazing rate.

Since the early 1990s several 'voluntary' codes of practice and policy documents have been developed in the UK to help companies improve their standards of corporate governance—to make companies more accountable to shareholders and other stakeholders. The Cadbury Report, the Greenbury Report, the Hampel Report, the Turnbull Report, the Higgs Report and their accompanying codes of practice are introduced in Chapter 3. Although the codes of conduct and recommendations contained in the related policy documents are voluntary, companies that are listed on the stock exchange have to disclose the extent to which they comply with the codes. Fears of damage to companies' reputation arising from the potential exposure of corporate governance weaknesses renders it difficult for listed companies not to comply. A good example of this relates to the separation of chairman and chief executive. UK companies not complying with the Combined Code (1998) in this area will be branded as having weak corporate governance checks and balances. The 'comply or explain' approach to corporate governance is explored in Chapter 3. We now turn to discuss a different theoretical framework for corporate governance, namely transaction cost theory.

Transaction cost theory

An exposition of transaction cost theory, describing its historical development, may be found in Williamson (1996). He stated that transaction cost theory was, '... an interdisciplinary alliance of law, economics, and organization ...' (Williamson, 1996, p. 25). This discipline was initiated by Cyert and March's (1963) *A Behavioural Theory of the Firm*, a work that has become one of the cornerstones of industrial economics and finance theory. Theirs was an attempt to view the firm not as an impersonal economic unit in a world of perfect markets and equilibria but rather as an organization comprising people with differing views and objectives. Transaction cost theory is based on the fact that firms have become so large that they, in effect, substitute for the market in determining the allocation of resources. Indeed, companies are so large and so complex that price movements outside companies direct production and the markets co-ordinate transactions. Within companies, such market transactions are removed and management co-ordinates and controls production (Coase, 1937). The organization of a company (e.g., the extent of vertical integration) seems to determine the boundaries beyond which the company can determine price and production. In other words, it is the way in which the company is organized that determines its control over transactions.

Clearly, it is in the interests of company management to internalize transactions as much as possible. The main reason for this is that such internalization removes risks and uncertainties about future product prices and quality. It allows companies to remove risks of dealing with suppliers to some extent (e.g., by owning both breweries and public houses, a beer company removes the problems of negotiating prices between supplier and retailer). Any way of removing such information asymmetries is advantageous to company management and leads to reduction in business risk for a company. There are non-trivial and prohibitive costs in carrying out transactions in the marketplace, and it is therefore cheaper for companies to do it for themselves through vertical integration. The same analysis applies equally well to the case of oil companies in their various stages of production, from oil exploration, to refining and eventual retail distribution.

Traditional economics considers all economic agents to be rational and profit maximization to be the primary objective of business. Conversely, transaction cost economics attempts to incorporate human behaviour in a more realistic way. In this paradigm, managers and other economic agents practise 'bounded rationality'. Simon (1957) defined bounded rationality as behaviour that was intentionally rational but only limitedly so. Transaction cost economics also makes the assumption of 'opportunism'. This means that managers are opportunistic by nature. The theory assumes that some individuals are opportunistic, some of the time. The result of assuming bounded rationality and opportunism is that companies must:

> ... organize transactions so as to economize on bounded rationality while simultaneously safeguarding the transactions in question against the hazards of opportunism.
>
> (Williamson, 1996, p. 48)

Opportunism has been defined as 'self-interest seeking with guile' and as 'the active tendency of the human agent to take advantage, in any circumstances, of all available means to further his own privileges' (Crozier, 1964, p. 265). Given the problems of bounded rationality and opportunism, managers organize transactions in their best interests, and this activity needs to be controlled. Such opportunistic behaviour could have dire consequences on corporate finance as it would discourage potential investors from investing in companies. Immediately, we can see similarities here between agency theory and transaction cost economics, as both theories present a rationale for management to be controlled by shareholders. We now examine the ways in which transaction cost theory and agency theory are similar.

Transaction cost theory versus agency theory

Difficulties in disentangling agency theory and transaction cost economics have been acknowledged in the literature (see, e.g., Gilson and Mnookin, 1985). Williamson

(1996) addressed the extent to which agency theory and transaction cost theory provided different views of the theory of the firm and of managerial behaviour. He concluded that one of the main differences between agency theory and transaction cost theory was simply the use of a different taxonomy (i.e., using different terminology to describe essentially the same issues and problems). For example, transaction cost theory assumes people are often opportunistic, whereas agency theory discusses moral hazard and agency costs. Agency theory considers managers pursue perquisites whereas in transaction cost theory managers opportunistically arrange their transactions. Another difference is that the unit of analysis in agency theory is the individual agent, whereas in transaction cost theory the unit of analysis is the transaction. However, both theories attempt to tackle the same problem: 'how do we persuade company management to pursue shareholders' interests and company/shareholder profit maximization, rather than their self-interest?' They are simply different lenses through which the same problems may be observed and analysed. We now present a third 'lens', that of stakeholder theory.

Stakeholder theory

Stakeholder theory has developed gradually since the 1970s. One of the first expositions of stakeholder theory, couched in the management discipline, was presented by Freeman (1984), who proposed a general theory of the firm, incorporating corporate accountability to a broad range of stakeholders. Since then, there has been an abundance of writing based on stakeholder theory, across a wide array of disciplines (see, e.g., Donaldson and Preston, 1995). The role of companies in society has received increasing attention over time, with their impacts on employees, the environment, local communities, as well as their shareholders, becoming the focus of debate. Social and environmental lobby groups have gathered information on business activities and have targeted companies that have treated their stakeholders in an unethical manner.

Stakeholder theory may be viewed as a conceptual cocktail, concocted from a variety of disciplines and producing a blend of appealing sociological and organizational flavours. Indeed, stakeholder 'theory' is less of a formal unified theory and more of a broad research tradition, incorporating philosophy, ethics, political theory, economics, law and organizational social science (Wheeler et al., 2002). A basis for stakeholder theory is that companies are so large, and their impact on society so pervasive that they should discharge an accountability to many more sectors of society than solely their shareholders. There are many ways of defining stakeholder theory and 'stakeholders', depending on the user's disciplinary perspective. One commonality characterizing all definitions of stakeholders is to acknowledge their involvement in an 'exchange' relationship (Pearch, 1982; Freeman, 1984; Hill and Jones, 1992). Not only are stakeholders affected by companies but they in turn affect companies in some way. They hold a 'stake' rather than simply a 'share' in companies. Stakeholders include shareholders, employees, suppliers, customers, creditors, communities in the vicinity of the company's operations and the general public. The most extreme proponents of stakeholder theory suggest that the environment, animal species and future generations should be included as stakeholders. The stakeholder relationship has been described as one of exchange, where the stakeholder groups supply companies with 'contributions' and expect their own interests to be satisfied via 'inducements' (March and Simon, 1958). Using this analytical framework, the general public may be viewed as corporate stakeholders because they are taxpayers, thereby providing companies with a national infrastructure in which to operate. In exchange they expect companies as 'corporate citizens' to enhance, not degrade, their quality of life (Hill and Jones, 1992). Indeed, every stakeholder represents part of the nexus of implicit and explicit contracts that constitutes a company. However, many writers refer to 'stakeholders' simply as those who have a legitimate stake in the company, in the broadest sense (Farrar and Hannigan, 1998).

In the UK the Corporate Report (ASSC, 1975) was a radical accounting proposal for its time, which suggested that companies should be made accountable for their impact on a wide group of stakeholders. The way that the Corporate Report hoped to achieve this was by encouraging companies to disclose voluntarily a range of statements aimed for stakeholder use, in addition to the traditional profit and loss account, and balance sheet. The additional statements included a statement of value added, an employment report, a statement of money exchanges with government, a statement of transactions and foreign currency, a statement of future prospects and a statement of corporate objectives. This was the first time that such an all-encompassing approach to financial reporting was considered seriously by a professional UK accounting body. The report excited substantial controversy, although its impact was negligible at the time. One reason for the apparent dismissal of the Corporate Report was the change of government, with the Conservative Party coming to power in 1979 and advocating a more free market approach than the Labour Party. In more recent years, however, a stakeholder approach to accounting and finance has become more acceptable, particularly in light of the change of government from Conservative to Labour in 1997 and the growing emphasis on an 'inclusive' society. Indeed, Wheeler and Sillanpää (1997) explained the importance of developing a stakeholder society and highlighted the need for companies to be accountable to a wide range of stakeholders. Their book was endorsed by Tony Blair, the UK Prime Minister, as the 'right' approach to industrial activity.

Linked to stakeholder theory is the idea of corporate social responsibility, which is explored in Chapter 9. This is becoming a major issue for companies in the current political and social climate. Companies are being actively encouraged by social and environmental lobby groups to improve their attitudes toward stakeholders and to act in a socially responsible manner. One motivation for encouraging corporate social responsibility derives from a belief that companies have a purely moral responsibility to act in an ethical manner. This 'pure ethics' view assumes that companies should behave in a socially responsible way, satisfying the interests of all of their stakeholders, because this is 'good'. This is intuitively appealing. Quinn and Jones (1995) defined this approach as 'noninstrumental ethics', arguing that company managers have no special rules that allow them to ignore their moral obligations as human beings and that, whether ethical behaviour is profitable or not, it must be adhered to. They provided strong analytical arguments that agency theory could only be applied effectively if four moral principles were adhered to: avoiding harm to others; respecting the autonomy of others; avoiding lying; and honouring agreements. Indeed, they claimed that the principal–agent model could only hold if it was embedded in the setting of these four moral principles. Why should the 'moral obligation' to 'keep a promise' to maximize shareholder wealth be any more important, or supersede, basic human principles, such as avoiding harm to others? In other words:

> How can one be morally bound to an agreement to ignore one's other moral obligations?
>
> (Quinn and Jones, 1995, p. 36)

This argument formed the basis of their exposition of 'agent morality', where agents must first attend to their basic moral duties as human beings, as they have no special dispensation from moral obligations. Only after meeting these moral obligations could they attend to their obligation to maximize shareholder wealth.

Company law, however, makes a purely ethics-motivated approach to business impractical, as companies have a legal and fiduciary obligation to shareholder wealth maximization.[5] Similarly, institutional investors have a legal, fiduciary obligation to maximize the returns of their clients. These legal obligations mean that the business case for corporate social responsibility is the only realistic approach for company management. The legal system has been shown to be a significant barrier to the non-instrumental ethics case for business in the US (Quinn and Jones, 1995). The basic philosophy of separate legal personality of companies, as famously encapsulated in the *Salomon versus A. Salomon & Co. Ltd* decision (see Farrar and Hannigan, 1998), is incompatible with a framework that makes directors personally accountable for their behaviour. Even the latest review of company law in the UK, which has attempted in its various drafts to stress the needs for business to be accountable to stakeholders, has ultimately resigned corporate social responsibility to a back seat, based on the 'materiality' of social, environmental and ethical risks to the business. In other words, companies should only take account of these factors, in so far as they affect the bottom line. We discuss the implications of the Modernising Company Law (2002) review for corporate social responsibility and socially responsible investment, within the context of corporate governance, in Chapter 9. It is almost impossible to pursue ethical business unless it is demonstrated to be

---

5 A 'pure ethics' motive attracts derision from many members of both the professional and academic community, who view it as completely impractical and unrealistic. For example, one of our academic colleagues, who will remain nameless, dismisses a pure ethics approach as the 'pink fluffy bunny' view of corporate governance.

profitable, not only because of the attitudes of managers and shareholders but also because of our legal system and corporate governance structures. It would take more than a change in attitude to reconstitute company law in the UK and elsewhere. We now discuss the extent to which stakeholder theory and agency theory may be considered together, rather than be viewed as mutually exclusive.

Stakeholder versus agency theory

Is it possible that companies can maximize shareholder wealth, in an agency theory framework, at the same time as satisfying a broad range of stakeholder needs? In other words, 'is there any consistency between stakeholder theory and agency theory?' The importance of this question, and related questions, cannot be over-stated, given the pervasive impact that businesses have on society in our consumer-led, multinational-driven world. Yet the answer remains elusive. New frameworks for business which depict a 'sustainable organization' culture within a corporate community and which also recognize the interdependencies and synergies between the company, its stakeholders, value-based networks[6] and society are emerging from the academic literature. Such an approach to business seeks to maximize value creation, through simultaneous maximization of economic, social and ecological welfare. Some academic work has provided empirical evidence that stakeholder management leads to improved shareholder value (Hillman and Keim, 2001).[7] However, stakeholder theory has long been vilified as the anathema of shareholder-based agency theory (e.g., Sternberg, 1998). We revisit this perspective, embodied in the work of Milton Friedman, in Chapter 9. From this viewpoint, the only moral obligation facing managers is to maximize shareholder return, as this results (in an efficient market) in the 'best' allocation of social resources (see, e.g., Drucker, 1982; Jensen, 1991). The continual friction between these two theoretical frameworks was discussed by Shankman (1999), who pointed out that agency theory has for a long time represented the dominant paradigm for business and that the conflict between agency and stakeholder theories of the firm can be characterized as:

> . . . an ongoing struggle between economic views of the firm which are decidedly silent on the moral implications of the modern corporation, and ethicists who place the need for understanding ethical implications in a central role in the field of business ethics.
>
> (Shankman, 1999, p. 319)

Indeed, on a theoretical basis, there are significant differences between the two

---

6 Wheeler et al. (2002) used the term Value Based Networks (VBNs) to refer to new communities that are being created from a desire (or need) to create and increase value.

7 Hillman and Keim (2001) used an index to measure stakeholder performance for companies, known as the Kinder, Lydenburg, Domini Index. This Index was compiled by an independent rating service that focuses exclusively on ranking approximately 800 companies according to nine areas of social performance.

theoretical paradigms, which at first sight render the two theories irreconcilable. For example, Shankman (1999) described stakeholder theory, but not agency theory, as normative in orientation, showing that the whole theoretical and philosophical underpinnings of the two theories were at variance. Nevertheless, there is a growing perception among theorists and practitioners that these two paradigms may be compatible (Wheeler et al., 2002) and that an altered approach to their theoretical derivation may allow them to be treated within one framework. For example, Shankman (1999) argued that agency theory may be subsumed within a general stakeholder model of companies, as:

(i) stakeholder theory is the necessary outcome of agency theory and is thus a more appropriate way to conceptualize theories of the firm;

(ii) agency theory, when properly modified, is at best a narrow form of stakeholder theory;

(iii) the assumptions about human behaviour and motivation implicit in agency theory are contradictory; and

(iv) all theories of the firm must uphold an implicit moral minimum that includes certain fundamental rights and principles and assumptions of human behaviour that may very well require other traditional theories of the firm to be modified or even reconceived.

Similarities between the theoretical standpoints are evident on close examination. For example, it is the manager group of stakeholders who are in a position of ultimate control, as they have decision-making powers allowing them to allocate the company's resources in a manner most consistent with the claims of other stakeholder groups (Hill and Jones, 1992). This means that it is company management who are ultimately responsible for satisfying stakeholders' needs and expectations. Using agency theory terminology, given their unique position of responsibility and accountability, managers' interests need to be aligned not only with shareholders' interests but also with the interests of all other stakeholder groups. As stated in Hill and Jones (1992):

> ... there is a parallel between the general class of stakeholder–agent relationships and the principal–agent relationships articulated by agency theory. Both stakeholder–agent and principal–agent relationships involve an implicit or explicit contract, the purpose of which is to try and reconcile divergent interests. In addition, both relationships are policed by governance structure.
>
> (Hill and Jones, 1992, p. 134)

Balancing the needs and interests of different stakeholder groups is notoriously difficult. This should not however be used as an excuse for making no effort to achieve such a balance. Hill and Jones (1992) also pointed out that many of the concepts and language of agency theory could be applied equally well to stakeholder–agency relationships. Overall, they argued that principal–agent relationships, as defined by agency theory, could be viewed as a subset of the more general class of stakeholder–agent relationships. Indeed, in developing 'stakeholder–agency theory' they sought to develop a modification of agency theory aimed at accommodating theories of power arising from a stakeholder perspective. They argued that stakeholder-derived and agency theory perspectives on organizational phenomena, which have been viewed as mutually exclusive interpretations, may indeed be interpreted in one model, by making a series of assumptions about market efficiency.

The moral discourse for company management implied by agency theory and stakeholder theory is vastly different. As Quinn and Jones (1995) explained, adopting one perspective (that of agency) leads to a discourse based on self-interest, whereas adoption of the other leads to a discourse of 'duty' and social responsibility. Unless these two perspectives can be merged in some way, the managerial discourse cannot be expected to combine fully the extremes of profit-seeking self-interest and moral responsibility to society.

As discussed above, the only realistic compromise solution to this problem is to adopt the business case, rather than the pure ethics case. The business case for managers to adopt a stakeholder-oriented approach is based on the notion that 'good ethics' is 'good business' and that employing ethics as a strategic management tool increases the present value of the firm (Blanchard and Peale, 1988; Kotter and Heskett, 1992; Quinn and Jones, 1995). This is, according to Quinn and Jones (1995), an example of 'instrumental ethics' whereby managers choose an approach of corporate social responsibility in order to maximize shareholder wealth. As argued earlier, this is really the only approach to ethics that makes sense in the modern world, given the extant legal and regulatory environment confronting businesses. Unless corporate social responsibility and accountability enhance shareholder wealth, neither company management nor large institutional investors, nor small-scale shareholders would ever endorse it as a realistic approach to corporate activity. It is more realistic to accept that ethics have to be profitable in order to be acceptable to businesses. But why should this not be the case? People are generally ethical, therefore ethical behaviour should be rewarded in a free market and unethical behaviour punished in an Adam Smith environment (see, e.g., Boatright, 1999).[8] This was certainly the case with Enron when managerial, unethical behaviour became public knowledge, as we can see from the case study in Chapter 2.[9]

---

[8] Boatright (1999) explains that Adam Smith's invisible hand may, in an ethical environment, distribute wealth to socially responsible, ethical companies and distribute wealth away from unethical companies, through the free market mechanism.

[9] There are, however, problems with the instrumental ethics case, or business case, for corporate social responsibility, as it is difficult to see how a company is being truly 'moral' if it is only pursuing ethicality for reasons of self-interest. See Quinn and Jones, 1995, for an in-depth discussion of this dilemma. For example, they comment that, 'Discussions about stock price movements, instrumental ethics, and shareholder wealth maximization obscure the true moral argument' (p. 28). They also make the point that ethics is 'hard to fake'.

It seems increasingly likely that creating value for stakeholders by businesses focusing attention on maximizing value for local communities, employees and environmental impacts (to name but a few) may be synonymous with creating financial value for shareholders. Ignoring the needs of stakeholders can lead to lower financial performance and even corporate failure. Corporate social, ethical and environmental performance are being viewed increasingly by investors as indicators of management quality and proxies for performance in other areas of the business. A company that is well managed is likely to have a good environmental management system and high levels of stakeholder dialogue and engagement. Indeed, the efforts made by many companies to increase the quality and quantity of cross-stakeholder dialogue is impressive. Camelot plc is a salient example of a company attempting to demonstrate an eagerness to embrace stakeholder dialogue and active engagement with diverse stakeholder groups (see Illustration 9.3 for a full discussion of this company's approach to stakeholders). However, this may be due to the company's heightened vulnerability in the area of ethics, given its core business of gambling. Nevertheless, any company with bad stakeholder relations could be characterized by poor management and consequently poor financial performance. This is one scenario—and one that is being accepted more widely in practice. There is, however, a large element of scepticism concerning the genuine improvements in stakeholder accountability arising from the increase in dialogue, as we see from the discussion in Chapter 9 (e.g., Owen et al., 2001).

An essential aspect of this debate is the extent to which satisfying the needs of a divergent group of stakeholders can also lead to satisfaction of the ultimate objective of shareholder wealth maximization. Throughout Part III of this book we attempt to demonstrate that in the long term there is little inconsistency between the ultimate objective of agency theory and the practice of a stakeholder approach. We consider that it is only by taking account of stakeholder as well as shareholder interests that companies can achieve long-term profit maximization and, ultimately, shareholder wealth maximization. This belief is principally based on a growing body of literature and empirical evidence that suggests that corporate accountability which takes into account a broad range of social, ethical and environmental factors is conducive to financial performance. We attempt to show at different points in this text that businesses can be ethical and profitable, by considering the growing wealth of literature endorsing a positive relationship between corporate social responsibility and corporate financial performance.

Chapter summary

In this chapter we have discussed the broad spectrum of definitions of corporate governance that exist in the literature, ranging from a narrow, agency theory definition to broader, stakeholder-oriented definitions. We have also provided our own definition for the purposes of this book, which adopts a stakeholder-oriented approach to corporate governance but one which, as we have discussed, does not necessarily contradict an agency theory approach. We have also outlined three theoretical frameworks used for discussing and analysing corporate governance and have examined the extent to which they overlap. Having outlined some theoretical issues in corporate governance, we now turn to a discussion of the practical agenda for corporate governance reform. Our first task is to look at what happens when corporate governance fails, as in the case of Enron. This case clearly demonstrates a need for corporate governance reform. We then proceed to examine the ways in which corporate governance may be improved by targeting a range of mechanisms, checks and balances.

Questions for reflection and discussion

1 Read the definitions of corporate governance provided in this chapter. What would be your own, preferred definition of 'corporate governance'?

2 Which theoretical framework discussed in this chapter do you believe presents the most appropriate explicit framework for corporate governance, and why?

3 Do you think that agency theory and stakeholder theory are striving toward the same goal?

4 Read the discussion on the instrumental and non-instrumental ethics case for corporate social responsibility. Do you think either of these approaches is viable in today's business environment?

Chapter 2

Enron: a case study in corporate governance failure

Aim and objectives

This chapter presents a case study of the Enron saga, in order to highlight the consequences that arise from the failure of corporate governance mechanisms. The specific objectives of this chapter are to:

- appreciate the importance of effective corporate governance and the consequences of weak corporate governance;

- consider the factors that led to the collapse of Enron;

- explain why the case of Enron has encouraged corporate governance reform worldwide.

Introduction

In the previous chapter we defined corporate governance and introduced a number of theoretical frameworks that have been used to analyse corporate governance issues. We now provide a detailed case study of the collapse of Enron, in order to enhance the reader's appreciation of why corporate governance is essential to successful business and social welfare. The Enron saga presents a poignant illustration of what happens when corporate governance is weak and when the checks and balances are ineffective. The case also illustrates the problems of controlling human nature. However good corporate governance is from a cosmetic point of view and however good a company's apparent financial performance, if there is unethical behaviour at the highest level, little if anything, can avoid eventual disaster.

The collapse of Enron

In 2001 Enron became a household name—and probably in most households in most countries around the world! On 2 December 2001 Enron, one of the 10 largest companies in the USA, filed for Chapter 11 bankruptcy (a type of court protection giving the company management time to make arrangements with their creditors). In the following months, more and more evidence emerged of corporate governance weaknesses and fraudulent activity. Countries across the world have been unsettled and disturbed by the shock of this event and are now examining their own corporate governance systems in micro-detail, looking for similar weaknesses and potential Enrons. 'Enronitis' has spread across the globe like a lethal virus, infecting every company and every shareholding institution, worrying even the smallest shareholder and unnerving the financial markets. In this case study we examine the downfall of Enron in detail, looking at the reasons for the collapse and commenting on the corporate governance problems that were rife within the company.

Corporate governance failure and corporate collapse can happen in the strongest company. Investors, employees and creditors can be seduced by a company's reputation and success and can throw caution to the wind. If economic agents were rational, as they should be according to economic and finance theory, this sort of blindness could never happen. But it does. Investors do not always behave rationally, and human behaviour and psychology are factors that are difficult to incorporate in a finance model or an economic theory. Polly Peck and Coloroll were cases of irrational behaviour in the UK in the 1980s, when investors missed vital information in the accounts of these companies, pertaining to huge contingent liabilities. As soon as this information became public knowledge, both companies collapsed (Smith, 1996b). We first consider the way in which Enron built up its glittering reputation and the success that it encountered before crashing in such a monumental fashion.

Laying the foundations

Enron was a Houston-based energy company founded by a brilliant entrepreneur, Kenneth Lay. The company was created in 1985 by a merger of two American gas pipeline companies. In a period of 16 years the company was transformed from a relatively small concern, involved in gas pipelines, and oil and gas exploration, to the world's largest energy trading company (*The Economist*, 28 November 2002). Deregulation of the energy market in the USA allowed utilities to choose their energy supplier. The 1980s saw deregulation of the market for natural gas in the USA, and deregulation of the wholesale electricity market followed in 1992 (*The Economist*, 26 February 1998). Deregulation had a far-reaching impact, allowing energy providers to diversify into other areas of the industry and become more competitive. Deregulation of energy in the UK had a similar effect, forcing providers to compete on price in order to attract supply contracts. One of the effects of deregulation was to create a market in energy trading, similar to a futures and options trading floor, where deals were struck between suppliers and clients on a continual basis.

Glittering success

Enron's success was phenomenal. By 1998 Enron had eight divisions including Enron Energy Services (EES) and Enron Capital & Trade (ECT). In 1994 ECT sold $10 million of electricity. By 1997 the company was selling $4 billion, which constituted almost a fifth of the North American wholesale market. Yet it only produced a small proportion of this itself. In 1998 Enron held $23 billion in assets (see *The Economist*, 26 February 1998 for these and other figures). In January 1998, Enron sold a 7% share of EES to two pension funds for $130 million. From 1990 Enron's total return to shareholders ran far in advance of the index. In July 1998 Enron announced a $2.3 billion takeover of Wessex Water in the UK. Indeed, Rebecca Mark, then in charge of Enron's new water business, commented that they intended to be one of the two or three dominant players in the business (*The Economist*, 30 July 1998). In 1999 Enron's sales reached $40.1 billion. By 2000 the company's revenues reached over $100 billion (*The Economist*, 8 February 2001). In February 2001 the company's stock market value was $60 billion (*The Economist*, 29 November 2001). Enron became famous for its dexterity in handling risk management derivatives, as well as for its abilities in the area of commodity trading derivatives. Indeed, the company was proud of having 'invented' weather derivatives in 1997 (*The Economist*, 15 June 2000). Another area where Enron was praised for its innovation and success was in Internet-based business. At the end of 1999, Enron launched its Internet-based trading platform, EnronOnline. The venture was massively successful with 5,000 trades taking place online every day valuing about $3 billion (*The Economist*, 28 June 2001). However, the chief executive of Enron, Jeffrey Skilling, dismissed this success by saying that the Internet business was just a better form of telephone, which was the way the company did business successfully before.

Toward the end of its life, Enron had transformed itself from an energy company to a predominantly financial and energy trading company, trading financial derivatives as well as energy contracts and effectively running a gas pipeline on the side (*The Economist*, 29 November 2001). Success was so great at Enron that the words over the door as visitors entered the Houston headquarters were changed in 2001 from:

'The world's leading energy company'

to:

'The world's leading company'

Perhaps a quote from Dante would have been better:

'*Lasciate ogni sparanza voi ch'entrate!*'[1]

This sort of self-confidence and pride is a clear example of counting chickens before they are hatched.

---

[1] The translation of this is 'Abandon all hope ye who enter here!' It is the last sentence of the inscription over the entrance to Hell in the *Divina Commedia*, 'Inferno' canto 3, 1.

Early worries

An article in *The Economist* (26 February 1998) raised queries as to the permanency of Enron's success. Causes for concern were, first, the different speeds of deregulation in different states in America and, therefore, the ability to achieve free competition in all of the states relatively quickly. Second, there were growing concerns that Enron may not have been well enough equipped to deal with the smaller customers it was taking on. Another main concern, expressed in many newspapers and professional literature, was that the company's management team were arrogant, overambitious and even sycophantic. Some even suggested that Kenneth Lay was like a cult leader with staff and employees fawning over his every word and following him slavishly (*The Economist*, 1 June 2000). This is not a healthy way to do business and indicates an ethical and moral problem at the head of the company. Such cases of unethical behaviour are associated with bad corporate governance and should be taken as warning signs. A prophetic, ironic and almost visionary comment begs quotation:

> *Arrogance . . . is Enron's great failing . . .* And how does Mr. Lay respond to this charge? . . . Mr. Lay speaks glowingly of the heyday of Drexel and of its star trader Michael Milken, whom he counts as a friend: they were accused of arrogance . . . but they were just being 'very innovative and very aggressive'. *The comparison is not especially well chosen*, for it is worth recalling what then happened: Mr. Milken ended up in jail for pushing the law too far, and the arrogant Drexel collapsed in a heap of bad debts and ignominy. *For all its arrogance, Enron is hardly likely to share that fate: but hubris can lead to nemesis, even so.*
>
> (*The Economist*, 1 June 2000, emphasis added)

This quotation proved to be a poignant forecast of later events at Enron, as well as prophetic in terms of the reasons for the company's downfall.

Signs of distress

In 1997 Enron wrote off $537 million, mainly in order to settle a contract dispute over North Sea Gas. The company also became notorious for relying too heavily on non-recurring items, such as asset sales, to reach its target of 15% annual growth in earnings. The company purchased Portland General Electric, a utility company in Oregon that held access to the California market. By buying into the Californian retail electricity market when the State deregulated electricity, the company seemed to be expanding too far. Furthermore, they had little success in penetrating the market and were only able to attract about 30,000 new customers in the whole State. This was not enough to merit their massive advertising campaign (*The Economist*, 23 April 1998). It seems that Enron's success in controlling the energy market came more from its dexterity in energy derivatives trading than its abilities in the core business. The company seems to have overstretched itself as a trader in commodities. In 2001, Dynegy, a competitor in the energy industry, was committed to a merger with Enron but backed out when Enron's accounting problems began to emerge. Indeed, not everyone was seduced by Enron's success. One investment firm, Reed Wasden, had been sceptical of Enron for a number of years. They pointed out that the company's trading margins had collapsed from 5.3% in 1998 to under 1.7% in 2001 (*The Economist*, 6 December 2001).

The fall . . . and fall . . . of Enron

In August 2001 the chief executive, Jeffrey Skilling, left the company following concerns about the company's management and about his outburst of 'asshole' at an analyst who dared ask him a tricky question (*The Economist*, 6 December 2001). By late autumn it became clear that Enron was suffering serious financial problems with discussion over a takeover or bankruptcy (*The Economist*, 1 November 2001). Toward the end of October 2001, Moody's credit rating agency cut Enron's rating to barely above that of junk bonds. In November 2001 Standard & Poor's downgraded Enron's debt to junk bond status. Unfortunately, Enron's debt contracts included clauses stipulating that the company would have to make additional payments to debtholders if the company was downgraded (*The Economist*, 6 December 2001). On one day alone, 30 October 2001, Enron's shares fell by 19% (*The Economist*, 1 November 2001).

Enron's brilliance in derivatives trading fuelled its demise, as the company lost $1.2 billion in capital from a failed hedging deal with a private equity fund. The company had to sell 55 million shares. A severe lack of transparency in Enron's balance sheet meant that no one was aware of this and other off-balance-sheet liabilities until it was too late. Despite such serious problems, even as late as November 2001, there was a general perception that the company was too big to fail and would weather the storm (*The Economist*, 1 November 2001). However, by the middle of November 2001 it was clear that the company was doomed. More than 20 class action lawsuits had already been filed. The main accusations covered fraud and material misstatement in the companies' financial reports. Kenneth Lay himself commented that the company had been overgeared, with extensive use of debt capital on the balance sheet (*The Economist*, 15 November 2001). Furthermore, the company was accused of insider trading. Indeed, Enron top executives sold over $1 billion of Enron shares to other investors. Even though Enron's annual reports indicated financial prosperity, it was clear that Enron's management knew a lot more than they were letting on, making hay while the sun shone. This is a clear illustration of information asymmetry and agency problems, with insider investors profiting from better information than outsiders.

On 2 December 2001, the great Enron filed for Chapter 11 bankruptcy. Kenneth Lay resigned in January 2002. In August 2002, Michael Kopper, an assistant to the former finance director of Enron, pleaded guilty to charges of wire fraud and money laundering. On 2 October 2002, Andrew Fastow, former finance director of Enron, was charged with: money laundering; securities, wire and mail fraud; and conspiracy to inflate Enron's profits and enrich himself at the company's expense (*The Economist*, 3 October 2002).

Creative accounting at Enron and its impact on the accounting profession

Transparency is an essential ingredient for a sound system of corporate governance. In Chapter 6 we examine the role of transparency in corporate governance in more detail. The USA has been dubbed the strongest capital market in the world, with the highest standards of integrity and ethicality. What went wrong? Both the audit function and the accounting function in Enron were fraudulent and opaque. However, Enron's collapse has had repercussions on the whole of the accounting and auditing profession, not just in the USA but worldwide. Enron's accounting was anything but transparent. Confidence in the company collapsed in 2001, when it became clear that their accounts were not only unreliable but fraudulent. Arthur Andersen, one of the Big Five, has now disappeared, partly as a result of its involvement in Enron's fraudulent accounting and auditing. However, Enron was not Andersen's first major problem. They had already paid out millions of dollars in settlements following inaccurate and weak auditing on a number of companies including Sunbeam, Waste Management and Discovery Zone (*The Economist*, 15 November 2001). In 2000, Andersen collected $25 million for auditing Enron's books in addition to $27 million for consulting services. This seems excessive and demonstrates a notorious problem of conflicts of interest between the auditing and consultancy arms of accounting firms. We return to this issue in more detail below.

Examples of Enron's devious accounting abound. The company recorded profits, for example, from a joint venture with Blockbuster Video that never materialized (*The Economist*, 7 February 2002). In 2002, Enron restated its accounts, a bad sign in itself and a process that reduced reported profits by $600 million (*The Economist*, 6 December 2001). Indeed, the process resulted in a cumulative profit reduction of $591 million and a rise in debt of $628 million for the financial statements from 1997 to 2000. This triggered an investigation by the Securities & Exchange Commission (SEC) into the auditing work of Andersen, Enron's auditors. The difference between the profit figures was mainly attributable to the earlier omission of three off-balance sheet entities. Such profit inflation allowed the company to increase its earnings per share figure (EPS). EPS is simply the total earnings figure divided by the number of shares. The company's exaggerated focus on its EPS was certainly a factor in its eventual decline, as Enron stated in its 2000 annual report that this main aim was to focus on EPS. This is a common strategy and one which can lead to manipulation of accounting numbers in attempts to inflate the EPS figure (*The Economist*, 6 December 2001). The pressure on companies in the USA and elsewhere to increase their EPS year on year has been blamed for corporate short-termism (see Chapter 1 for a discussion of short-termism, p. 17). It also provides directors with an irresistible temptation to cheat the figures! Not only did the company clearly manipulate the accounting numbers to inflate the earnings figure, but it was found to have removed substantial amounts of debt from its accounts by setting up a number of off-balance sheet entities. Such special purpose entities are non-consolidated, off-balance-sheet vehicles that have some legitimate uses, such as the financing of a research and development partnership with another company. However, they can also be used to hide a company's liabilities from the balance sheet, in order to make the financial statements look much better than they really are (*The Economist*, 2 May 2002). This was certainly the case for Enron. It meant that significant liabilities did not have to be disclosed on Enron's financial statements, as they were almost attributable to another legal entity (but not quite). To anyone, this is an obvious example of fraudulent, premeditated and unethical management. Furthermore, about 28% of Enron's EPS was shown to have come from gains on sales of securitized assets to third parties connected to Enron (*The Economist*, 6 December 2001).

All this begs the question, 'why did Enron's auditor allow this type of activity?' They had to have been aware of it. Perhaps Andersen considered the transactions were relatively too small to be considered material. However, this is becoming less of a reasonable excuse (*The Economist*, 6 December 2001). In December 2001 the chief executive of Andersen, Joseph Berardino, stated that the firm had made an error of judgement over one of the off-balance-sheet entities created by Enron (*The Economist*, 20 December 2001). One 'special purpose' vehicle in particular, called Chewco, again created by Enron to offload liabilities for off-balance-sheet financing purposes, was cited as being a chief culprit, as it did not provide Andersen with adequate information. Clearly, had Andersen had this additional information, they would have forced Enron to consolidate Chewco into their accounts. However, such ignorance on the part of Andersen may not be adequate support for its lack of action. According to Enron, Andersen had been carrying out a detailed audit of the main structured finance vehicles, which made the auditing firm guilty of acting too slowly and inadequately (*The Economist*, 20 December 2001).

In January 2002, Andersen fired the partner in charge of Enron's audit, David Duncan, as he was found to have ordered the disposal of documents even after the SEC had subpoenaed the firm as part of its investigation into Enron. However, David Duncan clarified that he was not working in isolation, but was in constant contact with Andersen's headquarters. Furthermore, Enron itself ordered the shredding of vast quantities of documentation concerning the company's financial liabilities. The firm was criminally indicted by the Department of Justice for shredding documents relating to Enron. In March 2002, Andersen pleaded not guilty in a federal court to charges of obstruction of justice by document shredding (*The Economist*, 21 May 2002). Documents pertaining to Enron were not only shredded in Houston but also in London! Berardino resigned as chief executive of Andersen in March 2002. On 15 June 2002, Andersen was convicted of obstruction of justice. It is difficult for some to see how a company (as opposed to a person) can be found guilty of a crime, but certainly in the USA there is a perception that companies may be associated with unethical behaviour, in the same way as individuals (see *The Economist*, 13 June 2002, for a discussion of this issue). Such an approach makes corporate social responsibility a moral, human obligation, as companies are considered to be equivalent to people in a moral sense. We explore this issue in more detail in Chapter 9. The fall of Enron was the biggest corporate collapse ever, and the downfall of Andersen the most significant death of an accounting firm ever.

Conflicts of interest are a frequent problem in the audit profession. Independent appointment of the company's auditors by the company's shareholders is frequently replaced by subjective appointment by company bosses, where the auditor is all too often beholden to the company's senior management. Further, there are conflicts of interest arising from interwoven functions of audit and consultancy. Special, cosy relationships are built over time between companies and their auditors, which can again compromise independent judgement and cloud the auditing function. Such conflicts of interest impinge on the corporate governance function. Improvements in the audit function are clearly emphasized by the Enron case (*The Economist*, 7 February 2002). Creating a division between the auditing and consultancy arms of auditing firms may help. Indeed, a complete ban on auditing firms offering both services to the same client may be implemented. KPMG and Ernst & Young, PricewaterhouseCoopers and Deloitte Touche Tohmatsu have all decided to separate their auditing and consulting arms (*The Economist*, 7 February 2002). Another solution may be to instigate the rotation of auditors so that special relationships between auditors and their companies may not be allowed to develop. We discuss these possible routes to ensuring the effectiveness of the audit function in Chapter 6. Until now audit companies have been essentially self-regulated. They have used a process of peer review to check their procedures. The oversight bodies have been weak and lacking in regulative clout (*The Economist*, 7 February 2002). The Sarbanes–Oxley Act of July 2002 has taken a hard line on the regulation of auditing. The new Act restricts the consulting work that accounting firms are allowed to carry out for their audit clients. The Smith Report (2003) has also attempted to deal with these issues, as we see in Chapters 3 and 6.

The Financial Accounting Standards Board (FASB) in the USA has been forced to reconsider its position on off-balance-sheet financing, a subject that has troubled them for years. Especially, the FASB is reviewing its rules on how to account for special purpose entities (financing vehicles), such as those created and used by Enron. Attempts to address such issues in the past have been halted by aggressive lobbying (*The Economist*, 7 February 2002). Not surprisingly, one important lobbyist was Richard Causey, Enron's former chief accountant (*The Economist*, 2 May 2002). The FASB rule in place at the time of Enron's fall was that a company could keep a special purpose vehicle off its balance sheet, as long as an independent third party owned a controlling equity interest equivalent to at least 3% of the fair value of its assets. The FASB has, post-Enron, considered raising that number to 10% (*The Economist*, 2 May 2002). The Enron saga has added fuel to the process of international harmonization of accounting standards. The International Accounting Standards Board (IASB) is in the process of developing internationally acceptable standards for accounting worldwide. The strong card that the USA has traditionally played, in setting the agenda for international accounting, has been severely weakened by the shock waves from Enron. Under international accounting standards, the removal of material liabilities from Enron's balance sheet via its special purpose entities would not have been allowed, as the rules are harsher. The rules-based approach to accounting traditionally applied by the USA has also come under fire, as it provides companies with an incentive to comply with the letter but avoid the spirit of the rules. A more principles-based approach, such as that adopted in the UK, would probably encourage companies to comply more in substance than in form.

Further, there are two accounting standards in the UK that protect investors from the type of creative accounting practised by Enron. First, there is the fifth accounting standard 'Reporting the Substance of Transactions'. This ensures that quasi-subsidiaries, such as Enron's special purpose entities, are presented in the group's accounts so that the commercial effects of controlling operations, not owned by the company in a technical sense, are clarified. Second, there is the twelfth accounting standard, which deals with contingent liabilities. Companies in the UK have to disclose a description and a quantification of the effect of each and every contingent liability (see Ryland, 2002). Having suffered severely from Polly Peck and Coloroll, the UK has ensured that these potential black holes in accounting are dealt with. Surely this is encouraging for UK investors, as these two standards make a UK Enron less likely.

The Sarbanes–Oxley Act, brought in quickly in July 2002, also attempted to address accounting fraud through regulation. Chief executives and chief financial officers now have to 'swear' that to the best of their knowledge their latest annual reports and quarterly reports neither contain untrue statements, nor omit any material fact (*The Economist*, 15 August 2002). Such new legislation should encourage directors to act ethically and monitor their own financial accounting practices more carefully. They are now personally liable for cases of fraudulent, creative accounting. But is regulation really the answer? Is it not more worrying for shareholders to feel that the directors of companies they 'own' are so untrustworthy that they have to be tied down in this way, not having the integrity to regulate themselves?

The aftermath

There are distinct similarities between the downfall of Enron and the collapse of Long Term Capital Management, an infamous hedge fund in the USA run by Nobel Prize-winning financial economists. Both companies demonstrated financial wizardry, trading immense quantities of derivative contracts and becoming excessively confident, indeed arrogant, about their abilities to beat the market. Indeed, although Enron had substantial abilities in the hedging field, these can collapse—and did—when the market started to fall. The general decline in stock markets around the world in 2001 had a negative influence on Enron's hedging success. The collapse of Enron also bore similarities to those of Maxwell and Polly Peck in the UK, as these companies also revealed significant audit failures. The personal suffering caused by Enron's collapse has been extensive. When Enron filed for bankruptcy many employees lost their savings as well as their jobs (*The Economist*, 28 November 2002). The pensions of Enron's employees were invested in Enron shares, so massive loss in future income for such pensioners is another important consideration. This emphasizes the social implications of corporate collapse and weak corporate governance.

One of the main effects of Enron's collapse has been on the general confidence of the government, corporate and professional bodies, and investors in companies' activities and management integrity. The effects of Enron have been so far-reaching that the term 'Enronmania' has been coined to refer to the reaction among company bosses and investors to fear (indeed terror!) that companies with characteristics similar to Enron may share its fate (Ryland, 2002). Indeed, the whole case raises the question, 'how could such a huge and successful company have avoided scrutiny for so long and managed to fool investors and creditors?' For the Federal Reserve, the concern was 'how could a company with such huge debts avoid regulatory checks and balances?' The immediate remedy for this situation was the Sarbanes–Oxley Act, which was produced and signed by the President in July 2002. However, an ongoing cause for concern is the choice between a regulated or a more voluntary corporate governance environment. As some countries, such as the USA, adopt a regulated approach to corporate governance reform and react in a regulative manner to corporate governance problems, other countries, such as the UK, consider that a more principles-driven and voluntary approach is more appropriate. The Higgs Report (2003) reviewed corporate governance in the UK and made proposals for improvements in boardroom practice, but avoided any attempt to introduce regulation. This is typical of the UK's more voluntary approach to corporate governance reform and is the UK's response to Enron, *inter alia* (see, e.g., *The Economist*, 31 October 2002). We discuss the 'comply and explain approach' to corporate governance in Chapter 3.

A reflection on the corporate governance problems in Enron

Severe corporate governance problems emerge from the Enron wreckage. Unfettered power in the hand of the chief executive is an obvious problem and one that characterized Enron's management. Separation of the chairman and chief executive role is not common in the USA. This is a technique that is so successful in the UK as a means of improving the effectiveness of a company's board of directors that its application in the USA would benefit American companies and particularly American shareholders! As we see from Chapters 3 and 4, the Higgs Report (2003) has further strengthened the relevance of this initiative to corporate governance in the UK. The function of the non-executive directors in Enron was weak as they did not detect fraudulent accounting activities through their internal audit function. Indeed, the internal audit committee failed completely in policing their auditors. Serious conflicts of interest have arisen involving members of Enron's internal audit committee. For example, Wendy Gramm was the chairman of Enron's audit committee and her husband, Phil Gramm, a senator, received substantial political donations from Enron. Also, Lord Wakeham was on the audit committee at the same time as having a consulting contract with Enron (*The Economist*, 7 February 2002). These examples show that people in responsible positions, who should have detected unethical activities, were themselves not independent.

There were numerous illustrations of unethical activity within the Enron Organization that continued to come to light long after its downfall. For example, in May 2002 it became clear from documents released by the Federal Energy Regulatory Commission that Enron's energy traders developed and used strategies, or tricks, to manipulate the markets in which California bought electric. One trick, the 'Death Star', involved arranging power sales to flow in opposite directions, so that Enron could collect fees for transporting electricity when it had not done so! (*The Economist*, 9 May 2002).

Overall, corporate governance in Enron was weak in almost all respects. The board of directors was composed of a number of people who have been shown to be of poor moral character and willing to conduct fraudulent activity. This was the genuine root of the company's corporate governance failure. If the leadership is rotten how can the rest of the company succeed in the long run? Also, the non-executive directors were compromised by conflicts of interest. The internal audit committee did not perform its functions of internal control and of checking the external auditing function. Furthermore, the company's accounting and financial reporting function failed miserably. Both the financial director and the chief executive were prepared to produce fraudulent accounts for the company. The corporate crimes perpetrated by members of the Enron hierarchy are unnerving. How could the company survive so long with such unethical activities being carried out at the highest level? Why did no one notice? Where they did notice problems, why did they not report the company? How could the company's auditors allow such a travesty of justice? The questions raised by the Enron saga are far more numerous than the solutions offered.

There have been a proliferation of books on the downfall of Enron, seeking to explain why events transpired as they did.[2] As we have seen, the USA and the UK reacted strongly to Enron's collapse and corporate governance has been hurled to centre stage, as a result of the terrible weaknesses at the heart of Enron's corporate governance system. The long-term effects of Enron will hopefully be a cleaner and

---

[2] The following represent just a few of the titles that have arisen as a result of the Enron debacle: Barreveld (2002), Cruver (2002), Elliott and Schroth (2002), Fox (2003) and Fusaro and Miller (2002).

more ethical corporate environment across the globe. Continuous updating of corporate governance codes of practice and systematic review of corporate governance checks and balances are necessary to avoid other Enrons in the future. As in the famous (or infamous) UK novel, *The Clockwork Orange* (by Anthony Burgess), systems of controlling juvenile delinquents only worked superficially, as they forced a change in behaviour but did not alter the individuals' character and attitudes. The chief miscreant in the novel still wanted to behave amorally, but could not due to the treatment he had received. In a similar way, preventing unethical behaviour within companies through cold, legalistic and mechanistic means cannot alter a person's general approach. In our own research into the attitudes of institutional investors toward corporate governance issues, we found that generally fund managers and directors considered unethical behaviour could not be controlled easily. For example, one corporate governance representative in a large investment institution in the City of London commented that:

> ... if people want to be fraudulent there is nothing in the current system to stop them— and if they are clever and fraudulent then they will get away with it for even longer and probably get rich on it.

Clearly, corporate governance checks and balances can only serve to detect, not cure, unethical practices.

Chapter summary

In this chapter we have used the case of Enron's downfall to illustrate the importance of 'good' corporate governance. The case study has shown that not only does weak corporate governance affect the company it also affects society as a whole. The system of checks and balances that supports corporate governance needs to function effectively. The Enron case highlights the essential functions of non-executive directors, audit and disclosure, as well as ethicality of management. Indeed, we make the point that all the checks and balances within the corporate governance system have the ultimate aim of controlling and monitoring company management. The corporate governance mechanisms cannot prevent unethical activity by top management, but they can at least act as a means of detecting such activity before it is too late. When an apple is rotten there is no cure, but at least the rotten apple can be removed before the contagion spreads and infects the whole basket. This is really what effective corporate governance is about. We aim to explore the various checks and balances, and mechanisms by which good corporate governance ensures successful business and social welfare maximization in the rest of this book.

Questions for reflection and discussion

1 Read a selection of newspaper articles and academic writings on the collapse of Enron. Do you think that the Enron management behaved in an unethical manner? If so, do you think that a better system of corporate governance checks and balances would have detected their unethical behaviour before it was too late and avoided the company's collapse?

2 Do you think that the role of non-executive directors, auditors, the internal audit committee and the board of directors are all equally important as mechanisms of 'good' corporate governance? If not, which mechanism do you consider is the most important?

3 To what extent do you agree that 'When an apple is rotten there is no cure, but at least the rotten apple can be removed before the contagion spreads and infects the whole basket. This is really what corporate governance is about.' Discuss your views.

4 Summarize the corporate governance problems in Enron. Do you think they are all of equal importance? If not, which corporate governance problem do you feel contributed the most to the company's downfall?

5 The response to Enron (and other recent corporate collapses) from the UK and from the USA are extremely different. Which approach do you prefer? Which do you think will be more effective in the long run? Explain your answer with reference to academic and/or professional articles you have read.

6 To what extent do you think a UK Enron is likely to occur? Discuss the reasons for your answer.

Chapter 3

Corporate governance reform in the UK

Aim and objectives

This chapter considers the process of corporate governance reform within the UK environment. The specific objectives of this chapter are to:

- introduce the UK corporate governance codes of practice and policy documents;

- appreciate the importance of the 'comply or explain' approach to corporate governance reform adopted in the UK;

- discuss the importance of a link between corporate governance and corporate financial performance.

Introduction

In Chapter 2 we considered the fall of Enron and the case it presented for corporate governance reform. Although Enron has initiated further changes to UK corporate governance, a process of reform has been under way for a decade. This does not imply, however, that inherent corporate governance problems do not persist in UK business. Directors continue to be rewarded for poor performance and even failure, as we discuss in Chapter 4. Nevertheless, the UK is generally acknowledged as a world leader in corporate governance reform. This was not a predetermined strategy but the result of a growing interest in corporate governance issues within the board-room, the institutional investment community and the Government. It was in part a reaction to scandals, such as the Maxwell case (see Illustration 3.1), and in part a result of introspection by boards and shareholders following economic decline in the early 1990s. The publication of the Cadbury Report (1992) represented the first attempt to formalize corporate governance best practice in a written document and to make explicit the system of corporate governance that was implicit in many UK companies. The renowned Cadbury Report has set the agenda for

Illustration 3.1

The Maxwell affair 1991

Robert Maxwell's abuse of power resulted in a scandal that was named the greatest fraud of the 20th century (Stiles and Taylor, 1993). Maxwell built up his corporate empire over time, but took on too much debt and pursued fraudulent activities in order to survive. The empire was founded mainly on two companies which were publicly quoted: Maxwell Communication Corporation and Mirror Group Newspapers, as well as a large number of private companies. After Maxwell's assumed suicide it emerged that he had taken money out of the pension funds of his public companies in order to finance his other activities. He was estimated to have stolen £727 million from the pension funds of the two public companies, as well as from the companies' assets. Also, an estimated £1 billion was lost from shareholder value after the public companies crashed.

There were a number of corporate governance problems relating to the Maxwell affair that have been flagged up as reasons why Maxwell was able to abuse his position so spectacularly. One problem was the lack of segregation of positions of power. Robert Maxwell was both *chief executive and chairman* of Maxwell Communication Corporation from 1981 to 1991. He also held the positions of chairman and chief executive in Macmillan Publishers from 1988 to 1991. Such undivided control is now considered to represent inarguable corporate governance weakness. A second problem was that although Maxwell appointed *non-executive directors* to the board, they did not appear to perform a truly useful and independent function. The non-executive directors were reputable people and helped to give the company an aura of respectability. However, they did not alert shareholders to lack of transparency in Maxwell's financial activities. Furthermore, the *audit function* did not perform effectively. The auditors were in a position to observe movements of funds from the pension fund to the company, but did not seem to notice such activities in practice. Although there is an acknowledged expectations gap in auditing, this sort of audit failure is not acceptable. The *pension fund trustees* also failed to examine Maxwell's financial activities in sufficient detail. Clearly, trustees are responsible for pension fund monies and should have been in direct control of transferral of funds between the pension fund and the sponsoring company. So why did they allow money to be moved from one source to the other? Similarly, the pension fund *regulators* failed to investigate and control Maxwell's activities, probably as a result of the complexity of the 'empire'.

However, the Maxwell case raises another important issue that is central to corporate governance, that of ethics. No amount of corporate governance checks, balances, codes of practice or even regulation can change a person's character. In 1969 Robert Maxwell agreed a takeover bid for his company at the time, Pergamon Press, from Leasco, a US financial and data-processing group. However, the discussions collapsed after Leasco questioned the profits at Pergamon Press. An enquiry by the Department of Trade & Industry ensued which revealed that the profits depended on transactions with the Maxwell family's private companies. The resultant report by the Department of Trade & Industry concluded that, ... *notwithstanding Mr. Maxwell's acknowledged abilities and energy, he is not in our opinion a person who can be relied on to exercise proper stewardship of a publicly quoted company*. Nevertheless, Maxwell rose from the ashes and went on to set up another business concern. But leopards do not change their spots. How can ethics in the boardroom be monitored and controlled? The latest efforts to sharpen the function of the audit committee in UK listed companies (Smith Report, 2003) and to improve the role and effectiveness of non-executive directors (Higgs Report, 2003) may help to monitor and control directors' activities more closely in the future.

corporate governance reform in the UK and is the forerunner of numerous policy documents, principles, guidelines and codes of practice in the UK and elsewhere.

From a finance or 'agency theory' perspective, the corporate governance problem involves aligning managers' interests with those of their shareholders. As we saw in Chapter 1 there are a number of ways in which a shareholder (the principal) can monitor and control company management (the agent) including: shareholder voting at AGMs; one-to-one meetings between a representative fund manager and an investee company director; the takeover mechanism; shareholder resolutions; the threat of divestment. We also commented that institutional investors in the UK have an important role in monitoring company management. Their stake in UK listed companies is expanding continuously, amounting to about 70% at the end of the 20th century (the Hampel Report, 1998). As we discuss in Chapter 5 the potential role that institutional investors can play in corporate governance has been empha- sized in UK policy documents and accompanying codes of best practice since the early 1990s. However, shareholder activism is not the only way in which company management are controlled and governed. There are a number of other ways includ- ing: the fiduciary responsibility that is imposed on directors by company law; the legal requirement for an annual independent external audit of the accounts of the company; the overseeing by the Financial Services Authority (FSA); the Stock Exchange 'model code' on directors' share dealings; the Companies Act regulations on directors' transactions; the 'City Code' on takeovers and mergers; and voluntary corporate governance codes of practice. There were some spectacular cases of company failure and corporate abuse of power in the late 1980s and early 1990s, which created an incentive for corporate governance reform in the UK. One example is summarized in Illustration 3.1, where we discuss the corporate governance failures associated with the Maxwell case. Despite these regulatory checks and balances, and the efforts of shareholders, it has been deemed necessary to provide a series of corporate governance policy documents and codes of best practice in the UK, to help companies and institutional investors improve corporate governance.

We now introduce each of the initiatives within the agenda of UK corporate governance reform. We do not at this point delve into the detailed content of each report and set of recommendations, as they are covered in later chapters when we discuss individual initiatives in more depth.

The Cadbury Report 1992

As a result of public concern over the way in which companies were being run and fears concerning the type of abuse of power prevalent in the Maxwell case *inter alia*, corporate governance became the subject for discussion among policy makers. In this sense the formation of the Cadbury Committee may be seen as reactive rather than proactive. However, it is important to remember that the Cadbury Report was compiled on the basic assumption that the existing, implicit system of corporate governance in the UK was sound and that many of the recommendations were merely making explicit a good implicit system (see Cadbury Report, 1992, p. 12, para. 1.7). The Cadbury Report and its accompanying Cadbury Code (1992) derived their names from Sir Adrian Cadbury, who chaired the committee that produced them. The Council of the Stock Exchange and the Accountancy Profession set about establishing the Cadbury Committee, *The Committee on the Financial Aspects of Corporate Governance* which produced its report and accompanying Code of Best Practice at the end of 1992. The Cadbury Code was not legally binding on boards of directors. Nevertheless, one of the rules in the Stock Exchange *Yellow Book*[1] at the time of its publication was a 'statement of compliance' with the Code. The result of this was that all companies publicly quoted on the Stock Exchange had to state in their annual reports whether or not they had implemented the Code in all respects. If they had not complied with the whole Code, then they were compelled to make a clear statement of the reasons why, detailing and explaining the points of non-compliance. The implication was that the companies' shareholders then had the opportunity of deciding whether or not they were satisfied with the companies' corporate governance system. Three general areas were covered by the Cadbury Report and its accompanying Code, namely: the board of directors; auditing; and the shareholders. The Cadbury Report focused attention on the board of directors as being the most important corporate governance mechanism, requiring constant monitoring and assessment. However, the accounting and auditing function were also shown to play an essential role in good corporate governance, emphasizing the importance of corporate transparency and communication with shareholders and other stakeholders. Lastly, Cadbury's focus on the importance of institutional investors as the largest and most influential group of shareholders has had a lasting impact. This, more than any other initiative in corporate governance reform, has led to the shift of directors' dialogue toward greater accountability and engagement with shareholders. Further, we consider that this move to greater shareholder engagement has generated the more significant metamorphosis of corporate responsibility toward a range of stakeholders, encouraging greater corporate social responsibility in general. There is no denying the substantial impact that the Cadbury Code has had on corporate Britain and, indeed, on companies around the world. By the late 1990s there was strong evidence to show a high level of compliance with the Cadbury Code's recommendations (see, e.g., Conyon and Mallin, 1997), partly due to the UK's 'comply or explain' approach, which we discuss on p. 57 in more detail.

The Greenbury Report 1995

A second corporate governance committee was created in response to public and shareholder concerns about directors' remuneration. There have been endless cases

---

[1] The *Yellow Book* provided the requirements of the Stock Exchange with which all listed companies had to comply. This has now been superseded by the overarching responsibilities of the FSA.

Illustration 3.2

Fat cats at British Gas 1995

The British Gas case is notorious both as a case of excessive executive remuneration and as a case of minority shareholder dissatisfaction. At the British Gas AGM on 30 May 1995 the views of individual shareholders were quashed by proxy votes from the company's institutional investors, in relation to the suitability of the company director, Cedric Brown, to run the company. One chief criticism was on his remuneration. Indeed, remuneration and compensation packages have attracted much attention in the UK, especially among minority shareholders. Despite strong sentiments among the smaller shareholders who attended the company's AGM in order to express their views and vote against the board, the votes of institutional investors supported the board, via proxy votes, even though their representatives did not attend. This was seen as unfair by many of the shareholders who attended and caused an outcry at the time. The case is especially memorable because a pig named Cedric, after Cedric Brown, was paraded outside the company during the AGM. The British Gas case is discussed in detail in a case study in the journal, *Corporate Governance: An International Review* (1996).

---

flagged up over recent years of excessive executive remuneration. *Fat Cat* incidents such as the notorious case of British Gas in the mid-1990s (see Illustration 3.2) attracted substantial media attention and distressed shareholders (usually small shareholders) of large public companies. The term 'fat cats' was coined to refer to directors who orchestrated huge remuneration packages for themselves, which bore little (if any) relation to performance. Shareholders in general have become extremely concerned about unseemly pay increases for company directors. Our own research into institutional investors' attitudes toward corporate governance has revealed executive remuneration to be one of the areas of greatest concern. For example, one pension fund director we interviewed commented that:

> What's different in corporate governance? Fat Cattery's different in the last few years and the publicity that goes with it. All these boards giving themselves big pay rises even when they fail ... Ultimately, we are partly responsible because we have got some votes and some shares.

It is interesting to see from the above quotation that institutional investors are beginning to appreciate more sharply their own responsibilities as owners for corporate excesses and lack of accountability, as well as their ability to influence corporate decision making.

At this point it is important to note that the aim of the Greenbury Report was not necessarily to reduce directors' salaries. Rather, it was to provide a means of establishing a balance between directors' salaries and their performance. The report recognized the importance for companies of offering salaries that were high enough to attract directors of adequate calibre, capable of running large, multi-national organizations. However, the report also highlighted deep concerns with directors' pay packages, especially in relation to share options and other additional sources of remuneration. The issue of executive remuneration and the impact of the Greenbury Report, as well as its successor, is considered in detail in Chapter 4.

The Hampel Report 1998

The Hampel Committee was the successor to both the Cadbury and the Greenbury Committees, taking on both the financial aspects of corporate governance and directors' remuneration. The Hampel Report was published in 1998 and the Combined Code (1998) arose from it. This Code brought together all the issues covered in Cadbury and Greenbury. The Combined Code (although redrafted since its original publication) is the currently applicable code of best corporate governance practice for UK listed companies. The recommendations of Hampel were along similar lines and on similar issues to Cadbury. An important contribution made by the Hampel Report was the emphasis attributed to avoiding a prescriptive approach to corporate governance improvements and recommendations. The Cadbury Report highlighted the importance of focusing on the spirit of corporate governance reform, and Hampel reinforced this by stipulating that companies and shareholders needed to avoid a 'box-ticking' approach to corporate governance. The Hampel Report emphasized the need to maintain a principles-based, voluntary approach to corporate governance rather than a more regulated and possibly superficial approach. This is typical of the UK approach to corporate governance and accounting as opposed to the US style of legislation, the rules-based approach. Indeed, the report stated:

> Good corporate governance is not just a matter of prescribing particular corporate structures and complying with a number of hard and fast rules. *There is a need for broad principles*. All concerned should then apply these flexibly and with common sense to the varying circumstances of individual companies. This is how the Cadbury and Greenbury committees intended their recommendations to be implemented ... Companies' experience of the Cadbury and Greenbury codes has been rather different. Too often they believe that the codes have been treated as sets of prescriptive rules. The shareholders or their advisers would be interested *only in whether the letter of the rule had been complied with*—yes or no. A 'yes' would receive a tick, hence the expression 'box ticking' for this approach.
>
> (The Hampel Report, 1998, p. 10, paras 1.11–1.12, emphasis added)

In some ways (such as the role of institutional investors in corporate governance) Hampel could be interpreted as being less demanding than Cadbury. Indeed, there is a widely held perception that the report represented the interests of company directors more than those of shareholders and that much of the positive impact from the Cadbury Report was diluted by the Hampel Report. Certainly, in the area of corporate social responsibility and corporate accountability to a broad range of stakeholders, there was a significant change in tack between the Cadbury

Report and the Hampel Report. The Hampel Report clearly felt the need to redress the balance between shareholders and stakeholders and made strong statements on these issues. For example, the Hampel Committee stated that:

> The importance of corporate governance lies in its contribution both to business prosperity and to accountability. In the UK the latter has preoccupied much public debate over the past few years. *We would wish to see the balance corrected*. Public companies are now among the most accountable organisations in society ... We strongly endorse this accountability and we recognise the contribution made by the Cadbury and Greenbury committees. *But the emphasis on accountability has tended to obscure a board's first responsibility*—to enhance the prosperity of the business over time.
>
> (The Hampel Report, 1998, p. 7, para. 1.1, emphasis added)

Although we agree that corporate governance in UK companies is exemplary in general and that the UK provides a benchmark for good corporate governance, we feel that such comments are suggestive of resting on laurels! UK companies should not be complacent. Accountability is one area where the corporate success of the future will be measured. Generally, we believe that Hampel was misguided in this area and in its perception of public, corporate and shareholder sentiment. As discussed in Chapter 1, there is a strong demand for greater accountability and there is also a growing perception that companies that are accountable to a broad range of stakeholders display better long-term performance. Although further research is required to demonstrate this link unequivocally, evidence is emerging that demonstrates that the approach of the Hampel Report was outdated and retrograde in this respect. These issues are revisited throughout the book, but especially in Part III.

An important contribution made by the Hampel Report related to pension fund trustees, as pension funds are the largest group of investors. Pension fund trustees were targeted by the report as a group who needed to take their corporate governance responsibilities more seriously. In particular, pension funds (and their trustees) were encouraged by the Hampel Committee to adopt a more long-term approach to institutional investment, in order to avoid short-termism for which UK companies are notorious. Pension funds were highlighted as the main culprits in placing short-term pressure on their investee companies. This discussion in the Hampel Report has been instrumental in encouraging an overhaul in the pension fund trustee's role, culminating in the recent Myners Review of the trustee's role and responsibilities (Myners, 2001). We deal with these issues in more detail in Chapter 5. In this area, the Hampel Committee clearly picked up on and developed the spirit of the original Cadbury Report.

Generally speaking, the Combined Code readdressed all the issues raised in previous reports, bringing the major points together and concluding with basic principles and provisions. The first draft of the Combined Code contained a series of Principles of Good Corporate Governance. It then detailed a series of provisions that represented ways in which the general principles may be achieved. The Code was structured in two parts. The first part dealt with companies and includes four sections of Principles covering: (A) Directors; (B) Directors' Remuneration; (C) Relations with Shareholders; (D) Accountability and Audit. The second part dealt with institutional shareholders and included three sections covering: (E) 1. Shareholder Voting; 2. Dialogue with Companies; and 3. Evaluation of Governance Disclosures. We can immediately see that all of these issues were dealt with in Cadbury and in Greenbury. However, the emphasis of the Combined Code was slightly different and the aim was to consolidate previous views into a consensus on what constituted 'good' corporate governance. Under each main principle there was a list of provisions, giving details of how the Principles may be attained.

The impact of the Combined Code (and its predecessors) on UK company directors and institutional investors has been far-reaching, especially in the area of investor relations and shareholder activism. Our own research into institutional investor attitudes toward corporate governance and accountability issues has highlighted the substantial effects that the process of corporate governance reform has had on institutional investor relations. In a decade, corporate attitudes toward their core investors have been transformed from relative secrecy to greater transparency. Similarly, the attitudes of institutional investors have been transformed from relative apathy toward their investee companies' activities to an active interest. We consider the impact of the Combined Code on UK companies and shareholders in Chapters 4–6.

As was the case for Cadbury and Greenbury, the Hampel Report could also be seen as reactive rather than proactive, as further significant UK corporate failures arose from weak corporate governance structures between the publication of the Cadbury Report and the Hampel Report. One of these was the fall of a major UK bank, Barings, which created shock waves through the corporate and financial communities throughout the UK and, indeed, across the world. Corporate governance failure has, in hindsight, been blamed as the main cause for the company's collapse. We summarize the fall of Barings in Illustration 3.3. Read it to grasp a feel for the type of corporate governance problems that may arise in companies unless the necessary checks and balances are in place.

Not only did the Barings case focus attention on corporate governance reform in a general sense but, due to the specific nature of the case, attention was also channelled toward the area of risk management and internal control. As a result, the Turnbull Committee was formed which published a report at the end of the 1990s devoted entirely to these issues.

The Turnbull Report 1999

The Combined Code (1998) dealt with internal control in Provisions D.2.1 and D.2.2. In these Provisions, the Code stated that company directors should conduct a review of the effectiveness of their internal control systems and should report this information to shareholders. The Turnbull Committee was established specifically to

Illustration 3.3

The fall of Barings 1995

The case of Barings Bank is important as it highlights the importance of 'good' corporate governance in the banking sector in the same way as the Maxwell case in the publishing industry. You will probably recall that Nick Leeson, a young trader at Barings in Singapore, destroyed the company by losing more than $1 billion by unauthorized trading of futures contracts (a type of financial derivative). He took them out speculatively, but the Japanese market turned the opposite direction from that expected at the time. He was released from jail a few years ago and the film, *Rogue Trader* (based on a book by Leeson himself) was produced. The film covers the whole story leading to the downfall of Barings and gives a useful and interesting insight into the way in which derivatives trading happens. The film depicts Leeson as a young man, coming from a very different educational and social background from most employees at Barings. He was thrown into the Singapore market (SIMEX) with relatively little experience. He was given the *dual position* of General Manager and Head Trader, being in charge of the actual trading (on the stock exchange floor) and of the trading accounts. This was against generally accepted principles, as it gave him too much control—it is similar to the problems of the same person acting as chief executive and chairman of a company. Indeed, lack of segregation of these roles is seen as one of the main failings leading to the fall of Barings. In the film he was placed in a favourable light—almost as an innocent who became more and more entangled in financial problems, unable to tell anyone. However, it is unlikely that he was behaving as innocently as the film makes out. It seems he made no financial gains for himself, but the temptations of gambling on the stock market—not using his own funds—was irresistible. On his arrival in Singapore he set up an 'errors and omissions' account, number 88888, which would take any differences in trading balances at the end of the month. After a couple of mistakes by his similarly young and inadequately trained trading staff he tried to 'trade out' of the losses, using money from the bank's clients, so that he would not be in trouble for the losses incurred. Luckily, the first couple of times he managed to clear the losses in the bank's errors account (about a million pounds!) and made huge speculative profits over and over again. It is important at this point to realize that he was only allowed to trade for the bank's clients and not on the bank's own account. No one (except his secretary) knew that he was trading for the bank, using clients' money. Here there is a parallel between Leeson and Maxwell (see Illustration 3.1), as Maxwell was illegally using funds from the pension fund. His confidence soared as he did not seem to be able to lose on the many gambles he made on yen options.

Leeson then started to take bigger risks. A large French client wanted to buy options contracts on the yen for a ridiculously low price, and in order to keep the client Leeson made the deal. It resulted in a massive loss which he transferred to the secret errors account. The client left anyway and went to Société Générale in France—he was obviously playing brokers off against each other. This left Leeson in a very difficult position. He had acted illegally and now decided to cover his losses by trading on the bank's account, as before, but this time it did not work. He made huge unauthorized trades on the Nikkei 225 stock index using the 'mystery account'. He made loss after loss against the yen, following the Kobe Earthquake in Japan, which rocked the stock exchange. He could not make up the losses. He eventually ran up a debt in yen options of about 400 million dollars. He escaped to a holiday resort leaving a message for Barings' managers to close the losing position—but they did not and the losses increased to about £830 million by February 1995. He thought they would solve it and never considered the bank may collapse. The police picked him up at an airport in Germany as he was flying back to the UK. Although

Nick Leeson behaved unethically, it was the bank itself that was chiefly to blame for allowing him to act in this way.

The bank's controls and monitoring procedures were insufficient. The management team in the UK seemed to have an unfounded confidence in their 'young star', and although they had the feeling there were problems they did not act to sort the situation out. They knew there was a very large client making huge losses and that Leeson was trading on the client's behalf with huge sums of money, but they did not realize that client 88888 was actually them! Leeson requested more and more funds from the UK London office to support his trading, but they believed he was covering margin payments for clients, not using the funds for his own trading. Still, if the bank had exercised the correct level of control, the situation could not have arisen. The *auditor* who visited was called back to London before she had finished the audit—so he escaped notice. There was a clear failure of the audit function. Although it was noted that he should not have been acting as manager of the trading floor as well as manager of the accounts, no moves were made to change this. The director in Singapore was keen on cost savings and did not want to pay out more salaries. Further, the director would not allow Leeson to have traders under him who were well qualified. He instead insisted that the staff were young and inexperienced and that Leeson could train them as they worked. This was another loophole in the system. By the time the London centre of Barings realized that there was a serious problem it was too late. The reasons for the fall of Barings and the Leeson affair can be summarized as:

- *On the part of Nick Leeson*: unethical behaviour, trading unlawfully.
- *On the part of Barings' senior management*: lack of segregation of Nick Leeson's duties; lack of supervision; lack of recognition of unusual profits; lack of understanding (London did simply not understand what happened in Singapore—the senior management did not understand the technicalities of derivatives trading); failure to conduct further investigations (audits not thorough enough and evident inefficiencies on the part of the auditor).

In a way we could say that Leeson was the scapegoat for Barings' lack of attention to detail. Although Leeson behaved unethically by trading without authorization and on the bank's account (absolutely against the rules) the bank was also much to blame for not having the internal control mechanism to constrain Leeson's activities. Since this affair (and others) there have been big moves to improve risk management within the banking sector. The corporate governance initiatives that have been adopted by companies in the UK to improve accountability and transparency have also been taken on by banks. Disclosure of risk-related information is immensely important for banks, as it is for other companies. Although we may not see the bank's 'lack of internal controls' as unethical behaviour, it is actually a *lack of responsible behaviour that is in itself unethical*. Therefore, the whole Leeson affair is not attributable solely to one individual's lack of ethics but to the corporate governance failure of the bank.

address the issue of internal control and to respond to these Provisions in the Combined Code. The report provided an overview of the systems of internal control in existence in UK companies and made clear recommendations for improvements, without taking a prescriptive approach. The Turnbull Report was revolutionary in terms of corporate governance reform. It represented an attempt to formalize an explicit framework for internal control in companies. Even though many other countries are now focusing attention on the systems of internal control and corporate risk disclosure within their listed companies, few have established a specific policy document or code of best practice dedicated to this issue. The USA, with its Treadway Commission (1987), paid attention to internal control, but the Turnbull Report has focused worldwide attention on this aspect of corporate governance. The Turnbull Report sought to provide an explicit framework for reference, on which companies and boards could model their individual systems of internal control. The framework was not meant to be prescriptive, given the problems of providing a common framework to companies in diverse industries that face an innumerable series of different risks and uncertainties. The aim was to provide companies with general guidance on how to develop and maintain their internal control systems and not to specify the details of such a system. We examine the elements of the explicit framework for internal control presented by the Turnbull Report in Chapter 6.

The Higgs Report 2003

Although the Cadbury Report and the Hampel Report stimulated substantial improvements in corporate governance in UK listed companies, certain areas have been highlighted for further examination. The fall of Enron spurred the UK and other countries into re-evaluating corporate governance issues, such as the role and effectiveness of non-executive directors. As we can see from the Enron case in Chapter 2, Enron's non-executive directors were ineffective in performing their corporate governance role of monitoring the company's directors and were subject to conflicts of interest. Even though the emphasis on non-executive directors in the UK has represented an improvement in UK corporate governance, the UK government post-Enron felt obliged to set up an enquiry to examine their effectiveness. In our own research we have detected an element of disillusionment with the effectiveness of non-executive directors as corporate monitors. One reason why non-executive directors are not fulfilling their potential is the difficulties of retaining their position. For example, one pension fund director we interviewed suggested that:

> There is a feeling that somebody ought to exercise constraint on boards. I don't think the system of non-executive directors is terribly successful. It is very difficult being a non-executive director because you actually have got to let the chief executive run the show—you cannot keep interfering, and that is the trouble. You don't want to interfere—you will get yourself voted out if you are too awkward.

The Higgs Report dealt specifically with the role and effectiveness of non-executive directors, making recommendations for changes to the Combined Code. The general recommendations included a greater proportion of non-executive directors on boards (at least half of the board) and more apt remuneration for non-executive directors. The report also concluded that stronger links needed to be established between non-executive directors and companies' principal shareholders. This would help to foster more effective monitoring of the notorious agency problem, as it would enhance the abilities of non-executive directors to represent shareholder interests and align the interests of shareholders and directors. One important practical recommendation of the Higgs Report was that one non-executive director should assume chief responsibility as a champion of shareholder interests. We return to the detailed implications and impact of the Higgs Report in Chapter 4.

The Smith Report 2003

As an accompaniment to the Higgs Report, another review was commissioned by the UK Government in response to the Enron scandal, *inter alia*, with the aim of examining the role of the audit committee in UK corporate governance. This Report was published in January 2003. The main issues dealt with in the Report concerned the relationship between the external auditor and the companies they audit, as well as the role and responsibilities of companies' audit committees. The creation of audit committees was a recommendation of the Cadbury Report and represented a clear means of monitoring company directors' activities. In the case of Enron, the failure of the audit committee and internal audit function were one of the principal causes of the company's collapse. Improvements in this area represent one way of keeping a check on the production of reliable and honest accounts. Nevertheless, some have suggested that the Report has not gone far enough. It has been suggested that a more prescriptive approach would have been preferable, which would, for example, prevent auditing companies from offering other professional services, such as consultancy or IT services, to client companies that they audit. However, the Smith Report preserved the UK tradition of a principles-based approach, attempting not to create a 'one size fits all' set of rules for listed companies. This would be counterproductive as not all companies would be in a position to comply. We discuss the detailed recommendations of the Smith Report in Chapter 6.

Redraft of the Combined Code 2003

In July 2003 the Financial Reporting Council approved a new draft of the Combined Code, as intended from the Higgs Report in January 2003. It was referred to as, 'the biggest shake-up of boardroom culture in more than a decade' (Tassell, 24 July 2003). Although the redrafted Code was not as prescriptive as Higgs' original recommendations, it retained much of the flavour of his concerns. Indeed, the redrafting was welcomed by both the corporate and institutional investment communities, despite their initial reactions to the Higgs' Report. The revised Code in fact retained almost all of the 50 recommendations contained in Higgs' original report. The language, not the message, was altered. The main reforms of the new Code included the following:

- at least half the board of directors should comprise independent non-executive directors;

- a company's chief executive should not become chairman of the same company, except in exceptional circumstances;

- the board's chairman should be independent at appointment;

- a Senior Independent Director (SID) should be appointed to be available to the company's shareholders, if they have unresolved concerns;

- boards should undertake a formal and rigorous evaluation of their own perform- ance, considering especially the performance and effectiveness of its committees and individual directors;

- institutional investors should avoid box ticking when assessing investee com- panies' corporate governance;

- companies should adopt rigorous, formal and transparent procedures when recruiting new directors;

- non-executive directors should only be reappointed after six years service, follow- ing 'a particularly rigorous review';

- non-executive directors can only continue after nine years' service following annual re-elections and should be considered no longer independent;

- boards should not agree to a full-time executive director accepting more than one non-executive directorship, or chairmanship, in a Top 100 company.

One of the main targets of the redrafted Code was to readdress executive remunera- tion, as the new version of the Code focused on forcing companies to avoid excessive remuneration which displayed little relation to corporate performance. The revised Code also placed an emphasis on shareholder activism as a means of furthering corporate accountability and transparency. We reproduce the most up-to-date draft of the Combined Code in the Appendix (p. 247). We now consider the reg- ulatory environment within which the UK codes of practice have been introduced.

Comply or explain

From the beginning of the process of corporate governance reform in the UK, a voluntary approach of 'comply or explain' has been chosen. This has been in keeping with the preferred approach of company law in the UK, which is one of self-regula- tion of the City of London financial institutions, as expressed in the Financial Services Act 1986 (Farrar and Hannigan, 1998). The Cadbury Report emphasized the importance of adopting an approach that encouraged compliance with a volun- tary code of best practice. As we saw from our discussion of the reports above, this approach was preferred to a statutory code mainly because it would be more likely to develop a 'good' corporate governance culture within UK companies. They would be encouraged to comply *in spirit rather than in letter* (Cadbury Report, 1992, p. 12, para. 1.10). This is an approach that has continued to the present day. It is not, however, an approach that has been adopted at a global level. The choice by many countries to adopt a more legalistic and statutory approach to corporate governance reform rests in part on the legal framework already in place in the countries themselves. This is an important issue that has generated a wealth of theoretical and empirical literature in the finance field and one to which we will return in some depth in Chapter 7. However, there is also a cultural influence on the choice of regulatory environment. The USA, as discussed earlier, prefers a more regulated, rules-based environment. This UK/US dichotomy is an important issue that is highlighted throughout this book, wherever relevant. In the UK, companies disclose details of non-compliance and provide a general compliance statement. For example, the Corus annual report of 2001 provided the following information:

> The board believes that during the period it has complied with the provisions of the Code of Best Practice with the following exceptions: (i) The reduction of notice periods for directors to one year or less. (ii) Currently the roles of chairman and chief executive are combined. This is a temporary situation, arising as a result of the resignation of the joint chief executives in December 2000.

In 2001 the FSA assumed control of company oversight, taking over the powers of the stock exchange listing rules. The FSA is an umbrella organization with the heavy responsibility of overseeing the activities of companies and financial institutions. The FSA is essentially the 'City watchdog'. However, the key issue for legislators concerning the future direction of corporate governance reform is the extent to which civil sanctions, such as the imposition of fines and the removal of director status for a predetermined time, should be supplemented by a 'heavier stick', namely the imposition of criminal sanctions, such as a period of imprisonment.

Applying the codes of practice to small companies

The Combined Code recognized that smaller listed companies may initially have difficulty in complying with some aspects of the Code. The boards of smaller listed companies who cannot, for the time being, comply with parts of the Code should note that they may instead give their reasons for non-compliance. However, the Hampel Committee also believed that full compliance by small companies would be beneficial. In particular, the appointment of appropriate non-executive directors should make a positive contribution to the development of their businesses. A report from the Department of Trade and Industry (DTI, 1999) entitled *Creating Quality Dialogue between Smaller Quoted Companies and Fund Managers* focused attention on the transferability of standards for 'good' corporate governance to smaller companies, especially the recommendations for better and more effective shareholder relationships.

The recent Generally Accepted Accounting Practice in the UK (GAAP, 2001) detailed the relevance of corporate governance for smaller quoted companies. The Cadbury Code made no distinction in its recommendations between larger and smaller listed companies. Hampel discussed whether a distinction should be made but concluded it should not, stressing that high standards of governance were as important for smaller listed companies as for larger ones. GAAP concluded that each company should be able to determine its corporate governance procedures in the best interests of the company. Smaller listed companies should not be forced to adopt corporate governance principles as this may be difficult for them. The Combined Code should not be prescriptive, but smaller quoted companies need to inform their shareholders of any ways in which they are not complying with the Code. Communication is the most important issue.

The Quoted Companies Alliance (QCA)[2] fights for the interests of thousands of companies that are not among the top 350 listed UK companies. It includes smaller companies, such as those in the Alternative Investment Market (AIM) and OFEX. In 2000 the Annual QCA Smaller Company Analyst Survey showed that the number of institutional investors prepared to invest in UK smaller quoted companies was declining for the second consecutive year. Improving corporate governance may be one way for smaller listed companies to attract more equity finance. This group prepared guidance in 1994 for smaller quoted companies aimed at identifying areas of the Cadbury Code that could prove difficult for smaller companies to implement. They suggested alternative recommendations that were more feasible. In April 2001 the QCA revised this guidance, providing alternative recommendations in the following areas: the role and number of non-executive directors, the constitution of audit committees, board meetings, the identification of a senior independent non-executive director, the size of the board and nomination committees.

Ranking corporate governance initiatives

As we can see from our above discussion, a broad range of corporate governance initiatives have arisen from the corporate governance policy documents and codes. However, there is little evidence relating to the relative importance of these initiatives. Are they all of equal importance to investors, for example? Solomon et al. (2000a) provided some empirical evidence that attempted to rank the various initiatives. They examined which corporate governance initiatives were considered to be of most importance to UK institutional investors. Table 3.1 summarizes the results.

These results were obtained from a questionnaire survey sent to an extensive

---

[2] The QCA was formerly known as the City Group for Smaller Companies (CISCO).

Table [3.1]   Institutional investors' views on specific corporate governance initiatives

Ranking	Initiatives	Average response
1	Appointment of *non-executive directors*	Strong agreement
2	*Splitting* of chairman/chief executive roles	Strong agreement
3	Appointment of *audit committees*	Strong agreement
4	Removing *rolling three-year contracts* for executive directors	Strong agreement
5	Company directors who deliberately produce misleading information should be made *personally liable* for their actions	Strong agreement
6	Establishment of *remuneration committees*	Strong agreement
7	The role of the audit committee in policing *negligence and fraud*	Strong agreement
8	Restrictions on *contract severance compensation* for directors	Strong agreement
9	*Increased voting rights* for shareholders	Strong agreement
10	Increased disclosure of *internal control* mechanisms	Agreement
11	*Training programmes* for newly appointed executive directors	Agreement
12	*Enhanced shareholder powers*	Agreement
13	Declaration of *voting policy* by institutional investors	Agreement
14	Greater *transparency in proxy voting* by institutional investors, concerning share ownership declaration	Some agreement
15	Restrictions on executive directors' *remuneration*	Some disagreement
16	*Limitations on proxy voting* by institutional investors	Strong disagreement

Reproduced by permission of Blackwell Publishers Journals

sample of UK institutional investors. The investors were asked the extent to which they agreed that each of the various initiatives had led to an improvement in corporate governance.[3] We can see that from the institutional investors' viewpoint, the appointment of non-executive directors was considered the most important and effective corporate governance initiative. Interestingly, this has been the target of the most recent review of corporate governance, the Higgs Report (2003), which endorses our research findings. In second place came the splitting of the chief executive and chairman role. These, from an agency theory perspective, represent effective ways of controlling the agents and are therefore likely to be seen as important by shareholders. Accountability by the investors themselves concerning their own role in corporate governance received less agreement as declaration of voting

[3] The respondents selected a score from 1 (strongly disagree) to 7 (strongly agree).

policy by institutional investors and greater transparency in their voting, as well as limitations on proxy voting, were ranked toward the end of Table 3.1. The institutional investors who responded clearly required company management to be accountable, but were not as interested in discharging their own accountability. This attitude has been reflected recently in calls by industry bodies for institutional investors to 'practise what they preach' and become more active in encouraging corporate governance reform. Interestingly, those initiatives ranked in first, second and third place in Table 3.1 have been shown in practice to represent areas where weaknesses can lead to corporate failure. The Enron case (presented in Chapter 2) involved serious weaknesses in the areas of non-executive directors, power held at the top, and the audit function. Similarly, the Barings case (see Illustration 3.3) displayed significant weaknesses in the areas of power distribution and audit. Other recent cases of corporate failure, such as WorldCom, were also attributable to weaknesses in the accounting and audit function. These findings therefore show that investors are most concerned about these areas of corporate governance, and with good cause.

Why is good corporate governance important?

Policy makers, practitioners and theorists have adopted the general stance that corporate governance reform is worth pursuing, supporting such initiatives as splitting the role of chairman/chief executive, introducing non-executive directors to boards, curbing excessive executive performance-related remuneration, improving institutional investor relations, increasing the quality and quantity of corporate disclosure, *inter alia*. However, is there really evidence to support these initiatives? Do they really improve the effectiveness of corporations and their accountability? There are certainly those who are opposed to the ongoing process of corporate governance reform. Many company directors oppose the loss of individual decision-making power, which comes from the presence of non-executive directors and independent directors on their boards. They refute the growing pressure to communicate their strategies and policies to their primary institutional investors. They consider that the many initiatives aimed at 'improving' corporate governance in the UK have simply slowed down decision making and added an unnecessary level of bureaucracy and red tape. As an example, read the short summary of Richard Branson's experiment with the stock market in Illustration 3.4. Such concerns need to be noted and debated. The Cadbury Report emphasized the importance of avoiding excessive control and recognized that no system of control can completely eliminate the risk of fraud (such as in the case of Maxwell, Illustration 3.1) without hindering companies' ability to compete in a free market (Cadbury Report, 1992, p. 12, para. 1.9). This is an important point, because human nature cannot be altered through regulation, checks and balances, as discussed in previous chapters.

Nevertheless, there is a growing perception in the financial markets that good corporate governance is associated with prosperous companies. Our own research

---

Illustration 3.4

Branson's flotation experiment in the 1980s

Richard Branson's affair with the accountability and corporate governance practices recommended by Cadbury was short-lived and tempestuous. Branson was the primary owner of his Virgin company from its creation. After some years, he was persuaded to gain a listing on the London Stock Exchange as this would provide him with valuable funds for his varied business ventures and endless new projects. However, the regular trips to the City of London to meet with institutional shareholders and discharge accountability to his shareholders cramped his style of business management. He withdrew from the stock market as soon as he could in the mid-1980s! He found that 'excessive' corporate governance hindered his decision making, slowing down his ability to 'make things happen'. For Branson, the problems of accountability to shareholders severely outweighed the benefits. Indeed, a common criticism wielded against corporate governance codes of practice and corporate governance reform in general is that it slows down decisions at company board level and makes running a company unnecessarily difficult, hindering innovation and creativity. These criticisms cannot be ignored. A balance needs to be achieved between accountability and transparency of operations and the ability of entrepreneurs to operate competitively and efficiently. However, Branson has once again been seduced by the City of London as he was considering floating a number of his Virgin firms raising as much as £2 billion in funds from shareholders in 2002.

---

has provided some evidence to support the agenda for corporate governance reform. The findings indicated that the institutional investment community considered both company directors and institutional investors welcomed corporate governance reform, viewing the reform process as a 'help rather than a hindrance'. Specifically, we focused on the attitudes of an extensive sample of UK unit trust fund managers toward corporate governance reform (see Solomon and Solomon, 1999). Table 3.2 provides the consensus of the institutional investors surveyed concerning corporate governance reform.

These findings endorse many of the issues discussed in this chapter relating to the agenda for corporate governance reform in the UK. They show, for example, that institutional investors agreed strongly with the Hampel view that corporate governance is as important for small companies as for larger ones. The results also indicated significant support from the institutional investment community for the continuance of a voluntary environment for corporate governance. The respondents' agreement that there should be further reform in their investee companies also added support to the ongoing reform process. Lastly, the institutional investors perceived a role for themselves in corporate governance reform, as they agreed that the institutional investment community should adopt a more activist stance. This is all encouraging. However, we now turn to the essential issue of whether improvements in corporate governance engender better corporate financial performance.

Table [3.2] Institutional investors attitudes toward corporate governance reform

Rank	Statements	Average response
1	I believe that high standards of corporate governance are as *important for smaller listed companies as for larger*	Strong agreement
2	I believe that corporate governance reforms should remain within a *voluntary framework*	Agreement
3	I believe that institutional investors should adopt a *more activist stance*	Agreement
4	I believe that there should be *further reforms in corporate governance* in our investee companies	Agreement
5	I believe that the directors of our investee companies are presently *overburdened* with corporate governance reforms	Slight disagreement
6	I believe that corporate governance reforms are more of a *hindrance than a help for UK company directors*	Disagreement
7	I believe that corporate governance reforms should be *regulated* through Government	Disagreement
8	I believe that corporate governance reforms are more of a *hindrance than a help for UK institutional investors*	Strong disagreement

Reproduced by permission of Blackwell Publishers Journals

Corporate governance and corporate performance

The ultimate test of whether or not corporate governance reform is having a positive impact on UK industry is whether or not there is a positive relationship between corporate financial performance and corporate governance. There is growing academic evidence to indicate that there is a significant statistical relationship between bad corporate governance and poor corporate financial performance. Indeed, it has been shown that US companies with weaker corporate governance structures (indicated by substantial agency problems) perform less well than companies with better corporate governance structures (see, e.g., Core et al., 1999). Some institutional investors have taken on the role of 'corporate governance doctors' and have profited from it. Lens (an American investment institution) experimented with the link between corporate governance and corporate performance in its approach to institutional investment. Lens is a fund established by Robert Monks and Nell Minow in the USA. This fund was set up as a vehicle for collective action. The fund was invested in companies with acknowledged weak corporate governance structures. Using extensive shareholder activism, the investee companies have been forced to improve their internal corporate governance, which has resulted in substantial increases in share valuation. This has led to excess returns to portfolio investment, well above the average market indices. Lens uses a strategy of investing in a company's shares, then negotiating and effecting change within the company. The fund has targeted such companies as Sears and Eastman Kodak (see Monks and Minow, 2001, for a discussion of Lens' successes). Recently, Lens has joined forces with a major UK institutional investor, Hermes, and has set up a similar fund in the European market, which is also succeeding in achieving substantial excess returns.

Chapter summary

In this chapter we have considered the development of policy documents and codes of practice for corporate governance in the UK, focusing on the work of the Cadbury Report, the Greenbury Report, the Hampel Report, the Turnbull Report, the Higgs Report and the Smith Report. It is important at this stage to note that corporate governance reform is not solely a UK issue but has taken centre stage in the international arena. Many countries around the world have followed in the footsteps of the Cadbury Committee and have developed corporate governance policy documents and codes of practice for 'good' corporate governance. Further, there have been several attempts to produce internationally acceptable standards of corporate governance at a global level, as we discuss in Part II. However, in the next chapter we turn to a discussion of the UK agenda for corporate governance reform in more detail, by examining the essential role played by boards of directors in corporate governance.

Questions for reflection and discussion

1 Analyse and debate the extent to which you consider the initiatives aimed at corporate governance reform in the UK represent an improvement to the system of corporate governance.

2 Read Illustration 3.4. Do you think that Richard Branson was right in his concerns that corporate governance reform slows down decision making and creates time-wasting, unnecessary bureaucracy?

3 How important do you think it is that the UK institutional investment community supports the agenda for corporate governance reform?

4 Do you agree with the view encapsulated in the Hampel Report that corporate governance reform is as important for smaller listed companies as for larger ones?

Chapter 4

The role of boards in corporate governance

Aim and objectives

This chapter examines the role of boards of directors in corporate governance, mainly from a UK perspective. The specific objectives of this chapter are to:

- explain the main initiatives introduced in the UK to improve the effectiveness of boards of directors;

- evaluate the impact of these initiatives on board function;

- discuss the findings of academic research relating to the effectiveness of boards as a corporate governance mechanism.

Introduction

In Chapter 3 we discussed the series of UK policy documents and codes of practice aimed at reforming corporate governance, initiated by the Cadbury Report (1992). The primary emphasis of the Cadbury Report was on the need for boards of directors within listed companies to be effective. This was considered by the Cadbury Committee as being a quintessential ingredient determining the UK's competitive position. The Cadbury Report reviewed the structure of the board and the responsibilities of company directors, making recommendations for best practice. The report recommended that company boards should meet frequently and should monitor executive management.

For a company to be successful it must be well governed. A well-functioning and effective board of directors is the holy grail sought by every ambitious company. A company's board is its heart and as a heart it needs to be healthy, fit and carefully nurtured for the company to run effectively. Signs of fatigue, lack of energy, lack of interest and general ill health within the board's functioning require urgent attention and care. The free and accurate flow of information in and out of the board is as essential to the healthy operating of the corporate body as the free and unhindered flow of blood is to the healthy functioning of the human body. From the burgeoning academic and practitioner literature on boards of directors, as well as from the recommendations of the various codes of practice, we have compiled a lighthearted 'recipe' for a 'good board' as follows:

Recipe for a 'good board'

The board should meet frequently

The board should maintain a good balance of power

An individual should not be allowed to dominate board meetings and decision making

Members of the board should be open to other members' suggestions

There should be a high level of trust between board members

Board members should be ethical and have a high level of integrity

There must be a high level of effective communication between members of the board

The board should be responsible for the financial statements

Non-executive directors should (generally) provide an independent viewpoint

The board should be open to new ideas and strategies (a 'learning board', Garratt, 1996)

Board members should not be opposed to change

The board must possess an in-depth understanding of the company's business

The board must be dynamic in nature

The board must understand the inherent risks of the business

The board must be prepared to take calculated risks: no risk no return

The board must be aware of stakeholder issues and be prepared to engage actively with their stakeholders

As education becomes increasingly important, board members should not be averse to attending training courses

Keep on a low heat and stir frequently!

An individual and interesting insight into board effectiveness was presented in *The Fish Rots from the Head* (Garratt, 1996). Garratt drew on his experiences on company boards as well as his experience as an academic to highlight problems within boards and make recommendations for corporate governance improvements in this essential area. One criticism he made was that boards spent too much time 'managing' (being professional managers) and insufficient time 'directing'. He defined 'directing' as showing the way ahead and providing leadership. There are numerous ways in which the effectiveness of the direction provided by a company's board can be improved. Below, we consider the many initiatives that have been recommended in order to ensure board effectiveness.

Splitting the role of chairman and chief executive

The Cadbury Report recommended that there should be a balance of power between board members such that no individual could gain 'unfettered' control of the decision-making process. Further, there should be a clear division of responsibility at the top of the company, ensuring this balance of power and authority. The Cadbury Report stipulated that if the roles of chairman and chief executive were not filled by two individuals, then a senior member of the board should be present who was independent. In 2003 the Higgs Report re-emphasized the importance of splitting the chairman and chief executive roles in UK listed companies. Higgs stated that, as a result of the Cadbury recommendations, approximately 90% of listed companies had actually split the roles of chairman and chief executive at the time of his report. This was indicative of Cadbury's lasting impact on the UK corporate community. However, Higgs recommended a change from Provision A.2.1 in the Combined Code which stipulated that:

> A decision to combine the posts of chairman and chief executive officer in one person should be publicly justified.
>
> (The Combined Code, 1998, p. 14)

To the far more rigorous version:

> The roles of chairman and chief executive should not be exercised by the same individual.
>
> (Suggested revisions to the Combined Code, 1998,
> Annex A of the Higgs Report, 2003, p. 80)

The essence of these recommendations, among others made by Higgs, was incorporated in the Combined Code in July 2003. We now look at evidence from the academic literature relating to the importance of these initiatives for effective corporate governance.

Research into split roles

According to the academic literature, splitting the role of chairman and chief executive is a corporate governance initiative that can reduce agency problems and result in improved corporate performance because of more independent decision making (Donaldson and Davies, 1994). In Chapter 1, we considered that agency problems could be lessened by mechanisms that aided monitoring of boards in order to align shareholder and management interests. Some studies have shown that splitting the role has indeed led to significantly higher financial performance (Peel and O'Donnell, 1995). However, it has been suggested that such improvements may be a case of wishful thinking and that the evidence is not persuasive enough to engender splitting the roles in practice (Daily and Dalton, 1997).

One area of the academic literature has focused on the relationship between top management turnover, corporate financial performance and the introduction of corporate governance initiatives, such as split roles into companies. In such studies, top management turnover has been used as a proxy for corporate governance quality, as a well-governed company is considered likely to remove ineffectual directors before they can do harm. A company with 'good' corporate governance mechanisms, such as split roles or an optimal balance of executive and non-executive directors, is likely to display more effective monitoring of management. However, high turnover of directors may not always involve replacing poor managers with better ones. There may be ulterior motives behind such replacements, which do not result in better people on the board. Nevertheless, if 'good' managers replace 'bad' ones, then we would assume that companies with higher top management turnover, better corporate governance mechanisms and more effective board members would display superior financial performance. Basing their analysis on these assumptions, Dahya et al. (2002) found that top management turnover was higher after Cadbury than before, but only in companies that had altered their board structure as a result of Cadbury. They also found that higher turnover of top management was statistically related to poorer financial performance, for an extensive sample of UK companies around the time of the Cadbury Report. They therefore deduced that:

> These results indicate that the increase in CEO turnover is not random; rather it is (inversely) correlated with performance: After controlling for performance, the likelihood that the CEO will depart his position is greater once a poorly performing firm comes into compliance with the key provisions of the Code. The answer to the question of whether the 'right' managers are leaving the firms appears to be yes, assuming, of course, that our measures of performance properly identify the right managers.
>
> (Dahya et al., 2002, p. 478, emphasis added)

These results provide a powerful mandate for corporate governance reform in the UK, as they endorse the positive impact of the chief Cadbury recommendations.

In the USA, boards of directors have been harshly criticized for not attaining a balance of power and therefore reducing board effectiveness. The board culture in the USA is considered to discourage conflict. This implies that the CEO (usually also the company chairman) wields excessive power and has ultimate control over decision making. Further, it is typical that US boards are excessively large, also reducing board effectiveness (see Jensen, 1993). Indeed, statistical evidence has shown that corporate performance and value were a decreasing function of board size (Yermack, 1996). For most companies, the CEO and chairman tend to be the same person. There is an emerging consensus opposing this practice, as expressed in the following statement:

> Some of the Sarbanes–Oxley rules for bosses and directors may be too cumbersome or prescriptive . . . A more useful idea is a toughening of checks and balances for bosses.

Best of all, American companies should adopt the common European practice of sep-
arating the jobs of chairman and chief executive, entrenching a check at the heart of their
corporate governance systems.

(*The Economist*, 28 November 2002, emphasis added)

This is one area of corporate governance where the UK is significantly more proactive than the USA, although senior independent directors substitute for split roles to
some extent on American boards.

The role of non-executive directors in corporate governance

As we saw from the case study in Chapter 2, the collapse of Enron during 2001
focused attention on the effectiveness of the non-executive director function. The
Higgs Report (2003) in the UK was clearly a knee-jerk response to the considerable
impact of ineffective non-executive directors in such companies as Enron. From an
agency theory perspective, the presence of independent non-executive directors
(frequently referred to as NEDs) on company boards, should help to reduce the
notorious conflicts of interest between shareholders and company management, as
they perform a monitoring function by introducing an independent voice to the
boardroom. However, it needs to be borne in mind that inside directors have an
essential role to play in achieving the appropriate balance between outside and inside
directors on boards, which is an essential ingredient for an effective board, as:

The inside directors provide valuable information about the firm's activities, while outside
directors may contribute both expertise and objectivity in evaluating the managers' decisions. The corporate board, with its mix of expertise, independence, and legal power, is a
potentially powerful governance mechanism.

(Byrd and Hickman, 1992, p. 196)

The Cadbury Report recommended that the board of directors should include a
minimum of three non-executive directors who are able to influence the board's
decisions. It stipulated that non-executive directors should provide an independent
view on corporate strategy, performance, resources, appointments and standards of
conduct. Further, the majority of non-executive directors should be independent of
management and free from any relationship that could affect their independence
(except their fees and shareholdings). Indeed, the Report stated that at least two
of the minimum requirement of three non-executive directors should be independent.
Several ways of ensuring the independence of non-executive directors have been
suggested. For example, the Cadbury Report discussed the fees payable to non-
executive directors, stipulating that a balance needed to be struck between
recognizing the value of the contribution made by non-executive directors and

avoiding compromising their independence. Another way was to encourage non-executive directors not to take part in share option schemes as this could also compromise their independence. The Cadbury Report also stressed that the appointment of non-executive directors was an important decision that should be taken via a formal selection process (using a nomination committee), again strengthening their independence. As well as the problem of independence, the Cadbury Report aired concerns about the supply of adequately qualified non-executive directors. This is an issue which has become increasingly problematic as more non-executive directors have been deemed necessary on boards.

The Hampel Report (1998) readdressed the role of non-executive directors but did not increase the desirable number of non-executives on the board. The balance of non-executive and executive directors recommended by the accompanying Combined Code (1998) remained unchanged from the number suggested in the earlier Cadbury Code. Both Codes stipulated that non-executive directors should comprise not less than one-third of the board. Indeed, it seems that the comments made in the Hampel Report, pertaining to the 'excessive' emphasis placed on the monitoring role of non-executive directors, was misguided. Specifically, the Report noted that:

> An unintended side effect has been to overemphasise the monitoring role [of non-executive directors].
>
> (The Hampel Report, 1998, p. 25, para. 3.7)

Such cases as Enron have underlined the dangers of an ineffective group of non-executive directors and the severe problems that can arise when their independence is compromised through conflicts of interest (see Chapter 2).

In April 2002 Patricia Hewitt, the UK Secretary of State, and Gordon Brown, the Chancellor of the Exchequer, commissioned Derek Higgs to prepare a review on the role of independent directors. This represented the UK equivalent of the Sarbanes–Oxley Act (2002), as it provided a response to the problems highlighted by Enron. The consultation document was published in June 2002 and requested responses from interested parties (such as the Stock Exchange, major institutional investors, the Institute of Directors). The terms of reference for the Higgs Review were set out in this consultation document. They specified that the objective of the review was to provide a short, independent investigation into the role and effectiveness of non-executive directors in the UK. The terms of reference also stated that, from the perspective of UK productivity performance, progressive strengthening of the quality and role of non-executive directors was strongly desirable. The terms of reference specified that the review should:

■ provide a picture of the population of non-executive directors in the UK at that time, focusing on who the non-executive directors were, how they were appointed and how a broader pool of prospective non-executive directors may be found;

- assess the extent to which the non-executive directors were 'independent' in practice;

- assess the effectiveness of non-executive directors in UK listed companies;

- assess the accountability of non-executive directors (i.e., their actual and potential relationship with institutional investors);

- assess a variety of issues relating to non-executive directors' remuneration;

- most importantly, proffer appropriate recommendations for strengthening the quality, independence and effectiveness of non-executive directors.

Lastly, the terms of reference stated that the review should:

- build and publish an accurate image of the status quo relating to non-executive directors;

- lead debate on non-executive director-related issues;

- make appropriate recommendations to the Government, or other relevant parties.

In keeping with the typical UK approach to corporate governance reform, we can see from the Higgs consultation document that the government intended to maintain a voluntary environment in the area of non-executive directors, avoiding regulation or legislation. The Government considered (in the terms of reference) that they required someone who was a leading figure in the City of London and who would provide an independent assessment of the current role and effectiveness of non-executive directors in UK listed companies. *The Economist*'s description of the man selected for the job was entertaining and evocative:

> Except that he is a devoted reader of the left-leaning *Guardian* newspaper, Derek Higgs is a typical member of the City of London elite. As astute deal-maker at the Warburg investment bank, an engaging dinner companion and comfortably rich, ... The sort of chap that British governments down the years have got to run committees to defuse political bombs with some sensible proposals ... If, as has been suggested this week, ministers are worried that he 'has not come up with anything radical enough', the surprise is that they expected anything else.
>
> (*The Economist*, 31 October 2002)

However, the final Higgs Report was published on 20 January 2003 and, contrary to expectations such as those expressed in the above quotation, it delivered some quite 'radical' suggestions. The full text can be viewed on the Department of

Trade & Industry (DTI) website.[1] Higgs' review was based on three pieces of primary research, specifically:[2]

- data on the size, composition and membership of boards and committees in the 2,200 UK listed companies, as well as the age and gender of their directors;

- a survey of 605 executive directors, non-executive directors and chairmen of UK listed companies conducted by MORI (the national polling agency) in August 2002;

- interviews of 40 directors in top UK listed companies carried out by academics in the field.[3]

First and foremost the Higgs Report recommended that at least half of a company's board of directors should be independent non-executive directors. This is a definitive development from the earlier codes of practice and one that conflicts with the Hampel Report's suggestion that the monitoring role of non-executive directors had been 'overemphasized'. He considered non-executive directors needed all the support possible to ensure they perform their role effectively and called for more non-executive director training. In many quarters this call was answered by discontent, as we can see from Illustration 4.1.

Another section of the Higgs Report was devoted to relationships with shareholders and contained a number of far-reaching (and controversial) recommendations, emphasizing that:

> The role of the non-executive director includes an important and inescapable relationship with shareholders.
>
> (Higgs Report, 2003, p. 67, para. 15.1)

This aspect of the Higgs Report made probably the most advanced and progressive recommendations, as he encouraged the linkage of two essential corporate governance mechanisms, namely the role of non-executive directors and the role of institutional investors. Such a linkage should be synergistic, as the combination of the two mechanisms should result in a much stronger monitoring instrument than when they function separately. The report recommended that one (or several) non-executive director(s) should take direct responsibility for shareholder concerns, effectively championing shareholder interests at board level. A related recommendation from the Higgs Report was for this senior non-executive director to attend regular meetings with the company's shareholders and for non-executive directors to be more closely involved with the process of shareholder engagement, which is continually

---

[1] The website address is http:www.dti.gov.uk/cld/non_exec_review/
[2] The data were supplied to the Higgs Committee by Hemscott Group Limited.
[3] They were Dr Terry McNulty (University of Leeds), Dr John Roberts and Dr Philip Stiles (both of the University of Cambridge).

Illustration 4.1

Educating NEDs

Cranfield School of Management and Henley Management College both offer training programmes for non-executive directors. However, despite calls from Derek Higgs for greater provision of training for non-executive directors (NEDs) both colleges are finding it difficult to fill their courses. Indeed, Cranfield had to cancel their two-day training seminar on the responsibilities of NEDs three times due to insufficient demand. Similarly, Henley abandoned a similar course for similar reasons. One reason certainly seems to be a feeling among board members that NEDs have no need for training. They are ready for the job in hand and have the adequate experience already. Forcing them to take courses and attend training sessions may simply be a time-wasting exercise, detracting from their main aim of serving on company boards. This attitude does, however, display a certain level of arrogance. To what extent can anyone ever claim to know everything about what they do? There is always more to learn. Some research findings have led some to the conclusion that the way NEDs are appointed represents the 'last Bastion of great British managerial amateurism' (Maitland, 2003). Such amateurism is a thing of the past in most areas of business today, as top management tend to be trained better than they have ever been. NEDs need just as much encouragement to take courses and receive training as anyone else with an important, responsible role to play in business. Certainly, another of Higgs' recommendations, to 'widen the gene pool' of NEDs, will be hard to meet unless adequate training is available and the encouragement to attend courses exists.

evolving between companies and their core institutional investors. Clearly, this is another way of augmenting the monitoring role of both non-executive directors and institutional investors. This recommendation arose from the impression that these two groups were operating separately and that they were missing an opportunity to strengthen their effectiveness by combining forces, as:

> ... only rarely do non-executive directors hear at first hand the views of major share-holders.
>
> (Higgs Report, 2003, p. 67, para. 15.5)

As soon as the Higgs Report was published there was a strong reaction from some members of the business community, specifically in relation to this recommendation. A senior representative from the Confederation of British Industry (CBI) was clearly concerned about potential conflicts of interest that may arise from this recommendation, when he commented that:

> This could lead to multiple splits in the board which every man and wife could come along and exploit. And that would be a madhouse.
>
> (Tassell et al., 2003, p. 1)

Adverse reaction to the Report seemed to be widespread throughout the business community, with Higgs' calls for greater accountability viewed as an infringement on company operations. For example, a poll of company directors in the Top 30 listed companies, immediately after the publication of the Report, indicated that the majority viewed this recommendation as potentially divisive and destructive in the boardroom (Tassell, 31 January 2003).

Another weighty recommendation in the Higgs Report was that executives should be indemnified against defending themselves from legal action by their own company. This recommendation also received an immediate negative response from insurance brokers who predicted a possible increase in insurance fees of 50% following its adoption (Tassell et al., 2003). However, from our research involving interviews with institutional investors, this recommendation has inspired little confidence. There was a general attitude among people we interviewed that such insurance would represent a waste of resources as it would simply involve executives insuring themselves against events that would never transpire.

There was also a call in the Higgs Report for modest pay rises for non-executive directors to reflect their growing range of responsibilities. The report stated that non-executive directors in the FTSE 100 companies were earning on average £44,000 per annum whereas those in companies outside the FTSE 350 were earning an average of £23,000 per annum. 'Low' levels of pay (in relation to the responsibilities and work-load of non-executive directors) were cited by Higgs as a chief reason why the task of recruiting non-executive directors of sufficient calibre had become onerous. Indeed, the Higgs Report indicated that there was no evidence of a 'magic circle' of non-executive directors, with boards controlled by a few individuals. Recent research has shown that only 95 directors of the 2,800 in the FTSE 350 held two or more posts on boards (Tassell et al., 2003).

The independence of the majority of non-executive directors on a board, introduced by the Cadbury Report, was re-emphasized by the Higgs Report, which sought to develop the Combined Code definition of independence to encompass the following general statement, accompanied by a detailed list of requirements:

> A non-executive director is considered independent when the board determines that the director is independent in character and judgement and there are no relationships or circumstances which could affect, or appear to affect, the director's judgement.
>
> (Higgs Report, 2003, p. 37)

This is a further example of the far-reaching and ambitious nature of the Higgs review. It seems that, although the Higgs Report was conducted partly in response to such corporate governance failures as Enron and was therefore partly reactive in nature, the recommendations contained in Higgs were far-reaching and therefore more proactive than its predecessors. This was probably the reason why the Report caused such a stir in UK companies! In other words, whereas previous corporate governance reports and codes caused systems that were already implicit in UK listed companies to become explicit, the Higgs Report made recommendations for change that were not based solely on the existing, implicit framework of UK corporate governance. Generally, policy recommendations that require changes to the status quo are likely to meet with opposition, as they seek to transform peoples' attitudes.[4] Illustration 4.2 provides a cameo of some of the initial reactions to the Higgs Report, which demonstrated that the status quo within the City was being threatened.

We now turn to considering evidence from the academic literature concerning the usefulness of the non-executive director function.

Research into the role of non-executive directors

There is a growing body of academic literature relating to the function of non-executive directors and their contribution to 'good' corporate governance. However, there is no clear consensus in the literature concerning whether or not non-executive directors play a useful corporate governance role and whether or not they enhance shareholder wealth and financial performance. We look now at a selection of empirical evidence from the academic research in favour of the presence of non-executive directors on boards, as well as evidence against it.

Evidence in favour

From an agency theory perspective, non-executive directors may be perceived as playing a monitoring role on the rest of the board. There is a substantial quantity of academic literature indicating that boards of directors perform an important corporate governance function and that non-executive directors act as necessary monitors of management (e.g., Fama, 1980; Fama and Jensen, 1983). Our own research has shown that a high degree of importance is attached to the non-executive director function by the UK institutional investment community. We surveyed a large sample of investment institutions and the respondents ranked the presence of non-executives on boards as the most important corporate governance mechanism recommended in successive policy documents (see Table 3.1). Without the monitoring function of non-executive directors it would be more likely that inside executive directors would be able to manipulate their position by gaining complete control over their own remuneration packages and securing their jobs (Morck et al., 1988).

Some academic studies have shown that non-executive directors have monitored management effectively. An indicator that has been used to proxy for such monitoring efficiency is chief executive turnover, the implication being that more frequent turnover of chief executives leads to better corporate financial performance. Further, this may in turn be related to a greater proportion of non-executive directors on company boards. We saw earlier in this chapter that similar assumptions are made in testing the effectiveness of splitting the roles of chairman and chief executive. Their

---

[4] See Solomon and Solomon (2000) for a discussion of conceptual frameworks that may or may not challenge the status quo.

Illustration 4.2

Initial reactions to Higgs

The Higgs Report was published in January 2003. Higgs was invited by the Government to review the role and effectiveness of non-executive directors in UK corporate governance. From an agency theory perspective, the function of non-executive directors is to monitor company directors in order to improve their accountability to the company's shareholders and align the interests of these two groups.

Reactions from the corporate community

There was an immediate adverse reaction to the report within the business community, with Higgs' calls for greater accountability being viewed as an infringement on company operations. A poll of company directors in the top 30 listed companies, immediately after the introduction of the Report, showed they saw some recommendations as potentially divisive and destructive in the boardroom (Tassell, 31 January 2003). The aspect of Higgs that caused the greatest stir was the recommendation that there should be a senior independent director (a SID) to champion shareholder interests. Accompanying this concept was the suggestion that this shareholder-friendly non-executive director should attend the meetings between executives and their institutional investors. Higgs considered that non-executive directors should be more closely involved in the engagement process and that their monitoring role would be enhanced through greater contact with core investors. Fears that this could be divisive represent exactly the executive attitudes that Higgs sought to change. Resistance to such recommendations highlights a lack of align-ment between executives and their shareholders at the heart of corporate decision making, which is reminiscent of an agency problem. If more shareholder representation is seen as divisive, this could be a sign that directors are still far away in their objectives from their shareholders.

The recommendation by Higgs that the nomination committee of the board should be chaired by a SID rather than the chairman also sparked fiery corporate opposition. This was clearly a radical monitoring device that would prevent cronyism in appointments. Representatives from both the CBI and the Institute of Directors (ID) expressed serious concerns that this and other recommendations could be divisive. Again, if they were no agency problems inherent in businesses, this type of knee-jerk reaction would be less likely.

Another recommendation of the Higgs Report was that the largest UK listed companies should not appoint retiring chief executives as chairmen, as this could encourage boardroom complacency. Companies generally ignored this recommendation, with John Sainsbury being an outstanding example in their appointment of Sir Peter Davis in March 2003 (Flanagan, 2003). However, the director of the voting agency, Manifest, considered that removing Sir Peter, at the same time as the chairman was retiring, would create too much instability in the company. There are clearly two sides to this, and even the institu-tional shareholders were not in favour of Higgs' recommendations in this case (Tassell and Voyle, 2003). There was, however, suspicion in the press that chairmen of Top 100 companies who criticized Higgs' recommendations had not actually read the Report (Plender, 16 March 2003). Such apathy and complacency are symptomatic of an in-herent corporate governance problem.

Reactions from institutional investors

Surprisingly, it was not just the corporate community that reacted against Higgs' recom-mendations, even though his intentions were clearly to improve corporate accountability to shareholders. Strong reactions to the recommendations of the Higgs Report from the institutional investor community were voiced at the conference of one of the largest investor groups, the National Association of Pension Funds (NAPF), in Edinburgh in March 2003. Pension fund managers and pension fund trustees, who together represent the weight of the institutional investors community in the UK, expressed their opposition to one of Higgs' recommendations that at least half the board of a company should comprise independent non-executive directors, as 40% of the conference delegates voted against it (Tassell, 14 March 2003a). The head of investment of another large investor group, the Association of British Insurers (ABI), considered that without a 'critical mass of support' the revisions to the Combined Code suggested by the Higgs Report would not be advisable. Qualifying this, he commented that, although the 'comply or explain' approach to corporate governance reform provided a solid basis for change, it would become impotent without a critical mass of support. Companies would simply 'comply or do nothing!' This accompanied Higgs' own concerns, also voiced at the conference, that companies would either 'comply or breach' or 'comply and have their trousers taken down in the press'! (Tassell, 14 March 2003b).

Clearly, the initial reactions to Higgs' recommendations were strong and varied, coming from both the corporate and the institutional investor community. The amount of discussion and the level of dissatisfaction were considerable. But change is never easy: no pain no gain. Accountability will only improve if changes are made.

independent influence on the board should in such cases lead to the removal of ineffective chief executives. Indeed, Weisbach (1988) found evidence that the turnover of chief executives was more strongly related to company performance in companies characterized by a majority of non-executive directors.

The presence of outsiders on company boards is also thought to be positively related to corporate control activity, as outsiders can facilitate takeovers, thereby activating the takeover constraint that disciplines company management (Agrawal and Knoeber, 1996). In relation to hostile takeover bids, empirical evidence has been provided, showing that boards with a significant independent contingent benefit shareholders in the bidding process (Byrd and Hickman, 1992). Again, this endorses the presence of non-executive, outside directors on boards. Also, in relation to the positive effects for shareholders of non-executive directors' involvement on boards, Rosenstein and Wyatt (1990) found evidence of a positive share price reaction to their appointment.

Evidence against

Another school of thought in the academic literature considers that boards of directors *per se* are superfluous, as the market provides a natural solution to the notorious agency problem rendering internal mechanisms unnecessary (e.g., Hart, 1983). If boards are superfluous then, from this theoretical viewpoint, non-executive directors are merely another impotent element in an unnecessary structure. Proponents of this view consider that the 'market' disciplines company management naturally (e.g., through the threat of hostile takeovers and shareholder voting), thereby aligning managers' interests with those of shareholders.

In relation to the relevance of non-executive directors versus the relevance of executive directors, there is considerable debate in the academic literature. Some evidence endorses the position of executives in preference to non-executives on boards. For example, one empirical study investigated the wealth effects of inside, executive director appointments by management (Rosenstein and Wyatt, 1990). Using event study methodology, the paper reported a positive share price reaction to the announcement of inside director appointments. The findings stressed the important role that inside directors played in ratifying material corporate decisions and endorsing corporate strategies. However, the study also highlighted the relevance of the existing board composition to the effect of new appointments on share price, as they found that the market reacted more favourably to insider appointments, where there was a board imbalance displaying a high proportion of non-executive directors, and less favourably when the balance was skewed more to insiders. The paper concluded that the benefits associated with the appointment of a new inside director only outweighed the costs of such an appointment when managerial and shareholder interests were closely aligned (i.e., when there was no significant agency problem).

There is also a perception among some academics and practitioners that the involvement of non-executive, outside directors on boards can damage corporate governance by reducing entrepreneurship in the business and by weakening board unity. This was certainly the view expressed by many board directors in their initial response to the Higgs recommendations to broaden the role and effectiveness of non-executive directors in the UK. Higgs' suggestion to make non-executive directors the champions of shareholder interests met with immediate opposition. Despite supporters of the non-executive director role, such as Derek Higgs, some leading figures in the City of London consider that non-executive directors can do more harm than good and that their role should be abolished! (*The Economist*, 13 June 2002). Indeed, there is a potential for the appointment of non-executive directors to result in more cronyism and a more comfortable network of close ties and cosy relationships between directors of leading companies. Furthermore, accusations are made that the relatively new level of non-executive directors in UK business provides just more 'jobs for the boys' and the opportunity for an even firmer golden handshake than retiring directors receive already.

There is also evidence suggesting that non-executive directors have a negative, rather than a positive impact on corporate financial performance. The presence of outside directors on US boards represented one of seven mechanisms used to control agency problems examined by Agrawal and Knoeber (1996). They found persistent evidence of a negative relationship between the proportion of outside directors and the companies' financial performance. Their conclusion was that companies had too many outside directors on their boards. This is not encouraging evidence for supporters of the UK Higgs Report. However, the authors were 'puzzled' by this result. One explanation they proffered was that outside directors were often added to boards in companies that were already performing badly, in order to improve performance (a result also presented in Hermalin and Weisbach, 1988). The authors examined their findings and concluded that the causality ran from board composition to performance, and not in the opposite direction, dispelling this explanation. They commented that:

> One possible rationale is that boards are expanded for political reasons, perhaps to include politicians, environmental activists, or consumer representatives, and that these additional outside directors either reduce firm performance or proxy for the underlying political constraints that led to their receiving board seats.
>
> (Agrawal and Knoeber, 1996, p. 394)

Clearly, these authors would be unlikely to support the hypothesis that wider stakeholder accountability improves corporate financial performance. However, their results are interesting and beg further investigation. They emphasized the interdependence of various control mechanisms, such as the non-executive director function, and took account of such interrelationships in their analysis in order to avoid spurious results.

Getting the balance right

Overall, it seems that the majority of empirical evidence endorses the roles of both non-executive and executive directors, even though some results are conflicting. Both groups of directors bring different but essential skills to the boardroom. An effective board attains the appropriate balance between the two. The weight of evidence seems to endorse the monitoring role played by non-executive directors and supports the current UK and US policy of encouraging their effectiveness. This view is emphasized by Mace (1986), for example, who stated that many chief executives considered the most effective boards were those with a 'balance' of inside and outside directors. Too great a proportion of insiders or outsiders can swing the balance in the wrong direction, for example:

> If there are too many insiders, the management team can become excessively cohesive. This sets up a very dangerous situation because the directors tend to derive their judgement only from colleagues. The scarcity of outside directors restricts outside influence and leads to close-minded decisions. On the other hand, the addition of many outsiders brings new information and ideas and allows the entire board to make sound decisions. Outside directors provoke an independent and fresh review of long-term decisions, effectuate impartial, uncontaminated audits of managerial performance, and counterbalance the influence of top management. *Companies need strong, knowledgeable insider directors as well as independent outsiders in order to represent stockholders most effectively.*
>
> (Alkhafaji, 1989, p. 54, emphasis added)

In practice, although the market offers real incentives to solve the agency problem, they are not sufficient to satisfy fully the needs of shareholders and other stakeholder groups. Such corporate governance mechanisms as the presence of independent, non-executive directors are necessary to improve the quality of governance in listed companies.

Another question addressed in the academic literature asks whether or not non-executive directors who are alleged to be independent are truly independent, or whether their independence is debatable. Indeed, a degree of scepticism is displayed by many authors concerning non-executive directors' independence. One of the major problems highlighted in the literature arises from the role played by executive directors in appointing non-executives. This could clearly compromise their independence if the appointment process is affected unduly by cronyism (see, e.g., Waldo, 1985; Mace, 1986; Vancil, 1987). Short (1996) also debated this issue, concluding that far more research was required.

Who wants the job anyway?

As in many other areas of UK industry, recommendations for improvements, greater accountability on remuneration and many other factors are making such positions as that of a non-executive director less attractive to prospective newcomers. As we mentioned above, this was a concern detected in the Cadbury Report and covered in the Higgs Review. Indeed, there appears to be a growing reluctance to become a non-executive director (*The Economist*, 31 October 2002). This is also the case in the USA where people are less and less inclined to become involved in companies as either inside or outside directors, given the potentially frightening repercussions from Sarbanes–Oxley. If non-executive directors are meant to bring impartiality into the boardroom, the question for legislators is the extent to which legal liability, including criminal sanctions, should attach to the role of non-executive directors. Clearly, it would be a significant disincentive to people considering a position as a non-executive director.

Such organizations as PRONED act as a type of professional dating service, matching prospective non-executive directors to suitable company boards. Their role is essential in ensuring the non-executive director function operates efficiently.

Executive remuneration

In the early 1990s people were not as familiar with the term 'corporate governance' as they are today. Even in leading business schools, discussion of corporate governance tended to centre around directors' pay and 'fat cats'. As we can see from this textbook, corporate governance is a far broader subject than that! However, the contentious issue of executive remuneration and the problems of setting pay at appropriate levels is an extremely important aspect of corporate governance. The need to establish directors' pay at a level that incentivizes management to pursue shareholder interests has been emphasized in the academic literature (Jensen, 1993).

Illustration 4.3

Is remuneration excessive?

Just a few tasty morsels of pay to chew on. Rose Marie Bravo at Burberry, the maker of fashionable raincoats, received a £6 million salary in 2002. Despite her hard work in transforming the company, the NAPF felt they could not condone the 'sheer largesse' of the executives' salaries in Burberry and the lack of any relation to performance (Boxell, 14 July 2003). The ABI expressed similar concerns. Ben Verwaayen, the chief executive of BT earned £3 million in 2002. Also in 2002, four executives at AWG, the utilities group, received special bonuses totalling £475,000 for their role in debt restructuring (Bream, 2003). Vittorio Radice, the ex-boss of Selfridges, was given a 'golden hello' of £1.15 million by Marks and Spencer. In April 2003 Alistair Dales received compensation of £889,457 when he agreed to retire early from Nationwide, on top of his basic salary of £301,000 and bonuses (Croft, 24 July 2003). But the problem doesn't seem to end when they leave the company. Sir Iain Vallance, the former chairman of BT, received almost £1.1 million over two years following his resignation as executive and appointment as 'president emeritus'. These are just a random handful of cases. A cursory glance at the media would reveal many more. The problem is by no means restricted to the UK. Frits Bolkestein, the EU Commissioner for the Internal Market and Taxation, has taken a hard line on executive remuneration at a pan-European level, commenting that, '... the remuneration for top dogs (and fat cats) in industry is out of all proportion ... I find the pay packages excessive.' He considers that prompt action is necessary for annual disclosure of remuneration policy, with shareholder approval of the policy, for listed companies throughout EU member states (see European Financial Services Regulation, 2003). What do you think about these levels of pay?

In this sense, executive remuneration is one more mechanism that can be refined to improve corporate governance.

The gap between executives' pay and that of workers on the factory floor has been shown to have widened in the past 20 years (see, e.g., *The Economist*, 15 November 2002). The Higgs Report quoted research findings that, on average, company chairmen in the FTSE 100 companies were earning £426,000 per annum at that time. This gives an indication of the salaries earned by senior board members. A scatter of contentious salary packages is collated in Illustration 4.3. Directors have received unreasonable amounts of additional benefit (e.g., in the form of stock options), which has generated controversy. Further, some people have felt that such high rewards have not been accompanied by high performance. An opinion poll in 2003 performed by MORI revealed that 78% of those members of the public surveyed, considered that directors of large companies were paid too much (Blitz, 2003).

The Cadbury Report devoted some attention to executive remuneration, but it was the Greenbury Report and its accompanying Code of Practice, produced in 1995, that focused specifically on issues relating to directors' pay. As with the Cadbury Code, the Greenbury Committee proposed that all listed companies registered in the UK should comply with the code and report annually to shareholders on their level of compliance. The Code aimed to establish best practice in determining and accounting for directors' remuneration. The Greenbury Report (1995) may be seen as reactive rather than proactive in nature, as it responded to public sentiment. The Greenbury Committee consisted of leading investors and industrialists and the chairman was Sir Richard Greenbury. The group's terms of reference were: *To identify good practice in determining directors' remuneration and prepare a code of such practice for use by UK plcs*, with the aim of increasing accountability and enhancing performance. Also, full disclosure of remuneration and other related information was raised as requiring attention. One important aim of the Committee (and of the earlier Cadbury Code of best practice) was to create remuneration committees that would *determine pay packages needed to attract, retain and motivate directors of the quality required but should avoid paying more than is necessary for this purpose*. This was an initiative intended to improve transparency in this area. Such remuneration committees of (mainly) non-executive directors were established to determine the company's policy on executive remuneration and specific remuneration packages for the executive directors, including pension rights and any compensation payments. Clearly, the intention was to prevent executive directors from designing their own pay packages. The need for an independent remuneration committee has been highlighted in the academic literature as an essential mechanism to prevent executives writing and signing their own pay cheques (Williamson, 1985). The members of the remuneration committee should be listed each year in the committee's report to shareholders and the committee should make a report each year to the shareholders on behalf of the board. This report should also include full details of all elements in the remuneration package of each individual director by name, such as basic salary, benefits in kind, annual bonuses and long-term incentive schemes including share options, as well as pension entitlements earned by each individual director during the year.

Since Greenbury, there have been significant improvements in the quality and quantity of disclosure relating to directors' remuneration, with companies providing substantial quantities of information relating to their directors' remuneration in their annual reports. The revision of the Combined Code in July 2003, in the wake of the Higgs review on non-executive directors, incorporated a series of provisions aimed at preventing excessive executive pay (Tassell, 22 July 2003). The new draft aimed to avoid the upward ratchet of pay levels that do not correspond to performance. We now turn to the academic literature for evidence relating to issues of directors' remuneration.

Research into executive remuneration

There is a vast quantity of literature relating to executive remuneration. Clearly, it is not our intention to provide comprehensive coverage of this literature, but rather to give a flavour of the issues addressed and some of the salient findings. As for the relationship between remuneration and corporate performance, one academic study found strong statistical evidence linking excessive executive remuneration with 'bad' corporate governance and poor corporate performance in the USA (Core et al., 1999). Indeed a significant negative association was found between remuneration (arising from board and ownership structure) and corporate operating and share price performance, indicating that companies fared less well when their board structure allowed an imbalance of power leading to excessive chief executive remuneration. This paper made a policy recommendation that US boards should split the roles of CEO and chairman, in line with the recommendations of Cadbury, *inter alia*. Academic research has also shown a significant relationship between CEO compensation and the manner in which members of the board are appointed. Generally, the more control the CEO has over appointing other board members, the higher their remuneration tends to be (Lambert et al., 1993).

With respect to remuneration committees, Bostock (1995) found that the recommendation to establish remuneration committees produced a speedy response, with a large number of UK company boards establishing committees comprising relatively few executive directors. Further, Conyon and Mallin (1997) reported that by 1995, 98% of companies responding to a questionnaire survey had established a remuneration committee in response to the initial Cadbury recommendations.

In relation to the level of executive remuneration in different countries, another paper examined the progressive globalization of executive remuneration (Cheffins, 2003). The author debated that not only was remuneration harmonizing at an international level but it was also following US levels, which are traditionally higher than in other parts of the world. The paper reviewed the data on the remuneration of US executives, concluding that the pay packages of US chief executives were far more lucrative than those of executives in other countries around the world. The paper discussed a number of market-oriented drivers for executive pay convergence and linked this evolution to the steady convergence of global corporate systems toward a market-based structure: a more market-driven global corporate governance system may be characterized by more lucrative executive pay structures. One of the main issues raised was disclosure of executive remuneration. Cheffins (2003) considered that if tougher laws on disclosure of executive pay packages were introduced internationally this would advance the 'Americanization' of executive pay. Moreover, shareholders would be able to see the remuneration that incentivizes executives to maximize shareholder value. This would in turn help to reduce the 'agency cost' in those companies. Cheffins (2003) argued that a strong relationship between pay and performance could reduce the costs associated with shareholder monitoring. Such changes are certainly occurring at present, with the UK Government's introduction of legislation committing institutional investors to vote on directors' remuneration and requiring companies to make far more detailed disclosure on their policies on director remuneration. Nevertheless, it appears that 'Americanization' of pay may become a reality in the UK if Cheffins' (2003) model holds. Certainly, the remuneration package given to the director of US operations at HSBC in May 2003, which included a multimillion dollar pay-off if he was ever ousted and totalled $37.5 million over three years, is evidence of American-style remuneration packages crossing the Atlantic (Croft, 12 May 2003). However, unless such appealing packages are offered, it will be impossible to attract talent from the USA, which many UK companies are attempting to do (Gimbel, 2003). Indeed, equalization of executive remuneration is likely to occur at a higher, rather than a lower level.

In Chapter 6 we discuss the literature that links the disclosure of financial accounting information with remuneration policies, in order to demonstrate the importance of establishing a positive relationship between remuneration and performance.

Voting on directors' remuneration

One substantial change effected in UK corporate governance and accountability was the decision by many companies (following pressure from shareholders and lobby-ists, *inter alia*) to allow their shareholders to vote on directors' remuneration. In October 2001 the Government announced proposals to produce an annual directors' remuneration report that would be approved by shareholders. There has been a significant increase in UK listed companies that have allowed their shareholders to vote on directors' pay. Indeed, a survey indicated that 37% of blue-chip companies were considering allowing their shareholders to vote on directors' remuneration at their AGMs in 2002, compared with only 13% in 2001 (see Jones, 2002). The Government's Trade and Industry Secretary, Patricia Hewitt, produced a consul-tative document in 2002 dealing with directors' remuneration, which called for enhanced shareholder powers in this area. However, the actual powers shareholders gained by such a change were perhaps less far-reaching than one might imagine. The vote is only advisory. In other words, the company does not have to take any notice of the outcome, should it prefer not to. Shareholders do not have the opportunity to vote on the remuneration of individual directors. Further, some institutional in-vestors have reacted negatively to the proposal, as they see it as a means of passing the buck from directors to shareholders, forcing them to discharge accountability and responsibility rather than the companies, for pay levels (Mayo and Young, 2002). Nevertheless, as with many 'voluntary' areas of corporate governance, it would be unlikely for companies with good reputations to ignore such a demonstration of discontent from their shareholders. This greater level of shareholder involvement should result in improved accountability and more reasonable remuneration packages.

The emerging evidence indicates that shareholder activism in this area is having a significant impact on company management, with remuneration policies being altered following shareholder protests. We discuss the evidence in detail in Chapter 5, when we consider the effectiveness of institutional investor activism in monitoring managerial behaviour. Specifically, Illustration 5.2 looks at a number of cases of shareholder activism on remuneration policies.

Directors' training

Another board-related issue that has been the focus of policy recommendations is directors' training. Education and qualifications are becoming increasingly important in today's society. The required specific knowledge to play a role within an institution is essential if the organization is to operate efficiently. In order to create a dynamic 'learning' board (Garratt, 1996) that has a lively approach, conducive to good corporate governance, directors are encouraged to attend training courses. Indeed, this was a recommendation of the Cadbury Report, which stated that:

> The weight of responsibility carried by all directors and the increasing commitment which their duties require emphasise the importance of the way in which they prepare themselves for their posts. Given the varying backgrounds, qualifications and experience of directors, it is highly desirable that they should all undertake some form of internal or external training.
>
> (Cadbury Report, 1992, p. 24, para. 4.19)

The Hampel Report reaffirmed the Cadbury emphasis on directors' training, especially in the case of new directors who have relatively little experience. Hampel also highlighted the necessity of training for directors on relevant new laws, regulations and evolving business risks. As suggested in Cadbury, there is an important role for business schools to play in providing high-quality training and corporate governance education for company directors. This also presents an opportunity for further research, as it would be interesting to find whether there is a significant statistical link between director training and corporate financial performance.

A sympathetic viewpoint

Having reviewed the many areas where corporate governance reform has targeted boardroom practice, we may wonder if such changes have started to discourage people from entering the boardroom. It could be said that a director's job, certainly in the UK, is getting tougher. It is no longer enough to have 'come up through the company', 'learned from Dad' or 'have experience of the trade'. Training, qualifications and evidence of the ability to direct are now required. Worse still for directors, any whiff of fraudulent or unsavoury thoughts, let alone actions, may now lead to prosecution and even jail, as directors' liabilities have become more carefully spelled out in the aftermath of Enron and other corporate collapses. Corporate reputation, built up over decades, can be destroyed overnight. The Sarbanes–Oxley Act (2002) represented a turning point for directors as it specified personal liability and prison for directors found guilty of corporate crime. Although the Act applies directly to the USA, it has severe implications for directors in other countries who may have any business connections with US companies. However, liabilities acted as a deterrent to prospective board members before the Enron debacle. Alkhafaji (1989) argued that in 1980s' America, candidates were turning down board positions because of the liabilities involved, given a significant increase in lawsuits against boards of directors. However, he also considered that such lawsuits may have been self-inflicted, in terms of the following analogy:

> ... if board members do not use their expertise and knowledge in the best interest of the corporation and shareholders, then they are guilty of malpractice—just like negligent doctors. From a business viewpoint, the patient is the corporation, the doctor is the board, and the shareholders are the family that sues the board for malpractice.
>
> (Alkhafaji, 1989, p. 69)

Nevertheless, in today's environment, directors can no longer be confident of receiving a bulky pay package to compensate for their considerable liabilities. Director remuneration is forced further under the microscope, with investors in the UK now possessing the right to vote on directors' pay. Every detail of pay packages is disclosed in the annual reports—no stone is left unturned. In fact, with such an increasingly difficult job and such far-reaching responsibilities, it is amazing that there are still volunteers! However, even if remuneration has been curbed, or at least observed, it is not a pittance. Indeed, who would turn down such a large salary, however difficult the job and far-reaching the responsibilities? Perhaps directorships should be put out to tender? This is a proposal that would be unlikely to hold water in the City but one that, in a watered-down version, may be worth considering, as companies and shareholders strive for greater accountability and transparency.

Chapter summary

In this chapter we have considered the role of boards of directors in corporate governance, focusing mainly on UK listed companies. We have looked at the evolution of their role and the evolution of the UK codes of best practice in corporate governance and their accompanying policy documents, from the Cadbury Report in 1992 to the Higgs Report in 2003. Specifically, we have considered the importance of achieving a balance of power in company boards and drawn the similarity between a company board and the heart of the human body, its effective and healthy function being essential to the healthy functioning of a company. We have highlighted the growing importance of the role of independent non-executive directors in corporate governance, as they provide an independent view on corporate strategy and help to attain a balance of power. Lastly, the contentious issue of executive remuneration has been discussed, as has the empirical evidence linking excessive pay packages to weak corporate governance structures and poor corporate performance. In the UK, corporate governance has a sound base, but there is always room for improvement.

Companies should not rest on their laurels and should aspire constantly to fine-tuning their corporate governance checks and balances, in order to avoid a UK Enron and to improve accountability. The academic research in this area has provided mixed results on all issues relating to boards of directors. We saw, for example, the divergent evidence on the effectiveness of the non-executive director function in monitoring company management. There is clearly room for further research and a need to clarify the advantages and disadvantages of the various corporate governance initiatives in this area in order to inform policy.

Questions for reflection and discussion

1 Has the Higgs Report produced recommendations that are feasible in practice? Do you agree with critics who have suggested that the recommendations are divisive?

2 Do you consider that non-executive directors play a useful role in company boards? To what extent do you think the academic research has clarified this issue?

3 Do you think that there will be an 'Americanization' of executive remuneration? Support your arguments with examples from the press.

4 Compare and contrast the recommendations contained in the original Higgs Report (January 2003) with the revised Combined Code (July 2003). To what extent do you think the revised code is less prescriptive than Higgs intended? Do you think that his original recommendations have been watered down too far?

5 From reading the literature, do you agree with our 'Recipe for a good board'. Would you prefer a different set of 'ingredients'? Compile your own list, explaining which 'ingredients' you consider to be the most important.

6 To what extent has the empirical research been useful in providing clarity regarding the structure of the board of directors and the firm's financial performance?

Chapter 5

The role of institutional investors in corporate governance

Aim and objectives

This chapter explores the role of institutional investors in corporate governance, mainly from a UK perspective. The specific objectives of this chapter are to enable readers to:

- highlight the important monitoring role that institutional investors play in UK corporate governance;

- discuss the complex web of ownership that arises from institutional investment;

- consider ways in which institutional investors are becoming more active in corporate governance;

- assess the evidence on the impact of shareholder activism on corporate perform-ance and company value.

Introduction

In the previous chapter we investigated the role of boards in corporate governance. However, boards of directors are not the only people with responsibility for ensuring effective corporate governance. Shareholders, especially institutional investors, also have an important role to play. In the UK the four main types of institutional investor are pension funds, life insurance companies, unit trusts and investment trusts. The position of institutional investors in corporate governance, from a theoretical perspective, is complicated. From one viewpoint, institutional investors represent another powerful corporate governance mechanism that can monitor company management, as their influence on company management can be substan-tial and can be used to align management interests with those of the shareholder group. The ways in which shareholders can monitor management in an agency theory framework were introduced briefly in Chapter 1. The monitoring role of institutional investors is increasingly important as they have grown so large and influential, at the same time gaining significant ownership concentration. Indeed, ownership concentration has been acknowledged in the literature as an important mechanism which controls agency problems and improves investor protection (Shleifer and Vishny, 1997). Such concentration can however have negative effects, such as their access to privileged information, which creates an information asymmetry between themselves and smaller shareholders. Institutional investors can also worsen agency conflicts by their existence as a significant principal who mitigates the problem due to the dispersion of ownership and control, although the growing concentration of ownership is resolving this problem.

Nevertheless, the importance of the corporate governance role that institutional investors can play in monitoring company management has been stressed in the academic literature. For example, Agrawal and Knoeber (1996) emphasized that the involvement of institutional investors can have a positive effect on corporate financial performance:

> ... concentrated shareholding by institutions ... can increase managerial monitoring and so improve firm performance.
>
> (Agrawal and Knoeber, 1996, p. 377)

Further, Stapledon (1996) commented that:

> ... monitoring by institutional shareholders fits within a broad tapestry of devices and market forces which operate to reduce the divergence between the interests of managers and shareholders.
>
> (Stapledon, 1996, p. 17)

Indeed, a large intermediary, such as an institutional investor, can solve agency problems because of their ability to take advantage of economies of scale and diversification (Diamond, 1984). From the above discussion, it seems that institutional investors, as shareholders in companies, represent both the cause and the solution of the agency problem. Their presence as shareholders creates a divorce of ownership and control, whereas their increasing involvement in companies and concentration of ownership provides a means of monitoring management and actually solving agency problems. We now consider in depth the growth of institutional investment in the UK which has resulted in a transformation of the ownership structure of UK listed companies. This growth has led to a transformation from dispersed ownership to ownership concentrated in the hands of a small number of large institutional shareholders. We then consider the implications of this ownership transformation for corporate monitoring and corporate governance.

The transformation of UK institutional ownership

Ownership structure, once characterized by Berle and Means (1932) as 'dispersed', has in recent times become more concentrated. Indeed, the growing concentration of shareholding by a relatively small number of institutional investors is resulting in the evolution of a capitalist system in the UK and in the USA that bears little resemblance to the fragmented and dispersed stock market of Berle and Means (Hill and Jones, 1992; Monks, 2001). Mainly, this is a result of the gradual transference of ownership from individuals to investment institutions. Institutional investors are organizations with millions of pounds invested in the shares of listed UK and foreign companies, as well as in other forms of financial asset. As already mentioned, they include pension funds, life insurance companies, unit trusts and investment trusts.

We can see this pattern clearly in the changes in ownership structure in the UK over the past 40 years. The proportion of institutional shareholding in UK listed companies has grown gradually to the point where they now represent the dominant shareholder class (see, e.g., Briston and Dobbins, 1978; Dobson, 1994). At the end of 1992 insurance companies and pension funds accounted for 51.8% of share ownership of the UK stock market. Unit and investment trusts held 8.5% and banks held 0.2%. Individual shareholders held only 20% of UK listed company shares, while overseas investors accounted for 12.8% (International Investment Management Directory, 1993/94). Indeed, individual ownership of shares in UK listed companies has declined from 54% in 1963 to less than 18% in 1993. By 1993 institutional ownership had risen to 62% of ordinary shares (Stapledon, 1996). The stake held by institutional investors in the UK stock market has continued to grow, and the Hampel Report (1998) stated that:

> 60% of shares in listed UK companies are held by UK institutions—pension funds, insurance companies, unit and investment trusts. Of the remaining 40%, about half are owned by individuals and half by overseas owners, mainly institutions. It is clear from this that a discussion of the role of shareholders in corporate governance will mainly concern the institutions, particularly UK institutions.
>
> (The Hampel Report, 1998, p. 40, para. 5.1)

However, it is not just the growth of institutional ownership that has characterized the transformation of ownership structure, and consequently corporate governance, in the UK. It is also the increase in ownership concentration. Listed companies are increasingly owned by a small number of large institutions. The UK pension fund industry is now highly concentrated and represents the most significant group of institutional investors in the country. For example, in 1994 the largest five pension funds managed almost £66 billion of all occupational pension fund assets. Further, the largest 68 pension funds accounted for approximately 57% of the assets of all occupational pension funds (Faccio and Lasfer, 2000).

The power of the institutional investors started to grow in the UK with the formation of the Institutional Shareholders Committee (ISC) in April 1973. When this class of dominant, large-scale investors first began to emerge, Briston and Dobbins (1978) studied their growth and predicted the impact of this growth on share ownership and influences on decision making within firms:

> We suggest that the persistent growth in the ownership of industry by institutional share-holders will inevitably involve those institutions in managerial decision-making.
>
> (Briston and Dobbins, 1978, p. 54)

This increase in ownership concentration and the transferral of ownership from individuals to institutions has had important repercussions for corporate governance in the USA and the UK. Institutional investors have moved away from being a cause, as shareholders, of the agency problem to being a means of solving the agency problem. They are now in a prime position to monitor company management and help to align the interests of management with those of their shareholders. Indeed, institutional investors today are far more involved in all areas of corporate decision making and have been encouraged to take on a more active role by the recommendations in corporate governance codes of practice and policy documents. Instead of creating an agency problem via dispersed, detached ownership, this new, dominant breed of shareholder is presenting a solution to agency problems, as they are providing a means of monitoring company management. Nevertheless, there have been warnings to avoid excessive 'interference' by institutions in the day-to-day running of businesses (e.g., the Hampel Report, 1998). If they are not managing, they are definitely monitoring company management, which is a form of pseudo-management. Similarly, in the USA Smith (1996a) stated that institutional ownership of domestic equities surpassed 50% in 1992. He suggested that their influence had grown to such a degree that monitoring by these institutions was becoming known as shareholder activism—a term with which we are now far more familiar than we were at that time.

A complex web of ownership

One problem with institutional investors as monitors of company management is that they are not actually the shareholders! Their relationship with companies and with the true shareholders involves a complicated web of ownership and account-ability. The real shareholders are the clients of the institutional investment organ-izations. For example, most company employees are members of an occupational pension scheme. The pension scheme is run by a fund manager. The pension fund manager selects companies for the portfolio and purchases the shares, using the pooled funds entrusted to him by all the employees in the company. The employee is the ultimate 'owner' of the companies in which the pension fund manager invests.

It is the employee who will be the ultimate beneficiary of the investment (via eventual pension payments). If the pension fund manager does not ensure that the various investee companies pursue shareholder wealth maximization, pension payments will not be maximized. Therefore, from an agency theory perspective there is an added agency problem. Not only does the shareholder (the individual pension fund member) have to worry about the possibly divergent objectives of investee company management but they also have to worry about the activities of the pension fund manager. The same analysis applies for people who invest in a unit trust, or who hold life insurance or endowment policies. It is because of this complex web of ownership that institutional investors' responsibilities of ownership are so pronounced. They are not responsible for themselves but for others, their clients. The pension fund manager is in fact the agent of the pension fund member. Pooling (also referred to as 'collectivization', or 'institutionalization') of investment funds adds another layer of complexity to the issue of monitoring company management.

In pension fund management (as opposed to other forms of institutional investment) there is a further layer of complexity in the web of ownership and accountability. Not only is the pension fund manager an intermediary, operating between the 'true' shareholder and the investee company, but there is also a pension fund trustee. The trustee, according to pension fund law, is entrusted with ultimate responsibility over the pension fund assets. It is the pension fund trustee who has a fiduciary responsibility to ensure that the eventual pension is maximized and that the funds of pension fund members are invested as effectively as possible. This complex web of ownership and control, resulting from the structure of pension fund investment, is alluded to in the Hampel Report as follows,

> Pension funds are the largest group of institutional investors. The trustees of the fund are the owners of the shares; but in many cases they delegate the management of the investments, including relations with companies, to a fund management group. In these cases the actions of the trustees and their relations with the fund manager have an important bearing on corporate governance.
>
> (The Hampel Report, 1998, p. 41, para. 5.6)

From this we can see that the existence of intermediaries, such as trustees in institutional investment, can obscure the corporate governance monitoring function. One of the problems arising from this complex ownership structure is that there tends to be an emphasis on short-termism in investment. Institutional investors are notoriously interested in short-term profit maximization in order to make their returns look as healthy as possible in the short run. They therefore pressure companies to focus on short-term profits rather than long-term profits. This can be detrimental to long-term company survival, as companies need to invest in long-term projects in order to ensure they grow and prosper in the long run. Such short-termism has been thought to have plagued British industry in the latter half of the 20th century. As early as the 1930s, the short-term attitudes of institutional investors were acknowledged by John Maynard Keynes, who stipulated in the following lengthy discourse that:

> It might have been supposed that competition between expert professionals, possessing judgement and knowledge beyond that of the average private investor, would correct the vagaries of the ignorant individual left to himself. It happens, however, that the energies and skill of the professional investor and speculator are mainly occupied otherwise. For most of these persons are, in fact, largely concerned, *not with making superior long-term forecasts of the probable yield of an investment over its whole life, but with foreseeing changes in the conventional basis of valuation a short time ahead of the general public.* They are concerned, not with what an investment is really worth to a man who buys it 'for keeps', but with what the market will value it at, under the influence of mass psychology, three months or a year hence ... Thus the professional investor is forced to concern himself with the anticipation of impending changes, in the news or in the atmosphere ... The actual, private objective of the most skilled investment today is 'to beat the gun', as the Americans so well express it, to outwit the crowd, and to pass the bad or depreciating, half-crown to the other fellow.
>
> (Keynes, 1936, pp. 154–155, emphasis added)

One of the main pressures for such short-term corporate behaviour is the insistence of the increasingly powerful institutional investors. In particular, pension funds may be seen as the chief culprits. The fiduciary duties of pension fund trustees emphasize such short-term profitability. As stated in Hampel:

> It is often said that trustees put fund managers under undue pressure to maximise short-term investment returns, or to maximise dividend income at the expense of retained earnings; and that the fund manager will in turn be reluctant to support board proposals which do not immediately enhance the share price of the dividend rate. Evidence to support this view is limited ... but we urge trustees to encourage investment managers to take a long view.
>
> (The Hampel Report, 1998, p. 41, para. 5.6)

We can see from this section of the Hampel Report that an emphasis for long-termism rather than short-termism is another important aspect of the agenda for corporate governance reform in the UK. Indeed, agency problems arising from the relationship between institutional fund managers and their clients (the ultimate beneficiaries of the institutional funds) may lead to a great emphasis being placed on short-term profits at the expense of longer term issues of corporate governance (Short and Keasey, 1997). There is, however, little evidence from the academic literature to support ongoing short-termism among institutional investors. Myopic institutions theory, which suggested that institutional shareholders were more short-sighted in their investment decisions than individual investors, has gained little support. The theory was based on the idea that fund managers competed for

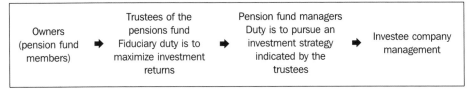

Figure [5.1]   Chain of share ownership in pension funds

clients and that their performance, in terms of return to investment, was used as a competitive indicator (Hansen and Hill, 1991). Indeed, institutional investors have now become so influential that their ability to divest from companies has been marred, such that they have been forced to become more long term (Graves and Waddock, 1994). This is because an 'exit' policy is far more expensive, as they have to accept substantial discounts in order to liquidate their holdings (Faccio and Lasfer, 2000). We summarize the complexity of pension fund share ownership in Figure 5.1, where the arrows signify the chain of ownership.

As we have seen from the above discussion, trustees are in an influential position in their pension funds. They have a fiduciary duty to maximize the investment returns for the members of the pension fund. They are responsible for the asset allocation decision and for the pension fund's investment policy. However, they are traditionally undertrained and unprepared for their hefty responsibilities. From his own research, Myners (2001) found that:

- 62% of trustees had no professional qualification in finance or investment;

- 77% of trustees had no in-house investment professionals to assist them;

- over half the population of trustees had received less than three days' training when they assumed their responsibilities;

- 44% of trustees had not attended any course since their initial 12 months of trusteeship;

- 49% of trustees spent 3 hours or less preparing for pension investment matters (implying that, given 4 meetings a year, trustees spent less than 12 hours a year on investment matters!).

Concerned by his findings, Myners commented that:

The review ... does, ... view the lack of investment understanding among trustees in general as a serious problem.

(Myners, 2001, p. 43, para. 2.27)

Indeed, one of the primary conclusions of the Myners Review was that trustees required far more preparation in order to take on their important role. One means of improving the trustee function and encouraging trustees to take a more active interest in their role may be to pay them. At present, few trustees are paid (except for items such as travel expenses to/from trustee meetings). Indeed, a survey by the *Financial Times* found that more than half of a poll of 50 from the top 100 UK listed companies did not pay their trustees (Targett and Gimbel, 2003). The implications and potential impact of increasing trustee compensation have been explored in Solomon and Solomon (2003b).

We now consider a significant trend in institutional investment, namely the growth of shareholder activism, which has accompanied the growth of institutional investment in the UK and has affected corporate governance significantly.

The growth of institutional investor activism

The role of institutional investors in corporate governance received significant attention in the Cadbury Report (1992) in a section devoted to shareholders' rights and responsibilities. Perhaps the most 'radical' aspect of the Cadbury Committee's work was its success in refocusing corporate governance not only on companies and the effectiveness of their boards of directors but also on the role that should be played by responsible shareholders, especially institutional investors. Specifically, the Cadbury Report stated:

> Given the weight of their votes, *the way in which institutional shareholders use their power to influence the standards of corporate governance is of fundamental importance*. Their readiness to do this turns on the degree to which they see it as their responsibility as owners, and in the interest of those whose money they are investing, to bring about changes in companies when necessary, rather than selling their shares.
>
> (The Cadbury Report, 1992, p. 50, emphasis added)

As a result of the Cadbury recommendations and successive corporate governance policy documents, ownership of shares can no longer be viewed as a passive activity, with institutional shareholders buying and selling shares as if they were gamblers in a casino, considering solely the financial benefit of the holdings (Keynes, 1936). Instead, institutional shareholders are now encouraged to play an active role in the companies they manage. They are no longer traders but *responsible* owners, taking an interest in their investment and maintaining it over time. In this respect it seems that Cadbury and its successors have initiated a paradigm shift in the City of London, which is having repercussions in stock exchanges across the world. Institutional investors, as well as the companies in which they invest, are recognizing the importance of their relationship with investee companies. Our own research, involving interviews with a large number of fund managers, has revealed a deep-rooted shift in approach toward institutional investment over the last decade, with institutional investors embracing an active, rather than passive, approach to investment. Further, our research has indicated that this transformation is unlikely to halt and should continue to grow in the future. In terms of specific recommendations on shareholder activism, the Cadbury Report suggested that institutional investors:

- should encourage regular one-to-one meetings with directors of their investee companies (a process referred to as 'engagement and dialogue');

- should make positive use of their voting rights; and

- should pay attention to the composition of the board of directors in their investee companies.

Institutional shareholders can also form representative groups and present resolutions to company management. This, however, is an extreme form of shareholder activism that is used in the USA but rarely in the UK. One of the only examples of a shareholder resolution in the UK occurred on an environmental issue, where shareholders compiled a resolution for BP-Amoco concerning their environmental practices. This is a rare and isolated event and in this country is usually inspired by a strong lobby on a social, ethical or environmental issue. We consider it in some detail in Chapter 10 (see Illustration 10.2). We summarize the forms of shareholder activism that institutional investors can employ to monitor company management and resolve agency problems in Figure 5.2.

Following Cadbury, the Myners Report (1995) emphasized the importance of developing a 'winning partnership' between institutional investors and their investee companies. Further, Monks (1994) emphasized the need for institutional investors to practise what he termed 'relationship' investing' with their investee companies. Another important initiative in the area of shareholder activism has been the

Figure [5.2]   Forms of shareholder activism

publication, in October 2002, of *The Responsibilities of Institutional Shareholders and Agents: Statement of Principles* for institutional investors by the ISC (2002).[1] The Higgs Report (2003) expressed support for this 'Code of Activism', requesting that it should be endorsed by the revised Combined Code (2003). The ISC Code established a benchmark for institutional investor practice in the areas of engagement and voting. The aim was principally to provide a reference point for institutional investors, such that activism would become more organized and less *ad hoc*. An interesting aspect of the Code was its recommendation that the process of shareholder activism should become dynamic in nature. In other words, it suggested that activism *per se* was inadequate and that institutional investors should monitor the effectiveness of their intervention in companies and their monitoring activities, in order to improve and refine their engagement, voting and related practices. Not only does such shareholder involvement benefit shareholders but it can also have a positive impact on other stakeholder groups. Illustration 5.1 provides a more philosophical perspective on shareholder activism, exploring sociological reasons why increased activism may contribute to society, in a broader context, by restoring the trust that has been lost in institutions, mainly as a result of scandals in the financial community.

Clearly, shareholder activism is an important means of monitoring company management and of restoring trust in financial institutions. We now discuss the role of voting by institutional investors.

Institutional investor voting

Until the 1990s the level of voting by institutional investors remained fairly low (Stapledon, 1995). However, the use of voting rights by institutional investors has increased significantly in recent years (Mallin, 1999). The NAPF has encouraged members to vote (NAPF, 1995), yet overall voting levels remain below 40% (Hampel Report, 1998). The Hampel Report featured an extensive discussion of the voting rights of institutional investors. Voting rights, as we discussed in Chapter 1, constitute an important component of a shareholder's financial asset. However, prior to the Cadbury recommendations, institutional investors had been neglecting to use their voting rights. The importance of the voting right as part of the institutional fund manager's responsibility was acknowledged in the Hampel Report as follows:

> The right to vote is an important part of the asset represented by a share, and in our view an institution *has a responsibility to the client to make considered use of it* …

---

[1] The members of this Committee are: the Association of British Insurers (ABI); the Association of Investment Trust Companies; the British Merchant Banking and Securities Houses Association; the National Association of Pension Funds (NAPF); and the Investment Management Association.

Illustration 5.1

Restoring trust

Reading the sociological literature in recent years provides a rather jaundiced view on the way in which British society is evolving. For example, the literature discusses a breakdown in 'social cohesion'. One of the main characteristics of this move to 'High Modernity' has been a breakdown in the level of trust in society. People seem to have lost the trust that they once had in institutions. This breakdown in trust is having serious implications for investment institutions. Trust in financial institutions has reached a low point. The publication of the Sarbanes–Oxley Act (2002) and the Higgs Report (2003) and Smith Report (2003) in the UK may be interpreted as attempts to salvage public trust: 'We do know what we're doing—honest! We are trying to put things right.' As Myners commented:

> ... the decline of trust is one of the greatest issues to affect not only the financial services industry but also the traditional professions. Lawyers, doctors, teachers, the clergy, they all have sufferered from the loss of trust in them and their work. Where does this come from? There are individual reasons in each profession—but the combination of transparency, scandal and bellicose consumers means that trust is the first casualty of the new social order.
>
> (Myners, 2003, p. 6)

Myners went on to explain that there are two sorts of trust in the financial markets that have collapsed. One is the personal trust held in a fund manager, to perform as well as possible for a client. The second type is the confidence once enjoyed by pension funds and other institutional investors. This confidence was based on the abilities of professional investors and fund managers to handle money safely and prudently. The main cause for decline of trust in this area is linked to the ongoing pensions crisis in the UK. It is becoming increasingly evident that vast numbers of people will not receive the pension they had hoped for when they retire. Maxwell did little to inspire confidence in pensions. A recent survey conducted by MORI, the UK national polling agency, revealed that one in four people did not consider that company pension schemes were worth joining. Further, the survey found that almost two-thirds of workers interviewed did not believe that companies could be trusted to honour pension commitments to their staff (Blitz, 2003). As we discussed in Chapter 1, unethical behaviour can only be checked by regulations and policy documents, it cannot be cured. Trust within the financial sector can only arise from self-regulation and ethical behaviour. So what is the answer? More regulation is one way of recapturing society's trust in financial institutions, but it is not a panacea *per se*. Myners suggests that greater accountability and transparency by financial institutions, concerning their fund management activities, provides the best way forward. As he states:

> We will trust again those institutions that make their internal and commercial processes as pellucid as possible. This means that transparent business—and through it, good governance and accountable relationships—is the key to rebuilding trust.
>
> (Myners, 2003, p. 6)

It is essential that, for investment institutions, pension funds and indeed the traditional capitalist system in the UK to be maintained, trust is restored. This can only be done by the institutions themselves. From this perspective, increased activism and participation by institutional shareholders, accompanied by communication of their activities to their clients and other stakeholders, provides an important means of regaining and recapturing trust. The philosophical aspects of institutional investment have been explored in some depth in McCann et al. (2003).

> We therefore strongly recommend institutional investors of all kinds, wherever practicable, to vote all the shares under their control, according to their own best judgement ...
> (Hampel Report, 1998, pp. 41–42, para. 5.7, emphasis added)

The accompanying Combined Code specified that:

> Institutional shareholders have a responsibility to make considered use of their votes.
> (Combined Code, 1998, para. E1)

In 1995 the NAPF produced a report entitled *The Powerful Vote* encouraging their members to exercise their voting rights. This was likely to have a significant impact on institutional investors' voting policies because most pension funds in the UK are members of the NAPF and most institutional investors are pension funds.

Overall, since the Cadbury Report (1992) there has been a transformation in the institutions' attitudes toward their voting rights, to such an extent that many institutional investors have established their own voting policies. However the impact of such policies on corporate governance in their investee companies is unclear, as:

> Several institutions have recently announced a policy of voting on all resolutions at company meetings. This has yet to be reflected in a significant increase in the proportion of shares voted, which has risen only marginally in the last five years.
> (Hampel Report, 1998, p. 41, para. 5.7, emphasis added)

Given the strength of the recommendations for institutional investor voting, there has been an ongoing debate concerning whether or not voting by institutions should be made mandatory. However, Hampel emphasized the importance of keeping the use of voting rights voluntary and not moving toward regulation:

> But we do not favour a legal obligation to vote. No law could compel proper consideration. The result could well be *unthinking* votes in favour of the board by institutions unwilling or unable to take an active interest in the company.
> (Hampel Report, 1998, p. 42, para. 5.7, emphasis added)

In relation to the question of whether or not voting by institutional investors should be made mandatory, one academic paper concluded that such regulation should be avoided as it would result in institutions 'paying lip service to votes' (Short and Keasey, 1997). Further, Stapledon (1996) argued that compulsory voting, already in force, for institutional investors in the UK would not be a 'worthwhile reform' (p. 287). He arrived at this conclusion by examining the impact of a compulsory voting requirement for the equity investments of non-public pension plans in the USA. Despite the more rules-oriented approach in the USA (discussed in Chapters 1 and 2) this mandatory voting policy resulted in fund managers creating formalized procedures and voting guidelines that were basically 'window dressing'. Stapledon also stipulated that disclosure of the direction of institutional investor voting should not be made mandatory (as had been deliberated by the UK Government in the mid-1990s) as he believed that institutional fund managers are principally accountable to their clients and not to other shareholders in the investee company, or other stakeholder groups. This perspective has been emphasized by the Code of Activism produced by the ISC, who stated that the duty of institutional shareholders is in the end to beneficiaries and not to the wider public (ISC, 2002). However, we feel that this argument does not fit comfortably within a broader, stakeholder approach to corporate governance. Not only do institutional investors have a responsibility to their clients but also, given the immense size of their collectivized assets, to society at large (see, e.g., Solomon et al., 2002, for discussion of this issue). We consider this viewpoint more fully in Chapter 10.

In 1999 the Newbold Committee was established by the NAPF to investigate the means by which votes were exercised by institutional investors in the UK. The Committee had to report its findings to the NAPF's Investment Committee and to make recommendations that would lead to improvements (where necessary) in the system of voting by institutional investors. This was targeted principally at pension funds but contained useful advice and recommendations for all types of institutional investor. Further, the recommendations were aimed at raising the level of institutional voting in the UK. Recently, there has been an intensification in shareholder activism, especially in the area of voting on remuneration policy. Early in 2003 the NAPF decided to form a joint venture with Institutional Shareholder Services, the influential US-based shareholder voting agency. The joint venture has been labelled Research, Recommendations and Electronic Voting. It provides detailed information on more than 22,000 companies in 80 markets around the world, with the aim of providing a basis for more active shareholding, through voting. Furthermore, there have been moves to encourage greater shareholder activism, or 'shareholder democracy', at a pan-European level, with the European Commission establishing a corporate governance action plan. The plan, linked to plans to improve company law within the European Union, aims to bolster shareholder rights, so that shareholders can use their voting rights more effectively. One initiative involves ensuring that shareholders throughout the European Union can participate in AGMs electronically and vote by proxy (Dombey, 2003).

Voting on remuneration policy
In Chapter 4, we discussed the introduction of voting on executive remuneration from the point of view of the board of directors. Here, we revisit this important new development from the perspective of shareholder activism and accountability. Since 2001, investors have been allowed to vote on remuneration policies in a growing number of companies. This does not mean they can now vote on the levels of pay of individual directors but rather on the policy designed for setting that remuneration. This is an area which is likely to witness increasing levels of activism and which demonstrates much greater accountability, both on the part of companies to their

shareholders and on the part of institutional shareholders to their clients. From a wider perspective, interest in directors' pay and proactive involvement by powerful financial institutions, are likely to result in improved accountability of companies and shareholders to other corporate stakeholders, such as employees and society. We provide a flavour of the intense shareholder activism on remuneration that has been taking place in Illustration 5.2.

Research into voting by institutional investors

The corporate governance literature has burgeoned in recent years, and the evolving role of institutional investors in corporate governance has not been ignored by academic researchers. In relation to voting, Stapledon (1995) shed light on the practical difficulties that can inhibit the exercise of voting rights by institutional investors. The paper also provided empirical evidence on the extent of voting by institutional investors prior to 1993. Stapledon emphasized that little evidence was available at that time on the voting practices of institutional investors. This was probably a reflection of the fact that institutional investors (*inter alia*) were not interested in voting their shares. He provided a summary of the empirical evidence on institutional investor voting in the UK as follows:

(i) Midgley (1974) surveyed an extensive sample of UK companies and found that only about 11% of votes were exercised. However, this included all types of investor (not just institutions).

(ii) Minns (1980) stated that in the 1970s institutional investors did not generally exercise their voting rights.

(iii) The ISC performed a study in 1990 and found that on average the total votes received by companies amounted to about 20% (including institutional and other investors). This was similar to, but a little higher than, the findings of Midgley's study from the 1970s. This report was not published and did not appear to break down the voting for institutions.

(iv) A second survey was conducted by the ISC in 1993. This was published (ISC, 1993), and the findings indicated that 24% of votes were exercised in a sample of top UK companies. Again, this indicated a rise in the exercise of voting rights over time.

Stapledon performed a series of interviews in order to gather evidence on institutional investors' voting practices. He found that voting practices among UK fund managers were diverse. Some institutional fund managers had always voted all of their shares. Others had only just started to vote on all issues since Cadbury in the early 1990s. Others were continuing to vote on major, contentious issues. The paper presented solid evidence that before Cadbury, voting was sparse and disorganized,

Illustration 5.2

Fat cat Slim

One of the most interesting and notable trends in UK business in 2002 and 2003 was the intensity of shareholder activism in relation to executive remuneration policies. In October 2001 the Government announced proposals for listed companies to produce an annual directors' remuneration report to be approved by shareholders. Since that time there has been a steady increase in companies allowing shareholders to vote on their remuneration policy. This has ushered in a spate of shareholder activism, with shareholders voting at AGMs in order to effect changes in these policies. The ABI and NAPF are two of the largest shareholder lobby groups in the UK, and much of the recent shareholder activism has been channelled through these two organizations. Another organization that is active in lobbying for shareholder 'voice' is Pirc, the corporate governance consultants.

There are a number of issues that shareholders have expressed views on. One has been to encourage companies to link remuneration more closely to performance. Shareholders and indeed the general public have been dismayed at companies who have rewarded failure. There have been numerous cases of executives receiving excessive remuneration packages in poorly performing companies (*Financial Times*, 4 June 2003). Another issue that has sparked shareholder action has been an encroachment of US-style remuneration packages crossing the Atlantic, as they are considered excessive. There are fears of contamination, as where one company chooses to go, the rest are likely to follow.

Let's take a snapshot of activism in the two months, May and June 2003. In May 2003 Kingfisher was targeted by the ABI and NAPF over its remuneration policy, as they condemned some aspects of the company's directors' remuneration packages as excessive and encouraged the company's shareholders to vote against them. The action was successful, as Kingfisher reacted by introducing tougher share option performance targets for the chief executive. They also lowered some of their directors' compensation for potential loss of office (Wendlandt, 2003). In the same month, HSBC staved off a shareholder rebellion concerning a controversial $37.5 million three-year remuneration package for Mr Aldinger, the bank's new director of operations in the USA. There was a shareholder outcry over his remuneration, with about 15% of shareholders abstaining or opposing his re-election to the board of directors. His remuneration package included, for example, a lifetime of free dental care and use of a company jet for personal holidays (Croft, 24 July 2003). One of the most tantalizing tales involved GlaxoSmithKline. According to Michelle Edkins, director of institutional relations at Hermes, the company had failed to appreciate that it had pushed its shareholders to the boundaries of their tolerance (Skapinker, 2003). Whereas institutional shareholders in the UK tend to have a preference for confidential discussions with investee company management, in this case they used their last resort, public shaming of the company. Shareholder dissatisfaction manifested itself in 63% of the company's shareholders voting against the company's remuneration policy, or abstaining, at the AGM.

In June 2003 Telewest bent over backward to avoid a disaster in its investor relations arising from their dissatisfaction with the company's remuneration policy. Specifically, shareholders criticized the board for deciding to pay the outgoing chief executive, Adam Singer, £1.4 million in severance (Kirchgaessner, 2003). Also in June 40% of Tesco's shareholders voted against the company's remuneration policy, or abstained. This was the third largest protest by shareholders at a large company AGM since the beginning of the year (Voyle and Tassell, 2003). Northern Foods was under fire in June for granting pay rises of more than 16% to two executive directors, even though the company's underlying profits had fallen significantly and its share price had seen a substantial drop in January. However, the company's remuneration committee retaliated to criticisms by stating that they intended to make an increasing proportion of their remuneration and incentive packages performance-related. Also in June almost a third of shareholders in Whitbread either abstained or voted against the company's remuneration report, due to their dissatisfaction with the continuation of two-year contracts for the company's executive directors. The NAPF was instrumental in firing up the shareholders before the company's AGM. Whitbread reacted by stating an intention to offer only one-year contracts to new executive directors (Boxell, 18 June 2003). Yet another case in the same month—46% of the shareholders of WPP Group opposed the company's remuneration report, or abstained their vote. The main problem was that Sir Martin Sorrell, the chief executive, had a three-year contract, whereas most companies are now turning to one-year contracts, as a result of shareholder concern. Further, Mr Sorrell was paid almost £1.6 million in 2002. Pirc estimated that his total remuneration package amounted to £65 million, if valued at the company's market share price (Harris, 2003).

It is clear that such public displays of shareholder dissatisfaction with executive remuneration policies and packages are having a deep impact on public attitudes, as a recent MORI poll found that almost 80% of those surveyed agreed that directors of large companies were overpaid. By July 2003 it was clear that such activism by the institutional shareholder community was having a substantial impact. Leading companies have been forced to increase the proportion of their executives' pay linked to performance, according to a survey. The survey indicated that two-thirds of chairmen in the FTSE 350 companies expected to increase the proportion of performance-related pay. Further, half of the chairmen surveyed stated that shareholder activism had forced them to review their remuneration policies (Tassell, 9 July 2003).

whereas by 1995 (three years after Cadbury) institutions were beginning to improve and formalize their voting policies.

An interesting point raised in Stapledon's (1995) paper was whether or not pension fund trustees had a duty to vote. He argued that under the contemporaneous legal framework, trustees and fund managers did not have any obligation to vote. However, whether they should be obliged through regulation, or a moral responsibility, to employ their voting rights was, he considered, an altogether different issue. Interestingly, a change to pension fund law has since stipulated that pension fund trustees have to (as from July 2000) disclose the extent to which (if at all) their fund managers exercise their voting rights in investee companies. Although this only forces trustees to disclose whether or not they instruct their fund managers to vote and does not make them vote, such disclosure *per se* can have an effect on voting practices.

Mallin (1996) compared the voting practices of UK institutional investors with those of US institutions. She carried out an extensive number of personal interviews with institutional fund managers, with the aim of canvassing their attitudes toward voting and discussing whether or not they had voting policies. Three categories of institutional voting policy emerged from the interview data:

(i) fund managers voted on all issues (routine and non-routine);

(ii) fund managers voted only on non-routine issues;

(iii) fund managers did not vote at all.

It appeared from the interviews that the first category was the most popular. However, fund managers who voted on all issues were not necessarily acting responsibly. It appeared that there were two types of fund manager who voted on all issues: 'box tickers' and those who actually considered their votes. The first group voted with the incumbent management on all issues without considering the issues carefully and perhaps voting against the management. In this case, the use of voting rights could hardly be considered effective from a corporate governance perspective. They are called box tickers because they are simply voting for the sake of voting and not reflecting on the impact of their votes. This is the sort of approach the Hampel Report warned could result from mandatory voting. Perhaps it is a negative result of recommendations of the Cadbury Committee. The second group did consider their votes carefully and decided in each case whether or not to vote with the incumbent management. This is a more responsible approach from a corporate governance perspective and is likely to result in far more effective monitoring of company management.

A later paper (Mallin, 2001) compared the voting practices of institutional investors across four countries. This study focused on the issue of whether or not voting was a fiduciary duty for institutional investors. Whereas Stapledon (1995) suggested that institutions were not bound to vote as part of their legal and fiduciary responsibilities, Mallin considered that they were. Indeed, she provided evidence that in the USA the right to vote was considered to be a fiduciary duty of institutional investors. The paper discussed the focus on encouraging institutional investors to exercise their voting rights since the early 1990s, as we have shown in the above discussion. On this issue the Newbold Committee had stated that voting was a fiduciary duty of institutional investors. Indeed, this Committee concluded that regular voting should be one of the first principles of proper conduct by the trustees of pension funds. Mallin concluded that, although the concept of voting as a fiduciary duty had long been accepted in the US, it had only been introduced in the UK relatively recently.

In our own research, we addressed voting via a questionnaire survey to UK unit trusts (Solomon and Solomon, 1999). We tested the hypothesis that UK unit trust managers were activist, were developing voting policies *vis-à-vis* their investee companies and were disclosing them to their clients and investee company directors. The questionnaire results showed that 72% of the respondents' institutions had a written voting policy for their investee companies. In relation to whether the unit trust managers had ever attempted to influence the decision-making process within their investee companies through private meetings, 84% responded that they had. A similarly strong indication of shareholder activism was whether the institutional investors had ever formed coalitions with other institutional investors, if an investee

Table [5.1]   Evidence on institutional investors and shareholder activism

Rank		Average response
1	Institutional investors should disclose their voting policy to their clients	Strong agreement
2	Companies should disclose, in a published form, the level of voting on each resolution at the last AGM	Strong agreement
3	Institutional investors should disclose their level of voting in their investee companies to their clients	Agreement
4	Institutional investors should be more actively involved in the management structure of their investee companies	Slight disagreement

Reproduced by permission of Blackwell Publishers Journals

company was in crisis: a clear indication of relationship investing. Again, 84% indicated that they had. Interestingly, one respondent, in a telephone discussion, expressed surprise at this question, saying that it tended to act well in advance of an imminent crisis. In Table 5.1 we can see how the respondents ranked a series of statements relating to shareholder activism.[2]

The institutional investors demonstrated strongest agreement with suggestions that they should disclose their voting policy to their clients, probably because this was the main group to whom they are accountable (as suggested by Stapledon, 1996). However, the same level of accountability did not extend to disclosure of their level of voting, as this received weaker agreement (statement 3 as ranked in Table 5.1). These findings also supported Hampel's concerns that institutional investors should not become involved in the day-to-day running of businesses in which they invest, as statement 4 was met by general disagreement.

Institutional investors and engagement

The Cadbury Report and the Myners Report (1995) stressed the importance of institutional investors holding regular meetings with executives of investee companies. The Hampel Report (1998) developed the recommendations made by the Cadbury Committee in this area. Hampel stated that earlier recommendations had been 'broadly welcomed' by companies and investors, although the Report did not provide any solid evidence of this. The accompanying Combined Code stipulated

---

[2]   They were asked to indicate the extent of their agreement/disagreement with four statements relating to shareholder activism, by selecting a score from 1 (strongly disagree) to 7 (strongly agree), with 4 indicating neutral.

that:

> Institutional shareholders *should be ready, where practicable, to enter into a dialogue* with companies based on the mutual understanding of objectives.
>
> (Combined Code, 1998, p. 24, para. E2, emphasis added)

The most recent corporate governance policy document, the Higgs Report, re-emphasized the important role that institutional investors can play in corporate governance through investor relations by commenting that:

> I endorse the Government's approach to more active engagement by shareholders.
>
> (Higgs Report, 2003, p. 70)

Further, the Higgs Report recommended a revision to paragraph E2 from the Combined Code (cited above) to the following, stronger version:

> Institutional investors *should enter into a dialogue* with companies based on the mutual understanding of objectives.
>
> (Higgs Report, 2003, Annex A, Suggested Revised Code, emphasis added)

The importance of active engagement between institutional investors and their investee companies was also stressed by the institutional shareholders' Code of Activism (ISC, 2002). This Code of practice stipulated that institutions had a responsibility to intervene in investee companies 'when necessary' in order to discharge their accountability to their own clients. Indeed, the Code highlighted several instances when institutional shareholders might wish to intervene in their investee companies, namely, when they had concerns about: the company's strategy; the company's operational performance; the company's acquisition/disposal strategy; non-executive directors failing to hold executive management properly to account; internal controls failing; inadequate succession planning; an unjustifiable failure to comply with the Combined Code; inappropriate remuneration levels (and related packages); and the company's approach to corporate social responsibility (ISC, 2002, p. 3). The Higgs Report also added another dimension to the debate over the corporate governance role and responsibilities of institutional investors. It drew attention to the lack of involvement that non-executive directors had in relationships between their companies and institutional investors as:

> ... only rarely do non-executive directors hear at first hand the views of major shareholders. The majority of non-executive directors ... never discuss company business with their investors.
>
> (Higgs Report, 2003, p. 67)

This was an issue which had not been raised by previous corporate governance recommendations and reports and which represented an area for significant improvement in the corporate governance monitoring mechanism.

As we saw in the discussion in Chapter 4, a chief recommendation of Higgs was for non-executive directors to attend some of the regular meetings that executive directors and the chairman hold with key shareholders, in their process of engagement and dialogue. However, the idea of improving links between institutional investors and investee companies' non-executive directors was not entirely new. Stapledon (1996) had pointed out that non-executive directors could not be truly independent unless they were connected to a powerful group outside the company which could counterbalance company management, such as institutional investors. Indeed, Stapledon considered a more far-reaching recommendation than that later proposed in the Higgs Report, as he suggested that UK institutional investors should appoint non-executive directors on boards and that these non-executives would monitor management more effectively.[3] He concluded that the Cadbury Report had not gone far enough in bringing two powerful monitoring mechanisms together, institutional investors and non-executive directors. However, Stapledon also explained that there were significant economic disincentives making such radical proposals unrealistic for Cadbury. One disincentive included the notorious free-rider effect, whereby institutional investors do not want to monitor management effectively for the benefit of their competitors. Perhaps the reason that Higgs was able to make more progress in this area was that the free-rider problem had diminished, with the growth of engagement and dialogue.

Almost all major institutional investors are now engaging actively with investee companies. They are now more interested in competing with each other by winning clients, as a result of having the best and most effective engagement strategies, rather than worrying about other institutions benefiting from their efforts. Engagement and dialogue have become an area for competitive advantage for institutions, as well as a means of monitoring management and improving corporate (and therefore portfolio) performance. Indeed, the Code of Activism (ISC, 2002) stressed that monitoring by institutional investors may require the sharing of information with other shareholders in order to agree a common course of action. The revised Combined Code, published in July 2003, has also led the way for greater shareholder activism, with a clearly defined role for institutional investors in promoting corporate governance reform. See Illustration 5.3 for a discussion of the impact of the revised Code.

There are also legal constraints on the engagement process. The Hampel Report raised potential problems with increased dialogue, such as risks of price-sensitive information being given to institutional investors. From a legal perspective, there are restrictions on the manner in which companies should disclose private information, especially risk-related information, to their core shareholders, as the process could be construed as insider dealing (Holland and Stoner, 1996; Solomon et al., 2000b). There have been various attempts to agree a legal definition of insider dealing, where the exploitation of price-sensitive information is the essential component

---

[3]   Similar recommendations for institutional investors in the USA were also made by Gilson and Kraakman (1991).

Illustration 5.3

The revised Code: a clear mandate for institutional investor activism

Despite the initial unfavourable reactions to Higgs' recommendations in January 2003 (see Illustration 4.2), by July 2003 both the institutional investment community and the corporate community had softened and decided on the whole to endorse a revised version of the Combined Code. The redrafted Code embraced the Higgs Report, changing the original language to appease business but not the spirit of his recommendations (see Chapter 3). The new Code encompassed all 50 of Higgs' recommendations, comprising 21 supporting principles, as opposed to 14 in the original Combined Code. Following the approval of the revised code by the Financial Reporting Council, Higgs commented that, 'The new code will encourage professionalism and objectivity in the boardroom. Shareholders will benefit from greater transparency and understanding of how boards work. The code will raise boardroom standards, drive company performance and help restore confidence in the listed company sector' (Tassell, 24 July 2003).

The revised Code received the endorsement of the UK business community, as Digby Jones, Director-General of the Confederation of British Industry (CBI), said the revised Code represented a 'Victory for common sense' that should strengthen boards and bolster the reputation of business, concluding that, 'The Financial Reporting Council has delivered a code that will encourage better corporate governance but not have damaging unintended consequences' (Tassell, 24 July 2003).

The institutional investment community, represented by its powerful lobby groups (the NAPF and the ABI) also supported the revised Code. Despite initial concerns among the institutional shareholders that Higgs' recommendations were too prescriptive, the final outcome was welcomed. The revised Code, expressed in softer language than the original report, was felt to have retained the essence, while avoiding the 'straitjacket of excessive prescription', according to Mary Francis the Director-General of the ABI. The role of institutional investors in endorsing the revised Code and pushing forward corporate governance reform is unquestionable. The new Code places the onus on shareholders to push forward corporate governance reform. More active shareholders should, with the support of the revised Code, be able to make deep-seated changes to their investee companies and to boardroom behaviour. Christine Farnish, chief executive of the NAPF, commented that, 'UK investors are increasingly ready to make their voices heard in Britain's boardrooms. We have already seen a number of high profile shareholder moves in some companies in order to encourage them to follow best practice. The new code establishes best practice firmly in the mainstream' (Fitzpatrick, 2003).

However, all has not been entirely rosy. Following the approval of the revised Code, there were widespread concerns that it might result in a massive increase in companies' disclosure burden (Tassell, 25 July 2003). This would be a result of the increased requirements for companies to disclose their level of compliance with the revised Code and explain any case of non-compliance.

(e.g., LSE, 1994). Further, there have been several attempts during the last decade to construct a statutory framework that could apply to the centuries-old phenomenon of insider dealing. The several specific statutory provisions that have emerged in this field seem to share the following generalized characteristics, when determining the parameters of legally (as opposed to ethically) unacceptable insider dealing. These characteristics can be encapsulated as follows:

- inside information relates to particular securities or to a particular issuer of securities, and not to securities generally or to issuers of securities generally;

- inside information is specific or precise;

- inside information has not been made public, which therefore covers information provided to institutional investors in one-to-one meetings with the managers of investee companies; and

- if inside information were made public, it would be likely to have a significant effect on the price of any securities.

As we can see, this draws a fine line for companies that enter into detailed dialogue with their core shareholders. Information can be passed to the shareholder that is not in the public domain, but the offence occurs if the information is 'price-sensitive' (i.e., if the information would affect share prices as soon as it became public). An early statutory attempt to deal with insider dealing was the Financial Services Act 1986, which stipulated that the user of the information does not need to make a profit to be considered for an offence. Therefore, the problem is how do companies know whether information is price-sensitive? It is very difficult for individuals to make the distinction between information that is price-sensitive and information that is not. The complexity of the area and the difficulty of defining price-sensitive information is perhaps best evident in the extremely small number of successful prosecutions that have taken place during the past decade. Having looked at the encouragements for increased engagement and dialogue, as well as constraints on the process, we turn to considering the academic research into the engagement process.

Research into engagement with institutional investors

Charkham and Simpson (1999) confirmed the emerging importance of the role of institutional investors in corporate governance. An extensive series of research interviews with companies and investment institutions has shown that the public disclosure of financial reporting information has been viewed as inadequate by institutional investors, who have therefore turned to private disclosure channels in many areas of financial reporting (Holland, 1998). This has led to the development of sophisticated systems of engagement between institutional investors and their investee companies, which cover many areas of financial reporting and corporate strategy. We addressed engagement and dialogue via a questionnaire survey to UK unit trusts (Solomon and Solomon, 1999). We tested the hypothesis that UK unit trust managers were encouraging relationship investing, supporting moves to encourage long-termism rather than short-termism in the UK system of corporate

Table [5.2]   Evidence on institutional investors and relationship investing

Rank		Average response
1	I believe that corporate activities that promote long-term relationship investing should be encouraged	Strong agreement
2	I believe that institutional investors should be more involved with the long-term strategic management of their investee companies	Agreement
3	I believe that the directors of our investee companies consider that the representatives from institutional investors change frequently and that they therefore have to educate them in the running of the business at each meeting	Agreement
4	I believe that the legal rights and responsibilities of institutional investors are sufficient to encourage and facilitate long-term relationship investment	Agreement
5	I believe that the directors of our investee companies resent the increasing time spent in meetings with institutional investors, as it detracts from their duties	Agreement
6	I believe that reforms in corporate governance lead to relationship investing	Agreement
7	I believe that stronger legal disclosure obligations placed on companies would encourage longer term investment commitment	Stong disagreement

governance. Table 5.2 presents responses to a question in which unit trust managers were asked to rank their attitudes toward statements on relationship investing.[4]

The results in Table 5.2 indicate clearly that institutional investors support longer and stronger communication and decision links with their investee companies. We can see that the respondents agreed unequivocally that corporate activities that promoted long-term relationships should be encouraged. This is a clear endorsement of the recent UK policy promoting institutional shareholder activism. As we saw from the results presented in Table 3.2, the institutional investors displayed a preference for a continued voluntary, rather than a regulated, corporate governance environment in the UK. This attitude is again reflected in the findings in Table 5.2.

From our interview research into institutional investors and corporate governance reform, we found that fund managers were engaging with their investee companies on a regular basis and were holding dialogue on a diverse range of corporate governance issues. Interviewees indicated that this level of engagement has been operating for several years and was continuing to grow. Further, we found that

---

[4] Investment institutions were asked to select a score from 1 (strongly disagree) to 7 (strongly agree).

dialogue was developing into an interactive, two-way process. Not only were institutional fund managers asking companies questions about their strategy and performance but also companies were initiating discussion and asking for advice from corporate governance specialists in investment houses (Solomon and Solomon, 2003a). Our research interviews also re-emphasized concerns raised in the Hampel Report that institutional investors were not business managers and should not assume the role of managing companies. On this issue, one of our interviewees, a corporate governance executive in a large investment institution, commented that:

> Investors don't want to run companies, they don't want to tell managers how to run companies, but they do like discovering what their clients are thinking.

Although quite a lot of literature has appeared on voting practices, less research has been conducted into the development of dialogue between institutional investors and their investee companies. This is partly due to the confidential nature of such information and partly due to the difficulties in obtaining data, but interviewing is really the only means of data collection for research in this area, as questionnaires cannot gain rich enough data, but interviewing is expensive and time-consuming. However, it is increasingly clear that institutional investors prefer the engagement route to the voting route as a means of influencing investee company management. Institutional investors prefer to discuss sensitive issues with companies behind closed doors, rather than embarrass companies by raising issues in public. Recent shareholder activism at AGMs on remuneration policy represents an exception rather than a rule and demonstrates the depth of dissatisfaction on this issue. Generally, fund managers consider that turning to voting rather than engagement is a last resort. As one of the institutional fund managers we interviewed commented, voting is equivalent to 'major heart surgery' in his view, as it is used only when other channels of engagement and dialogue have failed.

Factors affecting shareholder activism

A number of organizational factors seem to influence the extent to which institutional investors are active shareholders. For example, as with most issues in accounting and finance, size matters. Larger investment institutions have more resources available to allow them to focus on corporate governance issues, such as voting. Our interviews with investment institutions have shown that fund managers in larger institutions are more proactive in corporate governance affairs than those in smaller institutions.

Some institutional fund managers operate index-tracking funds whereas others can select the investee companies more freely in their portfolios. An index-tracking fund is one that invests in companies in a fixed proportion relative to their position and size on the stock exchange. They cannot vary their investment allocation unless the index that they are tracking is changed. For example, some funds will track the FTSE 100 and therefore will have to hold the companies included in that index in their portfolios. The aim is to achieve a return on investment at least equivalent to the index itself. Index-tracking investors are called passive investors as they do not choose the companies in the portfolio. Active institutional investors manage non-index-tracking funds. Intuitively, one may anticipate that passive investors would be less interested in corporate governance and would be less interested in the activities of their investee companies than active investors. However, the reverse seems to be the case. Indeed, passive investors are 'stuck with' their investee companies and cannot divest if they are dissatisfied with management. Therefore, it is in their interests to employ their voting rights and active dialogue to influence company management. In the literature, shareholder activism is considered to be particularly important for passive, index-tracking fund managers as they cannot divest their shares and therefore need to improve companies through direct activism (Monks, 2001). However, even funds that are not passive but have very large holdings cannot divest because of the potential impact of such action on the stock market.

It is also possible, theoretically, that different types of investment institution display different attitudes toward corporate governance. In other words, it is likely that institutional investors are not a homogeneous group with respect to corporate governance. Faccio and Lasfer (2000), for example, argued that pension funds had more incentive to monitor companies in which they held large stakes than other types of institutional investor, suggesting that they might be more activist. However, this was not borne out by their research findings, which instead indicated that pension fund activism was having little or no impact on companies.

Shareholder activism and financial performance

An essential issue in the whole debate about shareholder activism and the role of institutional investors in corporate governance is whether or not such intervention results in higher financial performance in investee companies. There are many studies that have attempted to address this issue, but the evidence is inconclusive, as we see from the following discussion. Also, most of the studies are on US data and have not focused on the UK. This issue needs to be addressed in order to vindicate the increasing involvement of institutional investors in corporate governance. It is clearly an implicit assumption of the Hampel Committee and other proponents of shareholder activism that institutional investors' intervention in investee companies produces higher financial returns. There is certainly a perception among the institutional investment community that activism brings financial rewards, as more efficient monitoring of company management aligns shareholder and manager interests and therefore helps to maximize shareholder wealth.

Academic research has produced mixed evidence on the impact of shareholder activism on corporate performance and company value. Some academic studies have found that institutional investors have a significant impact on top management turnover, which is interpreted as positive for corporate governance, as this tends to result in improved financial performance. Franks and Mayer (1994) showed this link for Germany, while similar evidence was presented for Japan by Kaplan and Minton (1994) and Kang and Shivdasani (1995). Further, some research has shown that block purchases of shares by institutional investors tended to result in an increase in company value, top management turnover, financial performance and asset sales (e.g., Mikkelson and Ruback, 1985; Shome and Singh, 1995; Bethel et al., 1998). Also, Strickland et al. (1996) showed that shareholder monitoring led to increases in company value. Nesbitt (1994) and Smith (1996a) found that pension fund activism had a significant positive impact on the financial performance of companies targeted by the funds.

There is also evidence to the contrary, as several studies have found only weak evidence of a relationship between holdings by institutional investors and corporate financial performance (Agrawal and Knoeber, 1985). Further, one study found that shareholder activism in the form of shareholder proposals did not seem to lead to an increase in company value and seemed to have no influence on corporate policy (Karpoff et al., 1996). Indeed, Faccio and Lasfer (2000) poured cold water on the perceived benefits of UK pension fund activism. They found no evidence that blockholding of listed company shares by occupational pension funds in the UK was positively related to profitability and company value. The paper employed a correlation matrix to discover whether there was a positive relationship between firm value and ownership structure. They found, in most cases, a weak, negative relationship and concluded that:

> We report that pension funds do not add value to the companies in which they hold large stakes. Our results cast doubt on the monitoring role of pension funds which are considered theoretically, on the one hand, to be the main promoters of corporate governance in the UK and, on the other hand, to be short-termist and dictate their rules to companies.
>
> (Faccio and Lasfer, 2000, p. 105)

The possible reasons they proffered for their results were, first, that occupational pension funds may not have a material effect on investee companies, because the blocks of shares that they held tended to represent relatively small fractions of the total values of the funds' assets. Second, they suggested that pension funds did not monitor because monitoring was costly, as this activity was not likely to result in a modification in the company's pay-off structure and did not therefore lead to net gains. Third, the authors suggested that perhaps pension funds avoided intervention because they did not wish to draw public attention to the investee company's problems. However, their overall conclusion was that pension funds were essentially passive and that this was the reason their holdings did not influence company value. Yet, their results used data from the mid-1990s. As we have seen from the discussion earlier in this chapter (p. 96), institutional changes, such as the change to trustee law, as well as successive corporate governance policy documents have exhorted pension fund activism. It is therefore likely that they have become less passive. Clearly, more research is required to establish the extent to which the situation has changed and the extent to which pension funds have become more active, influencing the performance and value of their investee companies. This finding does cause us to question the genuine contribution that pension funds can make as a corporate governance mechanism for monitoring company management. Indeed, the agency problems prevalent within pension funds, resulting from their complex web of ownership, as we saw earlier, have been considered to hinder pension funds' ability to monitor investee companies effectively.

It does need to be borne in mind that, despite the positive monitoring potential of institutional investors, their relative power in the stock market also bears some costs. One of the important principles of 'good' corporate governance, according to the Organization for Economic Co-operation and Development (OECD, 1999) Principles, is for all shareholders to be treated equally. As institutional investors in the UK, and elsewhere, gain larger stakes in companies and become more influential over company management through engagement and dialogue, their treatment by company management is likely to be preferential. This problem was debated in Shleifer and Vishny (1997), who emphasized that large investors, such as financial institutions, represented their own interests rather than the interests of the whole group of shareholders. This type of problem has been exemplified by cases such as British Gas, where there was a clear division between the views of the institutional shareholders and the individual shareholders (see Illustration 3.2). In some countries, by using their control rights, large shareholders can redistribute wealth from other shareholders, resulting in a significant cost to shareholders as a whole. Indeed, Shleifer and Vishny (1997) discussed a number of potential costs associated with the presence of large investors, such as institutions, namely: expropriation of other investors, managers and employees; inefficient expropriation through pursuit of personal (non-profit-maximizing) objectives; and incentive effects of expropriation on other stakeholders. However, these cases are more applicable to countries where large shareholders are related to founding families than to such countries as the UK where large shareholders tend to be financial institutions that follow ethical codes of practice and undergo substantial financial market regulation. We revisit these issues in Part II.

Chapter summary

In this chapter we have examined an important corporate governance mechanism, the role of institutional investors. More active shareholding can lead to better monitoring of company management and therefore to a lessening of the agency problem. Specifically, we have discussed the recommendations made by policy documents and codes of best practice in the UK on the issues of voting and engagement by institutional investors. We have also examined some of the empirical research, which

Illustration 5.4

Paws for thought: the responsibilities of share ownership

A new dog owner thinks about the merits of dog ownership. He looks forward to the love and affection he will receive from his 'best friend'. He thinks about walking in the hills with his new dog and throwing sticks for the dog to chase. If he buys a special breed of dog, he dreams of the prizes he is going to win parading his pedigree at shows. If he buys a racing dog, he meditates on the money he may win racing his fine greyhound. In a similar way, when an investor buys a share he becomes an owner of the investee company. Naturally, in purchasing a share the shareholder anticipates healthy future dividends and a promising capital gain. However, share ownership, like dog ownership, bears responsibilities. First and foremost a young puppy needs nourishment, vitamins, water. A responsible dog owner provides these. A shareholder has nourished the company with essential finance through his initial investment—but that is not the end of the story.

A responsible dog owner is not just concerned about his dog snapping at other members of the family but also worries that his cuddly pooch may snap at unrelated visitors, the unsuspecting postman of many a legend, or even his own employees, such as the window cleaner or nanny. In a similar way, a shareholder should not worry solely about the company's attitudes toward himself and his fellow shareholders but should also consider the company's relationship with other stakeholders connected with the company: the company's employees, suppliers, customers and debtors.

When a responsible dog owner leaves the house he is concerned that his beloved dog doesn't foul the public footpath. The mess would be dangerous to children, offensive to other walkers and generally unsightly. He ensures that the pile is cleared away. A responsible shareholder should have similar concerns. The company he owns should be discouraged from polluting the environment, from damaging the health of people in the local community, from creating unpleasant and unsightly surroundings for its neighbours. A responsible shareholder wants his company to behave in a socially responsible manner. He likes his investee company to have a glowing reputation, something to be proud of.

When the responsible dog owner exercises his dog in the park he is aware that he may slip his lead and sink his teeth into one of the toddlers playing on the swings. Dire consequences could arise from lack of responsibility here! The responsible dog owner is likely to keep Bonzo on a tight leash, to watch him carefully for signs of irritability, to muzzle him. He needs to calm and control the dog with careful words and even a whistle at times. The risks are great and efforts to avoid disaster are essential. Responsible shareholders are in a similar position. They need to ensure that systems are in place to monitor their companies' behaviour. They need to check the company's system of internal control and risk management. If there is cause for concern, the shareholder has a responsibility to voice his views rather than ignore worries or simply sell his shares. Responsible dog owners do not sell their dogs as soon as a problem arises. Even retiring greyhounds are not sold carelessly but placed with loving households that will provide the former star with a happy retirement.

However, there is also a breed of dog owner who does not treat his dog well, does not feed his dog, does not care about the dog's well-being and longevity. Some dogs are abandoned by the wayside, starved and neglected by their owners. These dogs often die early or are taken into care by other, more responsible dog owners. Often, if caught, the irresponsible dog owner is charged and fined. Again, an analogy can be drawn. The irresponsible shareholder neglects his company. Risks mount. Corporate social irresponsibility can ensue, unchecked by the apathetic shareholder. Companies collapse and shareholders lose their money. They do not win by neglecting their responsibility. It is hard work being a good dog owner. It is hard work being a responsible shareholder. Think before you buy!

suggests, generally, that there has been an increase in institutional shareholder activism and that this has had a positive effect on UK corporate governance and company value. Throughout the chapter we have introduced the idea that institutional investors have a responsibility as majority owners of companies to influence company management and take an active interest in their investment, rather than remain passive observers. In order to encourage debate on this issue particularly, we have included a light-hearted cameo of the responsibilities of share ownership in Illustration 5.4.

Questions for reflection and discussion

1 Assess the extent to which you consider UK institutional investors are active shareholders. In your discussion comment on whether or not they are developing longer and stronger communication and decision links with their investee companies.

2 Read Illustration 5.1. Do you believe that trust in financial institutions can be rebuilt through legislation? Do you have any suggestions as to the ways in which institutional investors might inspire greater confidence in society, following recent scandals?

3 Read Illustration 5.2. To what extent do you think that shareholder activism on remuneration policies is a positive step? Do you think the trend will continue? Have a look in the newspapers for the most recent examples of such activity. Do you consider that shareholder activism has a positive impact on corporate policy?

4 Read Illustration 5.4, 'Paws for thought'. Do you think this is a useful metaphor for discussing the responsibilities of shareholders? Or do you disagree vehemently with its implications?

Chapter 6

The role of transparency in corporate governance

Aim and objectives

This chapter discusses the ways in which corporate transparency contributes to corporate governance and the mechanisms by which companies may become more transparent. The specific objectives of this chapter are to:

- emphasize the essential role played by corporate disclosure and financial accounting information in corporate governance;

- define internal control, risk and risk management, and emphasize their role in effective corporate governance;

- appreciate the importance of the audit function in relation to corporate governance.

Introduction

Transparency is an essential element of a well-functioning system of corporate governance. Corporate disclosure to stakeholders is the principal means by which companies can become transparent. In this chapter we examine the role of disclosure in corporate governance. We then consider the importance of a company's system of internal control and the audit function in relation to corporate governance. Specifically, we discuss the initiatives recommended in UK corporate governance policy documents and codes of best practice that relate to these areas. The Enron debacle drew acute attention to the need for well-functioning audit committees and internal control systems, as we saw from the case study in Chapter 2. Weaknesses in these areas can easily lead to corporate failure, as they provide central monitoring mechanisms in corporate governance. Therefore, we examine the contribution that the audit function makes to corporate governance.

Disclosure and corporate governance

Disclosure is critical to the functioning of an efficient capital market. The term 'disclosure' refers to a whole array of different forms of information produced by companies, such as the annual report which includes the director's statement, the Operating and Financial Review (OFR),[1] the profit and loss account, balance sheet, cash flow statement and other mandatory items. It also includes all forms of voluntary corporate communications, such as management forecasts, analysts' presentations, the AGM, press releases, information placed on corporate websites and other corporate reports, such as stand-alone environmental or social reports (Healy and Palepu, 2001). Voluntary disclosure is defined as any disclosure above the mandated minimum (Core, 2001). Improvements in disclosure result in improvements in transparency, which is one of the most important aims of corporate governance reform worldwide (see, e.g., OECD, 1999, as discussed in Chapter 7). Increasing corporate transparency is a major initiative of corporate governance reform in the UK and elsewhere, as emphasized in the Cadbury Report:

> The *lifeblood of markets is information* and barriers to the flow of relevant information represent imperfections in the market ... The more the activities of companies are *transparent*, the more accurately will their securities be valued.
>
> (Cadbury Report, 1992, p. 33, emphasis added)

Increased and improved disclosure is likely to reduce agency costs as better information flows from the company to the shareholder, which in turn reduces information asymmetry. Indeed:

> Disclosure has long been recognised as the dominant philosophy of most modern systems. It is a *sine qua non* [essential aspect] of corporate accountability.
>
> (Farrar and Hannigan, 1998, p. 11)

From an agency theory perspective (see Chapter 1) the existence of information asymmetry results in managers being far more knowledgeable about the company's activities and financial situation than current or potential investors. This applies equally to stakeholder theory, as inadequate information places all stakeholders, not just shareholders, at a disadvantage. Without a structured system of disclosure, and in particular financial reporting, it would be very difficult for shareholders to obtain appropriate and reliable information on their investee companies.[2] Such

---

[1] The equivalent of the OFR in the US is the Management Discussion and Analysis (MDA) section of the annual report.

[2] The ways in which financial reporting address the problems of information asymmetry are analysed in Beaver (1989).

information asymmetry leads to moral hazard and adverse selection problems.[3] By ensuring frequent and relevant corporate disclosure, shareholders are in a better position to monitor company management. The accounting function is an essential aspect of a well-functioning corporate governance system. However, financial reporting *per se* is not the subject of this textbook.

Accounting has long been acknowledged as a necessary means of monitoring the shareholder–manager relationship according to the stewardship concept. From a historical viewpoint a widely held hypothesis stipulates that both accounting and auditing developed as a monitoring mechanism and that accounts have always been demanded by investors for decision-making purposes. Watts and Zimmerman (1986), in particular, highlighted the importance of financial reporting as a means of reducing information asymmetry. They discussed the agency theory approach of Jensen and Meckling (1976), *inter alia*, and showed that accounting plays a contracting role, as accounting is used in the nexus of contracts aimed at monitoring managers. Inefficiencies in the market for information have resulted in the need for mandatory disclosure by companies. One reason in the literature for disclosure regulation is that accounting information may be regarded as a public good, because existing shareholders implicitly pay for its production but have no means of exacting a share of this payment from new shareholders (Leftwich, 1980; Watts and Zimmerman, 1986; Beaver, 1989). This implies that potential investors and stakeholders are free riders on information, paid for by existing shareholders. This in turn leads to underproduction of information, which represents a form of market failure (Healy and Palepu, 2001).

Bushman and Smith (2001) described the role of financial accounting information in corporate governance, arguing that the use of externally reported financial accounting data in control mechanisms promotes the efficient governance of companies. However, we need to stress that this relates to the quality of the information disclosed, as in accounting terms it needs to be relevant and reliable.

For the sake of clarity, we need to draw a clear distinction between corporate disclosure (defined earlier) and financial accounting information. Financial accounting information represents one aspect of corporate disclosure, which has been defined as:

> ... the product of corporate accounting and external reporting systems that measure and publicly disclose audited, quantitative data concerning the financial position and performance of publicly held firms.
>
> (Bushman and Smith, 2001, p. 238)

---

[3] Adverse selection has been defined as an aspect of information asymmetry whereby those offering securities for sale practise self-selection, implying that securities of different 'quality' sell for the same price. Moral hazard, another product of information asymmetry, implies that the agent will attempt to benefit from the principal's inferior information set (see Beaver, 1989).

They couched their analysis in the finance paradigm of agency theory (see Chapter 1). They perceived financial accounting information as a control mechanism that aids outside investors in their quest to discipline investee company management, encouraging them to act in the interests of their shareholders. However, often in the real world, financial accounting information is manipulated by management, as we saw on p. 36 from Enron's use of off-balance-sheet vehicles. In such cases, financial accounting information can increase rather than reduce agency problems, as creative accounting deliberately clouds the image of the company. Nevertheless, disclosure that is 'honest' should lead to a more transparent organization, thereby reducing agency costs.

At this point it is useful to consider the legal aspects of corporate disclosure. In Chapter 3 we emphasized that the UK has adopted traditionally a comply and explain approach to corporate governance. Although financial reporting is a legal requirement for companies, the sanctions for companies that fail to disclose, or misrepresent information, are civil rather than criminal. A firmer environment, such as that introduced in the USA with the Sarbanes–Oxley Act (2002), would make directors more personally liable for the disclosure they produce. However, within the current UK legislative environment, companies that fail to disclose information adequately would find it difficult to maintain listing on the stock market or to attract investors. This should deter many directors from irregular accounting practices. We now turn to the findings of academic research in the area of disclosure and corporate governance.

Research into disclosure and corporate governance

Academic research indicates that investors perceive a value to corporate disclosure. There is a theoretical prediction that relevant and reliable disclosure by companies attracts institutional investors (Diamond and Verrecchia, 1991; Kim and Verrecchia, 1994). Indeed, increases in corporate disclosure have been shown to be associated with increases in ownership by institutional investors (Healy et al., 1999). Further, research in accounting has shown that regulated disclosure provides new and relevant information for investors (Kothari, 2001).

In relation to monitoring company management in an agency theory setting, how does financial accounting information help shareholders to monitor and control company management in an agency theory framework? One example of how accounting information is used to control management is through their remuneration, as the principal–agent model predicts that there is a direct link between company performance and managerial remuneration. As we saw in Chapter 1, one way of reducing agency problems is to establish explicit (and implicit) contracts between company management and their providers of finance. Such contracts require management to disclose relevant information that enables shareholders to monitor their compliance with these contractual agreements, so as to evaluate the extent to which management has utilized the company's resources in the interests of its shareholders

(Healy and Palepu, 2001). A large body of academic research has investigated the extent to which financial accounting information is used to determine management remuneration packages. We do not intend to provide an exhaustive coverage of the literature in this area, as an extensive review has been published (Bushman and Smith, 2001). However, it is worth noting, for example, that half of managerial bonuses were found to be determined by corporate performance, as reported in the financial accounts (Bushman et al., 1995). Further, research has shown that corporate performance measures have been used in evaluating managerial performance and that remuneration contracts depended significantly more on disclosed accounting measures than on share price (Keating, 1997).

As we can see from these findings, if publicly disclosed financial accounting information is used to determine management remuneration contracts, then it serves as a means of controlling company management and reducing the agency problem. However, as agency theory states that managers should maximize shareholder value, then surely managerial remuneration should more logically be determined by share price, not financial accounting information. This is the case to some extent, but research has shown that share price is only one of many factors found to influence remuneration contracts. This area of theory and research provides an insight into the current transformation of corporate governance in the UK, with respect to shareholder activism on executive remuneration. Principal–agent models imply that the shareholders should design a remuneration contract that is based on performance as disclosed in financial accounts, in order to align managerial incentives to their own (Bushman and Smith, 2001). Therefore, increasing shareholder activism on remuneration policy is likely to help shareholders to align managerial interests with their own. For the first time, in recent years, shareholders in UK listed companies have been able to implement a core corporate governance mechanism (i.e., their voting rights) to make the link between remuneration and performance (see Chapters 4 and 5).

The example we have used here is the most obvious means of using accounting information to reduce agency problems. Accounting information generally provides similar benefits (e.g., studying the profit and loss account and the balance sheet gives an insight into the stewardship of a company over a period of time). We now turn to a specialized area of transparency and corporate disclosure that relates to internal control.

Internal control and corporate governance

A company's system of internal control represents from an agency theory perspective another corporate governance mechanism that can be used to align the interests of managers and shareholders. Internal control has been defined as:

> The whole system of controls, financial and otherwise, established in order to provide *reasonable* assurance of: effective and efficient operations; internal financial control; and compliance with laws and regulations.
>
> (Rutteman Working Group, 1994, p. 1, emphasis added)

Note the use of the word '*reasonable*' in this quotation rather than a term such as 'absolute', as this definition implies that it is impossible to have complete insurance against risks. The Turnbull Report (1999) represented the culmination of several years' debate concerning companies' systems of internal control. The report was accompanied by a code of practice and recommendations for listed companies. Again, the recommendations are voluntary, but as with the Combined Code (2003, see Appendix), if companies do not comply with any aspect of the Turnbull recommendations, they have to state where the lack of compliance arises and explain why they have not complied in their annual reports. As with earlier corporate governance codes of practice, the Turnbull Report aimed not to transform companies' systems of internal control but to make explicit the systems of internal control, which many of the top-performing companies had developed, in order to standardize internal control and achieve best practice.

Without an effective system of internal control, companies can undergo substantial financial losses as a result of unanticipated disasters. The recent collapse of Enron has been attributed in part to a failure of the company's system of internal control (see Chapter 2). Similarly, the earlier cases of Maxwell (see Illustration 3.1) and Barings (see Illustration 3.3) involved weaknesses in internal control systems. Smith (1996b) discussed a number of cases of corporate failure and explained how inadequate systems of internal control, as well as investors' inadequate analysis of disclosed information, contributed to collapses such as Coloroll and Polly Peck. Companies need to establish a system for internal control so that they can manage risk effectively, thereby increase transparency. But how may we define risk?

Risk and risk prioritization

Risk has been defined as the possibility of loss as a result of the combination of uncertainty and exposure flowing from an investment decision or a commitment (Boritz, 1990). Uncertainty can however result in gain as well as loss. Unless companies and investors take risks they cannot expand. For example, foreign direct investment is essential for companies if they are to expand internationally but it involves significant risks. Although risk needs to be managed by organizations, it should not be eliminated. There are many different types of risk that face companies including financial risks (such as interest rate and exchange rate risk), environmental and social risks, and the risks arising from non-compliance with regulation. However, each company faces a different risk profile, and their prioritization of these risks is likely to vary. For example, a toy manufacturer will be faced with such risks as seasonal variation in consumer demand whereas an oil company will be concerned about the risks of oil tankers sinking and polluting areas of outstanding natural beauty, such as protected coastlines. The need for companies to prioritize risks was emphasized in a report by the Institute of Chartered Accountants in England and Wales (ICAEW, 1998).

As outlined in Chapter 3 the Combined Code (1998) dealt with internal control in Provisions D.2.1 and D.2.2, where it stated that company directors should conduct a review of the effectiveness of their internal control systems and should report this information to shareholders (Combined Code, 1998). The Turnbull Committee was established specifically to address the issue of internal control and to respond to these provisions in the Combined Code. Company management use the operating and financial review to disclose risk information and ways in which they are assessing and reducing risk. Such disclosure increases corporate transparency, thereby reducing agency problems.

An existing implicit framework for internal control
Despite practitioners' increasing interest in internal control, academic research has made little attempt to conceptualize a system of internal control that accommodates the issues associated with corporate governance. Individual companies have developed their own approaches to internal control and risk management. The risk management approach of British Aerospace has been documented in terms of corporate governance (see Meyrick-Jones, 1999). This approach involved: providing the main board with information on the risks within the group; facilitating internal control as well as providing the disclosure required for reporting, safeguarding the group's assets; and providing a set of rules that the companies within the group could use to assess risk. These, in turn, were expected to safeguard shareholder value (see also Groves, 1999; Thomas, 1999). Thus, although there may be generic categories for implementing risk control mechanisms, companies appear to have developed their own systems in order to meet their specific needs. Before the publication of the Turnbull Report, listed companies had been focusing generally on developing complex and detailed systems of internal control. However, as each company produced an individual system there had been concern that these different systems may not have been addressing internal control effectively. Although the general consensus was that standardization of internal control would be impossible as companies' risks varied so diversely, some common recommendations were deemed necessary. This was the aim of the Turnbull Report (1999). A need for formalizing the sets of procedures implemented across individual listed companies had arisen and the Turnbull Report represented an attempt to create an explicit framework for companies to refer to as a benchmark, when developing their own internal control strategies. For an excellent discussion of internal control see Blackburn (1999).

The Turnbull framework for internal control
The stated objectives of the Turnbull Report appeared to represent a conceptual framework that attempted to make the existing implicit corporate risk disclosure framework explicit. The aim of the framework was to:

> ... reflect sound business practice whereby internal control is embedded in the business process ...
>
> (Turnbull Report, 1999, para. 8)

In our research we summarized the chief components of the Turnbull framework for internal control in a diagram that represented the Turnbull framework (see Figure 6.1, adapted from Solomon et al., 2000b). The diagram showed that a company's system for internal control, according to Turnbull, included several stages. The first stage of the framework was *identification* which involved both the identification and prioritization of relevant risks. The recommendation from Turnbull corresponding to this stage of the framework was that in determining a company's internal control policies the board of directors should consider:

> ... the nature and extent of the risks facing the company.

As well as:

> ... the extent and categories of risk which it regards as acceptable for the company to bear.
>
> (Turnbull Report, 1999, para. 17)

The specific types of risk that should be identified explicitly were not specified in Turnbull, so it would be up to the company to identify the sources of risk that were relevant to them. The *estimation stage* of the conceptual framework depicted the assessment of the potential impacts of identifiable sources of risk. This was described explicitly as a consideration of:

> ... the likelihood of the risks concerned materialising.
>
> (Turnbull Report, 1999, para. 17)

At the *developmental stage* the company should develop its specific risk management strategy, tailored to match specific risks. Thus, the board should consider the:

> ... company's ability to reduce the incidence and impact on the business of risks that do materialise.
>
> (Turnbull Report, 1999, para. 17)

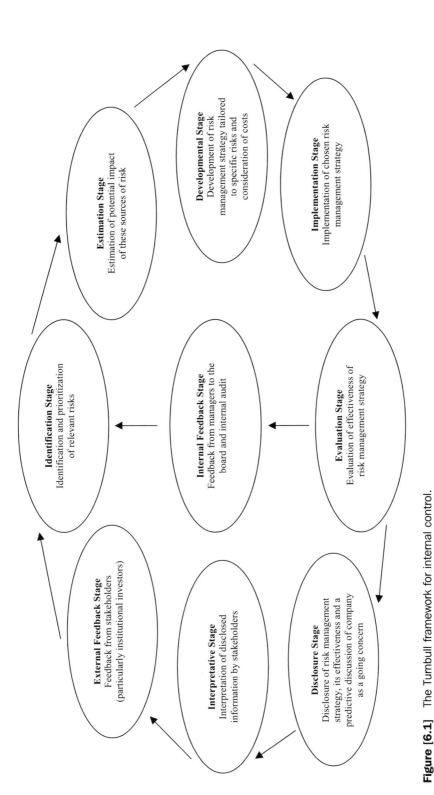

Figure [6.1] The Turnbull framework for internal control.

Adapted from Solomon et al., 2000b, reproduced by permission of Academic Press

This stage should also involve an evaluation of:

> ... costs of operating particular controls relative to the benefit thereby obtained in managing the related risks.
>
> (Turnbull Report, 1999, para. 17)

The development of a risk management strategy led naturally to the next stage of *implementation*, where the board put their chosen risk management strategy into operation. Following implementation, the internal control system was shown to involve an *evaluation stage* where the effectiveness of the implemented strategy was evaluated. This stage involved:

> ... effective monitoring on a continuous basis.
>
> (Turnbull Report, 1999, para. 27)

So as to ensure a dynamic and effective system of internal control, the evaluation stage flowed directly into an *internal feedback stage*, as frequent feedback in the form of reports from managers to the board, as well as (in some cases) an internal audit, to link evaluation to internal disclosure. Indeed, where companies do not operate an internal audit they should review the need for one at frequent intervals (Combined Code, 1998, D.2.2).

An outlet for the company's risk management strategy involves formal public disclosure to its stakeholders. This *disclosure stage* involves reporting information relating to the company's risk management strategy, its effects and success, as well as some predictive discussion of the company as a going concern. Despite the explicit guidance for an internal control framework, Turnbull provided remarkably little detail concerning the format of disclosure within the system of internal control. However, Turnbull provided detailed guidance concerning what should be discussed in an annual assessment preceding the company's public statement on internal control (Turnbull Report, 1999, paras 33 and 34). Indeed, the only explicit guidance on what should be disclosed stated that in their narrative statements companies should:

> ... as a minimum, disclose that there is an ongoing process for identifying, evaluating and managing the significant risks faced by the company.
>
> (Turnbull Report, 1999, para. 35)

This was followed by a suggestion that the company could choose:

> ... to provide additional information in the annual report and accounts to assist understanding of the company's risk management processes and system of internal control.
>
> (Turnbull Report, 1999, para. 36)

There was also a recommendation for some disclosure of the process that the company used to review the effectiveness of its internal control system, as well as information relating to the process it had applied to deal with *material* control aspects of any significant problems disclosed in the annual report and accounts. Of course, this left the decision on materiality to company managers, and it is this materiality decision that therefore governs the disclosure.

The last stage of the framework for internal control was one of *interpretation* of the disclosed material by stakeholders, which was intended to facilitate *external feedback* and control. This feedback should be incorporated in the first identification stage of the framework as a crucial aspect of the company's overall risk management strategy and system of internal control. The strengthening of communication and decision links between shareholders and investee companies, for example, is one sign that this feedback process is evolving (see Solomon and Solomon, 1999).

Although the main emphasis of the Turnbull Report was on the assessment, estimation, management and disclosure of financial risks, there was also an implication that companies should take account of non-financial risks in their systems of internal control. This broader agenda for internal control is discussed in Illustration 6.1.

Risk disclosure and corporate governance

Corporate risk disclosure represents an important, specific category of corporate disclosure. One of the main developments in the area of corporate disclosure for UK companies, linked to the general agenda for corporate governance reform, has been an increasing emphasis on corporate risk disclosure. This was highlighted by the publication of the Turnbull Report, which focused attention on this crucial aspect of the Turnbull framework for internal control. Emphasis on the reporting stage of the internal control system is essential, both for corporate accountability and for the future success of the business. Indeed, the USA and Canada recognized the need to improve corporate risk disclosure before the publication of the UK Turnbull Report (see Treadway Commission, 1987; Boritz, 1990; Courtis, 1993), and this need was also acknowledged a little later by interested parties in the UK (e.g., see Arthur Andersen, 1996). The Cadbury Report (1992) also highlighted the relevance of risk disclosure to the corporate governance agenda by suggesting that validating the company as a going concern and improving the disclosure of internal control should lead to improvements in the communication links between investors and their investee companies. Further, if the aim of company management is to reduce the cost of capital by raising confidence in the market, then the communication of risk management policies must be a significant factor. Improving information flows between companies and their shareholders represents one effective way of reducing information asymmetry, thereby lessening the agency problem inherent in UK corporate governance, as discussed in Chapter 1.

Illustration 6.1

Broadening the Turnbull agenda

In 2000 the Association of Chartered Certified Accountants produced a report that considered the relevance of risks other than solely financial risks from a Turnbull perspective (ACCA, 2000). This report is extremely interesting as it combines the importance of stakeholder issues with financial issues and extends the Turnbull remit to a broader community of stakeholders. The aim of the report is stated in a short introduction that says:

> This short report seeks to illustrate some of the wider implications of the Turnbull Report—especially as it relates to social, environmental and sustainable development risk issues. A number of involved practitioners set out their views on what Boards of Directors really do need to know about Turnbull—but probably won't be told by their finance director.

There are a number of short articles included in the report and we shall deal with them in turn.

Accountability, transparency, corporate social responsibility: a new mantra for a new millennium

This article represents the introduction to the report. It emphasizes that Turnbull is based on the '... adoption of a risk-based approach to establishing a sound system of internal control and on reviewing its effectiveness.' This should not be an additional 'extra-curricular' activity for company management but should instead be incorporated in normal, everyday management and corporate governance. The review highlights the fact that Turnbull is not intended to deal solely with financial controls but also with social and environmental issues. The way that such concerns are incorporated in a risk-based corporate framework is by the back door of 'reputation risk' issues. In other words, the reason why environmental and social issues are important for companies is because they can pose serious reputational risk by damaging corporate image. As a result of such reputational concerns, pension funds are now required to disclose the extent to which they invest according to social, ethical and environmental criteria. This is something we will be dealing with specifically in Chapter 10. The important point is that Turnbull requires a company board of directors to consider environmental, ethical and social issues as part of their compliance. Indeed, the authors state that, 'In our joint view, disclosure of broader risk-related issues is fundamental to the principles of accountability and transparency. Companies that hide behind a narrow definition of risk will be doing themselves a disservice, as the ability of stakeholders to penetrate that shield increases. As both Shell and Nike have found, openness is definitely the best policy when it comes to developing sustainable long-term relationships with stakeholders'.

Corporate governance in a CNN world (John Elkington and Peter Zollinger from SustainAbility)

CNN as an international new network is one media form that implies that reputational risk has a broader impact than ever before. The make-up and activities of corporate boards are in the spotlight more than ever before. Companies are now required to address such issues as health, the environment and ethics as part of their daily business decision-making process. Business leaders and boards are going to have to be able to pick up 'weak signals' in order to be globally competitive.

Turnbull and reputational risks: an investment view
(Craig Mackenzie from Friends & Ivory Sime, now ISIS)

This article emphasizes that Turnbull is a corporate governance issue. They comment that for a while institutional investors have been encouraged to influence companies by means of their voting rights as a part of their good corporate governance practice. Social, environmental and ethical issues have in the past been considered only for specialized investors. However, the new pension fund disclosure requirement has brought these issues to the forefront for mainstream investors.

Risk analysis and management: the role of dialogue (Simon Zadek from AccountAbility)

For Zadek, the author of this short article, the key to the Turnbull recommendations is stakeholder dialogue. It is vitally important for a company to know what its stakeholders require, what their concerns are and the issues that affect the business that are utmost in their minds.

Environmental and reputational risk in the annual report and accounts
(Roger Adams from ACCA)

Adams is a strong advocate of companies providing environmental information and is the accounting representative on many committees, such as the Global Reporting Initiative (GRI). Adams believes that it is important for companies to disclose environmental information in their annual reports. Being an accountant, he is particularly interested in the financial impacts. However, more qualitative-type disclosures such as poor ethical, environmental and employment practices, are also important for him. In particular, he advocates the disclosure of forward-looking reporting, in that financial reporting as we know is retrospective. Adams advocates disclosure that includes information on provisions for contaminated land, decommissioning of long-lived assets and contingent environmental liabilities.

The implications of Turnbull: a corporate view (Chris Tuppen from British Telecom)

Tuppen has been at the forefront of environmental disclosure at BT for many years. It is his view that social and environmental reports can be useful in the identification of risk. Also he considers that they should be included in the appropriate internal control mechanisms as suggested by Turnbull. For Tuppen there are two main risks to companies in the environmental and social sphere. The first includes liabilities resulting from past pollution, and the second concerns the company's reputation. For example, when BT was owned by the Government, people did not own their own telephones. They could only be hired from BT (which was part of the Post Office). An innovation in the 1970s was to produce a (by 1970s standards) 'trimphone' that was turquoise in colour (pathbreaking stuff at the time). The major innovation was that it was not only 'slim' but it had a neon dial. When these phones reached the end of their useful life BT found that they were radioactive. They dismantled them and the radioactive dials were stored in a warehouse somewhere, as BT did not know what to do with them. If this isn't an environmental/ethical/social risk what is?

Managing reputational risk (John Browne from PricewaterhouseCoopers)

Browne discusses the importance of managing reputational risk. In Browne's experience as a director of PricewaterhouseCoopers boards are as concerned about reputational risks as with financial loss *per se*. Browne considers at some length how it is important for companies to 'engage' with their stakeholders. To some extent this supports Zadek's views. In the Brent Spar incident in the early 1990s Shell wanted to dismantle an oil platform that had come to the end of its useful life. Shell wanted to dispose of it at sea. Greenpeace wanted it disposed of on land. A boycott of Shell products ensued. National governments became involved. Shell's reputation suffered badly. The scientific advice was to dispose of the platform at sea (!) implying that Greenpeace were misguided in their views. For Shell the main lesson was that it must manage its reputation and that stakeholder dialogue was essential. For further details check the Shell website which documents this fiasco in some detail.

Managing risk: a case study in the National Health Service (Nigel Woodcock)

Woodcock discusses the implications of Turnbull for the public sector. It is interesting to note that over the last 15 or so years the public sector has taken on many of the characteristics of the private sector. Corporate governance is no exception. This is in part due to an extensive privatization programme and the view by various governments that the market model is superior to the state model. Of particular interest here is that the direction of influence is not just private to public sector but also public sector to private sector, as non-financial indicators have been used for evaluating performance. For example, the railways should really be disclosing how many people have died on the railways each year! Indeed, this is now being considered. It is the ultimate in benchmarking performance. In a different paper, Belcher (2002) discussed the issue of 'corporate killing' as a corporate governance issue. Indeed, she stated that Turnbull opened the way for discussion on many more risk-related issues than the purely financial! To some extent, parts of the National Health Service have been privatized, with each hospital now in command of its own budget. There is no board of directors as such or shareholders, rather an NHS Trust exists in order to undertake a similar monitoring role. The Trust Board now has a statutory duty to certify that management has covered all risks in the management of the Trust and has systems in place to deal with these risks.

Turnbull and your company: identifying and managing the risks
(Rachel Jackson from ACCA and Chris Tuppen from British Telecom)

In the final section of this interesting report, Jackson and Tuppen provide a three stage model for identifying and managing risks. Stage 1 identifies the sources of risk. These risks may include:

- *Supply chain risks*. These are suppliers based in countries that have:
  - human rights abuses;
  - child-enforced labour concerns;
  - living wage issues.

  Suppliers that are:
  - high pollutants;
  - using unsustainable production technologies (e.g., forestry, fisheries, etc.);
  - involved with GMOs.

  If this is an area that you are interested in, B&Q DIY provide examples of how they have tried to overcome some of these problems (see their website or visit a store).

- *Operational risks*. Companies operating in countries with:
  - human rights abuses;
  - child and forced labour concerns;
  - living wage issues.

Also:

- ○ unsatisfactory employee satisfaction levels;
- ○ potential to contaminate land;
- ○ involvement with dangerous activities;
- ○ level of noise/visual pollution (e.g., brightly coloured outdoor clothing!);
- ○ compliance with environmentally and socially regulated processes;
- ○ location of sites (urban/rural).

- *Product risks*
  - ○ the use of unsustainable or hazardous raw material used in product composition;
  - ○ quantity and type of waste produced during production;
  - ○ end-of-life disposal methods;
  - ○ health and safety concerns related to product use;
  - ○ environmental effects from product use.

- *General societal expectation*
  - ○ disclosure of environmental and social performance via a report;
  - ○ certification to environmental and social standards;
  - ○ statement of business principles.

Stage 2 of the model evaluates the significance of these risks and Stage 3 considers how these risks may be managed.

Overall, we can see how this report brings stakeholder accountability and a much wider perspective on risk management and internal control into the corporate governance debate. This approach embodies stakeholder theory and inclusivity, as discussed in Chapter 1. We pick up on the broader agenda for corporate governance and the importance of an inclusive approach in Part III.

An 'ideal' framework for corporate risk disclosure

As can be seen from the earlier discussion of the Turnbull Report, the section of the report relating specifically to corporate risk disclosure was unspecific and short. Therefore, we developed a diagrammatic framework for corporate risk disclosure that presented several possible alternatives for an 'ideal' framework (Solomon et al., 2000b). The paper attempted to provide companies with a little more in the way of structure for their risk disclosure process. It is from Solomon et al. (2002b) that we reproduce the possible ingredients of an ideal corporate risk disclosure framework in Figure 6.2. The diagram incorporates six variable elements that interrelate to create the extant framework for corporate risk disclosure. One important element is whether corporate risk disclosure should remain in a voluntary environment or whether it should be made mandatory. Another element is the appropriate level of risk disclosure: Is the current level of information that is disclosed adequate or would increased corporate risk disclosure facilitate investment decision making? The most desirable location for risk disclosure within the annual report is also an important element of the risk disclosure framework. Is the OFR, for example, the most appropriate vehicle for risk disclosure? The review of modern company law currently under way is certainly pushing for this sort of information to be contained within

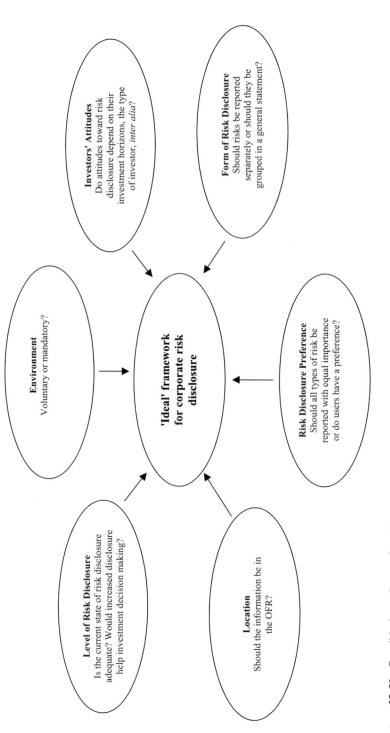

Figure [6.2] Possible ingredients of an ideal corporate risk disclosure framework

OFR = Operating and Financial Review. Adapted from Solomon et al., 2000b, reproduced by permission of Academic Press an augmented OFR (see Modernising Company Law, 2002). The framework also presents different possibilities for investors' risk disclosure preferences and the form of disclosure that certain risks should take. Should all types of risk be reported with equal importance? Should every risk be reported individually or should all risk information be grouped in a general statement for external reporting purposes? Is there a distinct preference for some types of risk information? Whether future developments in the risk disclosure framework will involve explicit guidance on specific risks remains to be seen. At present, it is unclear whether users of financial reports have strong preferences for the disclosure of particular types of risk. This issue requires clarification to inform future policy recommendations. Lastly, the framework considers whether investors' attitudes are influenced by specific factors. For example, are institutional investors' attitudes toward corporate risk disclosure influenced by their general attitudes toward corporate governance? Are their perceptions of corporate governance related to their requirements for risk information? Indeed, it is likely that there is a strong link between these issues, since internal control has recently become a central aspect of the UK agenda for corporate governance reform.

Having developed a framework that considered the possible ingredients of an ideal corporate risk disclosure system, it seemed important to gather some empirical evidence in order to establish the most desirable ingredients of an ideal framework. By obtaining empirical evidence, we were able to determine which of the possible ingredients constituted 'the' ideal corporate risk disclosure framework—at least from the perspective of one group of people. Some work had already been done on this area in the USA, as evidence indicated that there was a demand from institutional investors for disclosure of internal control information and that this type of information was considered useful to external decision makers (Hermanson, 2000). However, relatively little evidence has been collected in the UK. We therefore decided to canvas the views of an extensive sample of UK institutional investors in order to find out what their preferred or ideal framework was for corporate risk disclosure. Their views are important and influential given that the size of their stake in UK listed companies has grown substantially (recall the discussion in Chapter 5). To conduct the questionnaire survey, a sample of 552 institutional investors was drawn randomly from four sources. The sample comprised the four main types of investment institution: pension funds, investment trusts, unit trusts and insurance companies. The questionnaire was distributed between January and April 1999. Of the responses received, 97 (17.6%) were satisfactorily completed. The majority of respondents were from pension funds and insurance funds. Table 6.1 presents the responses to a question asking the investors to indicate the extent to which they agreed with a number of statements.[4] The table ranks the statements in order of mean average response, with the statement receiving the highest response at the top of the table.

---

[4] They were asked to select a score from 1 (strongly disagree) to 7 (strongly agree).

Table [6.1]   Institutional investors' attitudes toward corporate risk disclosure

Rank	Statements	Average response
1	I believe that increased corporate risk disclosure would help institutional investors in their portfolio investment decisions	Strong agreement
2	I believe that the best way of improving risk disclosure would be to report exposure to and management of different types of risk separately	Agreement
3	I believe that increased risk disclosure would improve the corporate governance of our investee companies	Agreement
4	I believe that financial risk information is more relevant to institutional investors than other risk information (e.g., product/service, compliance and environmental risks)	Agreement
5	I believe that the current state of risk disclosure by our UK investee companies is inadequate	Agreement
6	I believe that improvements in risk disclosure are essential to a company's reporting as a going concern	Agreement
7	I believe that the Operating and Financial Review (OFR) is the most appropriate vehicle for increased risk disclosure	Agreement
8	I believe that all types of risk affecting an investee company should be reported with equal importance	Some agreement
9	I believe that the best way for companies to improve risk disclosure would be to publish a general statement of business risk	Some agreement
10	I believe that increased risk disclosure would encourage the development of long-term relationships between institutional investors and their investee companies	Some agreement
11	I believe that corporate risk disclosure should be voluntary	Some agreement
12	I believe that corporate disclosure of risk information should be regulated through Government legislation	Disagreement

One important finding from this survey was that institutional investors endorsed the improvement in corporate risk disclosure and viewed such disclosure as decision-useful. The statement that received the highest mean average response concerned the relevance of risk disclosure to investors' portfolio investment decisions. The investors evidently felt that better risk disclosure improved their investment decisions. This provides a mandate for further improvements in corporate risk disclosure and is encouraging to policy makers. Further, the statement suggesting that the current state of risk disclosure by UK companies is inadequate also received support from the respondents, indicating that attention needed to be paid to this area. The results also indicated that the current voluntary framework of disclosure should be maintained. The institutional investors clearly preferred a voluntary, to a regulated, framework, as indicated in Table 3.2. Indeed, one questionnaire respondent remarked:

> ... these [corporate governance] reforms are generally acceptable, though the most important point to emphasize is the maintenance of self-regulation.

Another interesting finding was that, despite some published recommendations, the institutional investors appeared to prefer different risks to be reported and managed separately. They did not seem to favour an overall business risk report. Clearly, financial risks were shown to be of most relevance to the institutional investors. There was also some evidence to support the OFR as being the most appropriate vehicle for risk disclosure. It seems that on a practical level the Turnbull Report has had a far-reaching impact on corporate risk disclosure, as companies have been encouraged to comply with its recommendations by producing detailed reporting of their risks. Some examples of risk disclosure following Turnbull are presented in Illustration 6.2.

The role of audit in corporate governance

Within a company's system of internal control, the external audit represents one of the most indispensable corporate governance checks and balances that help to monitor company management's activities, thereby increasing transparency. The Cadbury Report emphasized that:

> The annual audit is one of the cornerstones of corporate governance ... The audit provides an external and objective check on the way in which the financial statements have been prepared and presented.
>
> (Cadbury Report, 1992, p. 36, para. 5.1)

From an agency theory perspective, the audit function represents another important corporate governance mechanism that helps shareholders in their monitoring and control of company management. The audit of a company's financial statements makes disclosure more credible, thereby instilling confidence in the company's transparency. Indeed, auditing has been considered to play a role in contract monitoring, as a company's auditors contract with debtholders to report any observed breaches of restrictive covenants and audited earnings numbers are used in bonus plans (Watts and Zimmerman, 1986). As we saw from reading the case of Enron in Chapter 2, failure of the audit function was one of the principal factors that contributed to the company's downfall. However, the existence of an 'audit expectations gap' needs to be acknowledged, as the audit function can only do so much where

Illustration 6.2

Examples of corporate risk disclosure after Turnbull

In the BP Annual Report (2000, p. 78) there was an illustration of disclosure relating to risk and the Turnbull Report, as follows:

> The Board Governance Policies include a process for the board to review regularly the effectiveness of the systems of internal control as required by Code Provision D.2.1. As part of this process, executive management presented a report to the November meetings of the Audit Committee, Ethics and Environment Assurance Committee and the Board about their system of internal control during 2000. The Report identified and evaluated seven significant risk categories, summarised the state of internal control and described the executive management's assurance process ... The Report also described enhancements implemented by executive management to their internal control systems during 2000. The Committees and Board reviewed this Report. In the Board's view, the information it received was sufficient to enable it to review the effectiveness of the company's system of internal control in accordance with the Guidance for Directors on Internal Control (Turnbull).

The Shell Transport and Trading Company Annual Report (2000) disclosed the following information:

> The approach in the Group to risk management and internal control ... which demonstrates that risk and control reporting was enhanced to provide from the beginning of 2000 a process designed to involve management in regular reviews of the risks that are significant to the fulfilment of the objectives of the business. These enhancements were designed to formalise the mechanisms for ongoing identification, evaluation, management and review of significant risks and the Directors consider that these internal control arrangements are compatible with the guidance for directors published in September 1999 (known as the Turnbull Report) in relation to the internal control provisions of the Combined Code.

The company was having a quarterly boardroom meeting to discuss risk. In contrast to this, Kingfisher (2001, p. 31) stated that they reviewed and assessed the Group's risks 'at least annually'. The reason for this may have been that Kingfisher operated in a more stable environment, showing that the Turnbull framework is a dynamic framework that is especially applicable to companies that are not stable. This type of review is a result of the Turnbull Report in that it was not happening before! Indeed, the company stated that since Turnbull:

> ... efforts to fully embed the risk-based approach to internal control are now being cascaded within the business.

This implied that Shell (a top company) was only establishing this type of internal control system as a result of Turnbull and that they had not been doing it before!

In the Diageo Annual Report (2001) the company stated that:

> Internal control: The directors acknowledge that they are responsible for the Group's systems of internal control and reviewing their effectiveness ... An ongoing process, in accordance with the guidance of the Turnbull Committee on internal control, has been established for identifying, evaluating and managing risks faced by the Group. This process has been in place for the full financial year and up to the date the

financial statements were approved. The risk management process and systems of internal control are designed to manage rather than eliminate the risk of failure to achieve the Group's strategic objectives. It should be recognised that such systems can only provide reasonable, not absolute, assurance against material misstatement or loss.

The statement went on to describe the main parts of the control system for each business. The auditors for Diageo were KPMG at the time.

The Corus Annual Report and Accounts (2000, p. 26) stated that:

Internal control: The directors are responsible for the Group's system of internal control and reviewing its effectiveness ... The Board has designed the Group's system of internal control in order to provide the directors with reasonable assurance that its assets are safeguarded, that transactions are authorised and properly recorded and that material errors are either prevented or would be detected within a timely period. However, no system of internal control can eliminate the risk of failure to achieve business objectives or provide absolute assurance against material misstatement or loss [note that this is very similar to the statement in Diageo's report].

The statement went on to describe the main parts of the control system for each business. The auditors were PricewaterhouseCoopers. These examples provide evidence that the Turnbull Report had an immediate and significant impact on corporate disclosure.

fraud is rife.[5] According to the Cadbury Report, it is important to bear in mind that the auditor's role is not to prepare the financial statements, nor to provide absolute assurance that the figures in the financial statements are correct, nor to provide a guarantee that the company will continue as a going concern, but the auditors have to state in the annual report that the financial statements show 'a' true and fair view rather than 'the' true and fair view. The Cadbury Report stressed that there was no question as to whether or not there should be an audit but rather how its effectiveness and objectivity could be ensured. We consider ways in which these may be ensured below.

Auditor independence

The Cadbury Report pointed out that auditor independence could be compromised due to the close relationship that is inevitable between auditors and company managers and due to the auditor's wish to develop a constructive relationship with their clients. Indeed, the Cadbury Report stated that:

The central issue is to ensure that an appropriate relationship exists between the auditors and the management whose financial statements they are auditing.

(Cadbury Report, 1992, p. 38, para. 5.7)

---

[5] The problem of the audit expectations gap is discussed in the Cadbury Report (1992, p. 37, para. 5.4) in relation to the Caparo Judgment.

The Cadbury Report stressed that a balance needed to be attained, such that auditors worked with, not against, company management, but in doing so they needed to serve shareholders. This is a difficult path to tread and one that is clearly bedecked with obstacles. Establishing audit committees and developing effective accounting standards were suggested as the most apt means of ensuring this balance is attained. We now look at a number of other issues relating to auditor independence.

Provision of non-audit services

Another problem raised in the Cadbury Report regarding the independence and effectiveness of the audit function involves the multiple services offered by auditors to their clients. Cadbury asserted that auditing tended to comprise only a part of auditors' business with their client companies. The desire for auditors to compete on price in offering a number of services, as well as their desire to satisfy their client's wishes, can lead to shareholder interests being sidelined. Auditing companies offer consultancy services and IT services to the companies that they audit. The immediate response to this is to prohibit auditors from offering other services, in order to prevent their objectivity from being compromised through inevitable conflicts of interest. However, as the Cadbury Report comments, such a prohibition could increase corporate costs significantly, as their freedom of choice in the market would be restricted. Consequently, a weaker recommendation was made in the Cadbury Report that companies should disclose full details of fees paid to audit firms for non-audit work, such as consultancy. Despite fears arising from the Enron case, the Smith Report (2003) was reluctant to deal with the issue in a proactive manner. The report stated that:

> ... we do not believe it would be right to seek to impose specific restrictions on the auditor's supply of non-audit services through the vehicle of Code guidance. We are sceptical of a prescriptive approach, since we believe that there are no clear-cut, universal answers ... there may be genuine benefits to efficiency and effectiveness from auditors doing non-audit work.
>
> (Smith Report, 2003, p. 27, para. 35)

This statement begs the question: Are the benefits of allowing auditors to provide non-audit services to their audit clients really greater than the possibly dire consequences that could arise from resulting conflicts of interest? The Enron case study highlighted the problems of restricted auditor independence. Research is needed in this area and plenty is currently under way. Rather than making specific recommendations on auditing practice the Smith Report seems to pass the buck on to the audit committee. The Smith recommendations centre around passing responsibility for auditor independence and objectivity on to the audit committee function.

Rotation of auditors

The Cadbury Report also discussed the possibility of establishing compulsory rotation of auditors, as this could be a means of avoiding cosy auditor–client relationships. However, the report concluded that the costs of such an initiative would outweigh the benefits, as it would result in a loss of confidence and trust between the auditor and their client company. The potentially negative attributes of a close relationship may be outweighed by the benefits, such as auditor's in-depth knowledge of the company's affairs. Again, since Enron, this has become a more important initiative worldwide.

Audit committees

The Cadbury Report recommended that all companies should establish audit committees. The Smith Report emphasized the essential role the audit committee should play in ensuring the independence and objectivity of the external auditor, as well as in monitoring company management. The Report provided detailed guidance on the role of the audit function and stipulated that the main role and responsibilities of audit committees should be to: monitor the integrity of companies' financial statements; review companies' internal financial control systems; monitor and review the effectiveness of companies' internal audit functions; make recommendations to the board in relation to the appointment of the external auditor and approve the remuneration and terms of engagement of the external auditor; monitor and review the independence, effectiveness and objectivity of the external auditor; and develop and implement policy on the engagement of the external auditor to supply non-audit services (Smith Report, 2003, p. 6, para. 2.1). Most significantly, the Smith Report highlighted the need for the audit committee to be proactive, raising issues of concern with directors rather than brushing them under the carpet. Further, the Smith Report stressed that all members of the audit committee should be independent, non-executive directors. Companies' annual reports should disclose detailed information on the role and responsibilities of their audit committee and action taken by the audit committee in discharging those responsibilities (Smith Report, 2003, p. 17, para. 6.1).

Research into the effectiveness of the audit function

The academic literature has provided mixed evidence on the effectiveness of the audit function, with respect to whether the audit adds value for investors and whether auditors' actions are independent of client interest (Healy and Palepu, 2001). There is evidence that shareholders consider audited accounting information to be credible because academic research has shown that share prices react to earnings announcements (Kothari, 2001). Further endorsement of the effectiveness of the audit function comes from research that has shown that providers of finance require companies to appoint an independent auditor before they will provide funds, even without regulation. One example comes from Leftwich (1983), who found that banks required companies to present audited financial information, again indicating that shareholders and other capital providers consider that the audit enhances credibility.

Our own research into the views of the UK institutional investment community toward corporate governance has provided less encouraging evidence on the usefulness and effectiveness of the audit function. Indeed, we found that there was general scepticism surrounding the role of the audit.[6] The institutional fund managers and fund directors we interviewed considered that auditors were not as informed as they should have been and that the audit was often more of a formality, having relatively little value for investors. For example, one head of corporate governance in a major investment institution commented that:

> We do have—not officially, not publicly—concerns about their independence overall ... you would be amazed at how, when you speak to auditors, from big firms as well as little firms, at drinks parties, at non-official events, and when they are in isolation (you would never get this if you had an audit conference), they often say that they are amazed that more does not come to light or that they often get their arm twisted by management—not from their own practice but of the companies they are auditing—to not worry about it, it is under control. I do find that quite alarming. What do you do about it? You cannot go out and say, 'Investment management believes that the auditing profession is completely corrupt!'.

If anything ever brought the credibility of the audit into question, this statement does! And coming from a major institution in the City of London! Furthermore, it was by no means an isolated view. If nothing else, this sort of view, so prevalent from our interview research, begs urgent research in the area. Not necessarily the type of abstracted empiricism that is so evident in the market-based accounting literature, but qualitative, interview evidence that provides an insight into how the institutional investment community really views the value of audit. Fortunately, our research also provided a ray of hope, which to some extent explained why audits continue to be supported by the investment community, as another interviewee commented that:

> ... *something is better than nothing* and one hopes that by going through the process most companies will say, 'Oh, my God, we didn't realise that we had that exposure or that we weren't doing this properly, or whatever. We will try and remedy it.'
> (Head of corporate governance at a leading investment institution, emphasis added)

As with any criticism of the accounting framework, there needs to be a consideration of what could take its place. There is a lot of academic literature in accounting that exposes serious flaws in our current system but offers no serious alternative.

---

[6] Our research has involved 25 interviews of members of the institutional investment community. However, these views on auditing have, to date, not been published anywhere else in the academic literature.

Overthrowing the status quo requires a viable system to replace it and a lot of support to impose the alternative.

Chapter summary

In this chapter we have reviewed the importance of transparency to the efficient workings of the corporate governance system. We have looked at the essential role that corporate disclosure, and specifically financial accounting information, plays in corporate governance and the ways in which these forms of information can help to solve the agency problem. We have also considered a specialized area of corporate transparency, that of internal control. Lastly, we discussed the role of the audit function in corporate governance and the ways in which these essential functions help to resolve agency problems. Such corporate failures as Maxwell, Barings and Enron have highlighted the need to improve the effectiveness of these functions. Indeed, we provide qualitative evidence from our own research, showing that there is a genuine lack of credibility regarding the usefulness of the audit function within the institutional investment community, which begs further research.

Questions for reflection and discussion

1 Discuss the importance to shareholders of the conceptual framework for corporate risk disclosure that is made explicit in the Turnbull Report.

2 Evaluate the extent to which you consider UK listed companies are complying with the recommendations of the Turnbull Report in spirit. In your answer make reference to the information disclosed in annual reports that you have examined as well as to academic papers and other published sources that you have read.

3 To what extent do you think that the Smith Report has produced recommendations that will improve the objectivity and independence of the external auditors?

4 Choose a company listed on the London Stock Exchange (preferably one in the Top 350). Download the latest annual report for this company from the Internet. Examine the information provided in the report on internal control, risk management and compliance with Turnbull. Evaluate the extent to which you consider the recommendations of Turnbull are being complied with in substance as well as in form.

5 Do you think there are real reasons why institutional investors should be concerned about the independence and genuine effectiveness of the audit function? Search newspapers and the Internet for cases supporting your view.

Part II

Global corporate governance

Chapter 7

An introduction to corporate governance systems worldwide

Aim and objectives

This chapter extends our discussion of corporate governance by introducing different types of corporate governance system prevalent throughout the world, highlighting the difficulties of categorizing such a diversity of systems. The specific objectives of this chapter are to:

- appreciate the diversity of corporate governance systems worldwide and consider the difficulties of forcing idiosyncratic systems into discrete categories;

- discuss the characteristics of the insider-oriented versus the outsider-oriented categorization for corporate governance systems at an international level;

- consider the influence of legal systems and other factors on the evolution of corporate governance systems;

- introduce the concept of a global convergence in corporate governance;

Introduction

In earlier chapters we focused on the UK system of corporate governance. Now we turn to considering systems of corporate governance in other countries around the world. Every country exhibits a unique system of corporate governance: there are as many corporate governance systems as there are countries. The system of corporate governance presiding in any country is determined by a wide array of internal (domestic) factors, including corporate ownership structure, the state of the economy, the legal system, government policies, culture and history. There are also a host of external influences, such as the extent of capital inflows from abroad, the global economic climate and cross-border institutional investment. The main determinants of a company's corporate governance system are ownership structure and legal frameworks. However, cultural and other influences are discussed where relevant and are highlighted in relation to specific countries' corporate governance systems.

Categorizing corporate governance: the Cinderella problem

The ways in which companies finance themselves and the structure of corporate ownership within an economy are considered to be principal determinants of a country's corporate governance system. We have seen from the discussion in Chapter 5 that in the UK institutional investors hold the majority of shares in listed companies. Since the 1970s there has been a reversal of share ownership, with individual shareholders becoming less important and institutional investors taking on a larger and larger proportion of UK equity in their investment portfolios. However, this pattern of ownership is by no means common to all countries around the world. The transformation of UK ownership structure has, as we have seen, had a substantial impact on corporate governance in the UK, as the change from dispersed to concentrated ownership has had implications for the way shareholders interact with their investee companies. Other countries are experiencing transformation of corporate governance but in many different ways, as we shall see in this and the following chapter.

Attempts have been made to categorize countries' corporate governance systems. However, such categorization is at best loose, and at worst incorrect, as it represents in some cases, oversimplification of extremely complicated financial systems. Trying to force a country's corporate governance framework into a neat category is reminiscent of the ugly sisters' attempts to squeeze their unshapely feet into Cinderella's shoe! Nevertheless, some broad categorization of corporate governance systems can be extremely useful for analytic purposes and allows analysis of the way in which countries interact with each other. Such categorization can be helpful in providing researchers with a hinge, on which they can rest their analyses and empirical work. As with any theorizing, practise may differ, but at least a useful framework is provided as a basis for discussion and further research.

One well-known and generally accepted means of categorizing corporate governance systems is the 'insider/outsider' model. Franks and Mayer (1994) and Short et al. (1998) discussed this categorization. The terms 'insider' and 'outsider' represent attempts to loosely describe two extreme forms of corporate governance. In reality, most systems of corporate governance fall somewhere in between these two, sharing some characteristics of both extremes. The polarization of corporate governance may have arisen from differences that exist between cultures and legal systems. However, as we shall see later in our discussion, countries are attempting to reduce the differences and there is a possibility that corporate governance will converge at a global level.

Insider-dominated systems

An insider-dominated system of corporate governance is one in which a country's publicly listed companies are owned and controlled by a small number of major shareholders. These may be members of the companies' founding families or a small group of shareholders, such as lending banks, other companies (through cross-shareholdings and pyramidal ownership structures) or the government. Insider systems are also referred to commonly as relationship-based systems in the literature, because of the close relationships prevalent between companies and their dominant shareholders. The possible superiority of insider corporate governance systems, such as those of Germany and Japan, has been an issue debated widely in the literature. Indeed, some researchers have discussed the benefits of replacing Anglo-Saxon styles of corporate governance with systems derived from those in Germany and Japan (Roe, 1993; Charkham, 1994). The tide, however, seems to be flowing in the opposite direction.

There are problems endemic to the insider-dominated mould. As a result of the close ties between owners and managers there is a reduced agency problem, which at first glance would seem a positive characteristic. There is less difficulty in aligning the interests of company management and the shareholders, often because they are the same people! However, other serious corporate governance problems arise. As a result of the low level of separation of ownership and control in many countries (e.g., due to ownership by founding families), there can be abuse of power. Minority shareholders may not be able to obtain information on the company's operations. There is little transparency and frequent abuse of the company's operations takes place. Opaque financial transactions and misuse of funds raised are typical of these systems. Indeed, for many East Asian countries, excessive ownership concentration structures and related corporate governance weaknesses have been blamed for the severity of the Asian crisis in 1997 (see Prowse, 1992; Rajan and Zingales, 1998; Johnson et al., 2000; Claessens et al., 2000). Corporate governance systems in East Asian countries fall more comfortably into the insider mould than the outsider model. Indeed, Johnson et al. (2000) emphasized the significance of East Asian legal systems in the crisis by showing that the weakness of the legal institutions for corporate governance had an important effect on the extent of depreciations and stock market declines in the Asian crisis. Weaker legal protection of minority shareholders in many East Asian countries allowed majority shareholders to increase their expropriation of minority shareholder wealth, in the event of a shock to investor confidence. Further, they showed empirically that corporate governance variables explained most of the variation in exchange rates and stock market performance during the Asian crisis (rather than macro-economic variables). We consider how a number of East Asian countries have sought to reform their corporate governance systems, often through changes to company law, since the Asian crisis in Chapter 8.

Outsider-dominated systems

The term 'outsider' refers to systems of finance and corporate governance where most large firms are controlled by their managers but owned by outside shareholders, such as financial institutions or individual shareholders. This situation results in the notorious separation, or divorce, of ownership and control, outlined by Berle and Means (1932). As we saw in Chapter 1, the development of agency theory arose from this separation, with its early exposition in Ross (1973) and Jensen and Meckling (1976). The agency problem is associated with significant costs to both management and the shareholder. The UK and the USA have been characterized traditionally in this mould. Another term used to refer to this type of system is market-based (see Zysman, 1983). They are also referred to frequently as Anglo-Saxon or Anglo-American systems, due to the influence of the UK and US stock markets on others around the world. Although companies are, in the outsider system, controlled directly by their managers, they are also controlled indirectly by the outsiders. Shareholders have voting rights that provide them with some level of control. They also have the ability to instigate engagement, which is becoming increasingly popular in the UK, as we saw in Chapter 5. These outsiders tend to be predominantly financial institutions, but also smaller individual shareholders. Until recently, as we saw in Chapter 5, larger shareholders such as financial institutions tended to be short-termist and rather passive in nature, preferring an exit strategy to a strategy of voice.[1] Increasingly in the UK and the USA, the large-scale institutional investors that characterize the outsider system are gaining a substantial influence over company directors. Indeed, it has been suggested that the outsiders in the UK and the US are becoming more like insiders, as the main institutional shareholders are gaining the largest proportion of shares in companies and are exacting strong influence on company management, taking on the role of an insider majority shareholder. The dominant characteristics associated with the traditional insider and outsider systems of corporate governance are summarized in Table 7.1.

Research into corporate governance systems worldwide

A growing area of the finance literature devoted to international comparisons of corporate governance systems seeks to explain the factors that determine countries' corporate governance. A paper by Shleifer and Vishny (1997) surveyed the extant research into corporate governance, focusing on the influence of countries' legal systems on corporate governance. Specifically, they investigated the relevance of

---

[1] This distinction was made by Hirschman (1970) in relation to companies and their consumers in an economic analysis. However, the notion of exit and voice has since been applied widely to the approach of shareholders to corporate governance.

Table [7.1]   Characteristics of insider and outsider systems

Insider	Outsider
Firms owned predominantly by insider shareholders who also wield control over management	Large firms controlled by managers but owned predominantly by outside shareholders
System characterized by little separation of ownership and control such that agency problems are rare	System characterized by separation of ownership and control, which engenders significant agency problems
Hostile takeover activity is rare	Frequent hostile takeovers acting as a disciplining mechanism on company management
Concentration of ownership in a small group of shareholders (founding family members, other companies through pyramidal structures, state ownership)	Dispersed ownership
Excessive control by a small group of 'insider' shareholders	Moderate control by a large range of shareholders
Wealth transfer from minority shareholders to majority shareholders	No transfer of wealth from minority shareholders to majority shareholders
Weak investor protection in company law	Strong investor protection in company law
Potential for abuse of power by majority shareholders	Potential for shareholder democracy
Majority shareholders tend to have more 'voice' in their investee companies	Shareholding characterized more by 'exit' than by 'voice'

investor legal protection and ownership concentration in corporate governance systems around the world. They adopted a narrow, agency theory perspective of corporate governance, associated with the 'finance' paradigm, examining corporate governance purely in terms of its contribution to solving the agency problem and its importance in helping companies to raise finance from shareholders. The paper emphasized that a high degree of legal investor protection was necessary to persuade investors to hand their money over to companies. Legal systems characterized by low levels of investor protection were found to be associated with poorly developed capital markets. The main problem was that, without strong investor protection, management could expropriate shareholders' funds. The paper outlined a number of ways in which this could happen. Managers could expropriate shareholders' funds by blatantly absconding with their money (e.g., where corporate ownership is in the form of pyramidal structures). Expropriation could also take a more subtle form, with managers using transfer pricing. However:

[a]n even more dramatic alternative is to sell the assets, and not just the output, of the company to other manager-owned businesses at below market prices.

(Shleifer and Vishny, 1997, p. 742)

One of the only ways for shareholders to counter weakness in legal investor protection is by being significantly large. The authors explained that if 'large' shareholders, such as institutional investors, can concentrate their shareholdings, then they can monitor management in investee companies by gaining enough control over the company's assets to earn 'respect' from the management. We have seen in Chapter 5 that institutional investors in the UK have become such powerful shareholders that they are now able to influence company management through engagement and dialogue, and therefore are able to monitor management through their actions. In this respect, the UK corporate governance system is taking on characteristics of an insider rather than an outsider system, with institutional investors becoming insiders who own and also control companies to some extent. However, the term 'large', in Shleifer and Vishny (1998), referred to holdings of over 25% and, despite their size and influence, institutional investors in the UK do not tend to hold such large stakes in individual companies. However, Shleifer and Vishny's assertion that large shareholders can only exercise control via voting rights, and therefore their level of control is determined by legal protection of voting rights, no longer applies in the UK, as engagement has usurped voting as a primary form of shareholder activism.

The most influential papers in the area of international corporate governance, to date, have been written by a group of authors (namely, La Porta et al., 1997). They explored in more depth the links between legal systems and corporate governance for a sample of 49 countries around the world. They explained that there were three general legal traditions operating across the globe. The French origin legal system is known to afford the lowest level of investor protection whereas the English origin legal system of common law affords the highest level of investor protection. The German and Scandinavian origin legal systems lie somewhere in between these two extremes. La Porta et al. (1998) studied the ownership structure of the 10 largest non-financial corporations for a cross-section of 49 countries, including 9 from East Asia. They found concentrated ownership structures in those countries that have traditionally fallen into the 'insider' mould. La Porta et al. (1999) studied the control structure of the 20 largest publicly traded companies in 4 East Asian countries (as well as 23 other countries around the world). Their evidence firmly supported the insider model for many East Asian economies characterized by a concentration of ownership, resulting in control of companies being held predominantly by a small number of owners, although less so in Japan and South Korea.

La Porta et al. (1999) investigated the ownership structure of large companies in 27 countries around the world in order to identify the ultimate controlling shareholders in those companies. Contrary to the portrayal of corporate ownership by Berle and Means (1932) which suggested that companies were owned by a widely dispersed group of shareholders and controlled by a small group of managers, this paper found evidence that the weight of companies were controlled either by families or by the state. Furthermore, they found little evidence of significant control by large financial institutions. The paper found that the shareholders with ultimate control tended to have power over their investee companies that was significantly greater than their cash flow rights. They seemed to have achieved this via the use of pyramids and participation in management. As well as outlining the differences between countries' corporate governance systems at an international level, much of the emerging literature focuses on the movement toward global convergence of corporate governance, toward one common framework. Debate centres around what characteristics this eventual system will portray.

Moving toward convergence?

International harmonization is now common in all areas of business. For example, in recent years we have observed strong moves toward international harmonization in the area of accounting and financial reporting, with the International Accounting Standards Board driving toward a comprehensive set of internationally acceptable standards for accounting. As a result of rising international trade and transnational business links, the development of internationally comparable business practices and standards is becoming increasingly necessary. The need for a global convergence in corporate governance derives from the existence of forces leading to international harmonization in financial markets, with increasing international investment, foreign subsidiaries and integration of the international capital markets. Companies are no longer relying on domestic sources of finance but are attempting to persuade foreign investors to lend capital. Corporate governance standardization is one way of building confidence in a country's financial markets and of enticing investors to risk funds. We now look at several initiatives aimed at standardizing corporate governance at a global level.

The OECD Principles

One of the most significant influences on corporate governance reform at a global level has been the introduction of several international corporate governance codes of practice. The first set of internationally acceptable standards of corporate governance were produced by the Organization for Economic Co-operation and Development (OECD, 1999). The OECD is an international organization, based in Paris. Its membership comprises 29 countries from all around the world. These principles represented a lowest common denominator of principles for 'good' corporate governance. Many of the principles displayed similarities to the Cadbury Code (1992) and covered such issues as equitable treatment of shareholders, shareholder responsibilities, transparency and disclosure in terms of corporate reporting and audit, the role and responsibilities of company boards of directors, and the importance of non-executive directors. For the purposes of the OECD Principles, corporate governance was defined as, 'that structure of relationships and corresponding responsibilities among a core group consisting of shareholders, board members and managers designed to best foster the competitive performance required to achieve the corporation's primary objective' (IMF, 2001). As we can see from this definition, the OECD attempted to describe corporate governance in the broadest terms, in order to embrace as many different forms of corporate governance system as possible. However, one of the problems with the OECD Principles and code of practice was their impotence, as they have no legislative power. Nevertheless, their impact has been substantial. Countries have used them as a reference point for self-assessment and for developing their own codes of best practice in corporate governance. In 1999 ministers representing the 29 countries in the OECD voted unanimously to endorse the OECD Principles (Monks and Minow, 2001). The World Bank has researched many countries around the world to assess the extent to which they have complied with the OECD principles, and all of these country assessments are available on the Internet.

The ICGN statement on the OECD Principles
The International Corporate Governance Network (ICGN) is an international organization comprising many groups interested in corporate governance reform. The organization represents the interests of investors, financial intermediaries and companies, *inter alia*. The organization promotes discussion on corporate governance issues and holds an annual conference for members, policy makers and academics, which acts as a forum for debate. The ICGN has been instrumental in promoting the OECD Principles and produced a statement to this effect in 1999. The statement confirmed the OECD Principles as the foundation stone of good corporate governance. However, they provided guidance for companies on how to put the Principles into practice, by presenting the essence of the Principles in a 'working kit' statement of corporate governance criteria. The ICGN approach to the OECD Principles was reproduced in Monks and Minow (2001).

The CalPERS principles
Another significant step to harmonize standards of corporate governance was taken by CalPERS, the California Public Employees' Retirement System, in the USA. CalPERS established a set of principles that they considered were the minimum standards with which all markets throughout the world should strive to comply (see CalPERS, 1999). The aim of these standards was to allow markets across the world to function freely and equitably for all investors. A global compromise in corporate governance was clearly a remit of these principles with the aim of creating a free, efficient and globally competitive market in all countries. A main characteristic of the principles was to attain increased and comparable levels of accountability (by companies to stakeholders) between countries. One primary emphasis of seeking to establish global convergence in corporate governance standards was to achieve

'long-term vision'. This would involve company managers in companies across the world creating long-term strategies.

The European Union

The European Commission of the European Union has spent a number of years deliberating about the ways in which it could provide guidance on corporate governance to its members. The report from the Centre for European Policy Studies (CEPS, 1995) documented the substantial reforms that have taken place in recent years in Western European countries' corporate governance systems. Within the European Union there has been, to date, no attempt to develop an overarching code of corporate governance best practice for member states. A detailed comparative study of existing corporate governance codes within European Union member states has been carried out that found substantial commonalities between the codes (Weil, Gotshal & Manges LLP, 2002). There are at present 42 corporate governance codes of practice existing in European Union member countries. However, differences that were found to exist were attributed to differences between the countries themselves. It is considered inadvisable by the European Union to force member states to harmonize as a result of regulation. The consensus is that harmonization should take place at a natural pace rather than through the imposition of a European Union-wide code of practice.

In June 2003 Frits Bolkestein, EU Commissioner for the Internal Market and Taxation, outlined the top regulatory priorities for the Financial Services Action Plan and corporate governance. He stated that the approach of the EU Commission was to provide essential measures at a pan-European level, at the same time encouraging better co-ordination among members' codes of conduct. The Commission is focusing on increasing transparency and disclosure, as well as improving the effective exercise of shareholder rights. The Commission requires listed companies in all EU member states to publish an annual statement of their structures and practices for corporate governance, which should as a minimum cover: the operation and powers of the shareholder meeting; the composition and function of the board and relevant committees; the national codes of conduct to which the company subscribes; and the steps taken for compliance along with an explanation for any failure to do so (European Financial Services Regulation, 2003). The Commission also requires institutional investors to disclose their policies for investment and the exercise of voting rights.

The Commonwealth guidelines

The corporate governance guidelines produced by the Commonwealth have focused attention in the last couple of years on the evolution of corporate governance systems in a number of developing African economies. However, there are relatively few studies that focus on African countries' corporate governance systems. Full details of the Commonwealth initiatives in promoting corporate governance harmonization are available on the Internet, on the Commonwealth website (http://www.thecommonwealth.org).

The outcome of corporate governance convergence

The ability of any international code of best practice to be applied successfully depends on the extent to which such varied systems of corporate governance can comply in practice with the recommendations. Each country has a system of corporate governance characterized by extremely different legal structures, financial systems and structures of corporate ownership, culture and economic factors. South Korea, for example, entered the OECD in 1996. The country has been characterized traditionally by corporate bodies with strong family control (the *chaebol* groups) and state influence. In addition, South Korea's legal protection of investors was, until the last few years, relatively low. Taiwan, although similar with respect to the extent of family ownership and control, is characterized by companies with extremely different board structures. Taiwanese companies have a supervisory system as well as a main board of directors. Such different existing corporate governance frameworks make the application of blanket codes of practice extremely problematic. Principles, such as those produced by the OECD, that are to be applied to countries with such different systems need to be flexible and not too prescriptive. Such differences as a unitary or a dual-board structure are not flexible and need to be accommodated in any initiative aimed at international standardization of corporate governance. Therefore, corporate governance reform at the global level needs to be effected with sensitivity for such international differences. It is important that countries can retain their individuality, while trying to harmonize their corporate governance standards to reflect good practice. Indeed, it is widely acknowledged that a 'one size fits all' approach is unrealistic, as 'alien practices cannot be transplanted or imposed' (Monks and Minow, 2001, p. 252). A problem for many policy makers and politicians is the potential for countries to be forced into Anglo-American style capitalism and corporate governance, when this is not the best route for them to take, given the characteristics of the economy. This is a sensitive political issue and one that requires careful treatment in all attempts to reform corporate governance. Nevertheless, investors can only be attracted to buy shares in foreign stock markets if they feel that basic standards of corporate governance, understandable at an international level, are being adhered to. In this sense the OECD has helped to further the development of stock markets around the world and is aiding capital market integration. There is however a body of academic research that has presented a case against corporate governance convergence. Mayer (2000) argued vehemently against corporate governance convergence suggesting that systems should remain inherently different so as to promote competition and take advantage of comparative advantage.

As we have seen from our earlier discussion (p. 149), both the insider and outsider systems possess advantages and disadvantages, and as both have proved successful it is difficult to argue relative superiority or inferiority. However, in recent years there have been moves toward some level of convergence. Countries with traditionally outsider-dominated systems have made significant efforts to reduce the main problem associated with outsider systems (namely, that of agency). We have seen from our detailed discussion of corporate governance reform in the UK that the agency problem has been dealt with via a broad range of initiatives, such as improving the effectiveness of non-executive directors, of the audit function, of the relationship between institutional investors and their investee companies. We have seen how ownership structure has been transformed by the increasing concentration of ownership in large financial institutions and the impact of this on control in companies. This agenda for corporate governance reform is not unique to the UK but has also been instigated in other outsider-dominated economies, such as the USA and Australia. Similarly, countries with traditionally insider-dominated systems of corporate governance have been attempting to alleviate some of the problems associated with their type of system. Many countries in East Asia have focused on improving the legal protection of minority shareholders. They have concentrated on improving corporate accountability by, for example, forcing companies to produce consolidated accounts. Further, traditionally insider-dominated systems have been encouraging greater dispersion of equity ownership. This has helped to cultivate a broader shareholder base and to encourage greater shareholder democracy.

The notion of a global convergence in corporate governance has been discussed in the literature in a number of ways. Overall, there seems to be a general *rapprochement* of corporate governance structures, with perhaps a trend toward a global compromise that may eventually lead to a worldwide system lying somewhere in between the traditional insider/outsider extremes. Theoretically speaking then, what would this global compromise involve? What characteristics would such a compromise adopt? Solomon et al. (1999) considered how an eventual global corporate governance compromise would look. They considered that, theoretically, a global convergence in corporate governance would be likely to take the most effective and successful characteristics from the existing systems around the world. Countries would eventually adopt those characteristics that would lead to the optimum balance between efficient business operations and an ethical, stakeholder-oriented society. They suggested that, from the direction of current trends and forces in international investment and current reforms in systems of corporate governance, an eventual global compromise would involve economies being mainly outsider-dominated but displaying characteristics of long-termism rather than short-termism. This would be an attempt to merge the competitive market forces of the traditional Anglo-American systems of finance and control with the more long-term styles of management and investment prevalent in the traditional insider systems of corporate governance. Figure 7.1 illustrates this view of global convergence in corporate governance by depicting a move from the extreme forms of the insider and outsider systems toward a similar and internationally accepted system of finance, investment and management.

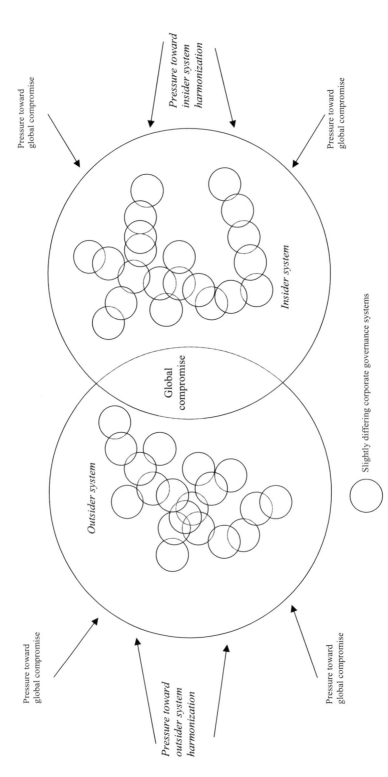

Figure [7.1] A global convergence in corporate governance

Reproduced by permission of Blackwell Publishers Journals

Pressure toward global compromise

Pressure toward insider system harmonization

Pressure toward global compromise

Insider system

Global compromise

Outsider system

Pressure toward global compromise

Pressure toward outsider system harmonization

Pressure toward global compromise

Slightly differing corporate governance systems

Country studies

As academic and professional research into corporate governance has grown progressively in recent years, academics and practitioners have started to study corporate governance systems across the globe. There has been a proliferation of country studies, investigating the process of corporate governance reform for an individual countries. The aims of these studies are varied but tend to focus on:

- defining the traditional system of corporate governance within a country and analysing the factors that have led to that system;

- comparing the country's system with other systems around the world and attempting to categorize the country as 'insider-dominated' or 'outsider-dominated';

- considering recent changes within the country's financial system and its relationship with other economies;

- evaluating the impact of recent changes on the country's corporate governance system;

- discussing the corporate governance system that will arise from recent developments and whether or not the country will comply with a general trend toward global convergence in corporate governance;

- suggesting the characteristics of a 'converged' system of corporate governance;

- using empirical evidence (econometric evidence, questionnaire evidence, interview evidence) to support the author's arguments.

In the next chapter we consider corporate governance in a sample of countries around the world, in the form of a 'reference dictionary'. We focus specifically on research into each country's corporate governance system. Clearly, we do not intend to provide an exhaustive coverage of all the countries, as this would be beyond the scope of the current text. We cannot possibly do justice to corporate governance in every country in one chapter of a general corporate governance text. However, we attempt to give a flavour of different systems of corporate governance around the world by illustrating the main forms of corporate governance system with selected examples. The choice of countries reflects to a certain extent our research interest in a number of East Asian economies.

Chapter summary

This chapter has introduced some of the international initiatives aimed at reforming and harmonizing corporate governance at a global level. We have discussed the publication by organizations such as the OECD of internationally acceptable standards for corporate governance. The OECD produced one of the first sets of international corporate governance standards which were intended to represent a lowest common denominator of corporate governance standards for companies around the world. We have summarized the principal characteristics of the 'insider' and 'outsider' extreme forms of corporate governance and shown that, despite the 'Cinderella problem', categorization can be a useful tool to enable further analysis and research. Further, we have discussed some of the literature relating to international corporate governance comparisons as well as a sample of the research that examines the factors that influence a country's system of corporate governance. Specifically, we have shown the importance of a country's legal system and corporate ownership structure in determining its corporate governance. Further, we have considered the extent to which a global convergence in corporate governance is possible and the type of system to which countries will aspire.

Questions for reflection and discussion

1 To what extent do you consider that the research into factors determining a country's corporate governance system is useful? Are you persuaded that corporate ownership structure and countries' legal systems have been more relevant to the evolution of corporate governance in countries around the world than factors such as culture and politics?

2 Do you think that the insider–outsider framework is a useful basis for analysing and discussing corporate governance systems in an international context?

3 *A global convergence in corporate governance is under way. In a few years there will be one internationally acceptable model of corporate governance that will be based on the US market-based, outsider-type system.* Do you agree with the above statement? Support your view with a discussion and refer to appropriate academic work and other published sources that you have read.

Chapter 8

A reference dictionary of corporate governance systems

Aim and objectives

This chapter illustrates the ongoing process of global corporate governance reform, using a sample of countries from around the world. The specific objectives of this chapter are to:

- illustrate the broad diversity of corporate governance systems worldwide by outlining the main characteristics of the systems in a selection of countries;

- outline the specific codes of practice and policy documents that have been developed in a sample of countries around the world and evaluate their impact, with reference to academic studies.

Argentina

A paper by Apreda (2001) provided evidence on two issues. First, it supported the allusion that there has been a marked shift in ownership and control in Argentina from large, family-owned domestic companies toward foreign groups and investment funds. Second, the paper provided evidence that while coping with corporate governance issues, Argentina has followed the common law countries' tradition, fostering a capital market-based financial system and swapping its corporate governance practices outright. The paper discussed the historical system of corporate governance in Argentina and its process of reform in recent years. The country was characterized by substantial family control and state ownership of companies, inefficient corporate operations and a closed economy. In the 1990s this situation changed dramatically with Argentina opening its borders to trade and investment and attempting to improve its system of corporate governance. Reform has included a privatization programme and a series of reforms of company law.

Australia

Stapledon (1996) compared the role of institutional investors in Australia with that of institutional investors in the UK. He explained that Australia has been characterized traditionally as having an outsider system of corporate governance, possessing the same basic characteristics as the UK. Despite this general similarity, there are significant differences between the two countries with respect to ownership structure and level of shareholder involvement in companies. The quoted corporate sector is not as significant in Australia as it is in the UK. Further, there is a higher incidence of founding family and intercompany ownership in Australia than in the UK. As in the UK, the two largest categories of institutional investor are the occupational pension funds and insurance companies (Stapledon, 1996). The early 1990s witnessed a growth in shareholder activism in Australia, with the introduction of the Australian Investment Managers' Group (AIMG), which provides a mechanism for collective shareholder action. Stapledon (1996) compared the level of institutional investor involvement in Australian companies with that in the UK, concluding that until the mid-1990s Australian shareholder activism was far less evident. He considered this was because Australian companies were effectively immune from intervention by institutional investors, as they tended to have a significantly large non-institutional shareholder base that controlled the company. Australia has its own code of corporate governance practice deriving from the Bosch Report (1995). Bosch (1993) described the development of the Bosch Report. From his discussion it seems that the Bosch Report followed the UK Cadbury Report (1992) closely.

Bahrain

Although Bahrain does not have a code of best practice for corporate governance, companies are established according to the Commercial Companies Law 2001 (Hussain and Mallin, 2002). This law requires that companies have a board of directors that acts in a responsible manner and that shareholders exercise their voting rights. In 2001 Hussain and Mallin conducted a questionnaire survey to investigate the status of corporate governance in Bahrain. They sent the questionnaire to all companies listed on the Bahrain Stock Exchange Market, finding that listed companies in Bahrain have in place some of the features of international corporate governance 'best practice'. However, they did question the effectiveness of the nomination committees and felt that company directors tended to be entrenched in their attitudes.

Belgium

In a paper examining corporate governance in Belgium, Wymeersch (1994) explained that Belgian companies were generally secretive and unaccountable to the outside world until a process of reform in 1991, when a series of amendments to Belgian company law focused on minority shareholder protection and rights. Also, corporate disclosure has been improved substantially. This is another example of an insider-type system becoming more market-oriented. Institutional investors in Belgium constitute about 20% of shareholding, with shareholder activism on the increase. However, the market for corporate control through takeover has been viewed as relatively undeveloped. There is a Belgian code of corporate governance, the Cardon Report (1998).

Canada

Daniels and Waitzer (1993) described the Canadian system in detail, emphasizing the importance of improving corporate governance in order to remain globally competitive and to attract foreign investment. An in-depth review of corporate governance was performed by Daniels and Morck (1996), which considered various policy options for the future development of Canadian corporate govern- ance. Their study showed that there was an element of outsider-type corporate governance in Canada, as some of Canada's largest companies and all its major chartered banks were widely held by a large number of small shareholders, each of whom had little effective control over managerial decision making. However, they also showed that this type of ownership structure was not common, quoting evidence that only 16% of the 550 largest Canadian companies were placed in this mould (Morck and Stangeland, 1994). Indeed, research has shown that most large Canadian companies were not widely held by investors. Rao and Lee-Sing (1995) found that in more than three-quarters of the Canadian companies they studied, one large shareholder controlled at least 20% or more of the voting shares. Corporate ownership was found to be concentrated significantly in the hands of company management, leading to management control over director appointments and cor- porate decision making. Although this situation removes the traditional agency problem to some extent, other problems are introduced, as managerial control can lead to the appointment of board members for reasons of friendship rather than merit. Indeed, Morck and Stangeland (1994) showed that Canadian companies whose dominant shareholders were their founders performed significantly worse than other companies of comparable age and size. Daniels and Morck (1996) stressed that improving corporate governance in Canada was essential, arguing that its absence would erode public confidence in Canada's financial markets and depress company share prices. This would result in Canadian companies experienc- ing difficulties in raising equity capital. These arguments may be applied to countries around the world in an attempt to support corporate governance reform. One way of improving corporate governance is to encourage monitoring of company manage- ment by institutional investors, as discussed in Chapter 5. Institutional investors controlled over 38% of Canadian companies in the mid-1990s (Rao and Lee-Sing, 1995), and that proportion has increased gradually. Their influence on corporate governance is likely to increase commensurately, as it has in the UK, Australia and other countries. Corporate governance reform in Canada was encouraged by the publication of the Dey Report (1994) and by the publication of a series of corporate governance standards by the institutional shareholder representative group, Pensions Investment Association of Canada (PIAC, 1998).

Chile

Following an upgrade of the legislative and regulatory framework dealing with corporate governance, Chile has become a standard setter for the entire Latin American region (Frémond and Capaul, 2003). Chile's system of corporate governance fits into the traditional insider model, with concentrated corporate ownership and pyramidal ownership structures. The stock market is quite large, with 249 companies listed on the Santiago Stock Exchange at the end of 2001. Frémond and Capaul concluded that Chile complied reasonably well with the OECD Principles for good corporate governance. Seven pension funds and insurance companies held 30% of total assets at the end of 2001. The evidence suggests that pension funds have influenced corporate governance in Chile, urging better disclosure of information by companies, as well as lobbying for the protection of minority shareholder rights. The country's legal system is based on French law, which is typical of insider-type corporate governance systems. However, a complete overhaul of company law in 2000 has strengthened the corporate governance framework, focusing on improving shareholder protection. However, in relation to corporate accountability to a broad group of stakeholders, Chile seems to be falling short as:

> Although the legal framework protecting stakeholders is fairly well developed, Chilean corporations still too often relate to their stakeholders in a confrontational manner, perpetrating the idea that entrepreneurs and stakeholders are rent-seeking individuals. Anecdotal evidence indicates that this approach often leads to corporate short-sightedness, which may jeopardize important opportunities for future economic development in Chile.
>
> (Frémond and Capaul, 2003, p. 9)

This suggests an acknowledged link between corporate social responsibility and corporate/economic performance, which we explore in Chapter 9.

China

As China is still a communist state, progress in the capital markets and in the area of corporate governance has been slower than in several other East Asian countries. However, as in many of the Central and Eastern European economies there has been a significant move toward a more liberal market system and a more transparent and 'Western' corporate governance system. In China, until recently, companies were owned chiefly by the Government. Consequently, China fits into the insider mould, with little separation of ownership and control. The Government owned Chinese companies and ran them. Recent reforms have initiated extensive privatization of these State Owned Enterprises (SOEs). Tam (2000) discussed the state of corporate governance reform in China and explained how SOEs have been privatized in some detail. SOEs were restructured into shareholding companies whose shares could then be traded on one of the two Chinese stock markets, the Shanghai and Shenzhen, which only opened in 1990 and 1991, respectively. One of the main corporate governance problems for Chinese companies has been to create a separation between company management and government, because the Government, as the principal owner of Chinese companies, has traditionally had a substantial influence over company activities and decision making. The notorious agency problems associated with outsider-type systems are now emerging in China, as they are in all countries with nascent equity markets and whose companies' capital structures are undergoing transformation. At face value it seems that corporate governance is improving considerably in Chinese companies. Company law in China specifies three levels of control over company activities: the shareholders' general meeting; the board of directors and supervisors; and company management. However, despite corporate governance reform progressing quickly there are evident weaknesses (Shi and Weisert, 2002). The shareholders' AGM has been considered impotent as managers tend to rubber-stamp decisions they made earlier, thus gaining control over the meetings. There is in practice a negligible amount of shareholder democracy. Further, insiders tend to gain positions on the boards of directors and supervisory board and simply become puppets for the controlling parties. Minority shareholders have few rights and their concerns are usually ignored by majority shareholders. As in all the countries we are studying, reform involves a long and difficult process that takes many years, even when the systems and structures are in place.

The Czech Republic

Mallin and Jelic (2000) summarized corporate governance changes in three countries in Central and Eastern Europe, making comparisons between the programmes of reform between the countries involved. They highlighted the commonalities and differences between the processes of change in the countries involved. For the Czech Republic they explained that during the communist regime Czechoslavakia was more tightly controlled than other Central and Eastern European countries. An agenda for corporate governance reform was instigated in 1991 that needed to be extremely ambitious in order to achieve privatization and an active market for corporate control. Shops and small business units were the initial focus of the privatization programme, with large-scale businesses being included over time. Despite reform, the state has retained substantial control over privatized Czech companies. In 1991, 400 Investment Privatization Funds (IPFs) were created that were intended to mimic Western mutual funds. Coffee (1996) found that IPFs and individual investors were mainly involved in the privatization programme. According to Mallin and Jelic (2000) it was unclear whether IPFs or banks will evolve as the dominant forces in Czech corporate governance.

An assessment of corporate governance in the Czech Republic was carried out by the World Bank and the International Monetary Fund (IMF, 2001). They explained that a major package of legislation affecting corporate governance was approved by Parliament for January 2001. This package included extensive changes to the country's Commercial Code, the Securities Act and the Auditing Act. As with most countries we are considering, changes to the legal framework are one of the main ways in which corporate governance reform is orchestrated, as a country's legal system is one of the most important factors influencing corporate governance. The assessment (IMF, 2001) stated that the changes to the Commercial Code were extensive, improving significantly the internal corporate governance mechanisms in the Czech Republic. However, they also suggested that, despite such changes, a number of institutional deficiencies implied that genuine improvements in corporate governance would take time. Such institutional deficiencies included a slow and inefficient court system. The report ended on a positive note:

> When implementation and enforcement of the new laws and regulations are strengthened, the Czech Republic will observe most of the principles on corporate governance.
>
> (IMF, 2001, p. 72)

France

The control of French companies tends to be divided between the state, company management and families. There is little dispersion of ownership and the system is clearly closer to the insider, rather than the outsider, model of corporate governance. The state has a powerful role in French companies, termed *dirigisme*, partly due to their necessary involvement in the redevelopment of industry following World War II (Monks and Minow, 2001). State control has included restructuring state-owned industries for policy purposes and ensuring that key industries remained under state control. Even listed companies are under state influence, as French financial institutions, such as banks and insurance companies, are state owned and/or controlled, and represent the major capital providers to private companies in France. An estimated two-thirds of French listed company shares are characterized by cross-company shareholdings, termed the *verrouillage* system. French boards are strong and control decision making in companies. They also interlock to a high degree. Monks and Minow (2001) provided statistics to show that, in 1989, 57 people accounted for one-quarter of all the board seats of the largest 100 listed companies in France. This is clear indication of director control. According to company law, French companies can choose either a unitary board (as in the UK) or a two-tier board structure (as in Germany), although most opt for a unitary board.

France has produced two codes of best practice in order to promote corporate governance reform (Viénot, 1995, 1999). The evidence suggests that companies have embraced the recommendations of the first report, as 92% of companies were applying the recommendations by 1999. Also, 30% of directors were classified as independent and 90% of boards had audit, remuneration and nomination committees (Monks and Minow, 2001).

Germany

German corporate governance has attracted significant interest from academics, as the German economy was extremely successful following World War II. Many attributed this success to the inherent differences between the German system of corporate governance and the Anglo-American system. The merits of the relationship-based, insider corporate governance system that has traditionally characterized German corporate governance have been heralded by many authors. The notorious short-termism problem, blamed for constraining British industry, was less evident in Germany, where long-term relationships between companies and their providers of finance led to long-term investment. This allowed companies to invest in long-term projects and enjoy a more secure financial environment. However, Edwards and Fischer (1994) questioned the extent to which superior economic performance was related to corporate governance in Germany.

In more recent times, such 'advantages' have become disadvantages for German companies, as they have not been able to attract capital from institutional investors in global markets, due to 'parochial governance practices that have obstructed shareholder rights' (Monks and Minow, 2001, p. 275). One initiative aimed at improving German corporate governance through better corporate transparency was the publication of a report by the *Deutsche Bundestag* (1998). Further, Germany produced a corporate governance code of best practice in January 2000, followed by an updated version in September 2001 (Government Commission, 2001). The code's stated aims were to present essential statutory regulations for the management and governance of German listed companies, as well as to contain internationally and nationally recognized standards for good and responsible governance. Clearly, achieving harmonization with internationally acceptable standards was a main driver of reform in Germany, as in most countries.

The German system of corporate governance is significantly different from the Anglo-American model in a number of respects. German companies are characterized by a two-tier board and significant employee ownership. The supervisory board, in theory, is intended to provide a monitoring role. However, the appointment of supervisory board members has not been a transparent process and has therefore led to inefficient monitoring and governance in many cases (Monks and Minow, 2001). Further, German corporate governance has been characterized traditionally by pyramidal ownership structures, with companies owning each other through a series of cross-shareholdings. There has also been a strong tendency toward employee representation, as a result of the Co-Determination Act of 1976, which stipulated that employees should be involved in the corporate governance mechanisms by being represented on supervisory boards. However, companies have rallied against the idea of co-determination since the 1970s, considering it infringed ownership rights (Alkhafaji, 1989). Employee representation at the heart of companies derives from an extremely different cultural attitude toward corporate governance from that operating in Anglo-Saxon economies. It is far more in keeping with a stakeholder, than a pure shareholder, approach to corporate governance.

Schilling (2001) discussed the recent changes in corporate governance in Germany, concluding that there are strong market forces pressuring for change in Germany. International institutional investment and increasingly open economies are forcing countries such as Germany to become more market-oriented. She suggested that there were moves toward a more equity-based system, with shareholders' involvement becoming increasingly important.

Hong Kong

Brewer (1997) discussed the evolution of Hong Kong's corporate governance system. This paper was written just before the handover of Hong Kong to China in June 1997. It is a professional rather than an academic paper and the author's discussion arises from his professional experience rather than from research. Brewer stated that, although Hong Kong appears to have an outsider system of corporate governance, it really has an insider system. He explained that in terms of company law, Hong Kong companies have imitated the UK model of a joint stock company. They have a broad base of owners, who delegate management of the business to a small number of company directors. However, the reality is very different. Ownership is not by a diverse range of outsiders who dominate control over the companies. Rather, in all companies, shareholding is concentrated and a small group of shareholders, or even a single shareholder, dominates the investee company management. Indeed, he states that up to 75% of a company's shares can be owned by management and friends of the management. There is therefore very little true separation of ownership and control, despite appearances. Two sets of corporate governance guidelines have been published in Hong Kong to promote corporate governance reform in the area of audit committee formation (HKSA, 1997) and boards of directors (SEHK, 1997).

Hungary

The evolving system of Hungarian corporate governance was discussed in Mallin and Jelic (2000). They explained that Hungary was more liberal than other economies in Central and Eastern Europe. A series of banking and accounting reforms took place in 1991 (see Pistor and Turkewitz, 1996). A privatization programme was initiated by the communist Hungarian Government in the early 1990s, and this programme of reform increased in pace as communism was dispensed with. As a result of the reforms the number of limited liabilities rose from 450 in 1988 to

79,395 in 1994. In the newly evolving Hungarian corporate governance system, banks appear to be taking on a major role.

India

India's Bombay Stock Exchange has the largest number of listed companies in the world. Yet, despite the size of the stock market in India, ownership remains concentrated in families and an insider-dominated structure seems to persist. However, Sarkar and Sarkar (2000) described the Indian system of corporate governance as a 'hybrid' of the outsider and insider model, as small shareholders participate in corporate governance. There is also significant institutional investor involvement in listed companies. Indeed, Sarkar and Sarkar (2000) found some evidence of a positive relationship between block shareholding by institutional investors and company value. They also provided evidence that the principal shareholders of Indian listed companies were: directors and their relatives, corporate bodies, foreign investors, Government-controlled financial institutions and the public. Their statistics indicated that about 43% of all sample companies had equity ownership by corporate bodies in excess of 25%. Directors and their relatives held about 21% of shares in private companies. This pattern of ownership results from the predominance of family ownership in listed companies.

India is following the global trend in reforming its corporate governance system. As in other countries a series of corporate scandals focused keen attention on corporate governance weaknesses (see Illustration 8.1). However, as a former colony of Britain, India has a UK-style legal system that offers a reasonable level of protection to minority shareholders in comparison with other East Asian countries. Since the second half of the 19th century, Indian industry has generally followed an English common law framework of joint stock limited liability (Goswami, 2000). The Confederation of Indian Industry (CII, 1998) have produced a code of practice aimed at reforming corporate governance. The adoption of a structural adjustment and globalization programme by the Indian Government in 1991 forced corporate governance policy attention on corporate governance issue. A survey of company directors in India showed that they were keen on reforming corporate governance in the wake of the Asian crisis and were focusing on improving the board of directors and investor relations (Solomon et al., 2003).

Indonesia

Indonesia represents a corporate governance system in East Asia with an emerging stock market. Most companies are family-owned and controlled. Indonesia's corporate governance fits neatly into the insider-dominated model and demonstrated severe cases of minority shareholder wealth expropriation following the Asian

Illustration 8.1

Scandal in India

A major fraud in the securities markets was uncovered in April 1992 in India. Harshad Mehta illegally led a cartel of bull players in the stock market to use liquidity provided by interbank credit and debit receipts to drive up the prices of certain company shares. The cartel succeeded in driving up the Bombay Stock Exchange Sensex index by almost 150%, due to the lack of depth and width of the Indian stock market as well as to the herding mentality of investors in the market (see Goswami, 2000). Specifically, he had diverted funds from the public sector firm Maruti Udyog Limited (MUL) to his own accounts, provoking a record fall in the index. In April 1992 the State Bank of India asked Mehta to return Rs 500 crores (1 crore = 10 million) that he had illegally put into the stock market (*Frontline*, 2002). As soon as Harshad's activities became public knowledge, the markets crashed. However, it was not until 1997 that a joint parliamentary committee could produce adequate evidence to link him to events. This affair demonstrated an urgent need to address transparency and the regulation of financial markets in India. The effects of Harshad's unethical activities have spilled over into the 21st century. In 1999 he was given a four-year jail sentence for defrauding MUL, but continued to appeal. However, he was arrested in 2001 for fresh fraud charges, the alleged misappropriation of 27 lakh (1 lakh = 100,000) shares of 80 companies (*The Hindu*, 12 January 2002). Do leopards change their spots? See the Maxwell case in Illustration 3.1 for further discussion of this issue. On New Year's Eve 2001, Harshad died from a massive heart attack, but still left questions relating to the scandal a decade earlier (*The Hindu*, 12 January 2002). At the time of his death he was still in judicial custody. His death has left many unanswered questions. Why did it take 10 years to bring him to justice? What weaknesses in the financial markets allowed such abuse to succeed? As in the UK and other countries, such examples of unethical behaviour set a clear agenda for corporate governance reform.

financial crisis. For example, managers diverted funds in order to finance a political party in the Indonesian PT Bank Bali, between 1997 and 1998. Further, group managers transferred currency losses from a manufacturing company to a group-controlled bank in Sinar Mas Group between 1997 and 1998, which effectively represented expropriation of wealth from the bank's minority shareholders and creditors (see Johnson et al., 2000). These cases present a clear mandate for corporate governance reform, as in many other countries.

Italy

Italian corporate governance fits well into the insider mould, with companies being predominantly family-owned, or owned through a structure of cross-company shareholdings. Further, the shareholdings are extremely concentrated. The main shareholder in Italian companies (termed a blockholder) exerts control over the company's management. Melis (2000) described the insider system as 'relationship-based' and discussed the possibility that Italian law has favoured family control rather than shareholder protection. This has deterred small shareholders from investing in Italian companies. Indeed, Italian corporate governance mechanisms have been found to be so underdeveloped that they significantly retard the flow of external capital to firms (see Shleifer and Vishny, 1997). The process of corporate governance reform in Italy has been called the Draghi Reform, a new corporate law produced in 1998 (Draghi, 1998). The Draghi Reform was aimed at regulating financial markets and corporate governance in listed companies and should lead to better investor protection. It is not a code of practice like Cadbury but is rather a legally binding series of amendments to company law. This is interesting as it seems that countries with less developed market systems (which are categorized as strongly insider in nature) have had to develop mandatory, regulated corporate governance reforms, rather than the voluntary codes that have been applied in more market-based, developed economies. In this way the nature of codes of practice reveal much about the character of countries' traditional systems and state of their financial markets. It is evident that emerging markets are reforming corporate governance by means of changes to their company law. Overall, Italy has been characterized by an almost non-existent market for corporate control and poor capital market orientation.

Japan

Japan fell traditionally into the insider-dominated group (Hoshi et al., 1991) and had a 'credit-based' financial system (Zysman, 1983), as the economy was characterized by intercompany shareholdings, intercompany directorships and frequently substantial bank involvement. Japan's economy, despite the reorganization following World War II is still to some extent characterized by the *zaibatsu*, a group of family-run businesses that emerged as early as the 17th century (Bison, 1954). These business enterprises have since evolved into the *keiretsu*, which are related closely through share ownership to one or more banks. In this type of system, there is little takeover activity and shares are not traded as frequently in market-based economies. More recently, the trend has been toward a more market-dominated Japanese system of corporate governance (Cooke and Sawa, 1998), perhaps as a result of pressures arising from recent economic problems. However, Japan and other East Asian economies still retain a different attitude toward business from Anglo-American-style economies, as expressed in the following:

> East Asian and particularly Japanese capitalist structures emphasise trust, continuity, reputation and co-operation in economic relationships. Competition is ferocious, but co-operation is extensive; the juxtaposition of apparently inconsistent forms of behaviour may strike those schooled in Anglo-American capitalism as irrational, but for the Japanese the tension actually enhances the strength of each. There is even a widely quoted phrase for it—*kyoryoku shi nagara kyosa*—literally 'co-operating while competing', so that out of the subsequent chaos comes harmony.

> (Hutton, 1995, p. 269)

Indeed, the differences between the corporate governance systems in Japan, the USA, the UK and continental European models have been summarized recently as follows:

> The continental European and Japanese model of corporate enterprises are somewhat similar, in that a sense of corporate solidarity with social harmony is expected and actually exists. The Anglo-American model, by contrast, is based on a respect for individuality as the societal norm; a key factor defining the structure of corporate enterprise is the notion of a contractual relationship between equal individuals. In this Anglo-American model, the governance of the corporation is based on the notion that shareholders are entitled contractually to claim the residual profit as the ultimate risk-takers of the corporation. In the continental European and Japanese models however, management and employees are recognised as institutionally cooperative in the context of corporate governance.
> (Corporate Governance Forum of Japan, 1999, pp. 210–211)

Hoshi and Kashyap (2001) considered corporate governance, finance and investment in Japan from a historic viewpoint and made predictions about the way in which corporate governance and the Japanese economy would evolve in the future. The authors presented substantial empirical evidence (from gathering financial data over long periods of time) to support their arguments. Before World War II Japan's corporate system was dominated by huge family-owned businesses (the *zaibatsu*). However, the Americans broke these companies up and reduced their powers over the economy and the Japanese market after the war ended. After the war and until the 1970s Japan's system of corporate governance still fitted well into the 'insider-dominated' mould. Companies in Japan were mainly financed by bank loans and as already mentioned the *zaibatsu* evolved into the keiretsu (literally 'relationship investing'). The banks that owned companies also sat on company boards and played an important role in monitoring company management. Companies were strongly influenced by their bank managers. There was little separation of ownership and control, and companies were disciplined by their banks. Many have suggested that this system of corporate governance was superior to the UK and US systems.

A pattern is emerging in Japan that is being repeated in many countries around the world. The system of corporate governance traditionally dominated by 'banks and bureaucrats' is being replaced gradually by a market-oriented system. A decade ago, when the *keiretsu* system of complicated intercompany shareholdings was still flourishing, companies were protected from shareholder influence. A series of aggressive liquidations of banks holdings in Japanese companies is breaking the close ties that banks and companies have traditionally enjoyed in Japan. There has also been a transformation of corporate ownership structures. Institutional investors are now estimated to own almost three-quarters of the equity market in Japan, reflecting the ownership structure in the UK. Further, Japanese institutional investors are beginning to recognize the financial benefits that may be gained from improved corporate governance. For example, Sparx Asset Management, Japan's only listed independent fund manager, has launched a $200 million fund. The fund's management is based on actively improving the corporate governance of investee companies and has been inspired by the involvement of CalPERS,[1] the activist US pension fund (Tassell, 28 July 2003). Therefore, the Japanese system of corporate governance is gradually moving much further toward a market-based, outsider-dominated system of ownership and control.

Despite recent changes, the empirical evidence indicates that Japan continues to fit more closely within an insider than an outsider system, if we consider the empirical evidence. Significant concentration of ownership in Japanese companies has been found by a number of studies. Although the corporate governance system is increasingly dominated by financial institutions, it is also characterized by concentration of ownership rather than wide dispersion, which implies that the agency problems associated with the market-based model are less prominent. For example, Prowse (1992) found that for a sample of Japanese firms in the mid 1980s ownership was highly concentrated with financial institutions being the dominant class of large shareholders. Indeed, they found that ownership concentration in Japanese companies was significantly greater than in US companies, which is consistent with Japanese companies fitting into the insider-dominated model of corporate governance. Berglof and Perotti (1994) also found Japanese companies to be characterized by significant concentration of ownership. It seems that the Japanese model is resembling the UK model as they are both being transformed into market-based systems, with a high proportion of ownership by financial institutions, which is concentrated rather than dispersed. Japan has issued guidelines on exercising voting rights (Pension Fund Corporate Governance Research Committee, 1998) and a series of corporate governance principles (Corporate Governance Committee, 1998).

Jordan

Jordan's system of corporate governance is insider-oriented with most companies on the Amman stock exchange being owned predominantly by founding families. Accountability and transparency are almost non-existent with minority shareholders' rights being insignificant. There is currently no code of practice for corporate governance in Jordan. However, corporate governance reform is high on the agenda in Jordan. The newly formed Arab Business Council is likely to focus attention on corporate governance issues, as reform will help to boost investor confidence in the Middle East (Alrawi, 2003).

---

[1] This comment was made by Mr Shuhei Abe, founder and chief executive of Sparx Asset Management (see Tassell, 28 July 2003).

Malaysia

Traditionally, Malaysia typifies the insider-based model of corporate governance, with most companies owned and controlled by founding families. Corporate governance problems have been blamed in part for the way in which Malaysia (and other East Asian economies such as South Korea) succumbed to the financial crisis of 1997. This realization has inspired corporate governance reform throughout East Asia. A policy document aimed at improving corporate governance practice in Malaysian companies was produced in 1999 (High Level Finance Committee Report on Corporate Governance, 1999). Ow-Yong and Kooi Guan (2000) discussed the potential impact of the first code of practice for Malaysian corporate governance, published in the same year. The most salient characteristic of the Malaysian code was its mandatory nature. Recall that the Combined Code (2003) in the UK is essentially voluntary, following the spirit of 'comply and explain' (see Chapter 3). Regulation appears to have been more necessary in Malaysia, as in the past minority shareholders have had few rights. It seems that the efforts taken by Malaysian regulators and market participants to improve the country's corporate governance framework have improved Malaysia's standing in the region, according to the results of a survey carried out by the Kuala Lumpur Stock Exchange (KLSE) and PricewaterhouseCoopers (KLSE, 2002). Further, the survey provided strong evidence that Malaysia's corporate governance practices have improved since the code's publication. Specifically, institutional respondents to the survey suggested that a greater separation of company management and ownership had been achieved, as well as clearer definition of the roles and responsibilities of managers and directors, greater focus on internal control and increased disclosure of corporate non-financial information. Attention has also been paid to encouraging growth in shareholder activism, with the establishment of the Minority Shareholder Watchdog Group by some large institutional investors.

The Netherlands

The Dutch system of corporate governance is characterized by a two-tier board. This is common to a number of countries worldwide. Under this structure, overall management is carried out by the executive board. This board is responsible for day-to-day running of the business and general corporate operations. There is then a supervisory board that acts like a watchdog. It supervises the conduct of the executive board and provides advice when necessary. The supervisory board, known as the *Struktuurvennootschap*, is compulsory for large companies but optional for smaller companies. A report on corporate governance in The Netherlands was printed in the journal *Corporate Governance: An International Review*. The report summarized the recommendations for corporate governance reform arising from the Committee on Corporate Governance in October 1996. This Committee produced a report that dealt with: the profile, constitution, duties, appointments and remuneration of the supervisory board; procedures of the supervisory board; the work of the board of directors; the functioning of the AGM and investors' role in the organization; compliance with the Committee's recommendations; the function of the auditors; and corporate disclosure. The report is commonly referred to as the Peters Report (Peters Committee, 1997).

Nigeria

Yasaki (2001) discussed the evolution of corporate governance in Nigeria. The author explained that, before Nigeria became independent, company management was not controlled or monitored by external agents but that in recent years this has changed. Nigerian companies are being increasingly called on to increase account-ability. Yasaki (2001) focused specifically on the Nigerian banking industry. The Commonwealth initiatives aimed at improving corporate governance, embodied in their *Principles for Corporate Governance in the Commonwealth: Towards Global and Economic Accountability*, are having a substantial impact on corporate Nigeria and other Commonwealth countries.

Poland

Lawniczak (1997) described the process of stock market creation that has occurred as a result of a government policy to liberalize the Polish economy. Lawniczak explained that the Polish model of mass privatization was characterized by the development of National Investment Funds (NIFs). The introduction of this process was the 30 April 1993 Law on National Investment Funds and their Privatization. This assigned over 500 small and medium-sized companies to 15 NIFs that control 60% of the companies overall. The state retained 25% corporate ownership and corporate employees were given the remaining 15%. The role of the NIFs has been to invest in companies created by restructuring state-owned enter-prises and in other Polish companies. The mass-privatized companies were not sold but transferred free of charge to the NIFs. The eventual aim is for the ownership of shares under the NIFs to be transferred to the general public (individual investors). Shares should eventually be traded freely on the Warsaw Stock Exchange. However, the road toward a free market in Poland has been rocky. There have been severe problems of conflicts arising between management firms and companies' supervisory boards. Indeed, the evolving corporate governance system has been termed a 'Bermuda Triangle', which describes the problems involved in the complicated NIF governance relationship.

Koladkiewicz (2001) discussed the most recent developments in the process of corporate governance reform in Poland. She concluded that in the past 10 years the basic skeleton of a new corporate governance system has been constructed. She showed that Polish banks have been prepared to provide companies with necessary capital but have not wanted to take on an active ownership role. She also considered that there are still problems arising from the close relationship between companies' supervisory boards and the political environment. She indicated that there should be less control of corporations' activities by the state.

Russia

Since the end of the Cold War, Russia has been opening up its financial markets and the Russian stock market has been developing. In a way, the changes in Russia have probably been too fast and furious for the economy to keep up with. The legal framework has been trying to catch up with the pace at which a market economy has been developing in Russia. In 1996, Yeltsin, the President of the Russian Federation, produced a document aimed at enforcing greater shareholder rights (Yeltsin, 1996). Jesover (2001) discussed corporate governance reform in Russia, explaining that the collapse of the communist state led to rapid embrace of a decentralized, free economy. However, businesses are struggling to adapt to the fast pace of change. The 1990s witnessed wide-scale privatization in Russia. Although a large proportion of Russian companies were transferred from the public to the private sector, the upheaval created many problems. Instability in ownership rights ensued. Most companies are characterized by an insider system whereby the company is controlled by a controlling shareholder. Monitoring of company activities by outsiders, such as institutional investors, has been weak. Jesover (2001) argued that, unless Russia improved corporate governance substantially, Russian companies would not be able to attract finance from abroad. Foreign investment is essential for the development of the Russian economy in the long term and its accession to global competitiveness. The author also went through the OECD Principles for 'good' corporate governance and considered how they matched up with the situation in Russia. The paper suggested that there had been wide abuse of power by Russian companies and many examples of corporate misconduct, which have had a devastating impact on the country's international reputation. The conclusion of the paper was that the reforms would take a long time because they involve not just institutional and corporate reform but also deep change in the society's culture. It appears from the paper that Russia has been taking significant steps toward reforming corporate governance. The Supreme Arbitrazh Court and the Federal Commission for the Securities Market have focused their attention on the need for corporate governance reform, which signifies a move in the 'right' direction.

South Africa

The first King Report (1994) was published in South Africa in order to formalize an ongoing process of corporate governance reform. It was a code of corporate practice and conduct that was based on a broad consensus of the South African business community. One of the most distinguishing aspects of South African corporate governance reform has been its focus on a more stakeholder-oriented approach.

Illustration 8.2

Differentiating between accountability and responsibility

In Chapter 1 we discussed the differences between an agency approach to corporate governance that focuses on corporate accountability to shareholders and stakeholder theory. Stakeholder theory suggests that companies should discharge an accountability to other groups of stakeholders, rather than shareholders alone. The Corporate Governance committee in South Africa has thought long and hard about these issues and has adopted a form of stakeholder approach to corporate governance, but one that draws an extremely important and interesting distinction between accountability and responsibility, as follows:

> One is liable to render an account when one is accountable and one is liable to be called to account when one is responsible. In governance terms, one is accountable at common law and by statute to the company if a director and one is responsible to the stakeholders identified as relevant to the business of the company. The stakeholder concept of being accountable to all legitimate stakeholders must be rejected for the simple reason that to ask boards to be accountable to everyone would result in their being accountable to no one. The modern approach is for a board to identify the company's stakeholders, including its shareowners, and to agree policies as to how the relationship with those stakeholders should be advanced and managed in the interests of the company.
>
> (King Report, 2002, p. 5)

The Committee was clearly emphasizing the need to satisfy shareholders, as long as it is not to the detriment of other stakeholders. However, this approach toward stakeholders may be seen by some as a backward step away from a broader corporate social responsibility agenda. The quote above begs many questions, such as: What is this 'modern approach'? What evidence is there that such a modern approach is successful? Does it not seem that such an approach to corporate governance is focusing on the 'interests of the company', whereas corporate governance is more about running companies in the interests of at least the shareholders and then possibly other groups of stakeholders? The King Report (2002) states that it takes an inclusive approach to corporate governance.

The first King Report (1994) included a code of business ethics for companies and their stakeholders, representing one of the most forward-looking codes of corporate governance practice. However, 2002 saw the publication of an updated report, again taking the title the King Report (2002) from the chair of the Corporate Governance Committee, Mervyn E. King. The 2002 King Report continued in the same vein, by focusing on a stakeholder approach to corporate governance. In Illustration 8.2 we discuss the South African approach to accountability and responsibility as defined in the King Report (2002) in more detail.

South Korea

From a corporate governance perspective, the case of South Korea is intriguing, as reform has been speedy and has engendered massive changes. Since the 1980s the

Korean political environment has been liberalized. A recent President of the Republic of South Korea, Kim Dae Jung, has made efforts to attract foreign funds to Korea, to make Korean business more transparent, to improve corporate governance and to make Korea a globally competitive economy. He initiated a policy of reform called *segyhewa*, or 'globalization'. Until well after World War II, Korea was occupied by Japan. This meant that Korean business was influenced substantially by the Japanese structure of business. As in Japan, the corporate ownership structure has been characterized by founding family ownership concentration. The Korean *chaebol*, or conglomerate business groups, have arisen from small family-run companies and are now global players (e.g., Hyundai and LG). Until very recently, the corporate governance structure in Korea has kept its traditional 'insider' character. There has been little separation of ownership and control in Korean companies as the owners and managers have tended to be the same people at the highest level. Indeed, outdated hierarchical business strategies have been blamed in part for the way in which South Korea succumbed to the Asian crisis in 1997. As the following quote suggests:

> ... anachronistic activities by chaebol were part of what caused Korea's economic crisis and the government has the responsibility to protect the rights of the people.
>
> Lee Yong-keun, Chairman of the Financial Supervisory Commission
> (*Digital Korea Herald*, 27 April 2000)

However, in more recent times efforts have been made to create more equity financing for business and therefore to extend share ownership to a wider community of shareholders—institutional investors and the general public. The Government has forced companies to reduce debt in their financial structures and to take on equity finance to a greater extent. The proportion of institutional investor ownership in Korea is now about 35%—a lot lower than in the UK but a lot higher than it was before. Another important aspect of Korean corporate governance is the historic influence of factors such as the state, culture and the legal system. We explore the influence of culture in more depth in Illustration 8.3. Until relatively recently, company law in Korea gave hardly any rights to minority shareholders (such as institutional investors). This is changing dramatically now. The Asian crisis in 1997 hit South Korea heavily and resulted in significant expropriation of minority shareholder wealth by majority shareholders in such companies as Samsung Electronics and SK Telecom (see Johnson et al., 2000). Such transfers of wealth highlighted a need for tightening of company law. The Government has had a substantial impact on company activities as state-owned banks have provided finance and the Government has instructed Korean companies on the strategic direction they wish them to take. Links with the state are now being lessened.

Illustration 8.3

The influence of culture on corporate governance

From a cultural point of view, Confucianism has had an important role to play in the conduct of Korean business. This religious tradition still dominates the Korean people, although the process of Westernization that is ongoing in East Asian countries is reducing Confucian influence. A hierarchical structure has always been characteristic of Confucianism, with family structures dominated by the 'father' of the household and women playing minor roles. This is changing but remains in existence. Solomon et al. (2002a) discussed the traditional, historic framework of corporate governance that prevailed in South Korea before the recent reforms in some detail. They explained that Confucianism emphasizes the importance of the family and provides moral guidance on how human relationships should be conducted (Song, 1997). Reflecting Confucian family structures, within the traditional Korean *chaebol*, power filters down from the chairman (the head of the *chaebol* owner family) to the most junior employees, through a top-down, hierarchical structure. Indeed, the hierarchical structure of the *chaebol* has been interpreted as military in nature (Song, 1997). As well as the writings of Confucius, Korean folklore, influenced by the Confucian tradition, has had a strong impact on business. The three values emphasized by Koreans are commitment, seniority and humility (Choi and Wright, 1994). In relation to corporate ethics, Ungson et al. (1997) explained that Daewoo, for example, emphasized 'coprosperity', which involved companies shouldering responsibility to give equal benefits to workers, suppliers, customers, partners and the Government—a true stakeholder approach. Solomon et al. (2002a) also explained the diverse range of initiatives that have been instigated in order to improve and develop the country's corporate governance system. The paper attempted to evaluate the success of the agenda for corporate governance reform. A conceptual framework was proposed to aid analysis of the reforms. A further paper (Solomon et al., 2002b) provided empirical evidence from a postal questionnaire and personal interviews conducted in Korea. The results indicated that institutional investors in South Korea were becoming far more active in corporate governance and were taking more interest in corporate governance issues. The paper also documented in some detail the recent amendments to Korean company law in terms of specific changes to the Korean Commercial Code (see also Hemmings and Solomon, 1998; Solomon et al., 1999). Overall, it appears that the pace of reform has been heightened since the Asian crisis. The Korean culture is changing, embracing a less hierarchical attitude to company management and encouraging companies to become more transparent and accountable. In a way it is sad to see a country's traditions being watered down. However, corporate governance, like society, is dynamic in nature. It is quite clear that if Korea wants to keep its status as a global business player, corporate governance reform is an essential tool to success.

Taiwan

Taiwan's system of corporate governance fits neatly into the insider mould, with the majority of companies characterized by family control and concentrated share ownership. The legal system in Taiwan derives from the German mould and therefore places the Taiwanese system somewhere between the Anglo-Saxon type system and the French law-based systems of stock markets and corporate governance (see, e.g., La Porta et al., 1997). However, the system of corporate governance in Taiwan is individualistic, with a board of directors accompanied by a group of supervisors, whose role is to provide an independent view to executive directors. On 15th October 2002, the Security and Futures Commission (SFC) of the Taiwan Stock Exchange (TSE) produced the first code of best practice on corporate governance, entitled *Practical Guidance on Corporate Governance for Listed and OTC* [Over The Counter] *Companies*. We examine some of the recent problems in Taiwanese corporate governance and the anticipated reaction to the new code of practice in Illustration 8.4.

Illustration 8.4

Corporate governance reform in Taiwan

Taiwanese companies have been branded with many of the negative characteristics associated with insider corporate governance systems. Crony capitalism, lack of corporate transparency, minority shareholder wealth expropriation and managerial abuse of power are all problems traditionally occurring in East Asian countries' systems of corporate governance. However, the notorious agency problem associated with outsider-dominated systems of corporate governance has, until relatively recently, been insignificant in Taiwan. As the TSE expands and shareholding gradually becomes more dispersed, agency problems are beginning to encroach on Taiwanese companies. It is therefore necessary for Taiwan to improve corporate governance standards in order to tackle these emerging problems of separation of ownership and control. Also in order to attract foreign capital, Taiwanese companies need to improve internal corporate governance standards, as international investment institutions require a minimum level of corporate governance and accountability before they are prepared to lend funds to foreign companies. Indeed, corporate governance has now become one of the main factors determining investment in Asian stocks, according to the latest research (McBride, 2002). As a result of the corporate governance reform process, in October 2002 Taiwan produced its first code of corporate governance best practice entitled *Practical Guidance on Corporate Governance for Listed and OTC Companies*. This document is voluntary in nature, although companies listed on the TSE are required to state whether or not they are complying with the guidance. The details of the document are very similar to those of the OECD and to the original UK Cadbury Code (1992). As a result of this new initiative, local Taiwanese newspapers have been full of commentary and discussion on corporate governance issues. One article enumerated all the reasons why corporate governance reform in Taiwan was likely to be difficult (Zun, 2002). Excessive control by founding family members was highlighted as probably the most significant problem. Systematic lack of transparency in Taiwanese companies arising from a desire to produce annual reports that provide an overly positive view for company analysts and shareholders has also been pinpointed as an obstacle to corporate governance reform. Indeed, Taiwanese companies have been widely associated with creative accounting and lack of transparency in their operations, as well as notorious and frequent cases of fraud by company management (*Taipei Times*, 15 July 2000, 18 July 2002). One of the principal problems with Taiwanese company accounts, according to foreign institutional investors, has been an unwillingness to disclose information relating to the companies' investments in mainland China (McBride, 2002).

Nevertheless, reform is progressing at a steady pace. In July 2002 TSMC (Taiwan Semiconductor Manufacturing Company) was the first Taiwanese company to establish a formal audit committee in the style of the Cadbury Report (Chang and Chan, 2002). Recently amended Company Law (2001) and the new guidance on corporate governance recommended that half of a company's board of directors should comprise independent directors. There are, however, concerns that there will be an inadequate supply of appropriate people to fill the role of independent director in all Taiwanese listed and OTC companies. Further, there are concerns that the presence of independent directors on boards will stifle creative and innovative activities: a common response to corporate governance checks and balances (Guan, 2002). In the wake of the corporate accounting scandals in the USA, the SFC in Taiwan has charged the TSE with tightening its scrutiny of financial reports of companies applying for a listing on the TSE or the OTC market. Further, the Accounting Research and Development Foundation in Taiwan is reviewing the current corporate accounting system in order to detect and correct any weaknesses. Further, many shareholders have been filing lawsuits against a number of noted accounting firms on suspicions that they may have collaborated with local companies in concealing financial losses and producing false annual reports.

Another initiative that has aided wider shareholder dispersion and encouraged foreign investment institutions to invest in Taiwanese companies is Taiwan's Qualified Foreign Institutional Investor (QFII) scheme. This scheme has been in place since the early 1990s, but is currently being disbanded. It allows all types of institutional investor to apply for a licence which, after giving a relatively small deposit to the Taiwan central bank, lets the institution trade freely in local shares up to an established limit. This scheme has been successful, attracting significant foreign investment. However, the investment process can be fraught with difficulties, as retrieving funds from Taiwan is not always easy, with foreign institutional investors faced frequently by long waits (*South China Morning Post*, 19 April 2002). Taiwan has been so serious about corporate governance reform that in December 2002 the government (the Executive Yuan) made improving corporate governance a national policy. The government has set up a new commission and task force under the Cabinet to supervise progress. Their initial aim is to produce a White Paper on government policy that will detail government policies designed to promote improvements in corporate transparency and governance (*Taiwan Business News*, 3 December 2002). A recent study investigated the attitudes of Taiwanese company directors toward corporate governance reform and found that they were strongly in favour of reform and wanted to see Taiwanese companies adopt internationally accepted standards of corporate governance, mainly with an aim to attracting international funds (Solomon et al., 2003b). Further, the paper indicated that Taiwanese directors were uncomfortable with the level of family control in Taiwanese companies and concluded that crony capitalism and managerial abuse of power needed to be curbed in order to make Taiwan internationally competitive. There are, however, many other factors influencing the speed of corporate governance reform in Taiwan and the country's ability to attract institutional investment from abroad. The political situation in Taiwan is extremely sensitive and the cultural roots are not necessarily conducive to an Anglo-American-style system of corporate governance. Indeed, the American Chamber of Commerce in Taipei has emphasised the need for Taiwan to pursue political stability and subordinate partisan politics to improving corporate governance, reducing corporate fraud and focusing on attracting foreign investment (Namgyal, 2001).

Thailand

Thailand represents an insider-dominated system of corporate governance with an emerging stock market. Again, Thailand's economy was affected severely by the

Asian crisis, and this has been attributed to corporate governance weaknesses, among other factors. Indeed, the whole crisis emanated from Thailand. In Summer 1997 there was a devaluation of the Thai baht, following a collapse of the property market. Following the crisis there was, as in many of the other Asian economies, significant expropriation of minority shareholder wealth. In the case of Thailand, managers in the Bangkok Bank of Commerce transferred huge funds offshore to companies under their control (Johnson et al., 2000). Since the Asian financial crisis, Thailand has been one of many countries to produce a code of best practice for the directors of listed companies (SET, 1998). Indeed, corporate governance weaknesses have been used partly as a scapegoat by the authorities in many countries since 1997.

United States

At the moment corporate governance is a hot topic in the USA. No one can think about corporate governance without turning immediately to the problems of Enron and WorldCom. If the USA has not got things right, being such an economically prosperous nation, what chance do smaller, poorer countries stand? Countries around the world have become introspective in their reaction to the problems in the USA, checking their own systems and corporate governance controls for similar Enron-type weaknesses. 'Enronitis' has spread across the world like a rampant virus. However, interest in US corporate governance is by no means new. The weight of literature and research in the corporate governance domain centres around the US system, or at least draws comparisons of countries' systems with that of the USA. Berle and Means' (1932) work was based on the US system of corporate governance. The first papers on agency theory (e.g., Jensen and Meckling, 1976) focused on the US corporate governance system. Similarly, much of the path-breaking work on boards of directors and corporate performance, the impact of outside directors on performance and the impact of mergers and takeovers came initially from US academics, as we saw in Chapter 4. Although the UK and the USA have outsider, market-based systems of corporate governance, these systems display many differences. Shareholder activism is different between the two countries, with US investment institutions presenting shareholder resolutions to companies far more frequently. As discussed in Chapter 4, the notion of splitting the chairman and chief executive roles in the USA has not been viewed favourably, as board culture is extremely different from the UK. Another difference that we have already discussed is in remuneration. Executive remuneration in the USA has been traditionally far more excessive than in other countries, such as the UK. Monks and Minow (2001) provided a detailed insight into US corporate governance. We will not cover the literature in detail here as much of it has been mentioned in comparisons with the UK system in earlier chapters. Table 8.1 summarizes some of the many corporate governance codes of practice and policy documents that have been published in recent years.

Table [8.1]   Corporate governance policy documents in the USA

Title	Organization	Year
Corporate Governance Market Principles	CalPERS	1998
Report of the NACD Blue Ribbon Commission on Improving the Effectiveness of Audit Committees	NYSE and NACD	1998
Report of the NACD Blue Ribbon Committee on CEO succession	NACD	1998
Core Policies	CII	1998
Statement on Corporate Governance	Business Roundtable	1997
GM Board of Directors Corporate Governance Guidelines on Significant Governance Issues	GM	1997
TIAA-CREF Policy Statement on Corporate Governance	TIAA-CREF	1997
Report of the NACD Blue Ribbon Commission on Director Professionalism	NACD	1996

Chapter summary

In this chapter we have provided a 'reference dictionary' of corporate governance in a selection of countries around the world. By compiling this dictionary, we have attempted to provide a flavour of the rich diversity of corporate governance systems internationally and the attempts that have been made in these countries to reform corporate governance. Clearly, there is a vast diversity of different systems, with many factors combining to determine a country's corporate governance environment, including legal framework, corporate ownership structure, culture and economic factors.

Questions for reflection and discussion

1 Select two countries from the 'reference dictionary' in this chapter and compare and contrast their systems of corporate governance. Research these countries' systems of corporate governance using newspapers, academic articles and the Internet. Consider the corporate governance reforms that have taken place there. To what extent do you feel these have been successful?

2 Read the OECD Principles on Corporate Governance (OECD, 1999). Choose two countries listed in the 'reference dictionary' and evaluate the extent to which you think they are adopting these principles? To assist you, there is a selection of country assessments on the World Bank website (http://

www.worldbank.org). These assess each country's success in complying with the Principles.

3 Choose a country that is not covered in the 'reference dictionary'. Search for information relating to corporate governance in the country of your choice, using the Internet and academic journals. Is this country reforming its system of corporate governance? If so, describe the ways in which this is occurring and the extent to which you think the country's evolving system of corporate governance is converging with other systems around the world.

4 Look at a selection of corporate governance codes of practice (using the Internet). Consider the different ways in which the codes deal with stakeholders. To what extent do you think corporate governance reform around the world is taking a genuine interest in stakeholder concerns?

Part III

Broadening the corporate governance agenda

Chapter 9

Discharging a broader corporate accountability

Aim and objectives

This chapter considers a broader agenda for corporate governance by extending the theoretical paradigm from a narrow agency theory perspective to encompass a stakeholder theory perspective. The specific objectives of this chapter are to enable readers to:

- consider the growth of corporate social responsibility in a broad philosophical and historical context, highlighting the potentially strong impact of corporate behaviour on a wide range of stakeholders;

- emphasize the importance of establishing a positive relationship between corporate social responsibility and corporate financial performance;

- discuss social, ethical, environmental and sustainability disclosure as one of the main ways in which companies can discharge their accountability to a wide range of stakeholders, with an emphasis on environmental reporting;

- discuss the use of stakeholder engagement to discharge broader corporate accountability.

Introduction

The preceding chapters have focused on corporate governance from a rather narrow, finance-dominated, agency theory perspective. In Part I we examined the ways in which corporate governance mechanisms, such as the board of directors, play a role in aligning the interests of shareholders and company management. However, recent years have witnessed a growing interest in corporate social responsibility. Growing fears of such high-consequence risks as global environmental disaster, terrorism and nuclear war have focused people's attention on environmental and social issues.[1]

---

[1] Giddens (1991) discussed the rise of what he termed 'high consequence risks', which include such potentially catastrophic events as nuclear war and global warming.

Policies and corporate governance initiatives have highlighted the importance of broadening the corporate governance agenda to incorporate a more 'inclusive' approach (i.e., an approach to corporate governance that focuses not only on the needs of shareholders but also on the needs and requirements of all corporate stakeholders). As discussed in Chapter 1, stakeholder theory has attracted increasing attention in recent years and the needs of stakeholders are being taken more seriously by businesses. Indeed, there is an emerging perception that shareholder and stakeholder theories are not dichotomous, as traditionally thought, but display many similarities and commonalities.

In the UK there has been a complete overhaul of company law in recent years, based on a belief that the existing documents had become outdated and less relevant for modern companies. The first drafts of the Modern Company Law Review appeared to be refocusing company law on social, ethical and environmental issues (now frequently referred to as SEE issues) and emphasized the broadening responsibilities of company directors in the UK (see Modern Company Law, 2000; Modernising Company Law, 2002). Indeed, the text of the accompanying White Paper reflected a paradigm shift in the way directors perceive their role in companies and in society. There were many references to company stakeholders included in the White Paper, representing an attempt to demonstrate a broadening corporate agenda, for example:

> The Review considered to whom directors should owe duties . . . the basic goal for directors should be the success of the company in the collective best interests of shareholders, but that the *directors should also recognise, as the circumstances require, the company's need to foster relationships with its employees, customers and suppliers, its need to maintain its business reputation, and its need to consider the company's impact on the community and the working environment.*
>
> (Modernising Company Law, 2002, Section 3.3, emphasis added)

However, the extent to which this shift in emphasis within the new versions of UK company law may really be viewed as a genuine change, in the discourse of company directors, is debatable. The final draft of the review inspired far less optimism for those wishing to pursue a stakeholder perspective, as any reference to stakeholder accountability was surrendered to a materiality constraint. Any suggestion within the law document stating that directors were responsible for managing and disclosing information pertaining to SEE issues was rendered important only if they were to prove material. In other words, directors were considered liable for SEE risks and were encouraged to disclose SEE information only when such issues were considered material, as:

> It will, of course, be for directors to decide precisely what information is material to their particular business.
>
> (Modernising Company Law, 2002, Section 4.33)

This means that if company directors consider an SEE issue is not material, then they are not liable and do not have to disclose information pertaining to it. Materiality is such an intangible, abstract notion that it would in practice be extremely difficult to prosecute a director on a point of SEE materiality. A series of interviews that we conducted with institutional investors and lawyers in the City of London revealed a deep scepticism over the potential impact of the review of company law in the area of SEE accountability. Indeed, one of the lawyers we interviewed commented that the new legislation was unenforceable in this area and was, in her opinion, simply a 'marketing ploy'. Certainly, institutional investors regard the social responsibility aspect of the Modern Company Law Review to be related to public relations rather than to financial return or genuine interest in SEE issues. Its eventual impact on corporate behaviour is certainly in question.

One initiative that has focused corporate attention on social responsibility and especially on SEE concerns within companies in the UK has been the guidelines on SEE disclosure published by the Association of British Insurers (ABI). The emphasis of these guidelines was on the responsibilities of directors for considering SEE issues in their general decision making within the company. Such emphasis on the SEE responsibilities of company boards was not new but picked up from writers and practitioners, such as Garratt (1996), who emphasized the importance of SEE issues to board effectiveness. More recently, Cadbury (2002) has highlighted the way in which companies are assimilating a socially responsible role. We now consider the emergence of corporate social responsibility, from a UK perspective, and its ensuing influence on business. We begin by delving into the historical roots of corporate social responsibility

Early roots of corporate social responsibility in the UK

Corporate social responsibility (often referred to as CSR in the literature) has existed for some time. Indeed, ever since the Industrial Revolution in Britain in the 18th century there has been a growing consciousness of the harm that irresponsible corporate behaviour can bring. The terrible living and working conditions of people involved in early industrialization moved many members of the 'higher classes' to write extensively on the evils of industry. The blast furnaces developed by Abraham Darby in Ironbridge and the cotton and woollen mills in the North of England were seen by visitors as inhuman environments for people to work in. Some writers described Abraham Darby's Coalbrookdale as the 'mouth of hell'. The poverty and appalling living conditions that millworkers suffered in Manchester horrified visiting academics and novelists. For example, Thomas Carlyle (1795–1881) passionately bewailed the suffering of the industrialized working class in the 1840s and was one of the first writers to produce novels encouraging a social consciousness (e.g.,

Past and Present). Other contemporary writers with similar intentions were Elizabeth Gaskell (1810–1865) and Benjamin Disraeli (1804–1881). Gaskell encouraged social reconciliation and a better understanding between employers and workers as well as between different classes of society. She observed the pitiful living conditions of the industrial workers in Manchester and was deeply affected by what she saw.

By Victorian times social-oriented movements were being established based on philanthropic and Christian values. There was a slow realization among certain circles of society that unethical corporate behaviour could have a detrimental influence on society. The founding of the Christian Socialist movement by philosophers, political economists, philanthropists and novelists was a step in the direction of corporate social responsibility. The early Christian Socialists were mainly middle-class intellectuals, writing between 1850 and 1870. Charles Kingsley (famous for writing *The Water-Babies*) and John Ruskin (an artist and architectural writer as well as an early political economist) were founders of the Christian Socialist movement. They were deeply affected by the working class misery they encountered on their travels. They were deeply concerned that the massive wealth arising from industrial activities was not necessarily generated by socially responsible business practices as:

> Any given accumulation of commercial wealth may be indicative, on the one hand, of faithful industries, progressive energies, and productive ingenuities ... or, on the other, it may be indicative of mortal luxury, merciless tyranny, ruinous chicane. Some treasures are heavy with human tears ...
>
> (Ruskin, 1862, p. 180)

These writers and philosophers tended to be unimpressed by industrialization and dreamed of returning to a peaceful, rural England without mechanization. As well as being early socialists in the political sense, their philosophy was deeply rooted in Christian principles. Their belief was that Christianity was the only foundation of Socialism and that a true Socialism was the necessary result of a sound Christianity. The writing that they produced reached a far wider public than purely social political literature in contemporary society because of the close relationship between the population and their church. Even though many may feel that such Christian-based ideologies are irrelevant in our predominantly multifaith society, the continuing influence of Christian Socialism is surprising. Today, the relevance of Christian Socialism is demonstrated by leading politicians such as Tony Blair and Stephen Timms belonging to the movement.

According to Boatright (1999) corporate social responsibility as a discipline in its own right (and the terminology surrounding it) originated in the 1950s. The consciousness of corporate social responsibility has grown continuously since the first roots of industrialization in England to the gradual growth of business around the world. The larger that companies have become, the greater their potential impact (good or bad) on society and, therefore, the greater the need for them to act in a socially responsible way.

One of the problems with discussing corporate social responsibility is in deciding whether we can treat a company in a similar way to a person: Can a company be attributed with ethics and morals? Is a company an entity, equivalent to a 'person', capable of behaving in a socially responsible or irresponsible manner? The problem is: How can a company, which is a collection of different people—employees and managers—be treated as a 'person' in its own right? There is an interesting discussion of the corporation as a moral subject in Lozano (2000), which shows the difficulties of making such an assumption and describes the way in which the debate has gone round in circles over time. Strong supporters of the idea of a company as a moral person are French (1979, 1984) and Goodpaster (1982, 1987).

The sole aim of companies to maximize profitability and maximize shareholder wealth has come seriously into question in more recent times. Pursuing profit at the expense of damage to the environment, local communities, employees and other stakeholders is not a route many people support any longer. The pure ethics case for business to act in a socially responsible manner was outlined in Chapter 1, where we showed that some writers consider that company management cannot subordinate basic moral obligations to shareholder obligations (Quinn and Jones, 1995). However, as we see from the following section, other writers disagree.

Friedman and corporate social responsibility

One person who has been demonized by proponents of corporate social responsibility is Milton Friedman. A free market economist, he believed that the *only* responsibility a company had to society was to maximize returns to its shareholders. He adopted a purely agency theory perspective of the company, believing that any attempts by companies to spend money on charitable donations, or attempt to satisfy stakeholders other than shareholders, were at best misguided (Friedman, 1962, 1970). A full discussion of Friedman's viewpoints *inter alia* may be found in Lozano (2000). Similarly, the work of Sternberg (1998) derided corporate social responsibility and echoed Friedman's sentiments. It is however hard to see that if corporate social responsibility makes companies more successful in the long term, as well as making companies more sustainable and accountable to society, this would not be in the long-term interests of shareholders as well as stakeholders. The crunch is whether or not corporate social responsibility engenders profits. As we emphasized in Chapter 1, it is unrealistic to assume that business managers will act in a socially responsible manner if this reduces profits. However, there is a growing body of literature that shows a positive relationship between corporate social/environmental performance and financial performance. We consider some of this literature in the following section.

Does corporate social responsibility improve financial performance?

There is a growing perception within the corporate and shareholder communities that companies that perform well in the social, ethical and environmental arena also perform well financially. Innovest Strategic Value Advisors, an organization that rates companies in more than 50 industries according to a wide spectrum of social, environmental and corporate governance issues, have provided evidence that companies with superior social and environmental ratings, as well as better corporate governance, also have the best performing shares (*Pensions Week*, 2003). In the academic literature there are a number of reasons given for a possible positive relationship between corporate social responsibility and corporate financial performance. One reason that corporate financial performance may be positively related to corporate SEE performance derives from the view that if company management act in a socially responsible manner they are more likely to possess the skills to run a company well, improving its financial performance and making it an attractive investment (Alexander and Buchholz, 1978). Our own research, based on extensive interview and questionnaire evidence, has certainly shown that the UK institutional investment community view SEE management as an important indicator of management quality more generally (Solomon and Solomon, 2002). Illustration 9.1 returns to the unfortunate case of Enron by using Enron's unethical activities to illustrate the possible link between management quality and management's behaviour in the SEE domain.

Another reason that company management would wish to concern themselves with SEE issues is in the case where their financial performance could be negatively affected by socially irresponsible behaviour. This view had underpinned initiatives aimed at improving internal control in the areas of SEE risk management (as endorsed by ACCA, 2000, see Illustration 6.1). It is however possible that a positive link may be found, simply because companies that have performed better financially may be better able to afford to act in a socially responsible manner, as suggested by McGuire et al. (1988) as they found that prior financial performance was a better predictor of corporate social responsibility than subsequent performance, again using US data. Academic research has found some support for a positive link between corporate social performance and financial performance. For example, Moskowitz (1972) found that the share returns of a small sample of US listed companies which he deemed were socially responsible had increased at a higher rate than major market indices.[2] Another study, which improved on earlier methodological approaches by including a variable in the analysis to take account of asset age, found weak evidence of a positive correlation between corporate social responsibility and financial performance for a sample of 61 US listed companies (Cochran and Wood,

---

[2] Moskowitz (1972) was the first to develop reputational indexes that list companies exhibiting remarkably 'good' or 'bad' social performance. Their usefulness has however been criticized as they measure perceived social performance rather than social performance *per se* (Ullman, 1985).

Illustration 9.1

Enron and ethics

We studied Enron's downfall in Chapter 2, analysing the various corporate governance weaknesses abounding in Enron and considered their contribution to its collapse. However, we did not consider the relevance of SEE accountability to Enron. There is a growing perception in the financial markets that SEE corporate performance is a good indicator of financial performance. Furthermore, there is a growing feeling that a company's management of SEE issues is indicative of the quality of the company's management in other areas. Enron was plagued with accusations of human rights abuse in India in the mid-1990s. Their handling of the situation raises several questions about the company's ethics and ability to manage risks effectively. In 1995 Enron's power project in Maharashtra in India encountered a long and bitter dispute with nationalist politicians. A change in the country's government after Enron's initial negotiations regarding foreign direct investment in India resulted in more nationalist leadership. The company was accused of corruption, lack of transparency, insensitivity to local citizenry and complicity in human rights abuses by police (*The Economist*, 1 June 2000). Protestors demonstrating against the company's new site were allegedly beaten by security guards hired by Enron. By 1998 controversy over the Indian project seemed to have been quelled (*The Economist*, 26 February 1998), which was a relief for the company. But did it leave a scar on the company's ethical profile? Perhaps more attention to this detail would have provided an important insight into the character of the senior management at Enron. Their handling of the situation left much to be desired and was perhaps indicative of things to come. Certainly, if companies' handling of SEE issues are indicative of their general management quality, this was not a positive sign for Enron.

1984). It is not our intention to attempt a comprehensive review of the literature in this area, but there are many more studies from the last 30 years that have found evidence of a positive relationship, including Bowman and Haire (1975), Belkaoui (1976) and Johnson and Greening (1994).

There are also numerous empirical studies that have found no evidence of a positive or a negative link. Such a result could be interpreted as positive evidence by those supporting corporate social responsibility: if acting in a socially responsible manner is costless in terms of financial performance, then surely from a pure ethics perspective it is better to pursue social responsibility. One reason proffered for an insignificant positive or negative relationship between corporate social responsibility and financial performance is couched in market efficiency arguments. If stock markets are efficient (in the sense of Fama, 1970) all new information relevant to the earnings outlook of a company is rapidly and accurately incorporated in share prices. Therefore, either information relating to SEE performance is not relevant to earnings, having no effect on financial performance, or the information is immediately impacted into share prices and reflects a trade-off between risk and return (Alexander and Buchholz, 1978). Indeed, Alexander and Buchholz (1978) found no significant relationship between social responsibility and stock market performance, using a set of rankings of social responsibility derived from the opinions of businessmen and students. An early review of some of the first empirical studies examining this issue concluded that economic performance was not directly linked in either a positive or a negative way to social responsiveness (Arlow and Gannon, 1982).

There are also a number of reasons given in the academic literature for a negative relationship between corporate social responsibility and corporate financial perform-ance. One view is that socially responsible companies may be at a competitive disadvantage due to the added expense incurred by socially responsible behaviour. Vance (1975) used students' rankings of companies according to social responsibility criteria to demonstrate a negative link between socially responsible behaviour and financial performance, as those companies perceived as the most socially responsible were the worst financial performers. Again, we are not going to attempt a compre-hensive view of the literature that provides empirical evidence of a negative relation-ship, but some papers worth reading are Shane and Spicer (1983) and Strachan et al. (1983). The implication for companies of a negative link would be that investors would avoid including socially responsible companies in their portfolio if they felt this would reduce their investment return. We return to this important issue in Chapter 10 when we discuss socially responsible investment and the extant evidence concerning the relationship between this type of investment and financial return. However, at this point it is worth mentioning that several studies have found evidence to conclude that improving a company's social performance does not discourage institutional investors from buying shares (Graves and Waddock, 1994).

One of the problems in comparing the results of the wide range of studies is the diversity of techniques used by the researchers. In short, all empirical research has limitations and there is no 'perfect' technique or methodology that can be applied. Whatever approach is adopted, there are always people who will doubt the findings. Nevertheless, the weight of evidence in the literature seems to point to a positive relationship between corporate social responsibility and corporate financial performance (e.g., as concluded by Griffin and Mahon, 1997). Furthermore, general perceptions concerning the relationship between corporate social responsi-bility and financial performance are important. It is clear from our own research that the most influential group of corporate stakeholders in the UK, the institutional investors, consider corporate social responsibility to have a significant positive effect on corporate financial performance. As one pension fund director pointed out:

> You can make a fast buck by ignoring corporate social responsibility but you can't run a long-term sustainable business without it!
>
> (Quoted in Solomon and Solomon, 2002)

Having discussed corporate social responsibility in a broad sense, we now discuss ways in which companies may discharge this social responsibility, focusing specific-ally on the finance and accounting arena. A wealth of academic literature has burgeoned in the areas of environmental, ethical, social and, more recently, sustainability reporting. There are a number of textbooks dedicated to these areas (e.g., Gray et al., 1993, 1996). It is not our intention to cover all of these issues in exhaustive detail; instead, we have chosen to use environmental reporting as an illustration of the way in which companies discharge their accountability in the SEE area. This seems a reasonable approach, as many of the theoretical arguments for and against environmental reporting can be applied equally well to social reporting. Further, environmental reporting was the first non-financial area of reporting to receive significant attention and is therefore the most developed.

Corporate environmental reporting

One of the first areas where companies have been encouraged to discharge a wider accountability has been the environment. In recent years environmental issues have attracted increasing attention from many sectors of society worldwide. The seeds of corporate environmental reporting (often abbreviated to CER in the literature) were sown by organizations such as the Coalition for Environmentally Responsible Economies (usually abbreviated to CERES), who provided the first guiding principles for companies wishing to discharge accountability to the environment. See Illustration 9.2 for an outline of the history of CERES.

Society's increasing awareness of environmental issues has encouraged companies to consider their interaction with the natural environment. This has led to increased calls for CER by such organizations as the European Federation of Accountants (FEE, 2000) and the Global Reporting Initiative (GRI, 2000). This growing demand is not a recent phenomenon. Earlier studies suggested that groups of users demanded and required environmental performance information in corporate annual reports (e.g., Deegan and Rankin, 1996).

Despite growing demand, it appears that the quality and quantity of CER has been considered insufficient to meet users' needs (see, e.g., Harte and Owen, 1992; Deegan and Rankin, 1996; Adams et al., 1995). Indeed, the United Nations Environment Programme concluded that:

> ... report-makers still have a long way to go before they can fully meet the emerging information needs of their key target audiences—and those of the rapidly growing ranks of report-users.
>
> (UNEP, 1996a, p. 43)

Significantly, most companies are still not reporting any environmental information, and where there is reporting it is mixed and inconsistent (KPMG, 2002). Not only is there an inadequate level of environmental reporting but some studies have found that most CER is of a descriptive, self-congratulatory nature, alluding more to good intentions than actual environmental programmes and rarely reporting any bad news about a company's relationship with the environment (Harte and Owen, 1992;

Illustration 9.2

CERES—the seeds of corporate environmental reporting

CERES was one of the early pioneers of environmental reporting, encouraging companies worldwide to discharge their accountability to the environment through the accounting framework. The organization took its name from the Roman goddess of fertility and agriculture. In 1988 the board of the US-based Social Investment Forum formed an alliance with environmental lobby groups in order to consider ways in which investment may lead to improvements in, rather than depletion of, the environment. Since that time CERES has become a worldwide leader in standardized CER and the promotion of transformed environmental management in companies. The CERES agenda was pushed forward by a number of corporate disasters. First, there was the case of *Exxon Valdez*, where a tanker poured thousands of gallons of oil into the ocean, destroying natural habitats and killing wildlife. Second, there was the disaster in Bhopal (India), where the Union Carbide plant suffered an explosion that resulted in poisonous gases entering the atmosphere and had terrible consequences for the local population. Both these cases horrified people worldwide and focused attention on corporate activities in relation to the environment and local communities. In 1989 CERES produced the 'Valdez Principles' (later renamed the 'CERES Principles'). These Principles comprised a 10-point code of corporate environmental conduct, to be endorsed publicly by companies as an environmental mission statement or ethic. The code carried the expectation for companies to report environmentally at regular intervals. Despite initial negative reactions from the corporate community, the 1990s witnessed an increase in CER and a deep change in corporate attitudes toward environmental, as well as social, issues. Companies began to recognize that their reputation depended on the way that they managed their impacts on the environment and on their stakeholders. Indeed, society as a whole began to be characterized by an 'environmental ethos', becoming more concerned about environmental issues and the future of the planet (Solomon, 2000). See the CERES website http://www.ceres.org/about/history.htm, for a detailed account of the development and impact of CERES.

Deegan and Rankin, 1996; Gray et al., 1996; Adams et al., 1998). We now consider a number of incentives and disincentives underlying CER, arising from the literature, as well as a number of factors characterizing corporate environmental reporting.

Incentives for corporate environmental reporting

Solomon and Lewis (2002) suggested that incentives for CER fell loosely within four categories (namely, a markets, social, political and accountability incentive). These arise from different perspectives held by different sectors of society, who require information for decision making.

From a free market perspective, demand for CER can be met through the market mechanism. Indeed, pressure from the marketplace is seen by some as one of the main incentives for CER (Macve and Carey, 1992). The existence of voluntary CER *per se* provides some support for a market motive, as where there is no legal requirement the production of information is likely to be in response to market demand. More substantially, a growth in socially responsible investment is creating an increasing demand for SEE disclosure by companies, as we discuss in the following chapter (Friedman and Miles, 2001). Indeed, our own research has shown that institutional investors are demanding improvements in SEE disclosure generally (Solomon and Solomon, 2002). However, if demand for CER is not being met, then market failures are likely to exist. We discussed the problems of market failure and information asymmetry in Chapter 6, in relation to corporate disclosure generally. Information asymmetry represents a serious form of market failure in CER, as in other areas of disclosure, as information that is voluntarily disclosed tends to have major inadequacies, often appearing to market the company rather than reveal problems relating to environmental issues. An issue as sensitive as the commercial use of the environment is likely to encourage secrecy, rather than transparency (Gray, 1992).

Stakeholder, legitimacy and political economy theory can be grouped under the category of social incentives for voluntary CER, according to Solomon and Lewis (2002). As we saw in Chapter 1, stakeholder theory involves recognizing and identifying the relationship between a company's behaviour and the impact on its stakeholders. The difficulties of balancing the needs of a diverse range of stakeholders has implications for CER, as companies struggle to provide appropriate and adequate information for these different groups. Nevertheless, the need to provide information to these stakeholder groups represents an incentive for CER.

Legitimacy theory also establishes an incentive for CER, stemming from the existence of a theoretical social contract between companies and society (Mathews, 1993). Companies need to demonstrate that they have a licence to operate. They need to legitimize their existence not just to their shareholder but also to society as a whole. From this perspective, voluntary CER represents a way in which companies can legitimize their existence to society (Lehman, 1983; RSA, 1995). Indeed, a company's licence to operate has been acknowledged as an important incentive for CER (RSA, 1995). Legitimacy theory has also been used to explain why companies may voluntarily disclose only positive aspects of their performance (Harte and Owen, 1992; Deegan and Rankin, 1996).

A third social incentive for CER arises from political economy theory, which centres around the social, political and economic framework within which human life takes place (Gray et al., 1996). From a CER perspective, political economy theory focuses on power and conflict in society, the specific historical/institutional environment of the society in which it operates and the acknowledgement that CER can reflect different views and concerns.

As well as the social and market categorizations of incentives for CER, there appears to be a political incentive, underlying the voluntary production of environmental information by companies. In other words, companies are encouraged to report environmentally due to political pressure. Political interest in environmental issues has been reflected in the creation over time of the Conservative Ecology Group, the Green Alliance, the Green Party, the Socialist Environmental and

Resources Association, the Tory Green Initiative and the Environment Agency. Large-scale integration of environmental issues into the political spectrum has led to the integration of environmental issues into all aspects of mainstream politics. We summarize incentives for CER as follows:

- to improve the company's corporate image;

- to market the company;

- to market company products;

- peer pressure from companies in the same industry;

- to comply with regulations;

- pressure from customers/consumers;

- to attract investment;

- as an acceptance of a change in society's ethics;

- to acknowledge social responsibility;

- as a result of company ethics;

- as a form of political lobbying;

- to meet the demand for environmental information.

A questionnaire survey of a large sample of organizations revealed that, from the above list, acknowledging social responsibility and marketing the company were viewed as the main reasons why companies produce corporate environmental information voluntarily (see Solomon and Lewis, 2002).[3] This is interesting as it shows that companies are believed to use CER to legitimize their existence, as discussed above. However, the results also suggest that companies are seen as being socially responsible in their disclosure.

Disincentives for corporate environmental reporting
As discussed above, the growth in CER has fallen short of satisfying users' requirements. Both the quality and quantity of the corporate environmental information disclosed by companies are considered to be inadequate on the whole. There is, however, a countervailing view in the literature that, if financial markets were genuinely interested in corporate environmental information, then more voluntary disclosure would take place and mandatory disclosure would be avoided (Perks, 1993). There must be reasons why CER continues to be viewed as inadequate.

---

[3] The total sample consisted of 635 organizations, which was broken down into three groups (namely, an interested party group, a normative group and a company group).

Why are companies not increasing the quantity and quality of their CER? Gray et al. (1993) gave a number of explanations for inadequate CER: absence of any demand for information, absence of a legal requirement, the problem that the cost would outweigh the benefits, and the possibility that the organization had never considered it. Further, several reasons why companies do not disclose certain information publicly were given by the World Industry Council for the Environment (WICE, 1984), including: the possibility of the information costing too much, companies wishing to report not possessing adequate information systems, and legal or customer confidentiality issues, or security implications. In practice, secrecy relating to environmental pollution has been considered to be significant and has been endemic to environmental legislation, as many statutes contain specific sections forbidding CER (Ball and Bell, 1995).

The role of the financial community has also been substantial in discouraging CER, as, until relatively recently, soft information in the area of SEE issues was awarded less status by institutional investors than it is today. Unless the financial community perceive a need for CER, reporting is less likely to be forthcoming (see, e.g., ACBE, 1996). Given recent developments in which social responsibility is being encouraged, the financial community's attitudes, particularly in the form of institutional investors, may change. Another possible disincentive for companies not addressing environmental issues may be inefficient management, because managers consider that environmental issues do not apply to the company and view environmental reporting as expensive. Further, management may be stuck in their ways and unable to accept a broader, more socially responsible agenda. Another reason, arising from a common sense view of companies, is that it would be irrational for corporations to disclose any information detrimental to them (Benston, 1982).

Given this discussion we can see that it is not surprising that companies have been unwilling to produce environmental information (Owen, 1992). The voluntary reporting framework also causes company management to feel exposed if they disclose more than their competitors. We summarize the possible disincentives for CER as follows:

- reluctance to report sensitive information;

- general lack of awareness of environmental issues;

- there is no legal obligation for companies to report environmentally;

- possible damage to companies' reputation;

- to avoid providing information to competitors;

- cost of disclosure;

- to avoid providing incriminating information to regulators;

- inability to gather the information;

- lack of awareness of competitive advantage;

- insufficient response feedback from stakeholders;

- companies generally believe they do not have an impact on the environment;

- users may not understand the information.

From their questionnaire survey, Solomon and Lewis (2002) found that a reluctance to report sensitive information was considered to be one of the most significant disincentives for CER. This is not surprising, especially if companies view SEE disclosure as a marketing tool. They are unlikely to market themselves by producing unfavourable information on their treatment of environmental issues, preferring instead to focus on the positive aspects. We now turn to a consideration of the contents and characteristics of CER, referring to the results of Solomon and Lewis (2002).

Users of corporate environmental reporting
A fundamental aspect of CER, as with financial reporting, is the identification of users. Although there is no consensus on the possible users of CER, the United Nations Environment Programme (UNEP, 1996) identified the following CER user groups: employees, legislators and regulators, local communities, investors, suppliers, customers and consumers, industry associations, environment groups, science and education, and the media. A number of other similar CER user groups were suggested by Gray et al. (1996): management, trade unions, potential employees, communities, pressure groups, national governments, local government, competitors, peers, industry groups and society in general. These groups overlap to a greater or lesser extent those user groups suggested by other organizations such as the Canadian Institute of Chartered Accountants (CICA, 1994), the World Industry Council for the Environment (WICE, 1994), the Confederation of British Industry (CBI, 1995) and Deloitte, Touche, Tohmatsu International (DTTI, 1993). A selection of possible users suggested in the literature is summarized below:

- legislators and regulators;

- local communities;

- employees;

- shareholders;

- customers;

- insurance companies;

- ethical investors;

- environmental groups;

- quangos;

- local government;

- potential investors;

- banks;

- media;

- suppliers;

- stock market;

- central government;

- industry associations.

From the findings of their questionnaire survey, Solomon (2000) showed that legislators and regulators, employees, local communities and ethical investors were considered to be the main recipients of corporate environmental information from companies.

Qualitative characteristics of corporate environmental reporting
In financial reporting, qualitative characteristics are essential for the production of decision-useful information (ASB, 1996). It is reasonable to suggest that the qualitative characteristics for financial reporting are also applicable to CER. Strong recommendations have been made for the qualitative characteristics that are established in financial reporting to be modified and applied in a structured way to CER (FEE, 2000). The application of qualitative characteristics from financial reporting to environmental reporting has been discussed in the literature (see, e.g., Gray et al., 1987; Macve and Carey, 1992; Gray et al., 1996). However, the usefulness for CER of those qualitative characteristics applied in financial reporting is debatable. Certainly, the characteristic of transparency is essential to all areas of corporate disclosure if it is to be useful. We have already stressed the importance of transparency for effective corporate governance. This characteristic is no less important in the area of environmental information than in the area of internal control of financial reporting. Certainly, the academic literature acknowledges that transparency represented one of the first qualitative characteristics to be applied to environmental reporting (see Gray, 1992; Gray et al., 1993). We summarize the possible qualitative characteristics for CER as follows:

- a true and fair view;

- understandability;

- relevance;

- faithful representation;

- reliability;

- freedom from error;

- consistency;

- valid description;

- substance over form;

- neutrality;

- completeness;

- corresponding information for the previous period;

- confirmation of information;

- timeliness;

- comparability;

- materiality;

- predictive value;

- prudence.

Solomon (2000) found from his survey evidence that the most important qualitative characteristics for CER were considered to be understandability, relevance, reliability, faithful representation, freedom from error, and a true and fair view. The paper used this to show a distinct similarity between the evolving framework for CER and the existing financial reporting framework.

Elements of corporate environmental reporting
It is unlikely that CER could bear similarity to financial reporting in the area of recognition and measurement, as the elements have to be different. Within the current financial reporting framework, a company has legally to own/control the assets on which it reports. Clearly, the natural environment cannot be owned or controlled in the same way as financial assets. Therefore, reporting on society's natural assets represents a completely different paradigm from that of financial reporting. Recognition and measurement in CER are probably most appropriately based on the elements of air, land, water and sound. However, an alternative view was proposed by CICA (1994), who considered that recognition and measurement should be based on the consumption of resources (processing, transportation and distribution) and the use and disposal of products. Other approaches to recognition and measurement criteria focus on actual environmental problems, such as global warming, ozone depletion, smog, acidification, neutrification potential, toxicology (both human and ecotoxicology), waste problems, biodiversity and others (odour, noise, light) (Muller et al., 1994). Jones (1996) suggested an inventory approach to

accounting for biodiversity, advocating the use of wildlife habitats (land or water, flora and fauna). Cowe (1992) advocated a hybrid approach combining natural elements and environmental problems, suggesting, for example: total energy used in heating, lighting and power; total fuel used for transport; total water used; volume of physical waste materials produced; and volume of waste output discharged into the atmosphere and waterways. Evidently, no consensus approach exists. We assume therefore that air, water, land and sound represent the most sensible elements for CER. Indeed, Solomon (2000) proposed these four elements in his questionnaire survey, finding that the respondents considered all the elements were important, but that water was the most significant element for environmental reporting purposes.

Verification of corporate environmental reports
As we discussed in Chapter 6, auditing plays an important role in transparency and therefore in corporate governance. Information needs to be verified in order to make it credible and therefore useful to interested parties. Verification is so important in financial reporting that it is compulsory. Solomon (2000) suggested that there are two fundamental questions that arise in relation to the verification of CER. These are, first, 'should voluntary corporate environmental disclosure be verified?' and, second, 'who are the most appropriate agents for verification?' In relation to the first question, there has been support for verification of environmental and social disclosure in the academic literature (Gray et al., 1987; Buck, 1992; Owen, 1992). It is unlikely that CER will be credible to the user unless the information is externally audited (Adams, 1992). In contrast, CERES (1992) advocated annual self-evaluation and the timely creation of generally accepted environmental audit procedures.

In relation to the second question, Perks (1993) suggested that the existence of a qualified independent body of auditors would add to the credibility of CER. He also suggested that financial audit arrangements could be used but qualifies this by considering that financial auditors lack independence and the appropriate expertise to deal with environmental disclosure. Welford and Gouldson (1993) suggested that accountants were appropriate agents for verification. Perks (1993) also emphasized the need to consider the expectations gap, discussed in Chapter 6, where society expects more from auditors than they provide in practice (Humphrey et al., 1992). However, Power (1991) proposed that accountants may not be the most appropriate professional body to undertake environmental audit and verification, as they may not have the appropriate experience and may be subject to pressures from company management. A selection of possible alternatives for verification are summarized below:

■ environmental consultants within their existing framework;

■ a registered auditor of the Environmental Auditors Registration Association;

■ scientists within their existing framework;

- internal management team;

- a new professional body that includes accountants, scientists and environmental consultants;

- accountants within their existing framework;

- verification is not necessary.

From his questionnaire survey on CER, Solomon (2000) found that existing frameworks for verification were generally preferred to a new body designed for the specific purpose. Specifically, respondents to the survey preferred the following verifiers: registered auditors of the Environmental Auditors Registration Association, environmental consultants within their existing framework and an internal management team.

Bearing the cost of corporate environmental reporting

Corporate environmental information tends to be provided free of charge to interested parties, with companies absorbing the full cost of disclosure. In financial reporting the company bears the cost of disclosure in return for its standing in law as a separate legal entity. Financial disclosure at no cost to the end-user was established in the Companies' Acts (see Mayson et al., 1998), applying principally to shareholders but usually to anyone requesting a report. However, this argument does not necessarily apply to environmental reporting. The costs of environmental disclosure may be substantial and are indeed 'material' for both compliance with legislation and for voluntary disclosure. Indeed, why would companies choose to pay for disclosure that is not mandatory and, worse, may have a negative impact on their reputation (Perks, 1993)? Companies that endorse the Ceres Principles support open environmental reporting and corporate accountability, which would imply that they should bear the entire cost. Solomon's (2000) survey demonstrated a consensus on companies bearing the full cost of environmental reporting.

Time period and communication of corporate environmental reporting

Corporate environmental information is usually disclosed via the annual report or a separate environmental report (usually annual), with the use of the media for any interim reporting (see Zéghal and Ahmed, 1990; Roberts, 1992; Mathews, 1993). The majority of environmental disclosure tends to appear in annual reports, and a number of companies have produced separate annual environmental reports for several years. In relation to time period, CERES (1992), DTTI (1993) and the CBI (1994) recommended that CER should be on an annual basis. The consensus view from Solomon's (2000) findings supported environmental disclosure in the annual report as presenting the most useful form of CER in terms of time period and communication.

The suggested content of corporate environmental reports

There have been a host of suggestions concerning the most desirable contents of CER. We summarize the possible basic contents of an environmental report as follows:

- environmental statement by company chairman;

- environmental policy statement;

- environmental strategy statement;

- environmental management system;

- management responsibilities for the environment;

- environmental audit;

- independently verified environmental disclosure;

- legal environmental compliance;

- research and development and the environment;

- company environmental initiatives;

- context of company environmental disclosure;

- product life cycle design;

- environmental reporting policy;

- product packaging;

- product impacts.

In addition to the characteristics of CER and its contents discussed above, there has been an increasing focus on risk-related aspects of CER, following the Turnbull Report (1999), as suggested in Chapter 6 (see Illustration 6.1). SEE risks are an increasingly important aspect of a company's system of internal control, as sudden events in these areas can turn latent environmental risks into material financial losses. The sinking of an oil tanker is a notable example. Having considered the ways in which companies may discharge their accountability for the environment to their shareholders and other stakeholders, we now consider the emerging importance of the sustainability agenda and its impact on corporate disclosure.

Sustainability and a stakeholder perspective

A stakeholder perspective is perceived as more consistent than such other theoretical frameworks as agency theory, with notions of corporate social responsibility. As discussed in Chapter 1, there have been many attempts in recent years to show that stakeholder and shareholder theories may be more compatible than theorists once believed. The concept of sustainability arises naturally from stakeholder theory. Sustainability and the concept of sustainable development are terms that have evolved over the last 20 years. There is at present no commonly accepted definition. Nevertheless, the Brundtland Commission (WCED, 1987) explained that sustainable development implies development that meets the needs of the present without compromising the ability of future generations to meet its own needs. An obvious interpretation of this is in relation to the environment, as where contemporary society chooses to meet its needs by depleting a natural resource, that same resource will be consequently unavailable to future generations. A preferred and more intuitively pragmatic definition has been provided stating that sustainability is value creation in three dimensions: economic, social and environmental (Wheeler et al., 2002). From an accounting and finance viewpoint, the novel notion of a triple bottom line was coined by Elkington (1998), which implied the inclusion in financial reports of SEE impacts. Similarly, the 'balanced scorecard' was an appealing term developed under the guise of sustainability (Kaplan and Norton, 1996). So, what impact have notions of sustainability had on companies and the information they disclose to their stakeholders? We consider this question in the next section.

Toward sustainability reporting

Interest in sustainability has encouraged companies to orient their disclosure toward a sustainability objective. There is as yet no clear definition as to what sustainability reporting is. However, the Global Reporting Initiative (GRI) has produced sustainability reporting guidelines, and the suggestion is that, for the GRI at least, sustainability reporting centres around economic, environmental and social performance: the so-called triple bottom line. This type of reporting is not new. There are examples of early joint stock companies reporting on their environmental and social activities for one reason or another. In relatively recent times (1970s) the accounting profession produced the Corporate Report (ASSC, 1975) which advocated a wider remit for accountants, as we discussed in Chapter 1. This included social and environmental disclosure. However, by the late 1980s and early 1990s companies were beginning voluntarily to disclose environmental information, even though this was mostly in environmentally unfriendly industries. Events such as *Exxon Valdez* and Bhopal *inter alia* gave social/environmental lobby groups the opportunity to encourage companies to disclose a range of information voluntarily. This in turn led to a need for some type of reporting guidelines, and to a certain extent the culmination of this increased reporting by companies can be seen in the GRI.

Every three years KPMG produce a survey of environmental reporting patterns. This began in 1973 with environmental reporting and in 1999 it began to look at sustainability reporting. The survey looks at reporting practices from the Top 100

Table [9.1] A summary of results from the KPMG surveys

Year	Companies producing a separate corporate environmental report (%)
1993	13
1996	17
1999	24
2002	28

companies in 11 countries. Table 9.1 summarizes its findings since 1993, indicating the proportion of companies that KPMG surveyed, which resulted in a separate corporate environmental report.

In the latest survey the UK has taken the lead over other European countries surveyed, with 49% of the Top 100 companies producing a separate environmental report. The survey also indicated that over 30% of the 100 companies sampled in 2002 had incorporated social and economic issues in their environmental reports, thereby moving the environmental reports more toward sustainability.

A number of initiatives have helped to encourage the growth of sustainability reporting. The Companies Bill arising from the recent review of company law (Modernising Company Law, 2002) required major public companies to produce an Operating and Financial Review (OFR). However, their requirements only applied to 'large' companies. Specifically, the Bill stated that companies have a duty to consider including matters in their OFRs, such as Section 75(2): the company's policies on environmental issues relevant to the company's business and the company's policies on social and community issues relevant to the company's business. These requirements are, however, subject to a materiality constraint, as discussed earlier in this chapter. The Bill also required that Section 73 company directors must comply with any rules about the manner in which the operating and financial review is to be prepared.

Further, the Green Paper entitled *Promoting a European Framework for Corporate Social Responsibility* (European Commission, 2001) presented the European Union's views on corporate social responsibility. It covered such issues as human resource management, health and safety at work and the environment. Of particular interest was that the discussion took place in terms of corporate social responsibility in an internal dimension and an external dimension. Not only did the report address multinational enterprises but also small and medium enterprises. The Commission hoped to see the development of social and environmental reporting by companies. The Commission is prepared to provide guidance to companies, particularly smaller listed companies.

Another initiative that has influenced sustainability reporting has been the foundation in 1991 of the Association of Chartered Certified Accountants (ACCA) UK awards for sustainability (initially environmental) reporting. By 2001, in order to reflect changes in disclosure practices of UK companies, the award schemes had been changed to sustainability reporting. The awards are divided into environmental reporting, social reporting and sustainability reporting. Each category has a winner. Shortlisted companies in the 2001 awards included: BP plc, Camelot Group plc, Co-op Insurance Services, Scottish Power and Shell International. Of particular interest was a commendation for Risk and Policy Analysts Ltd, is a small company with only 10 employees.

Disclosure is, however, not the only way that companies can discharge a broader accountability to a range of stakeholders. They can also involve themselves more directly with stakeholder groups through a process of active engagement and dialogue. We now turn to consider the ways in which this process is evolving.

Stakeholder engagement

An emerging trend in UK business is the growth of stakeholder engagement. Engagement with non-shareholding stakeholders has become the focus of recent research, with stakeholder engagement being described as:

> ... a range of diverse, qualitative information gathering methods.
>
> (Thomson and Bebbington, 2002, p. 20)

These information-gathering methods include questionnaire surveys, interviews, focus groups and public meetings (Owen, 2003). An acknowledged accountability requirement of the developing SEE engagement process between companies and stakeholders, and especially the process of SEE disclosure, is the emergence of dialogic[4] engagement (Owen et al., 2001; Thomson and Bebbington, 2002). Thomson and Bebbington (2002) built their theory on Freire's (1996) pedagogic concept, which emphasized the need for education to be dialogic rather than didactic, such that the teacher and the student learn from each other. He considered a dialogic education process as one that brings about liberation, transforming the world through a praxis. Thomson and Bebbington (2002) extended this concept to shed light on the potentially dialogic relationship between companies and their stakeholders in SEE disclosure via the process of stakeholder engagement but found little evidence of such dialogue. If the process is to lead to improved corporate accountability and greater corporate social responsibility, then it needs to become dialogic in nature. Indeed, the emerging literature that focuses on the role of stakeholder engagement in the SEE field tends to be sceptical of the accountability benefits of stakeholder engagement and considers the process to be undeveloped and sporadic (Owen et al., 2001; Adams, 2002). There is scepticism concerning the true value of the engagement process to the stakeholders themselves. Companies

---

[4] The term 'dialogic' has been defined as pertaining to a discussion, especially one between representatives of two political groups (*The Concise Oxford Dictionary*, 1995).

seem to be gaining considerable information from stakeholder engagement and are probably using the process to their advantage by gaining information for public relations and marketing (Owen, 2003). However, stakeholders seem to be gaining relatively little. The extent to which stakeholder engagement could enhance corporate accountability has been seriously questioned (Owen et al., 2001). It may be that the focus on stakeholder engagement is misplaced, as its impact is limited and companies have captured the process and turned it to their own advantage, as:

> Within the engagement processes we have been involved in, the scope of engagement was largely controlled by the organisation ... Whilst there was scope for active participation by stakeholders the dialogue was in the direction of stakeholders to the organisation. They appear to be a way for the organisation to learn about those outside, not for the stakeholders to learn about the organisation. These were not mutual learning exchanges and they did not develop meaningful dialogic exchanges.
>
> (Thomson and Bebbington, 2002, p. 29)

One of the most vigorous attempts to satisfy stakeholders through the engagement process has been conducted by Camelot, the Lottery operating company. Illustration 9.3 discusses their stakeholder engagement programme in detail.

In the stakeholder engagement literature the extent of SEE engagement between the (arguably) primary stakeholder group, the institutional investment community and their investee companies is often dismissed in favour of examining the involvement of other stakeholder groups.[5] However, we argue that, unless the primary shareholders, the institutional investors, are involved in SEE and are encouraging SEE disclosure because of their perception of a 'business case', significant developments in the SEE area will be hindered. The overemphasis on the 'ethics case' is likely to result in weaker lobbying of companies and a lack of genuine progress and commitment by the business community. This important change in attitude among the academic community, previously committed to the ethics case as a means of furthering the stakeholder and corporate social responsibility agenda, has been recognized in the recent literature as:

> At the present time we simply appear to be drowning in a sea of stakeholder rhetoric which, in the current political and economic climate, leads us up a blind alley as far as extending corporate accountability is concerned ... Given the absolute primacy awarded to the interests of financial capital by European legislatures it can be argued that, for those seeking to promote the cause of corporate accountability, *focussing attention on the operations of the capital markets, in particular the unaccountable power wielded by*

---

[5] We suggest that this dismissal of the primary shareholder group is due to a belief among some that the business case for SEE disclosure and SEE engagement is misplaced and that the ethics case, which focuses more strongly on the inclusion of other stakeholders in corporate social responsibility, is more important.

Illustration 9.3

Stakeholder engagement at Camelot

Camelot operates the National Lottery Company. The Company aims to raise money for good causes and their mission statement is 'To serve the nation's dreams through The National Lottery'. Camelot's primary business objective is to embed corporate social responsibility in order to meet its prime business objective, 'To deliver the target returns to good causes in a socially responsible way'. Camelot produced its first social report in 2002. It was the first company in the UK to apply the AA1000 standard.

The company has focused on developing and maintaining interstakeholder engagement. Camelot specifies its stakeholders as: the public, its employees, the community, its retailers, its suppliers, pressure groups, the environment and its shareholders. It is interesting that Camelot includes the shareholders at the end of its list in the social report—a striking difference from a traditional agency theory approach. For effective stakeholder engagement the company: arranges meetings between stakeholders; produces publications; organizes focus groups and events, such as seminars, conferences and receptions. The dialogue Camelot has nurtured between retailers and social lobby groups is a shining example of its work in this area. Retailers (typically small corner shops) have been confronted with children attempting to purchase tickets. The law does not allow anyone under 18 years old to participate in gambling, and buying lottery tickets falls into this category. This is a severe problem for retailers. How do they check younger peoples' age without appearing officious and potentially losing custom. Further, they could attract intimidating behaviour from some groups of young people by not allowing them to buy tickets. These sorts of difficulties are not always appreciated by social lobby groups who are attempting to prevent children becoming involved in gambling. Bringing these two important groups together helps to nurture more mutual understanding of the issues of concern. Camelot has arranged a series of meetings between representatives from retailers and lobby groups that have fostered better appreciation between the two parties. Further, Camelot has investigated ways in which it can curb the spread of gambling to children. For example, the company is introducing Lottery games for players on the Internet. This opens up greater potential for children to become involved in gambling as many have their own PCs at home. Therefore, Camelot has invested substantial funds in setting up an electronic age verification system, preventing children from playing the interactive games. Further, in relation to the broader ethical issue of tempting people of any age to spend excessive amounts on gambling, Camelot has invested in a country-wide electronic system that prevents people from spending more than a fixed amount at any one time.

On face value Camelot is making great strides in the area of corporate social responsibility. Its efforts are impressive and the structures are in place to deliver a high level of accountability to society. For a company whose very essence may be viewed by some as unethical, it is making massive efforts to alter public perceptions. However, balancing commercial objectives with such a self-acclaimed social responsibility aim is a hefty challenge to undertake. Further, there has been controversy from the start of the National Lottery about the organizations that have been selected to distribute funds to. The term 'good cause' is unspecific and extremely subjective. There has been a perception among some sectors of society that the Lottery may be seen as a silent tax, 'taking money from the poor and distributing it to the rich' in the form of more attractive arts, which only the rich can afford to participate in. This jaundiced view may have been dispelled by the company's recent efforts.

institutional fund managers, offers more hope of success than engaging in corporate controlled stakeholder dialogue processes.

(Owen, 2003, p. 27, emphasis added)

Perhaps another route to greater corporate accountability and social responsibility, such as institutional investor engagement, needs to be harnessed. As we saw in Chapter 5, institutional investors in the UK are arguably the most influential and therefore most relevant group of corporate stakeholders. We therefore expect engagement between institutional investors and their investee companies to be representative of the most evolved form of stakeholder engagement in UK companies on SEE issues. Indeed, our own research has shown that there is a sophisticated process of private disclosure on SEE issues that is already taking place between institutional investors and their investee companies (Solomon and Solomon, 2003a). We discuss the involvement of the institutional investment community in more detail in Chapter 10.

Chapter summary

In this chapter we have considered the growth in importance of corporate social responsibility from a historical perspective. We have also shown how this growth of interest has influenced companies and encouraged them to discharge a broader accountability to diverse stakeholders in the SEE arena. One of the main ways in which this accountability may be discharged is through reporting of SEE information, as shareholders and other corporate stakeholders require such information for decision making and for pure accountability purposes. We have used CER as a means of illustrating the characteristics of disclosure in these areas. Generally, the UK Government is pushing companies to disclose more SEE and ultimately sustainability information. There is, as we have discussed, a growing perception that good management of SEE issues is a reflection of good general management, which is helping to drive the sustainability agenda. Lastly, we have considered the evolving process of stakeholder engagement and the academic debate surrounding its genuine success in promoting corporate accountability to stakeholders.

Questions for reflection and discussion

1 Discuss the reasons why some companies undertake CER and others do not. What are the wider implications of companies not undertaking CER?

2 Download a corporate environmental report from the Internet from those short-listed by ACCA. Summarize the content of the report, focusing on the areas discussed in this chapter, highlighting both positive and negative aspects of the reporting.

3 Look at any company's latest social report on the Internet. Consider all the different stakeholder engagement techniques and strategies that the company is employing. Critically evaluate the usefulness of these techniques and strategies. What is your personal view of the company's success in discharging accountability to society and behaving as a socially responsible company?

4 Do you think that sustainability is achievable by companies in the UK?

Chapter 10

Socially responsible investment

Aim and objectives

This chapter considers the important role that institutional investors are playing in broadening the corporate governance agenda and in driving corporate social responsibility. The specific objectives of this chapter are to enable readers to:

- highlight the important role that institutional investors are playing in progressing corporate social responsibility and encouraging greater accountability to a broad range of stakeholders;

- consider the growth of socially responsible investment in the UK and elsewhere, highlighting the ways in which socially responsible investment has moved from a marginal to a mainstream area of institutional investment;

- discuss the potential implications of the socially responsible investment movement for companies, their stakeholders and ultimately for society.

Introduction

In the last chapter we considered a broader agenda for corporate governance by discussing the development of corporate social responsibility. We considered how companies can discharge accountability to a broad range of stakeholders through social, ethical, environmental (SEE) and ultimately sustainability reporting and stakeholder engagement. In this chapter we look at another very important aspect of this wider accountability and broader corporate governance. We turn to ways in which institutional investors can contribute to corporate social responsibility and to a greater accountability to stakeholders through their investment policies. Indeed, we show that institutional investors are playing an important role in progressing corporate social responsibility and have an important role to play in promoting more responsible business behaviour.

From a stakeholder theory perspective, companies are accountable to all stakeholders, not just their shareholders, as we showed in our definition of corporate governance in Chapter 1. As we discussed in Chapter 9, corporate environmental and social reporting represent ways in which corporate accountability to stakeholders may be discharged. There has been a growing awareness, or consciousness, in society that unless companies take account of the SEE issues in their business decisions, then future social welfare may be in question. Serious repercussions from socially irresponsible behaviour have highlighted the need to pay attention to and influence companies' actions. Exxon Valdez, Brent Spar, Nike and Huntingdon Life Sciences present just a handful of notorious examples that have shown companies in a negative light and have resulted in significant shareholder reactions. See Illustration 10.1 for a detailed discussion of the case of Huntingdon Life Sciences and its implications for socially responsible investment and corporate social responsibility. Corporate social responsibility has been encouraged by lobbyists who have pressured companies to improve their performance in the areas of the environment and human rights. They have also put pressure on shareholders, especially institutional investors, to become more involved in the SEE-related behaviour of their investees. However, it is not just outside pressure that has led companies to adopt a more stakeholder-oriented attitude. Experience has shown companies that they can suffer substantial financial losses as a result of SEE problems and incidents. The reputation risk attached to SEE incidents is tremendous, with share prices falling almost instantaneously in reaction to bad SEE news. As shown in Chapter 6, the Turnbull Report (1999) encapsulated an agenda to improve internal control in the area of non-financial as well as financial risks. Turnbull's recommendations have focused attention on a risk-driven approach to SEE management. Institutional investors are adopting a socially responsible investment mandate because of their perceptions of the importance of reputation risk arising from SEE misbehaviour. Indeed, CalPERS (California Public Employees' Retirement System), the largest and most influential investment institution in the USA, has opted to apply social criteria to all its investment decision making, stating that:

> ... equity in corporations with poor social and ethical records *could represent an excessive fiduciary risk* because such firms court boycotts, lawsuits, or labor activity.
>
> (Quoted in Monks, 2001, p. 134, emphasis added)

Another influential institutional investor in the UK, Friends Provident, has chosen to pursue socially responsible investment proactively, in part because it believes that this leads to enhanced returns for shareholders. The institution's chief executive commented, for example, that:

> Good corporate practice on human rights, child labour and environmental pollution is good for society, but it's also good for shareholders. As a large investor, it is right that we use our influence with companies to encourage responsible business practices while serving the financial interests of our customers.
>
> (Quoted in *Financial Times*, 7 May 2000)

If corporate social responsibility is to grow, the importance of the institutional investment community's role cannot be exaggerated. The power that institutional investors can wield as a force for good has been frequently acknowledged as:

> ... what we need is a means by which we can wield our influence over businesses to act responsibly ... Ethical and environmental investment is that means.
>
> (Hancock, 1999, p. 8)

As we discussed in earlier chapters, institutional investors hold the majority of UK shares. Consequently, unless they endorse corporate social responsibility through socially responsible investment, there will be little incentive for companies to act in a socially responsible manner. It is the pressure that these influential investors, the providers of finance, exert on the companies they own that decides corporate strategy to a certain extent. If these major shareholders put companies under pressure to behave in a socially responsible way then companies are likely to respond. If institutional investors reject socially responsible investment as an investment strategy, then companies will be unlikely to prioritize SEE issues in their business decisions. We can therefore see a strong link between socially responsible investment and corporate social responsibility. Institutional shareholders are in a position to pressure companies to behave in a more socially responsible manner and should, according to Monks' (2001) discourse on global investment, act as responsible owners. As early as the 1930s the influence of large investment institutions on society was acknowledged by John Maynard Keynes, who commented that:

> Of the maxims of orthodox finance none, surely, is more anti-social than the fetish of liquidity, the doctrine that it is a positive virtue on the part of investment institutions to concentrate their resources upon the holding of 'liquid' securities. It forgets that there is no such thing as liquidity of investment for the community as a whole. The social object of skilled investment should be to defeat the dark forces of time and ignorance which envelop our future.
>
> (Keynes, 1936, p. 155)

Therefore, even in the early 20th century, the ability of large shareholders to degrade or enhance social welfare was clearly acknowledged. We now turn to establishing a working definition of socially responsible investment.

Terminology and definitions

Over time the term used to describe what we now know as socially responsible investment has varied substantially. The most common term in general usage in the UK has tended to be 'ethical investment'. However, in recent years socially responsible investment has taken over as the primary term in theory and in practice. It implies a broader remit of definition, covering SEE issues. It is also more

Illustration 10.1

Shareholder activism on animal rights: the case of Huntingdon Life Sciences

The British have always been viewed as a nation of pet lovers. Nowhere could this be more obvious than in the case of Huntingdon Life Sciences (HLS). The company's failure to treat animals in its care with adequate respect has turned it overnight from a successful market leader in the biotechnology industry to a pauper, struggling to gain funding. The case is controversial and has inspired a broad range of emotional responses. A study of the problems experienced by HLS demonstrates unequivocally that lack of attention by a company to SEE matters can impact significantly on financial performance. In 1997 HLS was a company with a great future. The company was at the forefront of biotechnology, specializing in testing new chemicals, often on animals. The practice of vivisection is common in the production of chemicals and drugs. The term 'vivisection' means 'physical experimentation on a living animal … especially if considered to cause distress to the subject' (*Longman Dictionary*, 1984). Vivisection has aroused an emotional response from the British public for many years, who continue to be dismayed by information relating to animal tests. For example, in 2001 the European Commission's plans to test thousands of chemicals for toxicity, resulting in the death of at least 50 million animals resulted in an uproar from animal rights groups (Osborn, 2001). The animals that are used in tests include monkeys, rabbits, guinea pigs, mice, dogs, rats, hamsters, birds and fish. Generally, tests involve administering increasingly large doses of the chemical under test in order to observe the side effects. Such force-feeding causes bleeding from the eyes and nose, convulsions, vomiting, and a slow and painful death. All for the sake of scientific advancement and public protection.

In 1997 a documentary on Channel 4 entitled *It's A Dog's Life* provided video evidence that animals kept at the company's laboratories for testing purposes were undergoing terrible cruelty. For example, footage was shown of an HLS employee hitting a beagle. As soon as this information became public, the government threatened to revoke its licence to conduct animal experiments. All major pharmaceutical clients suspended contracts. In 1997 HLS's share price reached 117p, but by August 2000 this had fallen to 9p (Oakey, 2000). Given the dire financial situation that HLS found itself in, the company suspended trading in its shares in August 1998 in order to gain refinancing. The company called an extraordinary meeting and was successful in gaining approval for a £20.2 million refinancing package. Even this attempt to save the company was met by intense protests and lobbying (*Financial Times*, 2 September 1998). Five shareholders were thrown out of the meeting for persistent unruly behaviour. Animal rights lobbyists exerted terrific pressure on institutional shareholders and succeeded in 'persuading' major institutions to sell their shares in the company. Phillips & Drew, for example, sold its 11% stake in HLS in 2000, following a bomb threat, three years after the company's exposure (Skapinker, 2000). In December 2000 animal rights campaigners forced HSBC, the world's second largest bank, to sell its stake of almost 1% in HLS (Firn and Guerrera, 2000). Indeed, animal rights activism has been forceful to say the least, with activists from The British Union for the Abolition of Vivisection Reform Group threatening to protest outside the homes of HLS investors unless they sold their shares (Guerrera, 2000a). Pressure on UK investment institutions and banks was so intense that HLS repaid financing from UK financial institutions, such as the National Westminster, in order to release them from the embarrassment of association with the company. Instead, HLS turned to US institutions for financial backing in 2000 (Guerrera, 2000b). However, this did not deter lobbyists from the group Stop Huntingdon Animal Cruelty (commonly referred to as SHAC), who vowed to pursue the company and its new shareholders across the Atlantic. In December 2000 HLS lost its listing on the New York Stock Exchange (Firn, 2000) but gained approval to switch its stock market listing from the London Stock Exchange to the US NASD over-the-counter bulletin board market in January 2001 (Jenkins, 2001). In 2002, five years after the Channel 4 programme was broadcast, the US bank Stephens ended its backing of HLS (Firn, 2002). Animal rights activists pursued the world's largest insurance broker in the USA, Marsh, by attacking offices with smoke bombs and vandalizing a golf course (Bolger and Jenkins, 2002). They have even followed customers of HLS as far as Japan (Firn and Jenkins, 2003).

The problem is that however honourable the intentions of the activists may have been, they have certainly damaged their own cause, probably irrevocably. In the wake of scientific advances, animal rights activists may be viewed by some as reminiscent of the activities of the Luddites in an earlier era. Threats on employees and shareholders were enough to enrage supporters of animal research and scientist lobbies, but when these threats crystallized into action it was far easier for them to build defences. For example, six cars belonging to HLS employees were set on fire in August 2000. This type of activity clearly represented criminal behaviour, with the managing director of HLS commenting, 'How can people with such callous disregard for the safety of people purport to be campaigning for the welfare of animals' (The Guardian, 29 August 2000). The activists have clearly gone far too far. A professor of physiology at Oxford University has suffered two bombs being delivered to his home and his daughter being threatened with kidnap. In December 2000 a manager from the animal research centre at HLS was attacked outside his home. Chemicals were sprayed into his eyes and he was struck on the back (Eagle, 2000). It is hard for any reasonable person to be sympathetic to the cause of activists who inflict harm in this way. Not only has the company lost support from financial institutions in the UK but also pharmaceutical companies from foreign countries have been discouraged from investing directly in the UK. This could have serious repercussions in the long-term on the British economy. For some, the activities of animal rights groups range from the sublime to the ridiculous. A prime example of behaviour that was likely to remove rather than establish the credibility of such lobby groups as the Animal Liberation Front was the laying of a wreath for the guinea pigs bred for testing purposes at a farm in Newchurch (Griffin, 2000). This case is particularly interesting from the point of view of ethical relativism. Everyone has a slightly different opinion on what is 'right' and 'wrong', 'good' and 'bad'. Whereas some people feel strongly enough about animal rights and cruelty to animals to risk a prison sentence, others consider that any testing on animals is worthwhile and acceptable if it leads to improvements in the quality of human life. Animal rights activists have been referred to frequently as 'urban terrorists' in the press and by senior members of Government. The gulf between these extreme positions is hard to bridge, as there is no real meeting place. Nevertheless, the views of animal rights activists have been enforced in the market place, as even the largest institutional investors in the UK and USA have given in to pressure from lobby groups and divested their shares in HLS.

There has been a distinct backlash against animal rights activists as a result of their at times violent outbursts. For example, in 2000 all laboratories performing experiments on animals were granted official exemption, allowing them to keep the details of their work secret (The Independent, 16 September 2000). This decision arose from concerns for the safety of employees working in laboratories. In November 2000 Tony Blair attacked animal rights lobby groups, accusing them of 'anti-science attitudes' and warning that the Government would not allow 'blackmail' and physical assault to stand in the way of research (The Independent, 18 November 2000). Nevertheless, the latest reports into the use of monkeys in experiments have concluded that they are a 'regrettable necessity' but demonstrate concerns that there are ethical problems involved in using primates and suggest that such tests should be reduced wherever possible (Brown, 2003).

user-friendly than ethical investment, as the word ethical implies some subjective decision on the part of the investor. The term 'socially responsible' attempts to describe a form of investment that is less subjective and that 'should' be instigated by a 'responsible' society. The following definition of socially responsible investment illustrates the wide array of terms used to refer to the process of socially responsible investment:

> Social investing, social responsible investing, socially aware investing, ethical investing, values-based investing, mission-based investing . . . all describe the same concept. These terms tend to be used interchangeably within the investment industry to describe an approach to investing that integrates personal values and societal concerns into the investment decision-making process.
>
> (Steve Scheuth, Social Investment Forum, quoted in the *AccountAbility Primer*)

Another definition of the process of socially responsible investment, given in the *Primer* and quoted from the UK Social Investment Forum is that:

> Socially responsible investment combines investors' financial objectives with their commitment to social concerns such as justice, economic development, peace or a healthy environment.

This quote brings one of the most important issues in socially responsible investment to the fore: Is it possible to be ethical and still to make a profit? When we discussed corporate governance in earlier chapters we alluded to the importance of increasing corporate profitability by improving corporate governance. We stipulated that unless better corporate governance resulted in better financial performance, there would be little incentive to further the agenda for corporate governance reform. In Chapter 9 we provided evidence from the extant literature that suggests that corporate social responsibility leads to higher financial performance for companies. The same argument applies to socially responsible investment. However moral and ethical investors are, they do not tend to welcome a reduction in their investment return. Few people are prepared to accept a lower return to investment from investing in a socially responsible manner. Indeed, such a choice would be impractical, given that the majority of institutional investment involves pension funds and lower returns would result in impoverished pensioners in the future. Again, unless socially responsible investment produces returns that are at least equivalent to non-socially responsible investment, then socially responsible investment is unlikely to grow and prosper. We consider this issue later in this chapter. First, we discuss the type of issues with which 'ethical' investors are concerned. The issues that are important to socially responsible investors are shown in Table 10.1.

Nevertheless, a salient issue for institutional investors who wish to take account of SEE factors in their portfolio investment decisions is the extent to which a consensus can be reached on the relative importance of these factors. There is a general

Table [10.1]   Issues of importance to the socially responsible investor

Alcohol	Military/MOD contracts	Poor workplace conditions
Animal testing	Arms exports to oppressive regimes	Third World concerns
Gambling	Nuclear power	Tobacco
Greenhouse gases	Ozone depletion	Water pollution
Health and safety breaches	Pesticides	Tropical hardwoods
Human rights abuses	Pornography and adult films	Genetically modified food
Intensive farming	Road use/construction	Gene patenting

tendency for people to behave according to the philosophical concept of 'ethical subjectivism'. By this we mean that everyone has a different view of 'right' or 'wrong', and 'good' or 'bad'. It is therefore very difficult to decide on a set of ethical principles that may be applied to investments for a wide selection of investors. Indeed, by practising socially responsible investment investors are forcing a set of ethical principles on companies and by default on society as a whole. This is an interesting philosophical issue and one that is being explored in the academic work in order to appreciate the process of socially responsible investment and corporate social responsibility (Solomon and Solomon, 2003). So, what is the hard statistical evidence on socially responsible investment?

Some recent statistics on socially responsible investment

The UK has witnessed a substantial increase in socially responsible investment in recent years. Current figures indicate that £4 billion was invested in 'ethical' funds in August 2001. However, this is only a drop in the ocean when we consider that ethical funds are a minor area of socially responsible investment. Socially responsible investment now implies institutional investors taking account of SEE issues in their portfolio decisions, as an overarching umbrella investment criterion. Indeed, market research has indicated that 77% of the British public would like their pension funds to be invested in a socially responsible way, provided this did not harm financial returns (Targett, 2000). The extent of UK socially responsible investment has increased significantly in recent years, evidenced by the growth in the number of socially responsible investment funds offered by institutional investors. Recent evidence has suggested that almost 80% of pension scheme members require their schemes to operate an socially responsible investment policy (*The Ethical Investor*, November/December 1999). This trend toward more socially responsible investment has had a substantial impact on the institutional investment community, on pension fund trustees, on the managers of UK listed companies and on society in a wider context. As discussed in Chapter 5, pension funds hold the largest stake in the UK stock market, which shows the significant role they play in all areas of investment strategy, including social responsibility. Friedman and Miles (2001) and Sparkes

(2002) showed that institutional investors have embraced socially responsible investment as part of their mainstream portfolio investment strategies.

Socially responsible investment strategies

Screening
Until relatively recently the primary strategy for socially responsible investment had been screening. In making their portfolio investment decisions the fund managers of ethical funds within investment institutions 'screened' companies according to socially responsible criteria. There are two types of social screening, positive and negative. Positive (or aspirational) screening involves deciding what sort of companies would be a 'good' addition to the investment portfolio (Dobson, 1994). Negative screening involves fund managers avoiding companies that pursue certain activities. These may include: companies with negative environmental impacts; companies that provide strategic goods to repressive political regimes; companies that produce tobacco products, alcoholic beverages and weaponry; and companies involved in nuclear weapons or the production of nuclear power. Dobson commented that:

> Of all the social screens, environmental ones cause the least controversy . . . generally it is
> agreed that clean air, clean water and safe working conditions are desirable.
>
> (Dobson, 1994, p. 163)

As we saw in the area of environmental reporting in the previous chapter, the environment is the most mature form of non-financial, sustainability-oriented disclosure. This also seems to be the case in the area of socially responsible investment analysis.

Best in sector
Although socially responsible investment originally consisted of a screening strategy, more recent strategies have focused on a 'best in class' approach (Mansley, 2000), which means that socially responsible funds do not exclude whole sectors from their portfolios but include those companies in previously excluded sectors that are making the most effort to improve their social responsibility. The FTSE4Good index and other socially responsible investment indices around the world, such as the Jantzi index in Canada, which have been introduced in the last couple of years, adopt a best in class approach. This represents a realistic approach for socially responsible investment and one that is open to a much larger group of investors. However, from a 'deep green' perspective such an approach may be considered a cop-out, as shareholders can invest in a company in any industry, no matter what it produces, provided it has the best corporate social responsibility policies related to its industry peers. Having said that, the best in sector approach is perhaps the only

socially responsible stance possible for pension fund investment managers who are bound by legislation to provide stable returns without reducing the potential for portfolio diversification. It allows trustees to adopt socially responsible investment policies without compromising their fiduciary duties. As mentioned earlier a central issue for investors is whether socially responsible investment funds perform financially as well as, or better than, funds invested according to socially responsible investment criteria. However strongly investors desire to invest in a socially responsible manner, the prospect of lower financial returns on socially responsible funds would act as a disincentive for socially responsible investment.

Social, ethical and environmental engagement by institutional investors
In Chapter 9, we discussed the engagement process that is evolving between companies and stakeholders. In Chapter 5 we discussed engagement between institutional investors and companies on a range of issues. A sophisticated process of engagement and dialogue is also developing between institutional investors and their investee companies in the area of SEE information. Indeed, this type of engagement is becoming one of the most influential strategies used in socially responsible investment. Sparkes (2002) highlighted the growth in SEE engagement as a main indicator that socially responsible investment is moving away from the margin and into mainstream investment. We found evidence from a series of interviews with institutional investors that indicated that the process of engagement in this area has become formalized (Solomon and Solomon, 2003a). The interviews showed that engagement by institutional investors on SEE issues is evolving into a two-way process, with companies asking institutional fund managers questions as well as questions being directed toward companies by shareholders. As we saw in Chapter 5 engagement and dialogue between institutional investors and their investee companies now plays a major role in corporate governance. Such an investment strategy is equally important and effective for corporate governance in its broadest context, where it embraces corporate social responsibility. It is a more proactive approach for socially responsible investment than screening, as companies are pressured by their core investors to improve their SEE performance. Engagement represents a particularly important approach for index-tracking investors who cannot divest shares if they are dissatisfied with investee companies and, therefore, use engagement as a means of influencing company management.

As well as pressure from social and environmental lobby groups, the clients of investment institutions are also calling for their fund managers to engage on SEE issues. As we mentioned earlier on p. 214, company reputation is significantly affected by risks in the SEE area and institutional investors want to pre-empt the negative effects of such risks materializing wherever possible. Where risks materialize, significant financial losses can be incurred and SEE risks become financial risks. Often, in such cases, the institutional fund managers can no longer rely on engagement with the investee company but eventually turn to selling shares. A salient example of ethical problems within a company becoming public knowledge and leading to mass divestment of the company's shares by institutional shareholders is the case of Huntingdon Life Sciences. Refer to Illustration 10.1 for a full discussion of this case and its repercussions on shareholders and the company. We now turn to evidence pertaining to the crucial question: Is socially responsible investment profitable?

The financial performance of socially responsible investment funds

> There is no clear evidence from experience that the investment policy which is socially advantageous coincides with that which is most profitable ...
>
> (Keynes, 1936, p. 157)

An essential issue for institutional investors is whether socially responsible investment funds perform as well financially as funds without socially responsible characteristics. However strongly investors desire to invest in a socially responsible manner, the prospect of lower financial returns on socially responsible funds would act as a strong disincentive for socially responsible investment. As socially responsible investment is rising it is likely that investors believe they will make equal, if not higher, returns from socially responsible investment than from non-socially responsible investment investment. Certainly, in interviews that we have performed with fund directors this belief prevails, especially among the largest funds. Solomon and Solomon (2002) found strong evidence of a growing perception among the institutional investment community that socially responsible investment, as part of the mainstream investment strategy, enhances financial returns in the long term. Drexhage (1998) considered that investors and fund managers believe it is possible to make a difference while making a profit.

Boatright (1999) discussed the theoretical arguments underlying socially responsible investment. From a theoretical perspective there is some support for socially responsible funds outperforming non-socially responsible funds. First, from simple economic theory of demand and supply it is reasonable that if demand for socially responsible companies increases, then so will their price (i.e., the share price and therefore the market value of the company will rise). Similarly, if demand for shares in companies that are not socially responsible falls, so will their market value. This impact has been summarized as follows:

> ... investment demand for shares in institutions with such products as 'natural cosmetics' or positive employment policies may be stimulated. From the purely financial view, growth in such investor sentiment may be expected to produce gains in shares with a 'positive' ethical rating and losses on others ...
>
> (Luther et al., 1992, p. 57)

Second, from a free market perspective, socially responsible investment is an important issue, as it implies that funds may not be so easily raised by companies that are not socially responsible in their activities. Ultimately, if socially responsible screening continues to grow at its current rate we may see Adam Smith's (1838) 'invisible hand' distributing more funds to socially responsible companies and diverting funds from companies that do not act in a socially responsible manner (Boatright, 1999).

On the contrary, there are also a number of reasons from a theoretical perspective why socially responsible funds may indeed underperform non-socially responsible funds. Luther et al. (1992) suggested from a portfolio theory perspective that socially screened funds will attract lower returns because of a lack of diversification potential and higher transaction costs. Second, efficient markets theory also presents reasons for socially responsible fund underperformance. It is generally accepted that the UK stock market is semi-strong form-efficient, implying that all publicly available information is completely, immediately and accurately incorporated in share prices. This in turn implies that all share prices are a true representation of their inherent risks. This means that no investor can consistently beat the market by obtaining more, or alternative, information about a specific company or indeed about wider economic issues. Therefore, the only way in which an investor can obtain a higher return is by taking on greater risk or by gaining access to, and acting on, private/inside information, which is illegal. The implications for socially responsible investment are that actively evaluating company shares by any specific criterion (e.g., social responsibility) is a waste of resources as the traditionally accepted investment strategy for investors is to passively select a balanced portfolio, mirroring the market as a whole, rather than selecting shares actively according to such subjective criteria as socially responsible objectives. Only if the stock market is inefficient can there be potential gains from socially responsible investment as:

> The case for SRI, then, must be based on the claims that the market is inefficient and that the source of this inefficiency is a failure to recognize the significance of socially responsible activity in the evaluation of stock price.
>
> (Boatright, 1999, p. 111)

Existing academic empirical research has failed to find any statistically significant difference in the returns of socially responsible funds (e.g., Mallin et al., 1995). A number of empirical studies have been performed to evaluate the financial performance of UK socially responsible funds. Luther et al. (1992) isolated a sample of socially responsible unit trusts and found that five of the trusts offered a higher total return than the FT-All Share index. They found overall that half of the trusts studied outperformed the market and half underperformed. However, the use of an appropriate benchmark in such empirical work has provided cause for concern (see Luther and Matatko, 1994). Mallin et al. (1995) attempted to overcome this problem by using improved techniques to compare the performance of UK socially responsible investment funds not only with a market benchmark but also with non-socially responsible investment funds. Overall, they found that both socially responsible and non-socially responsible trusts seemed to underperform the market. However, they provided some weak evidence that socially responsible trusts outperformed non-socially responsible trusts. They attributed their findings to a type of 'bandwagon' effect:

> The weakly superior performance of ethical funds evidenced in the sample may have been a temporary phenomenon caused by an increased awareness and interest in ethical investment. This in turn led to increasing levels of demand for appropriate investment products establishing a premium in realised rates of return. Indeed, this phenomenon may still be continuing as ethical investment gains in acceptance.
>
> (Mallin et al., 1995, p. 495)

Using similar techniques, the most recent academic study by Gregory et al. (1997) showed that both socially responsible and non-socially responsible trusts under-performed the market but that underperformance was worse for socially responsible trusts.

From a more practical perspective, the development of benchmark indices for evaluating socially responsible fund performance should provide clarification on this issue. Williams (1999) stated that one of the future trends in UK socially responsible investment will be the development of dedicated performance bench-marks. Indeed, there has been a recent emergence of socially responsible investment stock exchange indices in the UK. The Ethical Investment Research Service (EIRIS) has developed five socially responsible indices, each of which indicates financial returns roughly equivalent to the FTSE-All Share Index for the period 1991 to 1998. Also, in 1998 the NPI Social Index was launched. It is likely that the emergence of new socially responsible investment indices will:

> . . . explode the myth that green and ethical investors have to accept that their investment performance will be disappointing.
>
> (Holden-Meehan, 1999, p. 35)

Williams (1999) stated that one of the future trends in UK socially responsible investment will be the development of dedicated performance benchmarks. The launch of the FTSE4Good index is an encouraging development for supporters of the socially responsible investment movement. But who are these supporters? We now look at whether or not there is evidence of a significant demand for SEE disclosure by companies arising from the interest of the institutional investment community in socially responsible investment.

A growing demand for social, ethical and environmental disclosure

In Chapter 6 we acknowledged the importance of corporate transparency as a means of reducing the agency problem and reducing information asymmetries. The disclosure function is just as important in the SEE area as in other areas. Linked to the growth of socially responsible investment is the need for adequate SEE information. The emerging emphasis on greater corporate accountability through greater disclosure of all types of risk to shareholders (as well as to the wider stakeholder community) is a clear indication that social-oriented information is becoming more important. From the perspective of socially responsible investment, the importance of recent disclosure recommendations, such as those stemming from the Cadbury Report (1999) and the Turnbull Report (1999), is the shift of focus away from solely financial aspects of internal control and toward consideration of non-financial risks, as:

> An effective risk management process addresses both financial risks (such as credit, market and liquidity risk) and non-financial risks (such as legal and environmental risk).
>
> (Stock et al., 1999, p. 41)

You may recall that we discussed the importance of non-financial risks in Chapter 6. It is likely that companies that do not behave in a socially responsible manner will be at risk from investor sentiment as well as potential unanticipated reputation risks, such as environmental disasters. It is now generally acknowledged that increased and improved information disclosure is not only essential for purely financial investment decisions but also for socially responsible investment. One signal that SEE disclosure is growing in importance is the recent publication of a new standard for companies, the AA1000 Standard (AccountAbility 1000, 1999), which provides a framework for companies to improve and disclose their performance as socially responsible companies. Other initiatives include recommendations from the Association of British Insurers (ABI) (Cowe, 2001) and the Global Reporting Initiative (GRI, 2000). This area has been covered in some detail in the previous chapter. The ABI has also published a set of guidelines on SEE disclosure directed at companies. This set of guidelines was prepared by a number of important institutional investor groups and attempts to represent the information requirements of the institutional investor community. Specifically, the guidelines stated that they would like company boards of directors to state in their annual reports whether or not the board:

- takes regular account of the significance of SEE matters to the business of the company;

- has identified and assessed the significant risks to the company's short and long-term value arising from SEE matters, as well as the opportunities to enhance value that may arise from an appropriate response;

- has received adequate information to make this assessment and that account is taken of SEE matters in the training of directors;

- has ensured that the company has in place effective systems for managing significant risks, which where relevant incorporate performance management systems and appropriate remuneration incentives.

Further, with respect to policies, procedures and verification, the ABI stated that they would like to see the following in the annual report:

- information on SEE-related risks and opportunities that may significantly affect the company's short and long-term value and how they might impact on the business;

- description of the company's policies and procedures for managing risks to short and long-term value, arising from SEE matters, and if the annual report and accounts state that the company has no such policies and procedures the Board should provide reasons for their absence;

- information about the extent to which the company has complied with its policies and procedures for managing risks arising from SEE matters;

- description of the procedures for verification of SEE disclosures. The verification procedure should be such as to achieve a reasonable level of credibility.

The needs of institutional investors and other shareholders for more disclosure of SEE information have been clarified in many institutional investor's written policy documents. For example, one institution provided the following in a document entitled *Responsible Shareholders: A Guide to Our Corporate Governance Views and Policies* (August 1998):[1]

> We expect the boards of the companies in which we invest to pay due regard to ethical and environmental issues and thereby protect and enhance long-term shareholder value. Companies should be able to demonstrate their commitment to responsible environmental policies. We believe that shareholders have a right to know about the activities of companies in the area of ethical and environmental issues. We will, therefore, support proposals for disclosure as long as the costs involved are reasonable.

In relation to corporate social disclosure and socially responsible investment, Harte et al. (1991) researched the sources of information used by socially responsible fund managers. The corporate annual report was found to be of little use in socially responsible investment decisions. The fund managers indicated that annual reports do not contain adequate information for screening companies on a socially responsible basis. The researchers concluded that there was a need for accounting policy makers to give a higher priority to issues of socially responsible information disclosure. Indeed, the fund managers suggested that companies should include more information in their annual reports on environmental impact, animal experimentation, community and social issues and trading interests in countries with repressive regimes. However, although these findings have substantial policy implications, the

---

[1] Confidentiality is maintained here as we are unsure whether or not this document is distributed in the public arena.

work has not been readdressed by the academic community until relatively recently. Friedman and Miles (2001) found from their research that the City of London was taking SEE issues far more seriously. In our own research we have found from extensive interviews within the institutional investment community that SEE matters are being treated as a mainstream issue and that fund managers are dissatisfied with the level of corporate disclosure of SEE information (Solomon and Solomon, 2003a). This is clearly an area where new research is needed to discover whether companies have responded in spirit, as well as in form, to information requirements of the ever-growing socially responsible investor population.

As well as greater disclosure of information on social responsibility issues, the development of longer and stronger communication and decision links between institutional investors and investee companies should help to improve information flows and increase the potential for socially responsible investment to continue growing. The role of fund managers within investment institutions is essential to the development of socially responsible investment, as:

> Now a third way has emerged—a positive, proactive policy of communication between institutions, fund managers and companies. This trend towards 'active dialogue' is very exciting ... Engaging in constructive discussions with companies on their ethical and environmental activities is what will ultimately make a sustainable difference.
>
> (Holden-Meehan, 1999, p. 25)

Solomon and Solomon (2002) argued that improvements in quality and quantity of SEE disclosure constitute part of a 'virtuous circle' of corporate social responsibility, arising from initiatives encouraging the development of socially responsible investment. As institutional investors take increasing account of social responsibility issues in their portfolio investment decisions, they will demand more information and companies will have to provide the information.

Socially responsible investment in an international context

socially responsible investment is not solely a UK concern and is increasingly important at a global level. We consider below some countries where socially responsible investment is growing in importance.

Socially responsible investment in the USA
The USA is a strong advocate of socially responsible investment. It is considered that ethical investment originated in the USA among a number of church groups and grew in importance with public reaction to the Vietnam War in the 1970s. In 1992 over US$500 billion of US institutional investment was invested accorded to some level of social screening. The latest figures indicate that more than $2 trillion (about

13%) of all US investment follows socially responsible criteria. Indeed, growth of socially responsible investment in recent years has been exponential. A 1999 report by the Social Investment Forum in the USA found that, since 1997, total assets under management in screened portfolios rose 183%. Another sign of the growing importance of socially responsible investment in the USA has been the development of the Domini 400 Social Index (DSI), used as a benchmark for measuring the performance of socially responsible portfolios. It includes the shares of 400 companies that have satisfied a multitude of social screens. From May 1990 to September 1992 the DSI was found to outperform the S&P500. The conclusion at that time was that socially responsible investing could produce higher returns than investment without social constraints but that these returns were riskier. Guerard (1996) found that there was no significant difference between the average monthly returns of US funds that were screened according to socially responsible criteria and those that were not for the period 1987 to 1994. Further, Guerard (1997) extended his earlier work and found no significant difference in the mean returns of socially unscreened and screened investment funds between 1987 and 1996. He took the implications of his findings further by suggesting that social screens may be a signal of better management and the generation of higher financial returns. Also, Kessler and Gottsman (1998) compared the total financial returns of companies in the S&P500 over a number of years with a series of subsets of the S&P500 over the same period. Environmental performance indicators were used as the basis for selecting the various subsets analysed, and those companies with apparently better environmental performance showed a slightly higher return than the overall return of the S&P500 companies as a whole.

Socially responsible investment in Canada
Several years ago 60 Canadian companies were chosen to constitute Canada's first index comprising 'socially responsible' companies (*The Economist*, 1 June 2000) called the Jantzi Social Index (after Michael Jantzi who developed it). The aim of the Index was to encourage managers to incorporate SEE considerations in their business decision making. The DSI screens out companies involved in tobacco, alcohol, gambling, weapons or nuclear power generation, whereas the new Jantzi does not screen out alcohol or gambling companies. Similarly, it does not exclude mining companies and forestry—as these represent the backbone of Canada's industrial activities. The index therefore represents a compromise, as the Jantzi is adopting the new 'best in class' approach, already evident in socially responsible investment funds in the UK.

Socially responsible investment in Australia
Recent research indicates that socially responsible investment is financially viable in Australia. Indeed, Knowles (1997) found that there were over $200 million invested in Australian socially responsible investment funds. Further, Spiller (1997) showed that financial returns from portfolios invested according to socially responsible

criteria could be just as high as from conventional investment portfolios. Further, a large institutional investor, Australian Ethical Investment Ltd, which currently manages over \$40 million states that it can offer investors competitive financial returns from four different socially responsible unit trusts. Of these unit trusts, one has returned 7.6% per year, while another has returned 8.3% per year.

Socially responsible investment in continental Europe

Butz and Blattner (1999) examined the hypothesis that, by adopting environmentally and socially responsible business practices, companies can achieve a higher than market return. The study compared the financial performance of 65 European securities over a two-year period with measures of their environmental and social performance. They found a significant positive correlation between environmental and financial performance but not between social and financial performance. However, they concluded that overall socially responsible investment should provide rates of return at least as high as those provided by traditional equity investment.

Socially responsible investment in Japan

In the last couple of years socially responsible investment has become an issue in Japan and other East Asian countries. The Japanese have been shocked by a number of cases of unethical business practice, and the investment institutions in Japan have now reacted by taking some account of SEE issues in their portfolio investment decisions. Instances of meat contaminated with BSE (commonly referred to as 'mad cow disease') being passed off to customers have been highlighted in the media across Japan. The growth of socially responsible investment in Japan is outlined in Solomon et al. (2003c).

The drivers of socially responsible investment

There is a broad range of factors driving socially responsible investment. Identifying the forces driving socially responsible investment is important, as it helps those who want to push the socially responsible investment agenda further identify which parties require more encouragement. In our own research we have attempted to discover what forces were principally motivating the socially responsible investment movement in the UK (see Solomon et al., 2002c). Were they drivers internal to companies or were they external drivers such as lobby groups? Lobby groups have been acknowledged as important drivers of socially responsible investment in the literature (Parkinson, 1994; Mansley, 2000). Was the church, for example, a significant driver of socially responsible investment? Non-passive and more socially oriented investment has been encouraged by church bodies as long ago as the Middle Ages (Monks, 2001). Indeed, the church developed some of the first ethical funds in the USA and the UK, and is still active in investing according to 'ethical' criteria (Parkinson, 1994). Many writers consider that socially responsible investment is being driven in part by an increase in interest in social responsibility in society in general, for example:

> ... growing awareness among the public at large of the broader consequences of how their investments are managed ...

(Mansley, 2000, p. 2)

Institutional investors themselves are likely to drive socially responsible investment as they are beginning to recognize the significant financial impacts in such areas as liability or reputation that environmental and social issues can have on investment portfolios (Mansley, 2000). The Government has also played an important role in driving socially responsible investment with its introduction of the new socially responsible investment disclosure requirement for pension fund trustees. This has already encouraged trustees to develop socially responsible investment policies for their pension funds and is acknowledged as a means of furthering corporate social responsibility (ACCA, 2000; Cowe, 2001; Solomon and Solomon, 2001). Trade associations such as the National Association of Pension Funds (NAPF) and the ABI are also involved in encouraging their members to be more proactive in corporate governance and socially responsible investment (NAPF, 1995; Cowe, 2001). Similarly, the recent Green Paper produced by the European Commission pressures for greater corporate social responsibility and emphasizes the important role that socially responsible investment has to play in furthering the corporate social responsibility agenda. A more cynical view suggests that an increase in consumerism in society resulting from a more luxurious standard of living has resulted in consumers requiring ethical funds as part of their desire for greater choice in commodities (Harte et al., 1991).

In Figure 10.1 we present a theoretical model that shows the various drivers of socially responsible investment and the importance of socially responsible investment as a driver of corporate social responsibility. In the model, a distinction is made between internal drivers and external drivers of socially responsible investment. Internal drivers include fund managers themselves, clients of the institutional investors (such as pension fund members) and (for pension funds) the actions of trustees. External drivers include lobby groups, the Government (and political parties competing for power), society's interest in corporate social responsibility, companies themselves wanting to promote socially responsible investment and such external bodies as the NAPF and the ABI.

As discussed earlier, one of the most important drivers of corporate social responsibility has to be socially responsible investment, as unless corporate owners require socially responsible behaviour from companies it is unlikely that companies will take corporate social responsibility seriously. We represent the importance of the role of socially responsible investment in corporate social responsibility by the arrow flowing from institutional investors to companies in Figure 10.1. The model does not attempt to rank the relative importance of each of these drivers but simply proposes a relationship. Our empirical evidence from institutional investors sheds light on

Figure [10.1]   Drivers of SRI and its role in CSR
Reproduced by permission of the Braybrooke Press Ltd

which drivers are considered to be of more/less importance in promoting the socially responsible investment agenda. Our findings arose from a postal questionnaire survey and face to face interviews. The questionnaire survey was conducted between August and December 2000 and involved distribution of a detailed questionnaire to the whole population of pension fund trustees who are members of the NAPF, amounting to a total of 891 organizations. We received responses from 162 pension fund trustees, providing a total response of 18%. Of the respondents 89

Table [10.2]   The drivers of SRI policies

Rank	I believe that the development of SRI policy by pension funds is motivated by	Mean
1	The impact of environmental and social lobby groups	Agreement
2	A general increase in interest in social responsibility in society in general	Some agreement
3	Political parties competing for power	Some agreement
4	Companies seeking to improve their reputation and corporate identity	Some agreement
5	The actions of the NAPF	Weak agreement
6	European Union legislation	Disagreement
7	The social dimension of European Union membership	Disagreement
8	The growing interest of pension fund trustees in SRI issues	Disagreement
9	The growing interest of pension fund managers	Disagreement
10	A demand from active pension fund members	Disagreement
11	A demand from retired pension fund members	Disagreement
12	The religious beliefs of the general public	Strong disagreement

Reproduced by permission of the Braybrooke Press Ltd

(10%) completed the questionnaire. Of the respondent institutions 83% had developed an socially responsible investment policy for their pension fund. The rest were either in the process of developing one or had decided not to develop a socially responsible investment policy. Also, 10 interviews were conducted in the summer of 2001. Table 10.2 summarizes the pension fund trustees' responses to a question about the extent to which they agreed/disagreed with a number of statements concerning the motivation of pension funds for developing a socially responsible investment policy.

The statistics show that the impact of environmental and social lobby groups was considered to be by far the most important driver behind the development of socially responsible investment policy by pension funds. Lobby group involvement in BP Amoco's interests in Alaska are a typical example of the way in which shareholders can be pressured and influenced by lobbyists' activities. Illustration 10.2 discusses the role of lobby groups in environmental issues, focusing on the case of BP Amoco. However, there was also some indication that a general increase in interest in social responsibility in society in general is motivating socially responsible investment policy development. Thus we can see from these findings that the parties involved in socially responsible investment who are internal to the investment institutions are not driving the socially responsible investment agenda; it is external parties, such as the Government and lobbyists. This is not encouraging as it implies that the people

Illustration 10.2

The role of lobby groups in corporate environmental issues: the case of BP Amoco in Alaska

The environment is a cause for serious concern to most people worldwide. Depletion of natural resources and pollution of the environment are considered by some to represent a time bomb that could ultimately render the Earth uninhabitable by humans, not to mention the millions of other species that share the planet with us. The debate about global warming and its potential consequences is well known. The destruction of the Earth's ozone layer due to pollution is undisputed, although the eventual impact is debatable. Certainly, many animal species are becoming extinct as a result of human interaction with the natural environment. Weather patterns are altering around the world. Although there have been global efforts to reduce pollution and 'clean up' industry, this is a difficult and controversial process. The usual problems apply. To what extent are we prepared to sacrifice high levels of corporate profitability, high rates of economic growth and wide choices in consumer goods in order to reduce our impact on the environment? People who make efforts to change their lifestyles to become more 'environmentally friendly' tend to be ridiculed by the majority and called 'greenies', 'tree-huggers' and the like. Some even consider such people wash less and have bad breath as a result of avoiding chemical products and eating organic, vegetarian food; but the dismissal of such a worthy cause through derision is worrying, given that its aims are for humankind, not the individual. Nevertheless, would most of us be satisfied with solar heating that worked intermittently? Would we be happy to sell our bright red sports car, trading it in for a bicycle? Somehow the local bus network does not give the same kick as revving the engine of a high-performance vehicle and speeding away from the traffic lights. How would we feel about not using our favourite deodorant anymore or doing without a cupboard full of expensive, exotic perfumes and face creams? The majority of people are satisfied with their high quality of life in the UK and elsewhere and would be unlikely to accept such changes. Going to work, bringing up children, cooking meals, coping with the everyday stresses—these constitute most people's everyday lives. It is hard in our hectic world to find the time to reflect on such imponderables as environmental degradation and sustain-ability. But the battle continues. The 'greenies' do not give up. There are many lobby groups that are influential worldwide, comprising individuals who believe passionately in preserving the planet for future generations. They are no longer in the background but have succeeded in influencing government policy in countries around the world. Things are changing. The Kyoto Protocol represented a worldwide attempt to combat the emission of greenhouse gases (Heal, 2000). However, withdrawal of the USA from this agreement was a massive step backward for lobbyists and reformers.

Nowhere are lobby groups more active and forceful than in the area of the environ-ment. Greenpeace is a worldwide organization that has fought for environmental protec-tion for many years. Oil companies are one of their many targets and BP Amoco's interests in Alaska represent one example of the most significant environmental issues in recent years. Not only did BP Amoco's presence in Alaska lead to forceful behaviour by lobby groups but it also resulted in one of the only cases of shareholder revolution in the UK. The Arctic National Wildlife Refuge (ANWR) in Alaska was deemed the largest unexplored, potentially productive onshore petroleum-producing basin in the nation in a report by the Energy Information Administration. However, it is also the last undisturbed area in the USA. The ANWR represents 8.9 million acres of land, designated a protected area by Public Law 2214 in 1960. The Alaska National Interest Lands Conservation Act created an additional 16 national wildlife refuges in 1980, which extended the area to 19 million acres. The area was also classified in 1980 as 'wilderness', which means that all types of development, including road building is prohibited (*Financial Times*, 27 June 2000). Thousands of caribou live in the area of wilderness (Heal, 2000). In April 2000 a multi-national alliance of environmental groups, including Greenpeace and the World Wildlife Fund, attended the AGM of BP Amoco in an attempt to prevent the company from drilling for oil in a remote area of Alaska (*Financial Times*, 11 April 2000). Sentiment was so strong that nine Greenpeace activists were arrested for trespassing at a BP Amoco oil exploration site in Alaska in a single week the same month (*Financial Times*, 13 April 2000). Indeed, environmental campaigners claimed 'unprecedented' support from share-holders, with about 13% of votes being cast at the AGM in favour of a Greenpeace-backed shareholder resolution. The resolution urged BP Amoco to cancel plans to exploit oil in Alaska's ANWR and to increase investment in solar energy (Ward, 2000). Despite such support, the resolution was at the time unsuccessful. However, BP Amoco has reduced the scale of its operations in Alaska (Buchan and Earle, 2002). Yet, the company's image was blighted. Oil spills in Alaska, due to ageing pipelines, have not enhanced BP Amoco's image. In July 2001 a corroded pipeline erupted, spilling over 400 gallons of crude oil onto the tundra (Earle, 2001). Since the problems in Alaska, BP Amoco has made a significant attempt to improve its image, becoming a pioneer company in environmental management, advertising its aims to develop new, renewable energy sources, such as solar power and wind energy. Indeed, the environment has become vastly important as a reputational issue for all UK companies and indeed for companies around the world (Fombrun and Shanley, 1990; Fombrun, 2000). As we have seen in Chapter 8, Corporate Environmental Reporting (CER) has grown significantly in recent years and there is evi-dence of a positive relationship between corporate environmental and financial perform-ance. The Alaskan case has continued to be a centre of controversy, becoming a political football. Even before he became President, George W. Bush stated emphatically that he wanted to develop the oilfield. This proposal was inspired mainly by his concerns about reliance on oil imported from the Gulf. He proposed opening around 8% of the ANWR to exploration and drilling (Durgin and Wolffe, 2000). However, energy analysts were not at all confident that this proposal would be successful, as falling energy prices would not provide enough funding to develop the required infrastructure to support the developments.

who are most closely involved in socially responsible investment do not appear to be interested in driving it forward. Lastly, the total rejection of religious beliefs as a socially responsible investment driver is interesting, given the church's involvement in early ethical investments. This demonstrates a complete transformation of society's ethics and values over the past hundred years, since the early years of ethical investment. People may pursue similar aims over time, such as social respon-sibility, but for allegedly different reasons.

Overall, the questionnaire data from our research indicated that there are a large number of significant socially responsible investment drivers, as suggested by Figure 10.1. However, there was a consensus on the overriding influence of lobby groups (which is related to society in general) and the Government (which again should theoretically represent the people).

Overall, it was clear from our results that internal drivers of socially responsible investment that are closely involved in institutional investment, such as fund

managers themselves, their members and trustees of pension funds, are not as interested in socially responsible investment as external parties. There are many possible
explanations of this. One is that pension fund managers in particular are concerned
about alienating corporate sponsors by pressuring them through active socially
responsible investment engagement. This could lead to them losing their fund management contracts (e.g., Coffee, 1991). Another explanation in relation to pension
funds is the concern of trustees about potential conflict between their fiduciary duties
and socially responsible investment. Whatever the reason, the primary force for
socially responsible investment is arising from outside the investment institutions.
This means that fund managers are in effect having socially responsible investment
thrust on them. If socially responsible investment is to have a sound future, it is
necessary for the driving force to also come from within the institutions themselves.
Unless fund managers, trustees and fund members believe that socially responsible
investment is in their financial interests as well as perhaps their normative, ethical
interests (which have to be subordinated to their fiduciary duties and need to meet
financial return targets), then socially responsible investment will not progress
substantially. As discussed earlier socially responsible investment is necessary if
corporate social responsibility is to be encouraged further. Therefore, a clear
policy recommendation for promoting socially responsible investment is to target
the internal drivers of socially responsible investment. By making fund managers and
trustees more aware of the financial (and non-financial) benefits of socially responsible investment they will be encouraged to take a proactive rather than reactive
stance. In other words, fund managers need to be pursuing socially responsible
investment actively as part of their own long-term investment strategy rather than
merely to satisfy the expectations of Government and lobbyists. Without this sort of
change, socially responsible investment will remain a box-ticking strategy that is
more in form than in substance.

Pension fund trustees and socially responsible investment

You may recall that in Chapter 5 we discussed the complicated web of ownership
that arises from the existence of pension funds. This ownership structure has
important implications for corporate governance and control. We considered a
diagram showing the accountability relationships between companies and their
shareholders, where the shareholder is in fact the member (client) of a pension
fund (Figure 5.1). The intermediaries include the pension fund trustee who is
responsible for the investment of the financial assets on behalf of the pension fund
member. There is then also a fund manager, appointed by the trustee on behalf of the
pension fund member, who manages the assets on a daily basis. From an agency
theory perspective, it is difficult for the individual member of the pension fund
to influence the investment strategy and decision making of the fund manager.
Accountability from fund managers to their clients is an area where significant
advances are required. The case of the University Superannuation Scheme (USS),

however, does indicate that pension fund members can influence the strategic management of the fund. A group of university professors in accounting joined forces and have succeeded in recent years in pressuring the USS to adopt an umbrella socially responsible investment policy for the whole pension fund. Indeed, a specialist socially responsible investment manager has been appointed to the fund whose sole responsibility is to monitor the extent to which the fund's investments comply with socially responsible investment criteria. However, this is probably an exception. Public sector pension funds such as the USS are traditionally more interested in society's needs and are more likely to adopt a stakeholder-oriented approach than private sector pension funds (see Monks, 2001 for a full discussion of the role and responsibilities of private and public sector pension funds).

The interesting question is whether or not pension fund trustees have a responsibility to adopt a socially responsible investment policy for their pension funds? We can see from the complexity of pension fund share ownership that the pension fund trustee has ultimate responsibility for the way in which the pension fund is invested. It is the pension fund trustee who decides on the investment strategy and who makes the investment allocation decision—the proportion of the fund to be invested in different financial assets (e.g., what proportion should be invested in equity and debt). If a socially responsible investment strategy is to be implemented, it is the trustee who has to make that decision and instruct the fund managers to pursue this strategy. The fund managers are simply employed by the trustee to manage the fund's assets. However, trustees seem in many cases to pass the responsibilities of equity ownership to their fund managers, stating that such responsibility has been 'delegated' to the fund managers and arguing that they are the ones with the expertise in the field. However, many will now argue that this does not exonerate them of all ownership responsibilities. Monks (2001) makes the point that the trustees are the true owners of the pension fund's investee companies and as such should ensure that they act as 'responsible owners'. As you can see this is a controversial and very complicated area of finance and corporate governance. What emerges from current research is that the trustees themselves appear to be confused as to their role in corporate governance and especially in the area of socially responsible investment.

One issue that remains unresolved at the moment is the role of pension fund trustees in corporate governance and in socially responsible investment. Trustees are extremely important people as they are ultimately responsible for the way in which workers' pensions are invested. Whether or not people have money to live on in their retirement is a result of decisions made by trustees. However, the amount of funds invested by pension funds is immense and represents the idle balances of most people in the UK. This financial power can be used for good or can be simply invested for financial return. It is evident from the earlier discussion that people are uncomfortable about their money being invested in companies that do not act in a socially responsible manner. There is a growing consciousness in society that buying shares in unethical businesses represents tacit support for unethical business practices. This appears to be increasingly unacceptable in the world we live in. The question therefore is whether or not pension fund trustees have a responsibility to society (as well as to their pension fund members) to ensure that funds are invested in a socially responsible manner. However, even if pension fund trustees want to adopt a socially responsible investment policy for the pension fund, they are faced with a significant problem: their fiduciary duty.

Trustees are concerned about breaching their fiduciary duties. Legal cases have found trustees guilty of not pursuing financial returns to the exclusion of all other investment motives. Trustees can be liable if they invest according to any criterion other than shareholder wealth maximization—in their terms of reference, the maximization of pension receivables for the members of the pension funds. If socially responsible investment results in suboptimal levels of pension payments then it would be in breach of the trustees' fiduciary duties as an investment strategy. However, it may be considered that trustees hide behind their fiduciary duty, as Monks stated:

> Under the rubric of 'fiduciary duty' much is justified. The unexceptionable fiduciary requirement that trustees may consider 'solely' the interests of beneficiaries is adduced to justify non-involvement in 'social' or 'political' investments. Activism is dismissed as being unrelated to adding long-term value to the trust portfolio.
>
> (Monks, 2001, p. 125)

This issue is very much a matter for debate at the moment and is very important to the pension fund community.

The *Cowan v Scargill* legal case inspired fear in trustees on any social issues.[2] This was the first legal case where ethical investment was considered. The case arose from the actions of the National Union of Mineworkers (NUM) Pension Scheme. Arthur Scargill, the notorious (or heroic) leader of the NUM decided that the fund should not invest in non-UK companies and should not invest in such other areas of the energy sector as oil and gas. However, this strategy was not adopted as there was substantial opposition from the trustee board. The main problem with this sort of proposed investment strategy is that it restricts the investment universe. As you will recall from the theoretical discussion in the last chapter, for optimum risk and return combinations the diversification of an investment portfolio is essential. Any restriction on investment choices due to an ethical (or other) investment policy restricts the risk reduction potential from portfolio diversification. Such a policy is therefore considered to contravene trustees' fiduciary duties as it makes the portfolio more risky and therefore potentially less profitable for the pension fund members. The judge Sir Robert Megarry concluded that, '... It is the duty of trustees, in the interest of beneficiaries, to take advantage of the full range of investments authorised by the terms of the trust, instead of resolving to narrow that range.'

---

[2] A full discussion of this case can be found in Mansley (2000).

However, this argument is not as valid for socially responsible investment now as it was in previous years. The increasing use of best in sector investment approaches rather than screening strategies has allowed institutional fund managers to invest ethically without restricting their investment universe. This new investment approach has made socially responsible investment available to a far wider range of investors.

The trustees' fiduciary duty to maximize pension fund return to investment is not the only restriction on their behaviour. The activities of company pension schemes are influenced to a great extent by the sponsoring company itself. The sponsoring company is the company whose employees are members of the scheme. For example, Marks & Spencer's (M&S) employees[3] are all members of the M&S Pension Scheme. M&S is the sponsoring company. The trustees of the M&S pension scheme appoint an institutional investment company. If the investment managers place too much pressure on companies to improve their performance (e.g., in the area of corporate social responsibility) through active engagement and dialogue, this could lead to companies turning against the investment managers. The sponsoring company may dismiss the fund manager as a result. It is not in the interests of the investment managers to lose clients, and they will therefore avoid any investment strategy that could upset relations with companies. This is a problem inherent in private sector pension funds due to their relationship with the sponsoring company, an issue discussed in Coffee (1991).

Sponsoring companies have also been affected by the new accounting regulation (FRS17) that forces them to disclose the details of their pension funds. In many cases (due in part to the slowdown in the stock market) corporate pension schemes have been making substantial losses in recent years. This is not something they relish revealing in their financial reports. A socially responsible investment policy may be seen as a further risk to pension fund performance that they would rather not take at present.

The discussion of the *Cowan v Scargill* case brings us back to the burning issue in socially responsible investment (and indeed in corporate governance), which we have made many times throughout this book. Does the adoption of a socially responsible investment policy lead to a reduction in investment return? In other words: Does ethical investment mean unprofitable investment? We have considered some empirical evidence from the academic literature that suggested in the main that socially responsible investment does not reduce financial returns. However, there is no definitive consensus on this subject and more research is urgently required. From interviews that we have conducted, there was a strong feeling from the

---

[3] As from March 2002 M&S decided to join many other companies in discontinuing final salary pensions to new pension fund members. This is a trend that is currently sweeping the pension market and is of great concern to most workers in the country. It does have implications for socially responsible investment—if companies cannot afford to run basic traditional pension schemes, how can they afford to take risks by experimenting with socially responsible investment strategies? This is certainly one possible argument against socially responsible investment.

professional investment community that not only does socially responsible investment not reduce returns to investment, it can also actually improve investment return. By encouraging companies to act in a more socially responsible way they can instead perform better financially. By avoiding reputational risks arising from socially irresponsible behaviour (such as environmental incidents or human rights abuses) companies can ensure more stable profitability. Better corporate performance leads to higher share values and therefore to better financial returns from investment. This scenario is perhaps a Utopian view of the results of socially responsible investment investment, and it remains to be seen whether or not such a 'virtuous circle' effect will manifest itself in practice.

Another way of looking at the trustee's role in socially responsible investment is as follows. If socially responsible investment improves investment performance over the long term, then it would actually be in breach of trustees' fiduciary duties *not* to pursue a socially responsible investment strategy. This is a very different approach. Although a little revolutionary it seems to be the approach that is rapidly being adopted by many core financial institutions at present.

From July 2000 all private occupation pension schemes have been subject to new pension fund regulation. Since then pension fund trustees have been required by law to disclose the extent to which (if at all) they practise socially responsible investment criteria in their pension fund. The Government had intended to introduce this regulation for a number of years. Why? This is the big question. It seems obvious that the Government feels that this sort of regulation could affect practice. It seems that they could only have introduced the regulation with the intention of encouraging further socially responsible investment. If the Government felt that socially responsible investment contradicted trustees' fiduciary duties, it is unlikely that they would have taken such steps. If socially responsible investment did conflict with trustees' duties, then it would be more likely that they pass a regulation making socially responsible investment illegal—this is not at all the case. Over the last decade the Government has been pressured by lobby groups to encourage corporate social responsibility and to improve social responsibility in all areas, as well as accountability.

It is quite possible that the new requirement to disclose whether or not pension funds adopt an socially responsible investment policy will actually act as an incentive for trustees to adopt such a policy. They will probably be embarrassed to state in their statement of investment principles that they do not adopt any type of socially responsible investment policy, given current sentiment. The recent report by ACCA on the wider aspects of risk considered that:

This [the new disclosure requirement] affects several hundred billion pounds of pension assets and is likely to cause a number of major pension funds to require their fund managers to give much greater emphasis to these issues.

(ACCA, 2000, p. 7)

Further, it has been suggested that the Pensions Act amendment has already had a substantial effect, as:

> This requirement [the new SRI disclosure requirement] has had a significant and wide-ranging impact on the investment community. The majority of trustees have incorporated reference to social, ethical and environmental (SEE) issues in their annual statements in 2001. Most of them have delegated responsibility for implementing this to fund managers which has added significantly to the growing Socially Responsible Investment (socially responsible investment) movement.
>
> (Cowe, 2001, p. 8)

Overall, it seems that by introducing the regulation the Government has succeeded in not only initiating further debate in the area, bringing socially responsible investment onto the agenda for pension funds but it has also encouraged pension fund trustees to adopt an socially responsible investment policy. Some institutional fund managers, however, objected strongly and considered that such policies are a back door means of influencing the City.

It seems from the evidence that trustees are somewhat confused about their role in socially responsible investment. Trustees' views seem to vary strongly depending on a number of organizational factors. Socially responsible investment is an important issue and one that is unlikely to go away. Indeed, given recent changes in institutional investors' strategies and policies it is more likely that socially responsible investment will increase in coming years. It is vital that trustees are made more aware of their role and that discussions take place in order to clarify their responsibilities. However, as Myners (2001) concluded, trustees are in a responsible position and have ultimate decision-making power for institutional investment strategy. He qualified this by showing that they were generally untrained, unprepared for their role and unpaid. Mainly as a result of Myners' conclusions, trustees are under increasing pressure to gain training in financial affairs and to devote more time and energy to their role as trustees. Surely, with the mounting pressures on trustees, social responsibility will represent simply another problem that they have to deal with. It may be more than they can take on at present. This issue was discussed in Solomon et al. (2002d). One solution to this and other problems may be to increase trustee remuneration, which would help them to treat their role in a more professional manner, as discussed in Chapter 3.

Chapter summary

In this chapter we have discussed the growth of socially responsible investment. We have shown that there is growing evidence in the academic and professional literature that socially responsible investment is no longer marginal but has become a mainstream strategy implemented by UK institutional investors across the board.

Specifically, we have examined the drivers of socially responsible investment, showing that they are mainly situated outside the financial community. We have discussed the problems faced by pension funds if they choose to implement a socially responsible investment strategy, due to their obligation to fulfil their fiduciary duty. However, having provided some evidence that socially responsible investment may enhance, rather than reduce, investment return, the radical suggestion that trustees should adopt socially responsible investment in order to fulfil their fiduciary duty may have a genuine empirical foundation. The most important aspect of this chapter has been to demonstrate that the institutional investment community, as well as the corporate community (as discussed in Chapter 9) are embracing issues of SEE accountability. This represents a deep change in the attitudes of business and financial institutions toward social responsibility, endorsing a broader remit for corporate governance than that encapsulated by pure agency theory. We can see from the discussion in Part III, that a broader agenda for corporate governance, which embraces a stakeholder theory approach, may no longer be viewed as inconsistent with value creation in the long run. As we discussed in Chapter 1 the gulf between a shareholder and a stakeholder approach to corporate governance may be less wide than has been considered in the past.

Questions for reflection and discussion

1 *The new socially responsible investment disclosure requirement for pension fund trustees has had a substantial impact on trustees' attitudes towards, and practice of, socially responsible investment. This impact is, through a virtuous circle effect, likely to lead to increased corporate social responsibility.* Explain and discuss the above statement with reference to the findings of academic papers and other published sources that you have read.

2 Investigate one of the following cases: Nike, Huntingdon Life Science, Shell and *Brent Spar*; or BP and renewable energy. Discuss the implications of these cases for the socially responsible investment movement. Did they have a positive or a negative impact on the attitudes of institutional investors toward socially responsible investment?

3 Spend some time developing your own diagrammatic image of the links between socially responsible investment, corporate social responsibility and the potential impact of socially responsible investment. Is yours a virtuous or a vicious circle?

4 Do you think that the institutional investment community will take an increasing interest in socially responsible investment? Or do you think socially responsible investment is a fashionable trend that will be dismissed in the near future?

Chapter 11

The future of corporate governance and accountability

In this book we have attempted to show how corporate governance has evolved over time into a discipline in its own right. In Part I we discussed the fall of the US giant Enron in a detailed case study, showing how its collapse focused global attention on corporate governance issues. We then analysed the process of corporate governance reform that has taken place in the UK over the last decade, paying special attention to the series of codes of practice and policy documents that this process has generated. We focused on the UK system of corporate governance, showing that the traditional separation of ownership and control, on which agency theory was constructed, has been transformed in recent times into a system characterized by institutional ownership concentration. Specifically, the growth in institutional ownership and the recognition that institutional investors need to acknowledge their power and responsibility in society has been a driving force in this transformation. Institutional investors are no longer passive shareholders but have become active drivers of corporate governance reform. In an agency theory framework, institutional investors have been transformed from shareholders whose existence engendered agency problems to a corporate governance mechanism, efficient at monitoring company management, thereby solving agency problems to a certain extent.

Part II explored the diversity of corporate governance systems around the world. We discussed the categorization of systems into the insider and outsider models. Further, we introduced the concept of a global convergence in corporate governance. We used a selection of countries to illustrate the wide range of different corporate governance systems around the world, the many factors determining these traditional systems and the gradual transformation of these systems due to a worldwide agenda for corporate governance reform.

In Part III we showed that companies are concerned increasingly not just with their shareholders' demands but also with the needs of a wide range of stakeholders. Company directors are discharging accountability to shareholding and non-shareholding stakeholders through the disclosure process and through stakeholder engagement programmes. There is a gradual broadening of the corporate governance agenda, characterized by a move away from a narrow agency theory view toward a broader, stakeholder-oriented view that embraces concepts of corporate social responsibility and sustainability.

The question for discussion in this last chapter is therefore: *Where do we go from here?* We consider below a number of issues, including: the future path for institutional investor activism, the future route for corporate governance from a global perspective and ways in which a broader agenda for corporate governance may continue to develop.

The future of institutional investor activism

It is clear from the evidence presented in this book that institutional investors are no longer passive, back-seat owners of companies. They can no longer ignore their responsibilities as shareholders. In the UK the investment institutions have realized that passive shareholding is not the route to shareholder wealth maximization. The actions of LENS and California Public Employees' Retirement System (CalPERS) in the USA and Hermes in the UK *inter alia* have shown that active shareholding and involvement in investee companies is financially rewarding. This type of instrumental ethics approach is a way of owning shares ethically and satisfying obligations to the ultimate beneficiaries of investment. Increasing shareholder activism (e.g., in the area of directors' remuneration) is clearly a case of ethical activism, as excessive re-muneration is an ethical as well as a financial issue. Institutional investors through portfolio investment are discharging an accountability first and foremost to their own clients but also to society as a whole. The free rider effect of their activism applies not only to all shareholders but also to society. Indeed, the writing of Monks (2001) and Sparkes (2002) *inter alia* has set a clear ethical agenda for institutional investors. From our discussion in Chapters 9 and 10 institutional investors have a clear mandate to grasp the nettle of socially responsible investment and corporate social responsibility. As owners of listed companies in the UK and around the world they need to act as socially responsible owners, satisfying the needs of a broad range of stakeholders as well as seeking maximum returns to investment for shareholders. It is vital that the trust in financial institutions that has been so sorely dented by recent scandals in the financial and corporate communities is restored. It is only by embracing greater shareholder activism and socially responsible investment that financial institutions can recapture this trust. Society needs to see change continuing. Without change, fewer and fewer people will choose to pay into a private pension or invest in the stock market, and capitalism as we know it today could decline immeasurably.

Another area where improvements are clearly needed is in the accountability of institutional investors to their clients. The disclosure by institutional fund managers to their clients, who are the ultimate shareholders, is not standardized and is generally not public. It is difficult for clients to influence their institutional fund managers. However, there have been growing calls from clients for greater share-holder activism by their institutional fund holders. This should continue to grow, with pension fund members, for example, receiving more transparent and under-standable information from their fund managers on a regular basis.

A global convergence in corporate governance

One of the most important issues for corporate governance is the extent to which harmonization in corporate governance standards will genuinely be achieved at an international level. In Chapter 7 we considered the possibility that countries may be moving toward a global convergence in corporate governance as well as toward some of the initiatives aimed at international harmonization of corporate governance, such as the OECD (1999) Principles. At the moment, the future is uncertain.

As some of the cases in Chapter 8 demonstrated, reform may be taking place around the world, but in many cases improvements may only be skin deep. In many cases, change has been instigated too quickly, as a knee-jerk reaction to events such as the 1997 Asian Crisis or the collapse of Enron. If reform is desirable, it needs to take place as part of a long-term strategy, rather than in the context of a quick fix. Ultimately, it remains to be seen whether countries' systems of corporate governance will harmonize their standards in line with the Anglo-Saxon model of corporate governance or whether a different, more individualistic model will be chosen. There is certainly a danger at present of Anglo-American-style governance being grafted onto corporate governance systems around the world, when the roots are not in place to support this model. There is a danger that countries with extremely different traditional styles of governance will be engulfed by a tide of market-oriented initiatives that may not be appropriate for their legal frameworks, their economies, their individual markets and their culture. A clear policy recommenda-tion that arises naturally from this discussion is for governments and policy makers around the world to look carefully at the eventual model they would like to see in their countries, before leaping into an inappropriate system and embracing a model that is not sustainable over the long term.

A continuing broadening of the corporate governance agenda

Throughout this book there has been a focus on the broadening agenda for corporate governance. We have provided plenty of evidence that companies are embracing a broader approach to corporate governance by discharging accountabil-ity to a wider range of stakeholders. Further, institutional investors are encouraging corporate social responsibility though active socially responsible investment strategies of engagement and dialogue with their investee companies. This raises the question: Are we really moving into a more accountable, socially responsible world? Perhaps corporate governance reform, corporate social responsibility and socially responsible investment are all signs that a moral consensus is forming around a more ethical approach to business. However, the continuing voluntary nature of reporting in the SEE area remains a cause for concern. It is clear from the discussion in Part III that recent research has revealed a market failure in the area of SEE information. Some level of standardization of SEE reporting seems overdue. Companies need guidance on the type and form of information that their shareholders and other stakeholders require. Similarly, shareholders and other stakeholders require information that is standardized and therefore comparable for accountability and decision-making purposes. Even if there is to be no mandatory disclosure, which is looking unlikely in the current environment given the views expressed in the recent review of company law, it may still be possible to issue a policy document, similar in strength to corporate governance documents, such as the Higgs Report (2003) and the Turnbull Report (1999), which focus specifically on corporate accountability in the SEE domain. Unless a more formalized approach is adopted in this area, massive resources will be wasted by shareholders and stakeholders, who will continue to seek information on SEE issues by other means, given the unreliability of the public disclosure process.

A more radical way of furthering SEE accountability arises naturally from the recent Higgs Report. Higgs' recommendations for one non-executive director in every listed company to assume the role of a senior independent director, or SID, who should represent shareholders' interests, could be extended to embrace social responsibility. Perhaps one non-executive director could take on the role of championing the interests of non-shareholding stakeholders (e.g., employees, local communities, environmental concerns). Higgs pointed out that there was little connection between non-executive directors and institutional investors. There is likely to be far less connection between non-executive directors and other stakeholders. This is a radical suggestion but one that could help companies to achieve greater stakeholder accountability by improving the board's understanding and appreciation of stakeholder concerns. It may be a more direct and more effective means of furthering stakeholder accountability than the process of stakeholder engagement which, as we have shown, has been criticized heavily for falling short of genuine improvements to stakeholder accountability. At present, it is highly unlikely that non-executive directors are involved in companies' programmes of stakeholder engagement. Perhaps encouraging one of the non-executive directors to attend meetings between the company and various stakeholder groups would be an effective means of improving corporate accountability within a broader corporate governance agenda. However, we would expect this suggestion to be met with strong reactions from corporate lobby groups. If they considered a SID would be divisive by introducing different objectives to the boardroom, this suggestion would be explosive.

Concluding comments

In this book we have attempted to show why corporate governance is *the system of checks and balances, both internal and external to companies, that ensures that companies discharge their accountability to all their stakeholders and act in a socially responsible way in all areas of their business activity.* As we saw in Chapter 8 the South African King Report (2002) drew a distinction between accountability to shareholders and responsibility to stakeholders, which seemed to lessen any impact the report may have on corporate social responsibility. Nevertheless, we feel that the approach embodied in the report carries the most forward-looking and progressive approach to corporate governance adopted by any code of practice. The Report summarized its philosophy as follows:

> ... successful governance in the 21st century requires companies to adopt an *inclusive and not an exclusive approach*. The company must be open to institutional activism and there must be greater emphasis on the sustainable or non-financial aspects of its performance. *Boards must apply the tests of fairness, accountability, responsibility and transparency to all acts or omissions and be accountable to the company but also responsive and responsible towards the company's identified stakeholders.*
>
> (King Report, 2002, p. 19, emphasis added)

This corporate governance policy document is admirable in its attempt to address a genuine stakeholder approach to corporate governance. The extent to which this approach is operationalized by boards of directors remains to be seen. It is not an unrealistic expectation that countries around the world will incorporate a similar approach to corporate governance and social responsibility in their core principles and codes of practice. Furthermore, voluntary codes of practice need to be accompanied by an agenda for modernizing company law, which attempts to support and encourage a broader, more inclusive system of corporate governance at a global level.

The last decade has witnessed vast changes in the definition and remit of corporate governance in the UK and around the world. The answer to our earlier question *where do we go from here?* is really another question *who knows where we will be 10 years hence?* No one can predict the future. We can only hope that reform will continue and that progress will continue to pay attention not only to the financial aspects of corporate governance but also to the creation of a more ethical business environment.

Appendix

The Combined Code on Corporate Governance (July 2003)

Preamble

1. This Code supersedes and replaces the Combined Code issued by the Hampel Committee on Corporate Governance in June 1998. It derives from a review of the role and effectiveness of non-executive directors by Derek Higgs and a review of audit committees by a group led by Sir Robert Smith.

2. The Financial Services Authority has said that it will replace the 1998 Code that is annexed to the Listing Rule with the revised Code and will seek to make consequential Rule changes. There will be consultation on the necessary Rule changes but no further consultation on the Code provisions themselves.

3. It is intended that the new Code will apply for reporting years beginning on or after 1 November 2003.

4. The Code contains main and supporting principles and provisions. The existing Listing Rules require listed companies to make a disclosure statement in two parts in relation to the Code. In the first part of the statement, the company has to report on how it applies the principles in the Code. In future this will need to cover both main and supporting principles. The form and content of this part of the statement are not prescribed, the intention being that companies should have a free hand to explain their governance policies in the light of the principles, including any special circumstances applying to them which have led to a particular approach. In the second part of the statement the company has either to confirm that it complies with the Code's provisions or—where it does not—to provide an explanation. This 'comply or explain' approach has been in operation for over 10 years, and the flexibility it offers has been widely welcomed both by company boards and by investors. It is for shareholders and others to evaluate the company's statement.

5.   While it is expected that listed companies will comply with the Code's provisions most of the time, it is recognized that departure from the provisions of the Code may be justified in particular circumstances. Every company must review each provision carefully and give a considered explanation if it departs from the Code provisions.

6.   Smaller listed companies, in particular those new to listing, may judge that some of the provisions are disproportionate or less relevant in their case. Some of the provisions do not apply to companies below FTSE 350. Such companies may nonetheless consider that it would be appropriate to adopt the approach in the Code and they are encouraged to consider this. Investment companies typically have a different board structure, which may affect the relevance of particular provisions.

7.   While recognizing that directors are appointed by shareholders who are the owners of companies, it is important that those concerned with the evaluation of governance should do so with common sense in order to promote partnership and trust, based on mutual understanding. They should pay due regard to companies' individual circumstances and bear in mind in particular the size and complexity of the company and the nature of the risks and challenges it faces. While shareholders have every right to challenge companies' explanations if they are unconvincing, they should not be evaluated in a mechanistic way and departures from the Code should not be automatically treated as breaches. Institutional shareholders and their agents should be careful to respond to the statements from companies in a manner that supports the 'comply or explain' principle. As the principles in Section 2 make clear, institutional shareholders should carefully consider explanations given for departure from the Code and make reasoned judgements in each case. They should put their views to the company and be prepared to enter a dialogue if they do not accept the company's position. Institutional shareholders should be prepared to put such views in writing where appropriate.

8.   Nothing in this Code should be taken to override the general requirements of law to treat shareholders equally in access to information.

9.   This publication includes guidance on how to comply with particular parts of the Code: first, *Internal Control: Guidance for Directors on the Combined Code*, produced by the Turnbull Committee, which relates to Code provisions on internal control (C.2 and part of C.3 in the Code); and, second, *Audit Committees: A Report and Proposed Guidance*, produced by the Smith Group, which relates to the provisions on audit committees and auditors (C.3 of the Code). In both cases, the guidance suggests ways of applying the relevant Code principles and of complying with the relevant Code provisions.

10.   In addition, this volume also includes suggestions for good practice from the Higgs Report.

11.   The revised Code does not include material in the previous Code on the disclosure of directors' remuneration. This is because 'The Directors' Remuneration Report Regulations 2002' are now in force and supersede the earlier Code provisions. These require the directors of a company to prepare a remuneration report. It is important that this report is clear, transparent and understandable to shareholders.

Code of best practice

Section 1   Companies

A   *Directors*

A.1   *The board*

MAIN PRINCIPLE

Every company should be headed by an effective board, which is collectively responsible for the success of the company.

SUPPORTING PRINCIPLES

The board's role is to provide entrepreneurial leadership of the company within a framework of prudent and effective controls which enables risk to be assessed an managed. The board should set the company's strategic aims, ensure that the necessary financial and human resources are in place for the company to meet its objectives and review management performance. The board should set the company's values and standards and ensure that its obligations to its shareholders and others are understood and met. All directors must take decisions objectively in the interests of the company. As part of their role as members of a unitary board, non-executive directors should constructively challenge and help develop proposals on strategy. Non-executive directors should scrutinize the performance of management in meeting agreed goals and objectives and monitor the reporting of performance. They should satisfy themselves on the integrity of financial information and that financial controls and systems of risk management are robust and defensible. They are responsible for determining appropriate levels of remuneration of executive directors and have a prime role in appointing, and where necessary removing, executive directors and in succession planning.

CODE PROVISIONS

A.1.1   The board should meet sufficiently regularly to discharge its duties effectively. There should be a formal schedule of matters specifically reserved for its decision. The annual report should include a statement of how the board operates, including a high-level statement of which types of decisions are to be taken by the board and which are to be delegated to management.

A.1.2   The annual report should identify the chairman, the deputy chairman (where there is one), the chief executive, the senior independent director and the chairmen and members of the nomination, audit and remuneration committees. It should also set out the number of meetings of the board and those committees and individual attendance by directors.

A.1.3   The chairman should hold meetings with the non-executive directors without the executives present. Led by the senior independent director, the non-executive directors should meet without the chairman present at least annually to appraise the chairman's performance (as described in A.6.1) and on such other occasions as are deemed appropriate.

A.1.4   Where directors have concerns which cannot be resolved about the running of the company or a proposed action, they should ensure that their concerns are recorded in the board minutes. On resignation, a non-executive director should provide a written statement to the chairman, for circulation to the board, if they have any such concerns.

A.1.5   The company should arrange appropriate insurance cover in respect of legal action against its directors.

A.2   *Chairman and chief executive*

MAIN PRINCIPLE

There should be a clear division of responsibilities at the head of the company between the running of the board and the executive responsibility for the running of the company's business. No one individual should have unfettered powers of decision.

SUPPORTING PRINCIPLE

The chairman is responsible for leadership of the board, ensuring its effectiveness on all aspect of its role and setting its agenda. The chairman is also responsible for ensuring that the directors receive accurate, timely and clear information. The chairman should ensure effective communication with shareholders. The chairman should also facilitate the effective contribution of non-executive directors in particular and ensure constructive relations between executive and non-executive directors.

CODE PROVISIONS

A.2.1 The roles of chairman and chief executive should not be exercised by the same individual. The division of responsibilities between the chairman and chief executive should be clearly established, set out in writing and agreed by the board.

A.2.2 The chairman should on appointment meet the independence criteria set out in A.3.1 below. A chief executive should not go on to be chairman of the same company. If exceptionally a board decides that a chief executive should become chairman, the board should consult major shareholders in advance and should set out its reasons to shareholders at the time of the appointment and in the next annual report.

A.3 Board balance and independence

MAIN PRINCIPLE

The board should include a balance of executive and non-executive directors (and in particular independent non-executive directors) such that no individual or small group of individuals can dominate the board's decision taking.

SUPPORTING PRINCIPLES

The board should not be so large as to be unwieldy. The board should be of sufficient size that the balance of skills and experience is appropriate for the requirements of the business and that changes to the board's composition can be managed without undue disruption. To ensure that power and information are not concentrated in one or two individuals, there should be a strong presence on the board of both executive and non-executive directors. The value of ensuring that committee membership is refreshed and that undue reliance is not placed on particular individuals should be taken into account in deciding chairmanship and membership of committees. No one other than the committee chairman and members is entitled to be present at a meeting of the nomination, audit or remuneration committee, but others may attend at the invitation of the committee.

CODE PROVISIONS

A.3.1 The board should identify in the annual report each non-executive director it considers to be independent. The board should determine whether the director is independent in character and judgement and whether there are relationships or circumstances which are likely to affect, or could appear to affect, the director's judgement. The board should state its reasons if it determines that a director is independent notwithstanding the existence of relationships or circumstances which may appear relevant to its determination, including if the director:

— has been an employee of the company or group within the last five years;

— has, or has had within the last three years, a material business relationship with the company either directly, or as a partner, shareholder, director or senior employee of a body that has such a relationship with the company;

— has received or receives additional remuneration from the company apart from a director's fee, participates in the company's share option or a performance-related pay scheme, or is a member of the company's pension scheme;

— has close family ties with any of the company's advisers, directors or senior employees;

— holds cross-directorships or has significant links with other directors through involvement in other companies or bodies;

— represents a significant shareholder; or

— has served on the board for more than nine years from the date of their first election.

A.3.2   Except for smaller companies, at least half the board, excluding the chairman, should comprise non-executive directors determined by the board to be independent. A smaller company should have at least two independent non-executive directors.

A.3.3   The board should appoint one of the independent non-executive directors to be the senior independent director. The senior independent director should be available to shareholders if they have concerns which contact, through the normal channels of chairman, chief executive or finance director, has failed to resolve or for which such contact is inappropriate.

A.4   *Appointments to the board*

MAIN PRINCIPLES

There should be a formal, rigorous and transparent procedure for the appointment of new directors to the board.

SUPPORTING PRINCIPLES

Appointments to the board should be made on merit and against objective criteria. Care should be taken to ensure that appointees have enough time available to devote to the job. This is particularly important in the case of chairmanships. The board should satisfy itself that plans are in place for orderly succession for appointments to the board and to senior management, so as to maintain an appropriate balance of skills and experience within the company and on the board.

CODE PROVISIONS

A.4.1   There should be a nomination committee which should lead the process for board appointments and make recommendations to the board. A majority of members of the nomination committee should be independent non-executive directors. The chairman or an independent non-executive director should chair the committee, but the chairman should not chair the nomination committee when dealing with the appointment of a successor to the chairmanship. The nomination committee should make available its terms of reference, explaining its role and the authority delegated to it by the board.

A.4.2   The nomination committee should evaluate the balance of skills, knowledge and experience on the board and, in the light of this evaluation, prepare a description of the role and capabilities required for a particular appointment.

A.4.3   For the appointment of a chairman, the nomination committee should prepare a job specification, including an assessment of the time commitment expected, recognizing the need for availability in the event of crises. A chairman's other significant commitments should be disclosed to the board before appointment and included in the annual report. Changes to such commitments should be reported to the board as they arise and included in the next annual report. No individual should be appointed to a second chairmanship of a FTSE 100 company.

A.4.4   The terms and conditions of appointment of non-executive directors should be made available for inspection. The letter of appointment should set out the expected time commitment. Non-executive directors should undertake that they will have sufficient time to meet what is expected of them. Their other significant commitments should be disclosed to the board before appointment, with a broad indication of the time involved, and the board should be informed of subsequent changes.

A.4.5   The board should not agree to a full-time executive director taking on more than one non-executive directorship in a FTSE 100 company, nor the chairmanship of such a company.

A.4.6   A separate section of the annual report should describe the work of the nomination committee, including the process it has used in relation to board appointments. An explanation should be given if neither an external search consultancy nor open advertising has been used in the appointment of a chairman or a non-executive director.

A.5   Information and professional development

MAIN PRINCIPLES

The board should be supplied in a timely manner with information in a form and of a quality appropriate to enable it to discharge its duties. All directors should receive induction on joining the board and should regularly update and refresh their skills and knowledge.

SUPPORTING PRINCIPLES

The chairman is responsible for ensuring that the directors receive accurate, timely and clear information. Management has an obligation to provide such information, but directors should seek clarification or amplification where necessary. The chairman should ensure that the directors continually update their skills and the knowledge and familiarity with the company required to fulfil their role both on the board and on board committees. The company should provide the necessary resources for developing and updating its directors' knowledge and capabilities. Under the direction of the chairman, the company secretary's responsibilities include ensuring good information flows within the board and its committees and between senior management and non-executive directors, as well as facilitating induction and assisting with professional development as required. The company secretary should be responsible for advising the board through the chairman on all governance matters.

CODE PROVISIONS

A.5.1   The chairman should ensure that new directors receive a full, formal and tailored induction on joining the board. As part of this, the company should offer to major shareholders the opportunity to meet a new non-executive director.

A.5.2   The board should ensure that directors, especially non-executive directors, have access to independent professional advice at the company's expense where they judge it necessary to discharge their responsibilities as directors. Committees should be provided with sufficient resources to undertake their duties.

A.5.3   All directors should have access to the advice and services of the company secretary, who is responsible to the board for ensuring that board procedures are complied with. Both the appointment and removal of the company secretary should be a matter for the board as a whole.

A.6   *Performance evaluation*

MAIN PRINCIPLES

The board should undertake a formal and rigorous annual evaluation of its own performance and that of its committees and individual directors.

SUPPORTING PRINCIPLE

Individual evaluation should aim to show whether each director continues to contribute effectively and to demonstrate commitment to the role (including commitment of time for board and committee meetings and any other duties). The chairman should act on the results of the performance evaluation by recognizing the strengths and addressing the weaknesses of the board and, where appropriate, proposing new members be appointed to the board or seeking the resignation of directors.

CODE PROVISION

A.6.1   The board should state in the annual report how performance evaluation of the board, its committees and its individual directors has been conducted. The non-executive directors, led by the senior independent director, should be responsible for performance evaluation of the chairman, taking into account the views of executive directors.

A.7   *Re-election*

MAIN PRINCIPLE

All directors should be submitted for re-election at regular intervals, subject to continued satisfactory performance. The board should ensure planned and progressive refreshing of the board.

CODE PROVISIONS

A.7.1   All directors should be subject to election by shareholders at the first annual general meeting after their appointment and to re-election thereafter at intervals of no more than three years. The names of directors submitted for election or re-election should be accompanied by sufficient biographical details and any other relevant information to enable shareholders to take an informed decision on their election.

A.7.2   Non-executive directors should be appointed for specified terms subject to re-election and to Companies Acts provisions relating to the removal of a director. The board should set out to shareholders in the papers accompanying a resolution to elect a non-executive director why they believe an individual should be elected. The chairman should confirm to shareholders when proposing re-election that, following formal performance evaluation, the individual's performance continues to be effective and to demonstrate commitment to the role. Any term beyond six years (e.g., two three-year terms) for a non-executive director should be subject to particularly rigorous review and should take into account the need for progressive refreshing of the board. Non-executive directors may serve longer than nine years (e.g., three three-year terms), subject to annual re-election. Serving more than nine years could be relevant to the determination of a non-executive director's independence (as set out in provision A.3.1).

B   *Remuneration*

B.1   *The level and make-up of remuneration*

MAIN PRINCIPLES

Levels of remuneration should be sufficient to attract, retain and motivate directors of the quality required to run the company successfully, but a company should avoid paying more than is necessary for this purpose. A significant proportion of executive directors' remuneration should be structured so as to link rewards to corporate and individual performance.

SUPPORTING PRINCIPLE

The remuneration committee should judge where to position their company relative to other companies. But they should use such comparisons with caution, in view of the risk of an upward ratchet of remuneration levels with no corresponding improvement in performance. They should also be sensitive to pay and employment conditions elsewhere in the group, especially when determining annual salary increases.

CODE PROVISIONS

REMUNERATION POLICY

B.1.1   The performance-related elements of remuneration should form a significant proportion of the total remuneration package of executive directors and should be designed to align their interests with those of shareholders and to give these directors keen incentives to perform at the highest levels. In designing schemes of performance-related remuneration, the remuneration committee should follow the provisions in Schedule A to this Code.

B.1.2   Executive share options should not be offered at a discount save as permitted by the relevant provisions of the Listing Rules.

B.1.3   Levels of remuneration for non-executive directors should reflect the time commitment and responsibilities of the role. Remuneration for non-executive directors should not include share options. If, exceptionally, options are granted, shareholder approval should be sought in advance and any shares acquired by exercise of the options should be held until at least one year after the non-executive director leaves the board. Holding of share options could be relevant to the determination of a non-executive director's independence (as set out in provision A.3.1).

B.1.4   Where a company releases an executive director to serve as a non-executive director elsewhere, the remuneration report should include a statement as to whether or not the director will retain such earnings and, if so, what the remuneration is.

SERVICE CONTRACTS AND COMPENSATION

B.1.5   The remuneration committee should carefully consider what compensation commitments (including pension contributions and all other elements) their directors' terms of appointment would entail in the event of early termination. The aim should be to avoid rewarding poor performance. They should take a robust line on reducing compensation to reflect departing directors' obligations to mitigate loss.

B.1.6   Notice or contract periods should be set at one year or less. If it is necessary to offer longer notice or contract periods to new directors recruited from outside, such periods should reduce to one year or less after the initial period.

B.2   *Procedure*

MAIN PRINCIPLE

There should be a formal and transparent procedure for developing policy on executive remuneration and for fixing the remuneration packages of individual directors. No director should be involved in deciding his or her own remuneration.

SUPPORTING PRINCIPLES

The remuneration committee should consult the chairman and/or chief executive about their proposals relating to the remuneration of other executive directors. The remuneration committee should also be responsible for appointing any consultants in respect of executive director remuneration. Where executive directors or senior management are involved in advising or supporting the remuneration committee, care should be taken to recognize and avoid conflicts of interest. The chairman of the board should ensure that the company maintains contact as required with its principal shareholders about remuneration in the same way as for other matters.

CODE PROVISIONS

B.2.1　　The board should establish a remuneration committee of at least three, or in the case of smaller companies two, members, who should all be independent non-executive directors. The remuneration committee should make available its terms of reference, explaining its role and the authority delegated to it by the board. Where remuneration consultants are appointed, a statement should be made available of whether they have any other connection with the company.

B.2.2　　The remuneration committee should have delegated responsibility for setting remuneration for all executive directors and the chairman, including pension rights and any compensation payments. The committee should also recommend and monitor the level and structure of remuneration for senior management. The definition of 'senior management' for this purpose should be determined by the board, but should normally include the first layer of management below board level.

B.2.3　　The board itself or, where required by the Articles of Association, the shareholders should determine the remuneration of the non-executive directors within the limits set in the Articles of Association. Where permitted by the Articles, the board may however delegate this responsibility to a committee, which might include the chief executive.

B.2.4　　Shareholders should be invited specifically to approve all new long-term incentive schemes (as defined in the Listing Rules) and significant changes to existing schemes, save in the circumstances permitted by the Listing Rules.

C Accountability and audit

C.1　　Financial reporting

MAIN PRINCIPLE

The board should present a balanced and understandable assessment of the company's position and prospects.

SUPPORTING PRINCIPLE

The board's responsibility to present a balanced and understandable assessment extends to interim and other price-sensitive public reports and reports to regulators as well as to information required to be presented by statutory requirements.

C.1.1   The directors should explain in the annual report their responsibility for preparing the accounts and there should be a statement by the auditors about their reporting responsibilities.

C.1.2   The directors should report that the business is a going concern, with supporting assumptions or qualifications as necessary.

C.2   *Internal control*

MAIN PRINCIPLE

The board should maintain a sound system of internal control to safeguard shareholders' investment and the company's assets.

CODE PROVISION

C.2.1   The board should, at least annually, conduct a review of the effectiveness of the group's system of internal controls and should report to shareholders that they have done so. The review should cover all material controls, including financial, operational and compliance controls and risk management systems.

C.3   *Audit committee and auditors*

MAIN PRINCIPLE

The board should establish formal and transparent arrangements for considering how they should apply the financial reporting and internal control principles and for maintaining an appropriate relationship with the company's auditors.

CODE PROVISIONS

C.3.1   The board should establish an audit committee of at least three, or in the case of smaller companies two, members, who should all be independent non-executive directors. The board should satisfy itself that at least one member of the audit committee has recent and relevant financial experience.

C.3.2   The main role and responsibilities of the audit committee should be set out in written terms of reference and should include:

—   to monitor the integrity of the financial statements of the company and any formal announcements relating to the company's financial performance, reviewing significant financial reporting judgements contained in them;

— to review the company's internal financial controls and, unless expressly addressed by a separate board risk committee composed of independent directors or by the board itself, to review the company's internal control and risk management systems;

— to monitor and review the effectiveness of the company's internal audit function;

— to make recommendations to the board, for it to put to the shareholders for their approval in general meeting, in relation to the appointment, reappointment and removal of the external auditor and to approve the remuneration and terms of engagement of the external auditor;

— to review and monitor the external auditor's independence and objectivity and the effectiveness of the audit process, taking into consideration relevant UK professional and regulatory requirements;

— to develop and implement policy on the engagement of the external auditor to supply non-audit services, taking into account relevant ethical guidance regarding the provision of non-audit services by the external audit firm, and to report to the board, identifying any matters in respect of which it considers that action or improvement is needed and making recommendations as to the steps to be taken.

C.3.3   The terms of reference of the audit committee, including its role and the authority delegated to it by the board, should be made available. A separate section of the annual report should describe the work of the committee in discharging those responsibilities.

C.3.4   The audit committee should review arrangements by which staff of the company may, in confidence, raise concerns about possible improprieties in matters of financial reporting or other matters. The audit committee's objective should be to ensure that arrangements are in place for the proportionate and independent investigation of such matters and for appropriate follow-up action.

C.3.5   The audit committee should monitor and review the effectiveness of the internal audit activities. Where there is no internal audit function, the audit committee should consider annually whether there is a need for an internal audit function and make a recommendation to the board, and the reasons for the absence of such a function should be explained in the relevant section of the annual report.

C.3.6   The audit committee should have primary responsibility for making a recommendation on the appointment, reappointment and removal of external auditors. If the board does not accept the audit committee's recommendation, it should include in the annual report, and in any papers recommending appointment or re-appointment, a statement from the audit committee explaining the recommendation and should set out reasons why the board has taken a different position.

C.3.7   The annual report should explain to shareholders how, if the auditor provides non-audit services, auditor objectivity and independence is safeguarded.

D   *Relations with shareholders*

D.1   *Dialogue with institutional shareholders*

MAIN PRINCIPLE

There should be a dialogue with shareholders based on the mutual understanding of objectives. The board as a whole has responsibility for ensuring that a satisfactory dialogue with shareholders takes place.

SUPPORTING PRINCIPLES

While recognizing that most shareholder contact is with the chief executive and finance director, the chairman (and the senior independent director and other directors as appropriate) should maintain sufficient contact with major shareholders to understand their issues and concerns. The board should keep in touch with shareholder opinion in whatever ways are most practical and efficient.

CODE PROVISIONS

D.1.1   The chairman should ensure that the views of shareholders are communicated to the board as a whole. The chairman should discuss governance and strategy with major shareholders. Non-executive directors should be offered the opportunity to attend meetings with major shareholders and should expect to attend them if requested by major shareholders. The senior independent director should attend sufficient meetings with a range of major shareholders to listen to their views in order to help develop a balanced understanding of the issues and concerns of major shareholders.

D.1.2   The board should state in the annual report the steps they have taken to ensure that the members of the board, and in particular the non-executive directors, develop an understanding of the views of major shareholders about their company (e.g., through direct face-to-face contact, analysts' or brokers' briefings and surveys of shareholder opinion).

D.2   *Constructive use of the AGM*

MAIN PRINCIPLE

The board should use the AGM to communicate with investors and to encourage their participation.

CODE PROVISIONS

D.2.1   The company should count all proxy votes and, except where a poll is
           called, should indicate the level of proxies lodged on each resolution and
           the balance for and against the resolution and the number of absten-
           tions, after it has been dealt with on a show of hands. The company
           should ensure that votes cast are properly received and recorded.

D.2.2   The company should propose a separate resolution at the AGM on each
           substantially separate issue and should in particular propose a resolu-
           tion at the AGM relating to the report and accounts.

D.2.3   The chairman should arrange for the chairmen of the audit, remunera-
           tion and nomination committees to be available to answer questions at
           the AGM and for all directors to attend.

D.2.4   The company should arrange for the Notice of the AGM and related
           papers to be sent to shareholders at least 20 working days before the
           meeting.

Section 2   Institutional Shareholders

E   *Institutional shareholders*

E.1   *Dialogue with companies*

MAIN PRINCIPLE

**Institutional shareholders should enter into a dialogue with companies
based on the mutual understanding of objectives.**

SUPPORTING PRINCIPLES

Institutional shareholders should apply the principles set out in the
Institutional Shareholders' Committee's 'The Responsibilities of Institutional Shareholders and Agents – Statement of Principles', which
should be reflected in fund manager contracts.

E.2   *Evaluation of governance disclosures*

MAIN PRINCIPLE

**When evaluating companies' governance arrangements, particularly those
relating to board structure and composition, institutional shareholders
should give due weight to all relevant factors drawn to their attention.**

SUPPORTING PRINCIPLES

Institutional shareholders should consider carefully explanations given
for departure from this Code and make reasoned judgements in each

case. They should give an explanation to the company, in writing where appropriate, and be prepared to enter a dialogue if they do not accept the company's position. They should avoid a box-ticking approach to assessing a company's corporate governance. They should bear in mind in particular the size and complexity of the company and the nature of the risks and challenges it faces.

E.3   Shareholder voting

MAIN PRINCIPLES

Institutional shareholders have a responsibility to make considered use of their votes. Supporting Principles Institutional shareholders should take steps to ensure their voting intentions are being translated into practice. Institutional shareholders should, on request, make available to their clients information on the proportion of resolutions on which votes were cast and non-discretionary proxies lodged. Major shareholders should attend AGMs where appropriate and practicable. Companies and registrars should facilitate this.

Schedule A   Provisions on the design of performance-related remuneration

1.   The remuneration committee should consider whether the directors should be eligible for annual bonuses. If so, performance conditions should be relevant, stretching and designed to enhance shareholder value. Upper limits should be set and disclosed. There may be a case for part payment in shares to be held for a significant period.

2.   The remuneration committee should consider whether the directors should be eligible for benefits under long-term incentive schemes. Traditional share option schemes should be weighed against other kinds of long-term incentive scheme. In normal circumstances, shares granted or other forms of deferred remuneration should not vest and options should not be exercisable, in less than three years. Directors should be encouraged to hold their shares for a further period after vesting or exercise, subject to the need to finance any costs of acquisition and associated tax liabilities.

3.   Any new long-term incentive schemes which are proposed should be approved by shareholders and should preferably replace any existing schemes or at least form part of a well-considered overall plan, incorporating existing schemes. The total rewards potentially available should not be excessive.

4.   Payouts or grants under all incentive schemes, including new grants under existing share option schemes, should be subject to challenging

performance criteria reflecting the company's objectives. Consideration should be given to criteria which reflect the company's performance relative to a group of comparator companies in some key variables such as total shareholder return.

5.   Grants under executive share option and other long-term incentive schemes should normally be phased rather than awarded in one large block.

6.   In general, only basic salary should be pensionable.

7.   The remuneration committee should consider the pension consequences and associated costs to the company of basic salary increases and any other changes in pensionable remuneration, especially for directors close to retirement.

Schedule B   Guidance on liability of non-executive directors: care, skill and diligence

1.   Although non-executive directors and executive directors have as board members the same legal duties and objectives, the time devoted to the company's affairs is likely to be significantly less for a non-executive director than for an executive director and the detailed knowledge and experience of a company's affairs that could reasonably be expected of a non-executive director will generally be less than for an executive director. These matters may be relevant in assessing the knowledge, skill and experience which may reasonably be expected of a non-executive director and therefore the care, skill and diligence that a non-executive director may be expected to exercise.

2.   In this context, the following elements of the Code may also be particularly relevant. (i) In order to enable directors to fulfil their duties, the Code states that:

—   the letter of appointment of the director should set out the expected time commitment (Code provision A.4.4); and

—   the board should be supplied in a timely manner with information in a form and of a quality appropriate to enable it to discharge its duties. The chairman is responsible for ensuring that the directors are provided by management with accurate, timely and clear information (Code principles A.5).

(ii) Non-executive directors should themselves:

—   undertake appropriate induction and regularly update and refresh their skills, knowledge and familiarity with the company (Code principle A.5 and provision A.5.1);

—   seek appropriate clarification or amplification of information and, where necessary, take and follow appropriate professional advice (Code principle A.5 and provision A.5.2);

— where they have concerns about the running of the company or a proposed action, ensure that these are addressed by the board and, to the extent that they are not resolved, ensure that they are recorded in the board minutes (Code provision A.1.4);

— give a statement to the board if they have such unresolved concerns on resignation (Code provision A.1.4).

3. It is up to each non-executive director to reach a view as to what is necessary in particular circumstances to comply with the duty of care, skill and diligence they owe as a director to the company. In considering whether or not a person is in breach of that duty, a court would take into account all relevant circumstances. These many include having regard to the above where relevant to the issue of liability of a non-executive director.

Schedule C Disclosure of corporate governance arrangements

The Listing Rules require a statement to be included in the annual report relating to compliance with the Code, as described in the preamble. For ease of reference, the specific requirements in the Code for disclosure are set out below. The annual report should record:

— a statement of how the board operates, including a high-level statement of which types of decisions are to be taken by the board and which are to be delegated to management (A.1.1);

— the names of the chairman, the deputy chairman (where there is one), the chief executive, the senior independent directors and the chairmen and members of the nomination, audit and remuneration committees (A.1.2);

— the number of meetings of the board and those committees and individual attendance by directors (A.1.2);

— the names of the non-executive directors whom the board determines to be independent, with reasons where necessary (A.3.1);

— the other significant commitments of the chairman and any changes to them during the year (A.4.3);

— how performance evaluation of the board, its committees and its directors has been conducted (A.6.1);

— the steps the board has taken to ensure that members of the board, and in particular the non-executive directors, develop an understanding of the views of major shareholders about their company (D.1.2).

The report should also include:

—   a separate section describing the work of the nomination committee, including the process it has used in relation to board appointments and an explanation if neither external search consultancy nor open advertising has been used in the appointment of a chairman or a non-executive director (A.4.6);

—   a description of the work of the remuneration committee as required under the Directors' Remuneration Reporting Regulations 2002, and including, where an executive director serves as a non-executive director elsewhere, whether or not the director will retain such earnings and, if so, what the remuneration is (B.1.4);

—   an explanation from the directors of their responsibility for preparing the accounts and a statement by the auditors about their reporting responsibilities (C.1.1);

—   a statement from the directors that the business is a going concern, with supporting assumptions or qualifications as necessary (C.1.2);

—   a report that the board has conducted a review of the effectiveness of the group's system of internal controls (C.2.1);

—   a separate section describing the work of the audit committee in discharging its responsibilities (C.3.3);

—   where there is no internal audit function, the reasons for the absence of such a function (C.3.5);

—   where the board does not accept the audit committee's recommendation on the appointment, reappointment or removal of an external auditor, a statement from the audit committee explaining the recommendation and the reasons why the board has taken a different position (C.3.6); and

—   an explanation of how, if the auditor provides non-audit services, auditor objectivity and independence is safeguarded (C.3.7).

The following information should be made available (which may be met by making it available on request and placing the information available on the company's website):

—   the terms of reference of the nomination, remuneration and audit committees, explaining their role and the authority delegated to them by the board (A.4.1, B.2.1 and C.3.3);

—   the terms and conditions of appointment of non-executive directors (A.4.4); and

—   where remuneration consultants are appointed, a statement of whether they have any other connection with the company (B.2.1).

The board should set out to shareholders in the papers accompanying a resolution to elect or re-elect:

—   sufficient biographical details to enable shareholders to take an informed decision on their election or re-election (A.7.1);

—   why they believe an individual should be elected to a non-executive role (A.7.2);

—   on re-election of a non-executive director, confirmation from the chairman that, following formal performance evaluation, the individual's performance continues to be effective and to demonstrate commitment to the role, including commitment of time for board and committee meetings and any other duties (A.7.2).

The board should set out to shareholders in the papers recommending appointment or reappointment of an external auditor:

—   if the board does not accept the audit committee's recommendation, there should be a statement from the audit committee explaining the recommendation and another from the board setting out reasons why they have taken a different position (C.3.6).

References

ABI (1997) *ABI Member Companies Mailing List*, Association of British Insurers, London.

ABI (2001) *Disclosure Guidelines on Socially Responsible Investment*, Association of British Insurers, London.

ACBE (1996) *Sixth Progress Report to and Responses from the President of the Board of Trade and the Secretary of State for the Environment*, Advisory Committee of Business and the Environment, London.

ACCA (2000) *Turnbull, Internal Control and Wider Aspects of Risk* (commissioned by the Association of Chartered Certified Accountants' Social and Environmental Committee), Certified Accountants Educational Trust, London.

AccountAbility 1000 (AA1000) (November 1999) *Accountability 1000 Framework: Exposure Draft*, AccountAbility, London.

Adams, C. A. (2002) 'Internal organisational factors influencing corporate social and ethical reporting: Beyond current theorising', *Accounting, Auditing & Accountability*, **15**(2), 223–250.

Adams, C. A., Hill, W. Y. and Roberts, C. B. (1995) *Environmental, Employee and Ethical Reporting in Europe* (ACCA Research Report No.41), Association of Chartered Certified Accountants, London.

Adams, R. (1992) 'Why is the environmental debate of interest to accountants and accountancy bodies?', in: D. Owen (ed.), *Green Reporting: Accounting and the Challenge of the Nineties*, Chapman & Hall, London.

Agrawal, A. and Knoeber, C. R. (1996) 'Firm performance and mechanisms to control agency problems between managers and shareholders', *Journal of Financial and Quantitative Analysis*, **31**(3), September, 377–397.

Alexander, G. J. and Buchholz, R. A. (1978) 'Corporate social responsibility and stock market performance', *Academy of Management Journal*, **21**(3), 479–486.

Alkhafaji, A. F. (1989) *A Stakeholder Approach to Corporate Governance: Managing in a Dynamic Environment*, Quorum Books, Westport, CT.

Alrawi, M. (2003) 'New Arab Council to Zero In on Corporate Governance', *Jordan Times*, 1 July.

Apreda, R. (2001) 'Corporate governance in Argentina: The outcome of economic freedom', *Corporate Governance: An International Review*, **9**(4), October, 298–310.

Arlow, P. and Gannon, M. J. (1982) 'Social responsiveness, corporate structure and economic performance', *Academy of Management Review*, **7**, 235–241.

Arnold, G. (1998) *Corporate Financial Management*, Financial Times Pitman Publishing, London.

Arthur Andersen (1996) 'What's the story? A survey of narrative reporting in annual reports', *Arthur Andersen*, Binder Hamlyn, London.

ASB (1996) *Derivatives and Other Financial Instruments* (discussion paper), Accounting Standards Board, Milton Keynes, UK.

ASSC (1975) *The Corporate Report* (Accounting Standards Steering Committee), Institute of Chartered Accountants in England and Wales, London.

Ball, S. and Bell, S. (1995) *Environmental Law* (3rd edn), Blackstone Press, London.

Barreveld, D. J. (2002) *The Enron Collapse: Creative Accounting, Wrong Economics or Criminal Acts?*, Writers Club Press, iUniverse Inc., USA.

Beaver, W. H. (1989) *Financial Reporting: An Accounting Revolution* (2nd edn), Prentice Hall International Editions, Upper Saddle River, NJ.

Belcher, A. (2002) 'Corporate killing as a corporate governance issue', *Corporate Governance: An International Review*, **10**(1), January, 47–54.

Belkaoui, A. (1976) 'The impact of disclosure of the environmental effects of organizational behaviour on the market', *Financial Management*, **5**(4), 26–31.

Benston, G. J. (1982) 'Accounting and corporate accountability', *Accounting, Organisations and Society*, **7**(2), 87–105.

Berglof, E. and Perotti, E. (1994) 'The governance structure of the Japanese financial keiretsu', *Journal of Financial Economics*, **36**, 259–284.

Berle, A. and Means, G. (1932) *The Modern Corporation and Private Property*, New York.

Bethel, J. E., Liebeskind, J. P. and Opler, T. (1998) 'Block share repurchases and corporate performance', *Journal of Finance*, **53**, 605–635.

Bison, T. A. (1954) *Zaibatsu Dissolution in Japan*, Greenwood Press, Westport, CT.

Blackburn, S. (1999) 'Managing risk and achieving Turnbull compliance', *Accountants' Digest*, **417**, October, 1–51.

Blanchard, K. H. and Peale, N. V. (1988) *The Power of Ethical Management*, Morrow, New York.

Blitz, R. (2003) 'UK Survey Shows Wide Distrust of Directors', *Financial Times*, 29 June.

Boatright, J. R. (1999) *Ethics in Finance*, Blackwell, Oxford.

Bolger, A. and Jenkins, P. (2002) 'Animal Activists Target Marsh', *Financial Times*, 13 August.

Boritz, J. E. (1990) *Approaches to Dealing with Risk and Uncertainty* (CICA Research Report), Canadian Institute of Chartered Accountants, Toronto.

Bosch Report, The (1995) 'Corporate practices and conduct', *Information Australia* (3rd edn), Woodslane Pty Ltd, Melbourne.

Bosch, H. A. O. (1993) 'Corporate practices and conduct: Setting standards for corporate governance in Australia', *Corporate Governance: An International Review*, **1**(4), 196–198.

Bostock, R. (1995) 'Company responses to Cadbury', *Corporate Governance: An International Review*, **3**(2), April, 72–77.

Bowman, E. H. and Haire, M. (1975) 'A strategic posture toward corporate social responsibility', *California Management Review*, **18**(2), 49–58.

Boxell, J. (14 July 2003) '"Fat Cat" Pay Issue Set to Dominate AGMs', *Financial Times*, 14 July.

Boxell, J. (18 June 2003) 'Whitbread "Fat Cat" Protest Vote', *Financial Times*, 18 June.

Bream, R. (2003) 'AWG to Stop Special Bonuses', *Financial Times*, 9 July.

Brewer, J. (1997) 'The state of corporate governance in Hong Kong', *Corporate Governance: An International Review*, **5**(2), April, 77–82.

Briston, R. J. and Dobbins, R. (1978) *The Growth and Impact of Institutional Investors* (a report to the Research Committee of the ICAEW), The Institute of Chartered Accountants in England and Wales, London.

Brown, P. (2003) 'Use of Monkeys in Research "Can Be Reduced"', *The Guardian*, 2 July.

Buchan, D. and Earle, J. (2002) 'BP Puts $600 million Alaska Oilfield in Cold Storage', *Financial Times*, 8 June.

Buck, J. (1992) 'Green awareness: An opportunity for Business', in: D. Owen (ed.), *Green Reporting: Accounting and the Challenge of the Nineties*, Chapman & Hall, London.

Burgess, A. (1962) *A Clockwork Orange*, Penguin Books, Harmondsworth, UK.

Bushman, R. M. and Smith, A. J. (2001) 'Financial accounting information and corporate governance', *Journal of Accounting and Economics*, **32**, 237–333.

Bushman, R., Indjejikian, R. and Smith, A. (1995) 'Aggregate performance measurement in business unit compensation: The role of intrafirm interdependencies', *Journal of Accounting Research*, **33**(Suppl.), 101–128.

Business Roundtable (September 1997) *Statement on Corporate Governance*, The Business Roundtable, Washington, DC.

Butz and Blattner (1999) *Socially Responsible Investment: A Statistical Analysis of Returns* (Sarasin Basic Report), Basle, Switzerland.

Byrd, J. W. and Hickman, K. A. (1992) 'Do outside directors monitor managers?', *Journal of Financial Economics*, **32**, 195–221.

Cadbury Code, The (December 1992) *Report of the Committee on the Financial Aspects of Corporate Governance: The Code of Best Practice*, Gee Professional Publishing, London.

Cadbury, A. (2002) *Corporate Governance and Chairmanship: A Personal View*, Oxford University Press, Oxford.

CalPERS (April 1998) *Corporate Governance Market Principles*, California Public Employees' Retirement System, Sacramento, CA.

CalPERS Corporate Governance Guidelines, The (1999) Part published in *Corporate Governance: An International Review*, **7**(2).

Cannon, T. (1994) *Corporate Responsibility. A Textbook on Business Ethics, Governance, Environment: Roles and Responsibilities*, Pitman, London.

Cardon Report, The (1998) *Report of the Belgium Commission on Corporate Governance*, Brussels Stock Exchange, Brussels.

Carlyle, T. (1909) *Past and Present*, R. A. Kessinger Publishing, London.

CBI (1994) *Introducing Environmental Reporting Guidelines for Business*, Confederation of British Industry, London.

CEPS (1995) *Corporate Governance in Europe* (CEPS Working Party Report No. 12), Brussels.

CERES (1992) *The CERES Principles*, Coalition for Environmental Responsible Economies, Washington, DC.

Chang, C. Z. and Chan, L. S. (2002) 'TSMC Establishes First Audit Committee', *Economy Daily*, 26 July [in Mandarin Chinese].

Charkham, J. (1994) *Keeping Good Company: A Study of Corporate Governance in Five Countries*, Clarendon Press, Oxford.

Charkham, J. and Simpson, A. (1999) *Fair Shares: The Future of Shareholder Power and Responsibilities*, Oxford University Press, Oxford.

Cheffins, B. R. (2003) 'Will executive pay globalise along American lines?', *Corporate Governance: An International Review*, **11**(1), January, 8–24.

Choi, C. J. and Wright, N. (1994) *How to Achieve Business Success in Korea: Where Confucius Wears a Three-Piece Suit*, Macmillan, Basingstoke, UK.

CICA (1994) *Reporting on Environmental Performance*, Canadian Institute of Chartered Accountants, Toronto.

CII (April 1998) *Desirable Corporate Governance: A Code*, Confederation of Indian Industry, New Delhi.

CII (March 1998) *Core Policies*, Council of Institutional Investors, Washington, DC.

Claessens, S., Djanklov, S. and Lang, L. H. P. (2000) 'The separation of ownership and control in East Asian corporations', *Journal of Financial Economics*, **58**, 81–112.

Coase, R. H. (1937) 'The nature of the firm', *Economica*, **4**, 386–405.

Cochran, P. L. and Wood, R. A. (1984) 'Corporate social responsibility and financial performance', *Academy of Management Journal*, **27**(1), 42–56.

Coffee, J. C. (1996) 'Institutional investors in transitional economies: Lessons from the Czech experience, in: R. Frydman, C. W. Gray and A. Rapaczynski (eds), *Corporate Governance in Central Europe and Russia*. Volume 1: *Banks, Funds, and Foreign Investors* (pp. 111–186), Central European University Press, London.

Coffee, J. C., Jr (1991) 'Liquidity versus control: The institutional investor as corporate monitor', *Columbia Law Review*, **91**(6), October, 1277–1368.

Combined Code, The (1998) The London Stock Exchange Limited, June, London, UK.

Combined Code on Corporate Governance, The (2003) Financial Reporting Council, July, London.

Company Law (2001) *Company Law* (amended on 12 November 2001), translated into English by Lee & Li, Attorneys-at-Law, Taipei, Taiwan.

Conyon, M. J. and Mallin, C. A. (1997) 'A review of compliance with Cadbury', *Journal of General Management*, **2**(3), spring, 24–37.

Cooke, T. E. and Sawa, E. (1998) 'Corporate governance structure in Japan: Form and reality', *Corporate Governance: An International Review*, **6**(4), 217–223.

Core, J. E. (2001) 'A review of the empirical disclosure literature: discussion', *Journal of Accounting and Economics*, **31**, 441–456.

Core, J. E., Holthausen, R. W. and Larcker, D. F. (1999) 'Corporate governance, chief executive officer compensation, and firm performance', *Journal of Financial Economics*, **51**, 371–406.

Corporate Governance Committee (May 1998) *Corporate Governance Principles*, Corporate Governance Forum of Japan, Tokyo.

Corporate Governance Forum of Japan (1999) 'Corporate governance principles—a Japanese view', *Corporate Governance: An International Review*, **7**(2), April.

Corporate Governance Handbook, The (1996) 'Supplement 1 on operating and financial review', Gee Professional Publishing, London.

Corporate Governance Report (1997) 'Corporate governance in the Netherlands', *Corporate Governance: An International Review*, **5**(4), October, 236–238.

Corporate Report, The, *see* ASSC (1975).

Courtis, J. K. (1993) 'Recent developments and frustrations in the corporate reporting process', *Corporate Governance: An International Review*, **1**(1), 18–25.

Cowe, R. (1992) 'Green issues and the investor: Inadequacies of current reporting practice and some suggestions for change', in: D. Owen (ed.), *Green Reporting: Accounting and the Challenge of the Nineties*, Chapman & Hall, London.

Cowe, R. (2001) *Investing in Social Responsibility: Risks and Opportunities* (ABI Research Report), Association of British Insurers, London.

Croft, J. (2003) 'HSBC Shrugs Off Shareholder Protest', *Financial Times*, 12 May.

Croft, J. (24 July 2003) 'Anger at Nationwide Executive's Pay-Off', *Financial Times*, 24 July.

Crozier, M. (1964) *The Bureaucratic Phenomenon*, University of Chicago Press, Chicago.

Cruver, B. (2002) *The Unshredded Truth from an Enron Insider: Enron, Anatomy of Greed*, Arrow Books, London.

Cyert, R. M. and March, J. G. (1963) *A Behavioural Theory of the Firm*, Prentice Hall, Englewood Cliffs, NJ.

Dahya, J., McConnell, J. J. and Travlos, N. G. (2002) 'The Cadbury Committee, corporate performance, and top management turnover', *Journal of Finance*, **57**(1), February, 461–483.

Daily, C. M. and Dalton, D. R. (1997) 'Separate, but not independent: Board leadership structure in large corporations', *Corporate Governance: An International Review*, **5**(3), 126–136.

Daniels, R. J. and Morck, R. (1996) 'Canadian corporate governance policy options' (Discussion Paper No. 3), *Industry Canada*, March.

Daniels, R. J. and Waitzer, E. (1993) 'Corporate governance: A Canadian perspective', *Corporate Governance: An International Review*, **1**(2), April, 66–75.

Deegan, C. and Rankin, M. (1996) 'Do Australian companies report environmental news objectively? An analysis of environmental disclosures by firms prosecuted successfully by the Environmental Protection Authority', *Accounting, Auditing and Accountability Journal*, **9**(2), 50–67.

Demirag, I. and Tylecote, A. (1992) 'The effects of organisational culture, structure and market expectations on technological innovation: A hypothesis', *British Journal of Management*, **3**(1), 7–20.

Deutsche Bundestag (March 1998) 'Law on Control and Transparency in the Corporate Sector', *Deutsche Bundestag*.

Dey Report, The (December 1994) *Where Were the Directors?*, Toronto Stock Exchange Committee on Corporate Governance in Canada, Toronto.

Diamond, D. and Verrecchia, R. (1991) 'Disclosure, liquidity, and the cost of capital', *Journal of Finance*, **66**, 1325–1355.

Diamond, D. W. (1984) 'Financial intermediation and delegated monitoring', *Review of Economic Studies*, **51**(3), 393–414.

Digital Korea Herald (27 April 2000) 'Top Financial Regulator Rejects Chaebol Demands for Regulation'.

Dobson, G. R. (1994) *The Global Investor*, Probus Europe, Cambridge.

Dombey, D. (2003) 'The Long March to Shareholder Democracy', *Financial Times*, 16 June.

Donaldson, L. and Davies, J. H. (1994) 'Boards and company performance—Research challenges the conventional wisdom', *Corporate Governance: An International Review*, **2**(3), July, 151–160.

Donaldson, T. and Preston, L. (1995) 'A stakeholder theory of the corporation: Concepts, evidence, and implications', *Academy of Management Review*, **20**(1), 65–91.

Draghi, M. (1998) 'Le Proposte della Commissione Draghi' (The Proposals of the Draghi Commission), *Il Sole 24 Ore On Line*, July.

Drexhage, G. (1998) 'There's money in ethics', *Global Investor*, **109**, 56.

Drucker, P. (1982) 'The new meaning of corporate social responsibility', *California Management Review*, **26**, 53–63.

DTI (1999) *Creating Quality Dialogue between Smaller Quoted Companies and Fund Managers*, Department of Trade and Industry, London.

DTTI (1993) *Coming Clean. Corporate Environmental Reporting*, Deloitte Touche Tohamatsu International, International Institute for Sustainable Development and SustainAbility Ltd, London.

Durgin, H. and Wolffe, R. (2000) 'Oilman Bush Focuses on a Burning Issue: But Not All Analysts Are Convinced by His Plans to Drill in an Alaskan Wildlife Reserve', *Financial Times*, 12 October.

Durkheim, E. (1952) *Suicide*, Routledge & Kegan Paul, London (first published in French in 1897).

Eagle, J. (2000) 'Chemical Attack on Animal Researcher', *Birmingham Post*, 23 December.

Earle, J. (2001) 'Alaska Oil Spill Ahead of Vote', *Financial Times*, 24 July.

Economist, The (26 February 1998) 'Electric Avenues'.

Economist, The (23 April 1998) 'Not As Billed'.

Economist, The (30 July 1998) 'Wet Behind the Ears'.

Economist, The (1st June 2000) 'The Energetic Messiah'.

Economist, The (15 June 2000) 'Buying a Financial Umbrella'.

Economist, The (8 February 2001) 'The Slumbering Giants Awake'.

Economist, The (28 June 2001) 'A Matter of Principals'.

Economist, The (1 November 2001) 'Houston, We Have a Problem'.

Economist, The (15 November 2001) 'See You In Court'.

Economist, The (29 November 2001) 'Upended'.

Economist, The (6 December 2001) 'The Amazing Disintegrating Firm'.

Economist, The (20 December 2001) 'Who Fiddled What?'.

Economist, The (7 February 2002) 'The Lessons from Enron'.

Economist, The (7 February 2002) 'When the Numbers Don't Add Up'.

Economist, The (2 May 2002) 'Badly In Need of Repair'.

Economist, The (9 May 2002) 'Bad News, Good News'.

Economist, The (21 May 2002) 'Picking Over Andersen'.

Economist, The (13 June 2002) 'Designed by Committee'.

Economist, The (13 June 2002) 'Prosecutor's Dilemma'.

Economist, The (15 August 2002) 'I Swear …'.

Economist, The (3 October 2002) 'But Not Forgotten'.

Economist, The (31 October 2002) 'Cleaning Up the Boardroom'.

Economist, The (15 November 2002) 'Executive Pay: The Background'.

Economist, The (28 November 2002) 'Investor Self-Protection'.

Edwards, J. and Fischer, K. (1994) *Banks, Finance and Investment in Germany*, Cambridge University Press, New York.

Eisenhardt, K. (1989) 'Agency Theory: An Assessment and Review', *Academy of Management Review*, **14**, 57–74.

Elkington, J. (1998) *Cannibals with Forks*, New Society, Gabriola Island, BC.

Elliott, A. L. and Schroth, R. J. (2002) *How Companies Lie: Why Enron is Just the Tip of the Iceberg*, Nicholas Brealey, London.

Ethical Investor, The (November/December 1999) Newsletter produced by the Ethical Investment Research Service (EIRIS), London.

European Commission (2001) *Promoting a European Framework for Corporate Social Responsibility* (Green Paper), European Commission, Brussels.

European Financial Services Regulation (2003) 'Bolkestein outlines top priorities for FSAP and corporate governance', *European Financial Services Regulation*, **4**, July, 1–2.

Faccio, M. and Lasfer, M. A. (2000) 'Do occupational pension funds monitor companies in which they hold large stakes?', *Journal of Corporate Finance*, **6**, 71–110.

Fama, E. F. (1970) 'Efficient capital markets: A review of theory and empirical work', *Journal of Finance*, **25**, 383–417.

Fama, E. F. (1980) 'Agency problems and the theory of the firm', *Journal of Political Economy*, **88**, 288–307.

Fama, E. F. and Jensen, M. C. (1983) 'Separation of ownership and control', *Journal of Law and Economics*, **27**, 301–325.

Farrar, J. H. and Hannigan, B. M. (1998) *Farrar's Company Law* (4th edn), Butterworths, London.

FEE (2000) *Towards a Generally Accepted Framework for Environmental Reporting*, European Federation of Accountants, Brussels.

Financial Times (2 September 1998) 'Huntingdon Investors Approve Refinancing'.

Financial Times (11 April 2000) 'Eco-Shareholders Target BP'.

Financial Times (13 April 2000) 'Five Protesters Arrested'.

Financial Times (7 May 2000) 'Friends Provident Backs Ethics'.

Financial Times (27 June 2000) 'Alaska Oil: The Debate Heats Up Again'.

Financial Times (4 June 2003) 'Curbing Failure's Rotten Reward'.

Firn, D. (2000) 'Huntingdon to Lose NYSE Listing', *Financial Times*, 22 December.

Firn, D. (2002) 'Silent Message to Animal Rights Activists', *Financial Times*, 10 January.

Firn, D. and Guerrera, F. (2000) 'Bank Drops Its Holding in Animal Tests Group', *Financial Times*, 12 December.

Firn, D. and Jenkins, P. (2003) 'Animal Activists Expand Campaign Against HLS', *Financial Times*, 14 March.

Fitzpatrick, N. (2003) 'Shareholders Targeted by New Code', *Pensions Week*, 28 July, p. 40.

Flanagan, M. (2003) 'Higgs Challenge as Davis to Step Up at Sainsbury', *The Scotsman*, 15 March.

Florence, S. (1961) *Ownership, Control and Success of Large Companies*, Sweet & Maxwell, London.

Fombrun, C. J. (2000) 'The Value to be Found in Corporate Reputation: The Public's View of a Company Not Only Acts as a Reservoir of Goodwill but also Boosts the Bottom Line', *Financial Times*, 4 December.

Fombrun, C. J. and Shanley, M. (1990) 'What's in a name? Reputation-building and corporate strategy', *Academy of Management Journal*, **33**, 233–258.

Fox, L. (2003) *Enron: The Rise and Fall*, John Wiley & Sons, Hoboken, NJ.

Franks, J. and Mayer, C. (1994) 'The ownership and control of German corporations' (manuscript), London Business School, London.

Freeman, E. (1984) *Strategic Management: A Stakeholder Approach*, Pitman Press, Boston.

Freire, P. (1996) *Pedagogy of the Oppressed*, Pelican, London.

French, P. (1979) 'The corporation as a moral person', *American Philosophical Quarterly*, **16**(3), 207–215.

French, P. (1984) *Collective and Corporate Responsibility*, Columbia University Press, New York.

Frémond, O. and Capaul, M. (May 2003) *Corporate Governance Country Assessment: Chile* (World Bank Report on the Observance of Standards and Codes). Available online at http://worldbank.org/ifa/rosc_chlcg.pdf

Friedman, A. L. and Miles, S. (2001) 'Socially responsible investment and corporate social and environmental reporting in the UK: An exploratory study', *British Accounting Review*, **33**, 523–548.

Friedman, M. (1962) *Capitalism and Freedom*, University of Chicago, Chicago.

Friedman, M. (1970) 'The Social Responsibility of Business is to Increase its Profits', *New York Times Magazine*, 13 September. Reprinted in Beauchamp, T. L. and Bowie, N. (1988) *Ethical Theory and Business* (pp. 87–91), Prentice Hall, Englewood Cliffs, NJ.

Frontline (2002) 'In Harshad Mehta's Wake: Harshad Mehta is Dead, but the Trail Goes On', (India's National Magazine).

Fukuyama, F. (1995) *Trust: The Social Virtues and the Creation of Prosperity*, Penguin Books, Harmondsworth, UK.

Fusaro, P. C. and Miller, R. M. (2002) *What Went Wrong at Enron: Everyone's Guide to the Largest Bankruptcy in US History*, John Wiley & Sons, Hoboken, NJ.

Garratt, B. (1996) *The Fish Rots from the Head*, HarperCollins Business, London.

Giddens, A. (1991) *Modernity and Self-Identity, Self and Society in the Late Modern Age*, Polity Press, Oxford.

Gilson, R. J. and Mnookin, R. (1985) 'Sharing among the Human Capitalists: An Economic

Inquiry into the Corporate Law Firm and How Partners Split Profits', *Stanford Law Review*, **37**, January, 313–397.

GM Board of Directors (June 1997) *GM Board of Directors Corporate Governance Guidelines on Significant Governance Issues* (2nd edn), General Motors, Detroit.

Goodpaster, K. E. (1982) 'Kohlbergian Theory: A Philosophical Counterinvitation', *Ethics*, April, 491–498.

Goodpaster, K. E. (1987) 'The Principle of Moral Projection: A Reply to Professor Ranken', *Journal of Business Ethics*, **6**, 329–332.

Goswami, O. (2000) 'The Tide Rises, Gradually: Corporate Governance in India', *Informal Workshop on Corporate Governance in Developing Countries and Emerging Economies, OECD Headquarters, Paris*.

Government Commission (2001) *German Corporate Governance Code* (translation), Government Commission, Dusseldorf.

Graves, S. B. and Waddock, S. A. (1994) 'Institutional owners and corporate social performance', *Academy of Management Journal*, **37**(4), August, 1034–1046.

Gray R., Bebbington, J. and Walters, D. (1993) *Accounting for the Environment*, Paul Chapman Publishing, London.

Gray, R. H. (1992) 'Accounting and environmentalism: An exploration of the challenge of gently accounting for accountability, transparency and sustainability', *Accounting, Organizations and Society*, **17**(5), 399–426.

Gray, R., Owen, D. and Adams, C. (1996) *Accounting and Accountability*, Prentice Hall, London.

Gray, R., Owen, D. and Maunders, K. (1987) *Corporate Social Reporting: Accounting and Accountability*, Prentice Hall, London.

Greenbury Report, The (July 1995) *Directors' Remuneration* (report of a study group chaired by Sir Richard Greenbury), Gee Professional Publishing, London.

Gregory, A., Matatko, J. and Luther, R. (1997) 'Ethical unit trust financial performance: small company effects and fund size effects', *Journal of Business Finance and Accounting*, **24**(5), June, 705–725.

GRI (2000) 'Sustainability reporting guidelines', available at the Global Reporting Initiative website, www.globalreporting.org

Griffin, J. and Mahon, J. F. (1997) 'The corporate social performance and corporate financial performance debate: Twenty-five years of incomparable research', *Business and Society*, **36**(1), 5–31.

Griffin, P. (2000) 'Wreath-Laying Marks Anniversary of Guinea Pig Raid', *Birmingham Post*, 2 September.

Groves, J. (1999) 'Identifying, developing and effectively implementing a risk management methodology which suits your company's operating strategy and corporate culture', *IIR Conference on Proactively Managing Business Risk and Ensuring Effective Internal Control in the Light of the Combined Code and the New Turnbull Committee Report, London, May*.

Guan, E. (2002) 'News Focus: SFC Sticks to Strengthen Corporate Governance', *Taiwan Business News*.

Guardian, The (29 August 2000) 'NIMAL Lab Staff Cars Set on Fire'.

Guerard, J. B. (1996) 'Is there a cost to being socially responsible in investing?', *Social Investment Forum Research*.

Guerard, J. B. (1997) 'Additional evidence of the cost of being socially responsible in investing', *Journal of Investing*, **6**(4), 31–36.

Guerrera, F. (2000a) 'Animal Rights Hit HLS Investors', *Financial Times*, 26 June.

Guerrera, F. (2000b) 'Huntingdon Seeks £34 million Lifeline in US. Drug Testing Group Sys

Attacks by Animal Rights Protesters Prompted it to Look Abroad', *Financial Times*, 16 August.

Hampel Report, The (1998) *The Final Report*, The Committee on Corporate Governance and Gee Professional Publishing, London.

Hancock, J. (1999) *Making Gains with Values: The Ethical Investor*, Financial Times/Prentice Hall, London.

Hansen, G. S. and Hill, C. W. L. (1991) 'Are institutional investors myopic? A time series study of four technology driven industries', *Strategic Management Journal*, **12**, 1–16.

Harris, C. (2003) 'WPP Shareholders Challenge Sorrell Contract', *Financial Times*, 30 June.

Hart, O. D. (1983) 'The market mechanism as an incentive scheme', *Bell Journal of Economics*, **14**, 366–382.

Harte, G. and Owen, D. (1992) 'Current trends in the reporting of green issues in the annual reports of United Kingdom companies', in: D. Owen (ed.), *Green Reporting: Accountancy and the Challenge of the Nineties* (pp. 166–200), Chapman & Hall, London.

Harte, G., Lewis, L. and Owen, D. (1991) 'Ethical investment and the corporate reporting function', *Critical Perspectives on Accounting*, **2**, 227–253.

Heal, G. (2000) 'Environmental Disaster: Not All Bad News', *Financial Times*, 30 October.

Healy, P. M. and Palepu, K. G. (2001) 'Information asymmetry, corporate disclosure, and the capital markets: A review of the empirical disclosure literature', *Journal of Accounting and Economics*, **31**, 405–440.

Healy, P. M., Hutton, A. and Palepu, K. (1999) 'Stock performance and intermediation changes surrounding sustained increases in disclosure', *Contemporary Accounting Research*, **16**, 485–520.

Hemmings, D. B. and Solomon, J. F. (1998) 'Corporate governance and stock market duration for South Korea and the USA', *Global Economic Review*, **27**(3), Autumn, 76–92.

Hermalin, B. E. and Weisbach, M. S. (1988) 'The determinants of board composition', *Rand Journal of Economics*, **19**, winter, 589–606.

Hermanson, H. M. (2000) 'An analysis of the demand for reporting on internal control', *Accounting Horizons*, **14**(3), September, 325–341.

Higgs Report, The (January 2003) *Review of the Role and Effectiveness of Non-Executive Directors*, Department of Trade and Industry, London.

High Level Finance Committee on Corporate Governance (February 1999) *The Malaysian Code on Corporate Governance* (High Level Finance Committee Report on Corporate Governance, Chapter 5), High Level Finance Committee on Corporate Governance, Kuala Lumpur.

Hill, C. W. and Jones, T. M. (1992) 'Stakeholder–agency theory', *Journal of Management Studies*, **29**, 134–154.

Hillman, A. J. and Keim, G. D. (2001) 'Shareholder value, stakeholder management, and social issues: What's the bottom line?', *Strategic Management Journal*, **22**, 125–139.

Hindu, The (12 January 2002) 'Cases Against Harshad Mehta to Continue'.

Hirschman, A. O. (1970) '"Exit", "voice" and "the elusive optimal mix of exit and voice"', *Exit, Voice and Loyalty: Responses to Decline in Firms, Organizations, and States*, Harvard University Press, Cambridge, MA.

HKSA (December 1997) *A Guide for the Formation of an Audit Committee*, Hong Kong Society of Accountants, Hong Kong.

Holden-Meehan (1999) *The Millennium Guide to Ethical and Environmental Investment*, Holden-Meehan, Bristol.

Holland, J. (1998) 'Private disclosure and financial reporting', *Accounting and Business Research*, **28**(4), Autumn, 255–269.

Holland, J. and Stoner, G. (1996) 'Dissemination of price sensitive information and management of voluntary corporate disclosure', *Accounting and Business Research*, **26**(4), 295–313.

Hoshi, T. and Kashyap, A. (2001) *Corporate Financing and Governance in Japan: The Road to the Future*, MIT Press, Cambridge, MA.

Hoshi, T., Kashyap, A. and Scharfstein, D. (1991) 'Corporate structure, liquidity, and investment: Evidence from Japanese industrial groups', *Quarterly Journal of Economics*, **106**, 33–60.

Humphrey, C., Moizer, P. and Turley, S. (1992) *The Audit Expectations Gap in the United Kingdom*, Institute of Chartered Accountants in England and Wales, London.

Hussain, S. H. and Mallin, C. (2002) 'Corporate governance in Bahrain', *Corporate Governance: An International Review*, **10**(3), 197–210.

Hutton, W. and Giddens, A. (2001) *On the Edge: Living with Global Capitalism*, Vintage, London.

Hutton, W. (1995) *The State We're In*, Vintage Books, London.

ICAEW (1998) *Financial Reporting of Risk: Proposals for a Statement of Business Risk*, Institute of Chartered Accountants in England and Wales, London.

IMF (July 2001) *Czech Republic: Financial System Stability Assessment* (IMF Country Report), International Monetary Fund, Washington, DC.

Independent, The (16 September 2000) 'Government to Keep Animal Testing Secret'.

Independent, The (18 November 2000) 'Blair Tells Violent Eco-Warriors They Can't Stop Science'.

International Investment Management Directory (1993/94), Euromoney Books/Global Investor, London.

ISC (1993) *Report on Investigation of Use of Voting Rights by Institutions*, Institutional Shareholders Committee, London.

ISC (2002) *The Responsibilities of Institutional Shareholders and Agents—Statement of Principles*, Institutional Shareholders Committee, London.

Jenkins, P. (2001) 'Huntingdon Set to Begin Trading on US Market', *Financial Times*.

Jensen, M. (1991) 'Corporate control and the politics of finance', *Journal of Applied Corporate Finance*, **4**(2), 13–33.

Jensen, M. (1993) 'The modern industrial revolution, exit, and the failure of internal control systems', *Journal of Finance*, **48**, 831–880.

Jensen, M. and Ruback, R. S. (1983) 'The market for corporate control: The scientific evidence', *Journal of Financial Economics*, **11**, 5–50.

Jensen, M. C. and Meckling, W. H. (1976) 'Theory of the firm: Managerial behaviour, agency costs and ownership structure', *Journal of Financial Economics*, **3**, October, 305–360.

Jesover, F. (2001) 'Corporate governance in the Russian Federation: The relevance of the OECD Principles on shareholder rights and equitable treatment', *Corporate Governance: An International Review*, **9**(2), April, 79–88.

Johnson, R. A. and Greening, D. W. (1994) 'Relationships between corporate social performance, financial performance and firm governance', *Best Paper Proceedings of the Academy of Management*, 314–319.

Johnson, S., Boone, P., Breach, A. and Friedman, E. (2000) 'Corporate governance in the Asian financial crisis', *Journal of Financial Economics*, **58**, 141–186.

Jones, M. J. (1996) 'Accounting for biodiversity: A pilot study', *British Accounting Review*, **28**(4), 281–303.

Jones, R. (2002) 'FTSE 100 Prepares for Shareholder Vote on Pay', *Investors Chronicle*, 25 January, p. 10.

Kang, J. K. and Shivdasani, A. (1995) 'Firm performance, corporate governance, and top executive turnover in Japan', *Journal of Financial Economics*, **38**, 29–58.

Kaplan, R. S. and Norton, D. P. (1996) *The Balanced Scorecard: Translating Strategy into Action*, Harvard Business School Press, Boston.

Kaplan, S. N. and Minton, B. A. (1994) 'Appointments of outsiders to Japanese boards: Determinants and implications for managers', *Journal of Financial Economics*, **36**, 225–258.

Karpoff, J. M., Malatesta, P. H. and Walkling, R. A. (1996) 'Corporate governance and shareholder initiatives: Empirical evidence', *Journal of Financial Economics*, **42**, 365–395.

Keasey, K. and Wright, M. (1993) 'Issues in corporate accountability and governance', *Accounting and Business Research*, **91a**, 291–303.

Keating, S. (1997) 'Determinants of divisional performance evaluation practices', *Journal of Accounting and Economics*, **24**, 243–273.

Kessler and Gottsman (1998) 'Smart screened investments: Environmentally screened funds that perform like conventional equity funds', *Journal of Investing*, **7**(3), 15–24.

Keynes, J. M. (1936) *The General Theory of Employment, Interest and Money*, Macmillan, Basingstoke, UK.

Kim, O. and Verrecchia, R. (1994) 'Market liquidity and volume around earnings announcements', *Journal of Accounting and Economics*, **17**, 41–68.

King Report, The (1994) *The King Report on Corporate Governance*, The Institute of Directors in South Africa, South Africa, 29 November.

King Report, The (2002) *The King Report on Corporate Governance for South Africa*, King Committee on Corporate Governance, Institute of Directors in Southern Africa, Parktown, South Africa.

Kingsley, C. (1984) *The Water Babies*, Puffin Books, Penguin Books, Harmondsworth, UK (first published in 1863).

Kirchgaessner, S. (2003) 'Telewest Fends Off Criticism by Shareholders', *Financial Times*, 13 June.

KLSE (2002) *Malaysian Corporate Governance Survey*, Kuala Lumpur Stock Exchange and PricewaterhouseCoopers. Available online at http://www.pwcglobal.com/pdf/my/eng/survrep/cgsurvey2002execsummary.pdf

Knowles, R (1997) *Ethical Investment*, Choice Books, Marrickville, New South Wales, Australia.

Koladkiewicz, I. (2001) 'Building of a corporate governance system in Poland: Initial experiences', *Corporate Governance: An International Review*, **9**(3), July, 228–237.

Kothari, S. P. (2001) 'Capital markets research in accounting', *Journal of Accounting and Economics*, **31**, 105–231.

Kotter, J. P. and Heskett, J. L. (1992) *Corporate Culture and Performance*, Free Press, New York.

KPMG (2002) *International Survey of Corporate Sustainability Reporting*, KPMG, Amsterdam.

Lambert, R., Larker, D. and Weigelt, K. (1993) 'The structure of organisational incentives', *Administrative Science Quarterly*, **38**, 438–461.

La Porta, R., Lopez-de-Silanes, F. and Shleifer, A. (1999) 'Corporate ownership around the world', *Journal of Finance*, **54**, 471–518.

La Porta, R., Lopez-de-Silanes, F., Shleifer, A. and Vishny, R. W. (1997) 'Legal determinants of external finance', *Journal of Finance*, **52**(3), 1131–1150.

La Porta, R., Lopez-de-Silanes, F., Shleifer, A. and Vishny, R. W. (1998) 'Law and finance', *Journal of Political Economy*, **106**, 1113–1155.

Lawniczak, R. (1997) 'A Polish experiment in corporate governance—The National Investment Funds (NIFs)', *Corporate Governance: An International Review*, **5**(2), April, 67–76.

Lee, L. (2002) 'Time for Taiwan to Act on Non-Performing Loans', *Taipei Times*, 23 August.

Leftwich, R. (1983) 'Accounting information in private markets: Evidence from private lending agreements', *The Accounting Review*, **58**(1), 23–42.

Lehman, C. R. (1983) *Stalemate in Corporate Social Responsibility Research* (Working Paper No. 3), Public Interest Section, American Accounting Association, Sarasota, FL.

Longman (1984) *Dictionary of the English Language*, Longman, Harlow, UK.

Lozano, J. M. (2000) *Ethics and Organizations*, Kluwer Academic, Boston.

LSE (February 1994) *Guidance on the Dissemination of Price Sensitive Information*, London Stock Exchange, London.

Luther, R. G. and Matatko, J. (1994) 'The performance of ethical unit trusts: Choosing an appropriate benchmark', *British Accounting Review*, **26**, 77–89.

Luther, R. G., Matatko, J. and Corner, D. C. (1992) 'The investment performance of UK "Ethical" unit trusts', *Accounting, Auditing and Accountability Journal*, **5**(4), 57–70.

Mace, M. L. (1986) *Directors: Myth and Reality*, Harvard Business School Press, Boston.

Macve, R. and Carey, A. (1992) *Business, Accountancy and the Environment: A Policy and Research Agenda*, Institute of Chartered Accountants in England and Wales, London.

Maitland, A. (2003) 'Importance of Training the NEDs', *Financial Times*, 7 July.

Mallin, C. (1999) 'Financial institutions and their relationship with corporate boards', *Corporate Governance: An International Review*, **7**(3), July, 248–255.

Mallin, C. A. (1996) 'The Voting Framework: A Comparative Study of Voting Behaviour of Institutional Investors in the US and the UK', *Corporate Governance: An International Review*, **4**(2), April, 107–122.

Mallin, C. A. (2001) 'Institutional investors and voting practices: An international comparison', *Corporate Governance: An International Review*, **9**(2), April, 118–126.

Mallin, C. A. and Jelic, R. (2000) 'Developments in Corporate Governance in Central and Eastern Europe', *Corporate Governance: An International Review*, **8**(1), January, 43–51.

Mallin, C. A., Saadouni, B. and Briston, R. J. (1995) 'The financial performance of ethical investment funds', *Journal of Business Finance and Accounting*, **22**, 483–96.

Mansley, M. (2000) *Socially Responsible Investment: A Guide for Pension Funds and Institutional Investors*, Monitor Press, Sudbury, UK.

March, J. G. and Simon, H. A. (1958) *Organizations*, John Wiley & Sons, New York.

Mathews, M. R. (1993) *Socially Responsible Accounting*, Chapman & Hall, London.

Mayer, C. (2000) 'Ownership matters', inaugural lecture given in Brussels.

Mayo, C. and Young, M. (March 2002) *Cool for Cats: The DTI's Proposals on Directors' Remuneration*, Simmons & Simmons, London.

Mayson, S. W., French, D. and Ryan, C. (1998) *Company Law* (12th edn), Blackstone Press, London.

McBride, S. (2002) 'Heard in Asia: Corporate governance becomes a strong factor for investors', *The Asian Wall Street Journal*, 18 July.

McCann, L., Solomon, A. and Solomon, J. F. (2003) 'Explaining the recent growth in UK socially responsible investment', *Journal of General Management*, **28**(3), summer, 32–53.

McGuire, J. B., Sundgren, A. and Schneeweis, T. (1988) 'Corporate social responsibility and firm financial performance', *Academy of Management Journal*, **31**(4), 854–872.

Melis, A. (2000) 'Corporate Governance in Italy', *Corporate Governance: An International Review*, **8**(4), October, 347–355.

Meyrick-Jones, J. (1999) 'Effective strategies to ensure you overcome the barrier of corporate culture when adopting a proactive risk management approach', *IIR Conference on Proactively Managing Business Risk and Ensuring Effective Internal Control in the Light of the Combined Code and the New Turnbull Committee Report*, London, May.

Midgley, K. (1974) 'How much control do shareholders exercise?', *Lloyds Bank Review*, **14**, 24–37.

Mikkelson, W. H. and Ruback, R. S. (1985) 'An empirical analysis of the interfirm equity investment process', *Journal of Financial Economics*, **14**, 523–553.

Minns, R. (1980) *Pension Funds and British Capitalism*, Heinemann, London.

Modernising Company Law (July 2002) White Paper presented to Parliament, Department of Trade and Industry, London.

Monks, R. A. G. (1994) 'Tomorrow's corporation', *Corporate Governance: An International Review*, **2**(3), July, 125–130.

Monks, R. A. G. (2001) *The New Global Investors: How Shareholders Can Unlock Sustainable Prosperity Worldwide*, Capstone Publishing, Oxford.

Monks, R. A. G. and Minow, N. (2001) *Corporate Governance* (2nd edn), Blackwell, Oxford.

Morck, R. and Stangeland, D. (1994) 'Large shareholders and corporate performance in Canada', unpublished manuscript.

Morck, R., Shleifer, A. and Vishny, R. W. (1988) 'Management ownership and market valuation: An empirical analysis', *Journal of Financial Economics*, **20**, 293–316.

Moskowitz, M. R. (1972) 'Choosing socially responsible stocks', *Business and Society Review*, **1**, 71–75.

Muller, K., de Frutos, J., Schussler, K-U. and H. Haarbosch (1994) *Environmental Reporting and Disclosures: The Financial Analyst's View*, European Federation of Financial Analysts' Societies, Edinburgh.

Myners (2001) *Institutional Investment in the United Kingdom: A Review* (The Myners Report), London.

Myners Report, The (1995) *Developing a Winning Partnership*, Department of Trade and Industry, London.

Myners, P. (July 2003) 'Trust is vital for good business', *Financial Times Fund Management*, 60.

NACD (November 1996) *Report of the NACD Blue Ribbon Commission on Director Professionalism*, National Association of Corporate Directors, Washington, DC.

NACD (November 1998) *Report of the NACD Blue Ribbon Commission on CEO Succession*, National Association of Corporate Directors, Washington DC.

Namgyal, T. (2001) 'AmCham Paper Calls for Pragmatic Cooperation', *Taipei Times*, 11 May.

NAPF (November 1995) *The Powerful Vote*, The National Association of Pension Funds Investment Committee, London.

Nesbitt, S. L. (1994) 'Long-term rewards from shareholder activism: A study of the "CalPERS effect"', *Journal of Applied Corporate Finance*, **6**, 75–80.

NYSE and NACD (December 1998) *Report of the NACD Blue Ribbon Commission on Improving the Effectiveness of Corporate Audit Committees*, New York Stock Exchange/ National Association of Corporate Directors, New York.

Oakey, D. (2000) 'Share Price Shocks: An Active Interest', *Investors Chronicle*, 18 August.

OECD (1999) *OECD Principles of Corporate Governance*, OECD, Paris.

Osborn, A. (2001) '50 Million Animals in Mass Test Plan', *The Guardian*, 27 October.

Ow-Yong, K. and Kooi Guan, C. (2000) 'Corporate governance codes: A comparison between Malaysia and the UK', *Corporate Governance: An International Review*, **8**(2), April, 125–133.

Owen, D. (1992) 'The implications of current trends in green awareness for the accounting function: An introductory analysis', in: D. Owen (ed.), *Green Reporting: Accounting and the Challenge of the Nineties*, Chapman & Hall, London.

Owen, D. L. (2003) 'Recent developments in European social and environmental reporting and auditing practice: A critical evaluation and tentative prognosis', *Cardiff University Staff Seminar Series in Accounting and Finance, 22 January*.

Owen, D. L., Swift, T. and Hunt, K. (2001) 'Questioning the role of stakeholder engagement in social and ethical accounting, auditing and reporting', *Accounting Forum*, **25**(3), September, 264–282.

Parkinson, J. E. (1994) *Corporate Power and Responsibility*, Oxford University Press, Oxford.

Pearce, J. A. (1982) 'The company mission as a strategic tool', *Sloan Management Review*, Spring, 15–24.

Peel, M. and O'Donnell, E. (1995) 'Board structure, corporate performance and auditor independence', *Corporate Governance: An International Review*, **3**(4), October, 207–217.

Pension Fund Corporate Governance Research Committee (June 1998) *Action Guidelines for Exercising Voting Rights*, Kosei Nenkin Kikin Rengokai, Tokyo.

Pensions Week (28 July 2003) 'Green Firms Perform Better Than Their Peers', p. 7.

Perks, R. W. (1993) *Accounting and Society*, Chapman & Hall, London.

Peters Committee (June 1997) *Corporate Governance in the Netherlands—Forty Recommendations*, Secretariat Committee on Corporate Governance, Amsterdam.

PIAC (1998) *Corporate Governance Standards* (4th edn), Pensions Investment Association of Canada, Toronto.

Pistor, K. and Turkewitz, J. (eds) (1996) 'Coping with Hydra—State ownership after privatisation', in: R. Frydman, C. W. Gray and A Rapaczynski (eds), *Corporate Governance in Central Europe and Russia. Volume 2: Insiders and the State*, Central European University Press.

Plender, J. (2003) 'Bank Bandwagon Hits a Bump', *Financial Times*, 16 March.

Power, M. (1991) 'Auditing and environmental expertise: Between protest and professionalism', *Accounting, Auditing and Accountability Journal*, **4**(3), 30–42.

Prais, S. (1976) *The Evolution of Giant Firms in Britain: A Study of the Growth of Concentration in Manufacturing in Britain 1909–1970*, Cambridge, UK.

Prowse, S. D. (1992) 'The structure of corporate ownership in Japan', *Journal of Finance*, **47**(3), July, 1121–1141.

Quinn, D. and Jones, T. (1995) 'An agent morality view of business policy', *Academy of Management Review*, **20**(1), 22–42.

Rajan, R. and Zingales, L. (1998) 'Which capitalism? Lessons from the East Asian Crisis', *Journal of Applied Corporate Finance*, **11**(3), fall.

Rao, P. S. and Lee-Sing, C. R. (1995) 'Governance structure, corporate decision-making and firm performance in North America', in: R. J. Daniels and R. Morck (eds) *Corporate Decision-Making in Canada* (Industry Canada Research Vol. V), University of Calgary Press, Ottawa.

Roberts, C. (1992) 'Environmental disclosures in corporate annual reports in Western Europe', in: D. Owen (ed.), *Green Reporting: Accountancy and the Challenge of the Nineties*, Chapman & Hall, London.

Roe, M. (1993) 'Some differences in corporate structure in Germany, Japan and the United States', *The Yale Law Review*, **102**, 1927–2003.

Rosenstein, S. and Wyatt, J. (1990) 'Outside directors, board independence and shareholder wealth', *Journal of Financial Economics*, **26**, 175–191.

Ross, S. (1973) 'The economic theory of agency: The principal's problem', *American Economic Review*, **63**, 134–139.

RSA (1995) *Tomorrow's Company* (Royal Society for the Encouragement of Arts, Manufactures and Commerce), RSA-Gower, Aldershot, UK.

Ruskin, J. (1862) 'The veins of wealth', *Unto This Last and Other Writings* (an essay, pp. 180–189), Penguin Books, Harmondsworth, UK (1997).

Rutteman Working Group (December 1994) *Internal Control and Financial Reporting, Guidance for Directors of Listed Companies Registered in the UK*, Institute of Chartered Accountants in England and Wales, London.

Ryland, P. (2002) 'Enronmania Sweeps Britain', *Investors Chronicle*, 8 February, p. 9.

Sarkar, J. and Sarkar, S. (2000) 'Large shareholder activism in corporate governance in developing countries: Evidence from India', *International Review of Finance*, **1**(3), 161–195.

Scheuth, S. (accessed 2002) *AccountAbility Primer*, Social Investment Forum, downloaded from www.socialinvest.org

Schilling, F. (2001) 'Corporate governance in Germany: The move to shareholder value', *Corporate Governance: An International Review*, **9**(3), July, 148–151.

SEHK (September 1997) *Guide for Directors of Listed Companies*, Stock Exchange of Hong Kong, Hong Kong.

SET (1998) *The SET Code of Best Practice for Directors of Listed Companies*, Stock Exchange of Thailand, Bangkok.

Shane, P. B. and Spicer, B. H. (1983) 'Market response to environmental information produced outside the firm', *The Accounting Review*, **58**(3), 521–538.

Shankman, N. A. (1999) 'Reframing the debate between agency and stakeholder theories of the firm', *Journal of Business Ethics*, **19**, 319–334.

Shi, S. and Weisert, D. (2002) 'Corporate governance with Chinese characteristics', *China Business Review*, **5**, 40.

Shleifer, A. and Vishny, R. W. (1997) 'A survey of corporate governance', *Journal of Finance*, **52**(2), June, 737–783.

Shome, D. K. and Singh, S. (1995) 'Firm value and external blockholdings', *Financial Management*, **24**, 3–14.

Short, H. (1996) 'Non-executive directors, corporate governance and the Cadbury Report: A review of the issues and evidence', *Corporate Governance: An International Review*, **4**(2), April, 123–131.

Short, H., Keasey, K., Hull, A. and Wright, M. (1998) 'Corporate governance, accountability, and enterprise', *Corporate Governance: An International Review*, **6**(3), 151–165.

Simon, H. (1957) *Models of Man*, John Wiley & Sons, New York.

Skapinker, M. (2000) 'In the Line of Fire—from all Directions: The "New Economy" and Stakeholder Pressure Are Making Life Ever More Difficult for Company Boards', *Financial Times Survey*, 31 March.

Skapinker, M. (2003) 'When Push Comes to Shove—We Shove', *Financial Times*, 6 June.

Smith Report, The (January 2003) *Audit Committees: A Report and Proposed Guidance*, Financial Reporting Council, London.

Smith, A. (1838) *The Wealth of Nations*, Ward Lock, London.

Smith, M. P. (1996a) 'Shareholder activism by institutional investors: Evidence from CalPERS', *Journal of Finance*, **51**(1), March, 227–252.

Smith, T. (1996b) *Accounting for Growth* (2nd edn), Century Business Books, London.

Social Investment Forum (1999). Available online at http://www.socialinvest.org

Solomon, A. (2000) 'Could corporate environmental reporting shadow financial reporting?', *Accounting Forum*, **24**(1), March, 35–61.

Solomon, A. and Lewis, L. A. (2002) 'Incentives and disincentives for corporate environmental disclosure', *Business Strategy and the Environment*, **11**(3), May–June, 154–169.

Solomon, A. and Solomon, J. F. (1999) 'Empirical evidence of long-termism and shareholder activism in UK unit trusts', *Corporate Governance: An International Review*, **7**(3), July, 288–300.

Solomon, A. and Solomon, J. F. (2002) 'The SRI dilemma for pension fund trustees: Some perceptions of their evolving role', *Business Relationships, Accountability, Sustainability and Society (BRASS)*, Working Paper Series No. 7, pp. 1–45.

Solomon, A. and Solomon, J. F. (2003a) 'Insights into social, ethical and environmental

[286] References

engagement by institutional investors', *Business Relationships, Accountability, Sustainability and Society (BRASS)*, Working Paper Series No. 7, pp. 1–35.

Solomon, A. and Solomon, J. F. (2003b) 'Commentary: Pension fund trustee payment debate', *European Financial Services Regulation*, July, 14–16.

Solomon, J. F., Hemmings, D. B. and Solomon, A. (November 1999) 'Evidence of a global compromise in corporate governance. Part II: Management of the crisis', in: Kap-Young Jeong and Jaewoo Choo (eds), *East Asian Economy Reconsidered*, ORUEN Publishing, South Korea.

Solomon, J. F., Solomon, A., Joseph, N. L. and Norton, S. D. (2000a) 'Institutional investors' views on corporate governance reform: Policy recommendations for the 21st century', *Corporate Governance: An International Review*, **8**(3), July, 217–226.

Solomon, J. F., Solomon, A., Norton, S. D. and Joseph, N. L. (2000b) 'A conceptual framework for corporate risk disclosure emerging from the agenda for corporate governance reform', *British Accounting Review*, **32**(4), December, 447–478.

Solomon, J. F., Solomon, A. and Park, C. (2002a) 'A conceptual framework for corporate governance reform in South Korea', *Corporate Governance: An International Review*, **10**(1), January, 29–46.

Solomon, J. F., Solomon, A. and Park, C. (2002b) 'The role of institutional investors in corporate governance reform in South Korea: Some empirical evidence', *Corporate Governance: An International Review*, **10**(3), July, 211–224.

Solomon, J. F., Solomon, A. and Norton, S. D. (2002c) 'Socially responsible investment in the UK: Drivers and current issues', *Journal of General Management*, November 2001.

Solomon, J. F., Solomon, A., Joseph, N. L. and Norton, S. D. (2002d) Who would be a trustee? The growth of SRI in UK pension funds', *New Academy Review*, **1**(4), winter, 98–104.

Solomon, J. F., Lin, S. W., Norton, S. D. and Solomon, A. (2003b) 'Corporate governance reform in Taiwan: Empirical evidence from Taiwanese company directors', *Corporate Governance: An International Review*.

Solomon, J. F., Solomon, A. and Suto, M. (2003c) 'SRI in Japan: Lessons from the UK experience' (Working paper), unpublished.

Song, B-N. (1997) *The Rise of the Korean Economy*, Oxford University Press, New York.

South China Morning Post (19 April 2002) 'Taiwan Template Tempts', p. 3.

Sparkes, R. (2002) *Socially Responsible Investment: A Global Revolution*, John Wiley & Sons, Chichester, UK.

Spiller, R. (1997) 'Death of the "Greed is Good" Era', in: R. Knowles (ed.), *Ethical Investment*, Choice Books, Marrickville, New South Wales, Australia.

Stapledon, G. P. (1995) 'Exercise of voting rights by institutional shareholders in the UK', *Corporate Governance: An International Review*, **3**(3), 144–155.

Stapledon, G. P. (1996) *Institutional Shareholders and Corporate Governance*, Clarendon Press, Oxford.

Sternberg, E. (October 1998) *Corporate Governance: Accountability in the Marketplace* (Hobart Paper No. 137), The Institute of Economic Affairs, London.

Stiles, P. and Taylor, B. (1993) 'Maxwell: The failure of corporate governance', *Corporate Governance: An International Review*, **1**(1), January.

Stock, M., Copnell, T. and Wicks, C. (1999) *The Combined Code: A Practical Guide*, Gee Publishing, London.

Strachan, J. L., Smith, D. B. and Beedles, W. L. (1983) 'The price reaction to (alleged) corporate crime', *The Financial Review*, **18**(2), 121–132.

Sykes, A. (1994) 'Proposals for internationally competitive corporate governance in Britain and America', *Corporate Governance: An International Review*, **2**(4), 187–195.

Taipei Times (18 July 2000) 'Corporate Scandal Old Hat in Asia'.

Taipei Times (15 July 2002) 'Asia Can Learn from Trials in the US'.

Taiwan Business News (3 December 2002) 'News Briefs: The Executive Yuan Decides to Improve the Island's Listed Firms' Corporate Governance'.

Tam, O. K. (2000) 'Models of corporate governance for Chinese companies', *Corporate Governance: An International Review*, **8**(1), January, 52–64.

Targett, S. (2000) 'Friends Plans to Give Ethical Lead' (Companies and markets), *Financial Times*, 8 May.

Targett, S. and Gimbel, F. (2003) 'Unpaid Trustees Run Most Company Pension Schemes', *Financial Times*, 6 January.

Tassell, T. (31 January 2003) 'FTSE 100 Chiefs Question Boardroom Reform Plans', *Financial Times*, p. 4.

Tassell, T. (14 March 2003) 'Higgs Qualifies Boardroom Reform', *Financial Times*.

Tassell, T. (14 March 2003) 'Warning on Revisions to Corporate Governance Code', *Financial Times*.

Tassell, T. (9 July 2003) 'Executive Pay Under Review After Shareholder Activism', *Financial Times*.

Tassell, T. (24 July 2003) 'Investors Urged to Adopt Higgs Standards', *Financial Times*.

Tassell, T. (25 July 2003) 'Corporate Code Will Increase Disclosure Burden', *Financial Times*.

Tassell, T. (28 July 2003) 'Japanese Fund to Improve Standards', *Financial Times Fund Management*, p. 5.

Tassell, T. and Voyle, S. (2003) 'Promoting the Exception that Moves the Rule', *Financial Times*, 15 March.

Tassell, T., Bolger, A. and Parker, A. (2003) 'Fear of Board Splits Over Higgs Code: Critics Argue Proposal Could Lead to Division and Confusion', *Financial Times*, 20 January, p. 1.

Thomas, S. (1999) 'Proactively managing business risk', *IIR Conference on Proactively Managing Business Risk and Ensuring Effective Internal Control in the Light of the Combined Code and the New Turnbull Committee Report*, London, May.

Thomson, I. and Bebbington, J. (2002) *Social and Environmental Reporting in the UK: A Pedagogic Evaluation* (working paper, Aberdeen Papers in Accountancy), Finance & Management, University of Aberdeen, Aberdeen.

TIAA-CREF (October 1997) *TIAA-CREF Policy Statement on Corporate Governance*, Teachers Insurance and Annuity Association-College Retirement Enquities Fund, New York.

Treadway Commission, The (1987) *Report of the National Commission on Fraudulent Financial Reporting*, New York.

Tricker, R. I. (1984) *Corporate Governance: Practices, Procedures and Powers in British Companies and Their Boards of Directors*, Gower Press, Aldershot, UK.

Turnbull Report, The (September 1999) *Internal Control: Guidance for Directors on the Combined Code*, Institute of Chartered Accountants in England and Wales, London.

Ullman, A. A. (1985) 'Data in search of a theory: A critical examination of the relationships among social performance, social disclosure, and economic performance of U.S. Firms', *Academy of Management Review*, **10**(3), 540–557.

UNEP (1996) *Engaging Stakeholders. 1: The Benchmark Survey*, SustainAbility Ltd/United Nations Environment Programme (Industry and Environment Office), London, UK.

Ungson, G. R., Steers, R. M. and Park, S-H. (1997) *Korean Enterprise: The Quest for Globalization*, Harvard Business School Press, Cambridge, MA.

Vance, S. C. (1975) 'Are socially responsible corporations good investment risks?', *Management Review*, **64**, 18–24.

Vancil, R. F. (1987) *Passing the Baton: Managing the Process of CEO Succession*, Harvard Business School Press, Boston.

Voyle, S. and Tassell, T. (2003) 'Tesco Mulls One-Year Contracts for Chiefs', *Financial Times*, 14 June.

Waldo, C. N. (1985) *Boards of Directors: Their Changing Roles, Structure, and Information Needs*, Quorum Books, New York.

Ward, A. (2000) '13% Back Greenpeace Move', *Financial Times*, 14 April.

Watts, R. L. and Zimmerman, J. L. (1986) *Positive Accounting Theory*, Prentice Hall International Editions, Upper Saddle River, NJ.

WCED (1987) *Our Common Future* (World Commission on Environment and Development, known as the Brandtland Commission), Oxford University Press, Oxford.

Weil, Gotshal & Manges LLP (January 2002) *Comparative Study of Corporate Governance Codes Relevant to the European Union and its Member States* (on behalf of the European Commission Internal Market Directorate General, Final Report), Weil, Gotshal & Manges LLP, Brussels.

Weisbach, M. S. (1988) 'Outside directors and CEO turnover', *Journal of Financial Economics*, **20**, 431–460.

Welford, R. and Gouldson, A. (1993) *Environment Management and Business Strategy*, Pitman, London.

Wendlandt, A. (2003) 'Kingfisher Bows to Shareholder Demands', *Financial Times*, 26 May.

Wheeler, D. and Sillanpää, M. (1997) *The Stakeholder Corporation*, Pitman, London.

Wheeler, D., Colbert, B. and Freeman, R. E. (2002) 'Focusing on value: Reconciling corporate social responsibility, sustainability and a stakeholder approach in a network world', paper *Denver Meeting of the Academy of Management, August.*

WICE (1994) *Environmental Reporting. A Manager's Guide* (World Industry Council for the Environment), International Chamber of Commerce, Paris.

Williams, S. (1999) 'UK ethical investment: A coming of age', *Journal of Investing*, summer, 58–75.

Williamson, O. E. (1985) *The Economic Institutions of Capitalism*, Free Press, New York.

Williamson, O. E. (1996) *The Mechanisms of Governance*, Oxford University Press, New York.

Wymeersch, E. (1994) 'Aspects of corporate governance in Belgium', *Corporate Governance: An International Review*, **2**(3), July, 138–152.

Yasaki, A. G. A. (2001) 'Corporate governance in a Third World country with particular reference to Nigeria', *Corporate Governance: An International Review*, **9**(3), July, 238–253.

Yeh, K, S. (1997) 'Board network structural change before and after initial public offerings in Taiwan', *Sun Yat-sen Management Review*, International Issue, 93–114.

Yeltsin, B. (1996) *Decree on Measures to Ensure the Rights of Shareholders* (Parker School of Foreign and Comparative Law, Legal Matters, Release No. 28), Columbia University, New York.

Yermack, D. (1996) 'Higher market valuation for firms with a small board of directors', *Journal of Financial Economics*, **40**, 185–211.

Yoo, S. and Lee, S. (1987) 'Management style and practice in Korean chaebols', California Management Review, summer, 95–110.

Zeghal, D. and Ahmed, S. A. (1990) 'Comparison of social responsibility information disclosure media used by Canadian firms', *Accounting, Auditing and Accountability Journal*, **3**(1), 38–53.

Zun, W. M. (2002) 'The difficulties of improving Taiwanese corporate governance', *Economy Daily*, 2 September [in Mandarin Chinese].

Zysman, J. (1983) *Governments, Markets and Growth: Financial Systems and the Politics of Industrial Change*, Cornell University Press, Ithaca, NY.

Index

The Wealth of Nations (Smith) 4
Welford, R. 203
Wessex Water 33
Wheeler, D. 24, 26
WICE *see* World Industry Council for the
    Environment Williams, S. 224
Williamson, O.E. 21–3
World Bank 154, 166
World Industry Council for the
    Environment (WICE) 199–200
WorldCom 61, 182

worldwide issues *see* global ...
Wright, M. 13
Wyatt, J. 77–8
Wymeersch, E. 162

Yasaki, A.G.A. 175
Yellow Book 48
Yeltsin, B. 176

Zimmerman, J.L. 121